PLEKHANOV

SAMUEL H. BARON

Plekhanov

THE FATHER OF RUSSIAN MARXISM

STANFORD UNIVERSITY PRESS · STANFORD, CALIFORNIA · 1963

Stanford University Press
Stanford, California

© 1963 by the Board of Trustees of the
Leland Stanford Junior University

Library of Congress Catalog Card Number: 63-10732

Printed in the United States of America

53,217

to Virginia

PREFACE

Few historical events have made so great an impact on the world as the Bolshevik Revolution. Seeking to comprehend this momentous event, students have turned attention to its antecedents, particularly to the hundred-year-long history of revolutionary movements in Russia, the ideas that inspired them, and the intelligentsia who created the ideas and led the movements. Among other illuminating works that have resulted are several valuable studies of the Social Democratic movement in Russia. However, no Western scholar has examined at any length the life and thought of G. V. Plekhanov, the Father of Russian Marxism. Even in the U.S.S.R. no such work has appeared since 1924, when many of the important documentary materials were not yet available. The studies of V. Vaganian and S. Vol'fson published in that year are not without merit, though they are marred by the authors' unquestioning acceptance of Marxian doctrine. Despite that, they have long since been relegated to oblivion in the U.S.S.R. as too sympathetic to their subject, and they are also virtually unknown in the West.

Yet Plekhanov's importance in Russian history is beyond dispute. Almost singlehandedly, he launched the movement that was to culminate in the Bolshevik Revolution. He laid the theoretical foundations of Russian Marxism in *Socialism and Political Struggle* (1883) and *Our Differences* (1885); and, according to Lenin, his book *On the Development of the Monistic Conception of History* (1894) "reared a whole generation of Russian Marxists." He was the dominant figure in the first Russian Marxian organization, the Gruppa Osvobozhdenie Truda (Emancipation of Labor Group), and almost all the leading personalities in the movement, including Lenin, began as his disciples. He was an editor of the important publication *Iskra* and was chiefly responsible for the program of the Social Democratic Labor Party that was adopted in 1903. Ever the defender of orthodoxy, Plekhanov was in the forefront of the struggles against various heresies that successively arose from the mid-nineties on. For two decades the Social Democratic movement centered around him, and he remained a figure to be reckoned with until the end of his life.

Moreover, Plekhanov was one of the most cultured men of his time. Not without reason has he been regarded as the last of that line of gifted individuals in the history of the Russian intelligentsia that began with Belinsky and Herzen. The liberal historian Kizevetter wrote of him: "No disagreement with the socio-political views of G. V. Plekhanov can dim in anyone's eyes either the brilliant literary talent or the powerful and original mind and the many-sided erudition of this remarkable writer." In Plekhanov, the best traditions of Russia's intelligentsia fused with the broader stream of European Marxism to produce a voluminous and variegated literary output. One of the most sensitive and creative of Marx's disciples, he not only wrote incisive analyses of contemporary affairs but also inaugurated Marxian literary criticism and pioneered in the extension of Marxian research into a number of other fields. A long chapter in the book provides an introduction to his studies in philosophy, history, and art.

Plekhanov began his revolutionary career at the age of nineteen. For five years, before beginning his thirty-seven-year exile, he was a hard-driving and effective organizer and agitator, an underground revolutionist who carried brass knuckles, practiced the use of the dagger, and slept with a revolver under his pillow. Once in the emigration, however, he lost touch with day-to-day politics, and he became more and more preoccupied with theory as he worked out his adaptation of Marxism to Russia. He devoted himself especially to the philosophical side of Marxism, to the defense of the tactics he deemed consistent with it, and to its employment for the investigation of a whole range of social and cultural phenomena. So great was Plekhanov's absorption in the life of the mind that a study of his life must in large part be a study of his thought. This consideration has led me to write what is primarily an intellectual biography.

Rather than limit myself simply to a consideration of Plekhanov's ideas, however, I have sought to give some understanding of the forces and experiences that shaped his moral and intellectual development: his family training, his education, and the radical milieu in St. Petersburg which transformed him into a revolutionist. I have devoted particular attention to his generally neglected years as a Narodnik, for it is against the background of Narodnik hopes and their frustration that one should view both Plekhanov's conversion to Marxism and the more general problem of the rise of Marxism in Russia. I have endeavored as well to trace the developments in the revolutionary movement that led to the establishment of the Emancipation of Labor Group, and the fortunes of this organizational vehicle of Plekhanov's first dozen years as a Marxist.

The greater part of the book may be viewed as the history of an idea; of the origins, vicissitudes, and ultimate defeat of the two-stage revolutionary scheme that constituted Plekhanov's adaptation of Marxism to the conditions of his backward native land. In the years after its creation, Plekhanov's formulation was repeatedly challenged, both implicitly by practices inconsistent with it and explicitly by theorists of every hue. Against these challenges, he strove to preserve intact his carefully articulated construction, which required a nice balance between economic and political struggle, between the bourgeoisie and the proletariat, between the Russian workers and their Social Democratic leaders, and between determinism and voluntarism. He believed he had succeeded until, in 1905, the revolution he had so long awaited disclosed the inner contradictions of his scheme. At that critical moment the bold innovator of another day failed to respond creatively, instead clinging to his discredited system and ultimately going down with it. Ever the advocate of secure theoretical foundations, Plekhanov's own assumptions proved disastrously faulty in the end.

Against the two great ideological deviations of his time, Eduard Bernstein's Revisionism and Lenin's Bolshevism, Plekhanov struggled more insistently than any other leader of orthodox Marxism. Yet, ironically enough, his campaign against Revisionism did much to facilitate the rise of Bolshevism; and later, when he turned his fire on Bolshevism, he himself imperceptibly slipped toward Revisionism. Not always able to keep the elements of his system in balance, he nonetheless made the best conceivable defense of orthodox Marxism. Still neither of his campaigns succeeded: Revisionism triumphed in the West, Bolshevism in Russia, orthodox Marxism nowhere. Plekhanov's fate offers a good deal of insight into orthodox Marxism's unsuitability either to the changing societies of the West or to such underdeveloped countries as Russia in the twentieth century.

Many dimensions of the eventful period of Russian history during which Plekhanov lived have been ably examined by others. For my study, I have not considered it necessary to deal more than cursorily with the general historical background. It goes without saying that such chapters as those on the 1903 Congress of the RSDLP and the revolutions of 1905 and 1917 present mainly the aspects of those events essential for an understanding of Plekhanov's thought and action. In turn, an appreciation of his thought and action helps to illuminate the events he participated in or reacted to. If this study makes clear Plekhanov's ideas, why he held them, how they influenced his party's and his country's destiny, and wherein they went awry, it will have achieved its purpose.

I first became interested in Plekhanov while working on a doctoral dissertation on the Emancipation of Labor Group under the sponsorship of Professor Gerold T. Robinson of Columbia University. Although several chapters of the book draw upon the dissertation, much the greater part is based upon research carried out in the years since its completion. I am pleased to acknowledge my indebtedness to the many institutions and individuals without whose assistance it would never have been possible to produce this work: to the Social Science Research Council and the Danforth Foundation for summer research grants; to Mme E. Batault-Plekhanova of Paris, for generously placing at my disposal unpublished manuscripts, letters, and photographs, for sharing her reminiscences with me, and for giving me permission to use pictures and quotations from *God na rodine*; to the International Institute of Social History in Amsterdam for permission to quote from manuscript materials and to use the group photograph of the socialist leaders at the Amsterdam Congress of the International; to the Oxford University Press for permission to quote from *Poems by Nicholas Nekrassov*, translated by Juliet Soskice (London, 1929); to the *Russian Review*, the *American Slavic and East European Review*, the *Journal of the History of Ideas*, and *Survey* for permission to use materials from articles by me which appeared in these journals; to the staffs of the Columbia and Harvard University Libraries, the New York Public Library, the Hoover Library, the British Museum, the International Institute of Social History, the Bibliothèque de Documentation Internationale Contemporaine, and the Leningrad Public Library for the many courtesies extended to me as I made use of their rich collections; and to Mrs. Lyle Purcell, for the conscientiousness and skill with which she typed the manuscript. I wish further to express my gratitude to Morris Watnick, for giving me the benefit of his comments on several chapters of the book; and to my friend John Kautsky, who also read parts of the book, and whose warm encouragement has meant a great deal to me. Finally, I am deeply indebted to my wife, not only for her aid with a multitude of details, but for the fortitude, good cheer, and devotion she has unfailingly shown in the course of this long and difficult journey.

GRINNELL, IOWA   S. H. B.
    January 1963

CONTENTS

The illustrations follow page 146

PLEKHANOV

1

THE FORMATIVE YEARS

By THE MIDDLE OF THE nineteenth century, the dynamism that Peter the Great once had imparted to his country had spent itself. Earlier the sponsor of innovation, the throne had long since become the guardian of tradition and order. Critics of the system, if they did not escape into self-exile, were intimidated or imprisoned. Frequent peasant disorders bespoke growing dissatisfaction in the countryside, but they were systematically suppressed. Those who would have changed the regime were powerless to do so. For their part, the governing authorities sought to give the impression that all was well in the best of all possible worlds. Then in the Crimean War (1853–56) Russia was routed by its more progressive adversaries, Britain and France. Humiliating military defeat disclosed the bankruptcy of the regime Tsar Nicholas I (1825–55) had sought so strenuously to preserve. The death of the Tsar, coinciding as it did with the military debacle, made it possible at last to move Russia off dead center.

The new Tsar, Alexander II (1855–81), instituted an extensive program of reforms aimed at the modernization of Russia. Chief among them was the abolition of serfdom in 1861, a move calculated both to pacify internal unrest and to facilitate economic development.* With these matters attended to, it was hoped, Russia's power and international prestige should be restored. No radical, Alexander envisaged a program of controlled change that should leave the monarch's autocratic power unimpaired. He and his aides also gave due consideration to the interests of the landed

---

* Other reforms relaxed the censorship of the press, created institutions of local self-government (the *zemstva*), liberalized both the judicial and military branches of the state apparatus, and promoted education.

gentry, the crown's chief social support. Somehow continuity was to be combined with change, conservation with modernization. But time was to prove that the reforms were incompatible with the preservation of the old power structure. Once set in motion, the process of change got out of control, bringing on developments that threatened to consign autocracy to the same fate as serfdom.

Freed by the Emancipation edict from personal dependence upon the landlord, the peasant remained a second-class citizen, still deprived of free choice of residence and occupation, bound by law to a village commune, and obliged to accept the land allotment it offered him. The land he received in settlements worked out by members of the local gentry* was likely to be poor in quality, inflated in price, and insufficient in quantity to meet his needs. A high birth rate reduced further the per capita holding in the last decades of the nineteenth century, while the tax load on the peasant increased. Accordingly, the majority suffered a decline in material well-being in the decades after the Emancipation. The large holdings that remained in the hands of the gentry and state excited the envy of a land-hungry peasantry convinced that the soil should belong to those who tilled it. *Jacqueries* flared through the countryside in later years, proving conclusively that the "Tsar-Liberator" had not solved the agrarian question.

In spite of the advantages the Emancipation statute conferred upon them, the gentry fared hardly better. Generally they retained half—the more fertile half—of their landed property, and were compensated handsomely for the portion they surrendered. To be sure, they now lacked the labor supply formerly theirs, and the implements for the cultivation of the soil, but these were reparable deficiencies. What the gentry lacked above all were habits of work, managerial experience, and the initiative and adaptability to acquire the one and the other. With the breakup of the old system of agrarian relations, the nobles were exposed as never before to the free play of economic forces. Powerless to understand the new economic order or to resist its effects, a large majority followed with variations the pattern of decline and fall so brilliantly limned by Chekhov in *The Cherry Orchard*.

As it turned out, the Alexandrine reforms increased opportunities for geographical and social mobility,† created a free labor supply, and gave new scope for economic initiative. State support to railroad building and to the establishment of credit institutions spurred the development of a market economy. Industrial activities grew in prominence from 1880 on.

---

* The land was transferred to the communes, which in turn parceled it out among the peasants. Title was held by the communal organization rather than by the individual peasant.

† Restrictions on peasant movement were gradually relaxed.

New branches of production arose; the scale of operations expanded; the pulse of economic life quickened. Out of the old near-feudal order, a capitalistic economy evolved that bid fair to transform Russia's social structure and perhaps even its political constitution.

Urban centers multiplied, and Russia's city population attained unprecedented proportions.* With a modern industrial economy in the making, the bourgeoisie assumed greater importance. The Tsarist government's policies favored its economic interests. Yet, socially and politically, the capitalist class remained much less powerful than its counterparts in England, France, and the United States. Whether it would be content indefinitely to accept its inferior status was a question of critical import.

In allotting land to the peasants, the reform architects had hoped to ward off the rise of an industrial proletariat and the turbulent class struggles associated with it. But overpopulation on the land and indigence in the village presently drove large numbers of peasants to seek employment in the towns. Though they often retained deep roots in the countryside, many were in due course converted into industrial proletarians. As in the early stages of the industrial revolution elsewhere, the living and working conditions of Russia's factory hands were atrocious. Besides, little social legislation was enacted, and the workers were forbidden to organize trade unions for their defense. Under the circumstances, it was vain to hope that class struggle could be avoided. Beginning as early as the 1870's, serious labor disturbances broke out in some of the major industrial centers. Even then, and more so later, Russia's revolutionists won a sympathetic hearing in the proletarian milieu.

The revolutionists came predominantly from the ranks of the intelligentsia.[1] This social group had no exact parallel in Western society; yet, paradoxically enough, it was itself a consequence of the Western impact upon Russia. The intelligentsia was the product of cultural contact between two unlike civilizations, a contact fostered especially since the time of Peter the Great. From then on, Russia's tradition-oriented and rigidly stratified society was exposed to the secular, dynamic ideologies that successively arose in the West. Advanced political and social ideas won a few followers in the eighteenth century and a larger number, including such brilliant figures as Aleksandr Herzen and Vissarion Belinsky, in the nineteenth. From the standpoint of Western values, the intelligentsia found Russian life barbaric. The fulfillment of their aspirations demanded a radical revision of its foundations. But since their ideals were derived from a fundamentally different social context, they had to contend not

* Nevertheless, Russia's population was still overwhelmingly rural even at the outbreak of the World War.

only with the power of the repressive state apparatus but also with the incomprehension of the common people to whose interests they were dedicated. Undaunted by repeated failures, they persistently searched for an "algebra of revolution"—that combination of ideas and forces that would transform their dream into reality.

In the decades after the Emancipation the strength of the intelligensia waxed. As Russia's modernization effort called for a greatly expanded professional corps—educators and engineers, lawyers and doctors, managers and technicians—students flocked to the institutions of higher learning.[2] Kept alive at the universities by earlier generations of students, radical thought showed no tendency to decline during Alexander's reign. The Tsar's innovations fell far short of the ideals of the intelligentsia and, in addition, provided no legal means for the realization of those ideals. The renewal of reaction after an attempt on Alexander's life in 1866 increased their alienation, spurring them to intensified oppositional activity. They sedulously cultivated the educated youth who were similarly inclined, and recruits from the universities flowed to the revolutionary movements. Among their number was Georgii Valentinovich Plekhanov.

Georgii was born on November 29, 1856,[*] in Gudalovka, a village in the central Russian province of Tambov. His father, Valentin, was a member of the gentry of Tartar extraction.[3] Before retiring to manage his estate, Valentin had a military career that included duty in the Crimean War and in the suppression of the Polish uprising of 1863. One of the elder Plekhanov's brothers was also an army officer, the other a district police commissioner in Tambov province. In the following generation, Georgii's three older brothers all entered the military service, and he himself initially favored the same profession. The future revolutionist sprang from a family with a strong tradition of loyalty to the Russian state.

By the economic measure Valentin Plekhanov belonged to the lower stratum of the landed gentry. He received as his inheritance 270 acres and perhaps fifty serfs. His first wife's dowry doubled his holding, but in 1858 the demands of his family—there were eventually twelve children—compelled him to sell that portion of the estate his wife had brought him. Three years later the abolition of serfdom deepened the family crisis, depriving the landowner of his customary source of labor and halving the estate again. After ten years of trying to manage what remained of his holding with paid labor, he abandoned the effort in 1871 and assumed an administrative post in one of the newly created zemstvo institutions. After his death two years later, his wife disposed of most of the remaining land.

[*] Throughout the book, dates are given according to the Russian Old Style calendar, which was thirteen days behind the Western Gregorian calendar.

The economic history of the Plekhanovs in these decades faithfully mirrored that of many another petty gentry family, except that Valentin did conscientiously attempt to manage his lands efficiently.

Despite the fact that he fared poorly under the old system, Valentin was unalterably opposed to the Emancipation reforms. He believed that the old social order corresponded to a natural hierarchy, in which those fit to command directed the efforts of the great majority, who were incapable of managing their own affairs. Lacking insight into the larger problems of the state and the nation, he never forgave Alexander II for upsetting the allegedly natural order of society. Valentin was proud of his noble status and military rank and profoundly resented the loss of his prerogatives with respect to the peasants. He had the satisfaction of predicting correctly—if for the wrong reasons—that the Tsar's innovations would harm both landlords and peasants alike.

The reminiscences of both his children and his former serfs agree in characterizing the elder Plekhanov as a severe, irascible, and sometimes violent man.* He was also one of those men who deliberately attempt to mold the character of their children, and some of his values became deeply imprinted upon Georgii. As a military man, he naturally set great store on manliness and courage. The story is told of his putting five-year-old Georgii on a spirited horse, handing him the reins, and turning the horse loose, shouting to the boy to hang on. Georgii passed the test, and this is not the only tale told of his pluckiness. In the same way that Valentin applied himself to the management of his estate, he set himself the task of making his children self-reliant, independent, and active. He instructed them never to call upon the servants to do anything they were capable of doing themselves. Intolerant of idleness, he would often say: "We shall rest when we die." Plekhanov responded well to the training his father gave. Physical courage and an ability to keep cool in the face of danger were to stand him in good stead in the early years of his revolutionary career. As an adult, he proved able not only to stand on his own two feet but to stand alone if necessary. The energy Valentin put into his estate was more than matched by the devoted service Georgii gave to the revolutionary movement. Like his father, also, he was outspoken, proud, yet aloof and reserved. (He is repeatedly described in the reminiscences of his followers as awesome, austere, and inapproachable, and it is notable that throughout his life he had few intimate friends.)

In his mature years, Plekhanov took considerable pride in the fact that

* He reminded one of his daughters of the elder Prince Volkonsky in *War and Peace*, who was nicknamed the Prussian King and resided on an estate called Bleak Hills. See V. V. Pozdniakova-Plekhanova, in L. Deutsch, ed., *Gruppa "Osvobozhdenie Truda,"* I, 84–85.

his mother was distantly related to the famous radical critic Belinsky. Maria Fedorovna, the daughter of an impoverished nobleman, was employed as a governess when she first met Valentin Plekhanov. Valentin was then a widower of forty-five, with seven children; Maria was twenty-two. The courtship was brief and they were married in 1855. Georgii was the first of their five children.

Maria, a gentle, modest, and tender person, had suffered humiliation and mistreatment at the hands of her stepmother, and perhaps for this reason was quickly moved to compassion for the suffering of others. More than half a century later, some of the former serfs remembered her with affection and gratitude. She was something of an intellectual and had studied at Smolnyi Institute on a government scholarship. Her teachers regretted that she could not go on to advanced studies, which at that time were closed to women in Russia. As a wife and mother, Maria undertook the early education first of her stepchildren and then of her own. After the death of her husband in 1873, she became a teacher in order to support her younger children.

The relationship between Maria and her first-born child was an especially warm one. She encouraged his obvious intellectual gifts, first telling him stories and then teaching him to read at an early age. Georgii devoured the books in the family library—mainly on military subjects. His father, somewhat taken aback at his son's appetite for books, urged him to take more exercise. It has been affirmed, with some little truth, that Plekhanov's "first teacher of revolution was undoubtedly his mother."[4] Maria Fedorovna was hardly a revolutionist even in spirit; but the sense of altruism and devotion to justice that she communicated to her son were of great importance. Georgii may have drawn the strength of his character from his father, but it was the standards derived from his mother that helped him to recognize and impelled him to oppose the evils of Russian political and social life.

Georgii's formal education did not begin until 1866, when, at the age of ten, he entered the second class of the Voronezh Military Academy. To obtain leave to enter the Academy, Georgii showed against his father some of the firmness of will that Valentin had been at such pains to instill. The father wanted Georgii to work toward a career in the civil service, in which there would, he thought, be greater opportunities than in the Army. But Georgii was determined to be an officer, and at last the father gave way, perhaps secretly pleased at his son's tenacity and resolution.

Plekhanov attended the Academy from 1866 to 1873. He was a well-liked and influential member of his class, and his intellectual and moral development was stimulated by some excellent teachers. His mother later blamed his revolutionary career on the freethinkers at the Academy.[5] The charge had at least some substance to it. In the early 1860's, with the spirit of liberalism in the ascendant, the Ministry of War came under the control of the reformer D. A. Miliutin. One result was the liberalization of the military schools. The emphasis on discipline was lightened, the curriculum broadened, and capable teachers hired, more or less irrespective of political persuasion. Among the outstanding faculty at the Academy in Plekhanov's time were M. F. de Pulé, a historian, and N. F. Bunakov, a well-known proponent of liberal pedagogical ideas.

Although not a revolutionist, Bunakov was sympathetic to opposition movements, and had earlier been dismissed from the Vologda gymnasium for his advanced political views. He had an exalted conception of the teacher's calling and believed that education should be made universal and compulsory. In the 1870's, he actively propagated his views through publications and work in teacher-training institutions. He was also active in adult education enterprises and helped organize the first peasant theater in Russia.* Forty years after his student days at Voronezh, Plekhanov said of Bunakov: "He instilled in me a love of literature, and he taught me to speak and write correctly, definitely, clearly, and simply."[6] Bunakov made Plekhanov conscious of his flair for writing. It is reported that after reading one of his compositions he told the boy, "Plekhanov, you will become a great writer." It was probably Bunakov who introduced Plekhanov to the writings of Belinsky, Chernyshevsky, and Dobroliubov, Russia's great triumvirate of radical literary critics, thus giving the young man his first acquaintance with the world of ideas that engrossed the intelligentsia. So strong an impression did Chernyshevsky make upon Plekhanov that in 1881 he paired the Russian with Marx as the writers who had most helped him to develop his mind in all respects.†

Perhaps the most important thing Bunakov conveyed to his students was his sense of responsibility to the Russian people. This is particularly brought out in a description of a stirring experience of his student days that Plekhanov recounted long years later. After 1870, when a new and

* Bunakov's activities were curtailed during the repressions of the 1880's, and in 1903, after publicly going on record in support of civil liberties, he was exiled. See D. Medynskii, *Istoriia russkoi pedagogiki* (Moscow, 1938), pp. 278–82.

† *Dela i dni,* No. 2 (1921), p. 86. Plekhanov made this confession in a letter to Lavrov, whom he included along with Chernyshevsky and Marx as his "favorite authors." In my view, Lavrov influenced Plekhanov much less than the other two; his inclusion of Lavrov is to be viewed more as an expression of gratitude for the many kindnesses Lavrov rendered him in the early 1880's. In the mid-eighties Plekhanov publicly declared his indebtedness to Chernyshevsky: "My own intellectual development was greatly influenced by Chernyshevsky; the analysis of his views was a major event in my literary life." *Sochineniia,* VI, 382.

reactionary director was appointed to head the Academy, following the increasingly conservative government policy, students would meet in one another's rooms in the evening to read in secret the forbidden works of radical authors. Plekhanov recalled one such occasion in his last year at the Academy, when a group met to read aloud the poetry of the famous radical poet Nikolai Nekrasov:

We had hardly finished "The Railroad" when a signal sounded calling us to drill. We hid the book and went to the armory with our weapons, under the strongest impression of what we had read. When we began to fall in, my friend S. approached me and, grasping the barrel of his gun, whispered, "Oh, if I could only take this weapon and go into combat for the Russian people!" These words, spoken furtively within a few paces of a strict military official, were deeply engraved on my memory.[7]

"The Railroad" is a poem filled with compassion for the sufferings of the people. It describes the toil and sacrifice, pain and death, of the workers constructing a railroad, in language calculated to call up a sense of identification of the reader with the cause of popular progress and welfare:

> We, in the heat, in the frost, strained our sinews
> Toiled with our shoulders eternally bent
> Lived in mud hovels, were sodden and frozen
> Fought with starvation, with scurvy were spent
>
> Cheated we were by the quick-witted foreman
> Flogged by the masters and ground in the soil
> All we endured and were patient, God's legions
> Peaceable children of toil
>
> Brethren, you now reap the fruit of our struggle
> We have been fated to perish and rot
> Do you still think of us sometimes with kindness
> Do you remember or not?[8]

Plekhanov had been brought up by his mother in the Orthodox faith, but in the freethinking atmosphere of the Academy he broke with traditional religion. Characteristically, he did not hesitate to express his new views. To the priest who taught sacred law he soon began to put searching questions, and the priest at first answered willingly. As word spread of what was going on, the students flocked to what had been a poorly attended class to hear the contest of wits. The priest soon became uneasy about the line of questioning, which brought into doubt matters that were supposed to be taken on faith, and after four or five sessions he called things to a halt, saying: "No, young man, let us leave off these disputes; otherwise our lessons on the law of God will be transformed into lessons on godlessness."[9]

Although Plekhanov distinguished himself scholastically in his first years at the Academy, he did less well in the upper classes, and in his final examinations placed only tenth among the twenty students who passed. He received the highest mark possible in geography, very good marks in Holy Scripture, French, and history, and mediocre marks in his other subjects, including all the science examinations. Along with six or seven other members of the class, he was awarded the lowest mark given in the area of conduct. Presumably both his indifferent academic record and his low mark in conduct were the result of his lack of interest in a great deal of the formal work of the school and his preference instead for extracurricular reading.

After his graduation in 1873 he registered in the Konstantinovskoe Military School in St. Petersburg. He was seventeen years old, and clearly not yet a revolutionary. Sympathy for the people and disbelief in God did not yet seem incompatible with a military career in the service of the Russian state. The ground had been prepared, however, and his political innocence failed to survive a half year in the capital. His interest in military science and drills waned as he devoted more of his time to Russian literature and literary criticism, pondering the questions raised by his reading and experience. During these months, he saw a good deal of his stepbrother Mitrofanov, an officer stationed at the capital, who had graduated from the General Staff Academy. In the company of Mitrofanov and his friends, Georgii brought into the open one of the chief questions over which he was brooding, that of whether one's proper duty consisted of loyalty to the Tsar or loyalty to the country.[10] If he were to enter military service, as had so many of his family, he might be called upon to act against the welfare of the Russian people. Could he, then, in good conscience forget his responsibilities to the people and serve the Tsar? He decided that he could not and withdrew from Konstantinovskoe after only one semester. At the beginning of 1874, he applied for and was granted permission to postpone his term of military service, and he then settled down to prepare for the entrance examinations to the Mining Institute in St. Petersburg.

Plekhanov's move did not represent a decision for a revolutionary career; nor was it, as has been suggested, "his first gesture as 'a repentant nobleman.'"[11] His behavior in the summer of 1874, which he spent with his mother on the estate in Gudalovka, though it indicated the advanced character of his outlook, was not yet that of a committed revolutionary. After her husband's death in 1873 Maria Fedorovna had returned to Gudalovka, hoping to manage the estate alone. This proved impossible, small though it now was, and at last she decided to sell all but forty acres. The peasants of Gudalovka expressed interest in purchasing the land, but they were outbid by a well-to-do merchant, and Maria, despite her sympathy for the peasants, was on the point of selling the land to the merchant when Georgii arrived. He was outraged at the impending transaction and threatened that if she let the land go to a stranger rather than to "our peasants," he would set fire to the merchant's storehouse and turn himself over to the authorities for judgment. Knowing that he meant what he said, Maria yielded.[12]

In reply to this demonstration of good will, the peasants shortly thereafter burned down the Plekhanov manor house,[13] apparently in the belief that the land would not really be theirs so long as the house of the former landowner remained standing. Then, having started the fire, they proceeded to commit foolhardy acts of bravery to save the family's furniture and other belongings. Plekhanov's conviction as to the irrationality of the peasants, later a major element in his social outlook, may have been partly rooted in these events.

The famous Russian anarchist Kropotkin, a classic example of a repentant nobleman, reveals the psychology of the type in his memoirs. Speaking of the pursuit of scientific knowledge, he says: "But what right had I to these highest joys when all around me was nothing but misery and struggle for a moldy bit of bread; when whatever I should spend to enable me to live in that world of higher emotions must needs be taken from the very mouths of those who grew the wheat and had not bread enough for their children?"[14] In Plekhanov's shift from a military career to that of a mining engineer there is no indication of the repentant sentiments expressed by Kropotkin. It is curious, however, that Plekhanov, with his undistinguished record in scientific subjects, chose mining engineering instead of languages and literature or social sciences, where his interests and talents had already been demonstrated. The explanation for the choice no doubt lies in the peculiarities of the radical spirit in Russia in the sixties and early seventies, with its addiction to utilitarianism, positivism, materialism, and science. Turgenev's nihilist, Bazarov, was a doctor and an amateur scientist. Lopukhov and Kirsanov, two of the central characters in Chernyshevsky's novel *What Is to Be Done?*, although they are devoted to the popular welfare, are concerned above all with the advancement of science. In the same work, Vera Pavlovna, who establishes a workshop organized on socialist principles, later embarks upon the study of medicine. Chernyshevsky saw no inconsistency between acquiring knowledge and serving the people; indeed, science appeared to be one of the most likely ways to improve the popular welfare. Such a formulation would have been particularly appealing to a youth with strong intellectual interests. And, as between natural science and literature or social studies, much greater prestige was attached to the former, because of its association with positivism and materialism, and its superficially more utilitarian character.

Some such considerations as these surely induced Plekhanov to transfer from military to scientific studies, from Konstantinovskoe to the Mining Institute, which, parenthetically, now bears his name. He remained enrolled in the school for only two years, however, and when he left the Institute it was not as a mining engineer but as a stalwart of the revolutionary movement.

2

"TO THE PEOPLE!"

Plekhanov first arrived in St. Petersburg in 1873 just as revolutionary populism was burgeoning into what would soon become the most substantial movement against Russia's established system since the Decembrist Conspiracy of 1825. From England in 1861, Herzen, already disillusioned with Tsar Alexander II, cried to the students in his newspaper *Kolokol* (The Bell): "To the people! . . . That is your place. . . . Prove . . . that out of you will come not clerks, but soldiers of the Russian people." At first ignored, Herzen's injunction received a positive response a dozen years later, thanks to a number of developments in the sixties which emphasized the failings of the Alexandrine regime against which he was protesting.

The arrest and imprisonment of a group of liberals who had dared to ask for a government responsive to the people's wishes, and the imprisonment of Chernyshevsky and a fellow literary critic, Dmitri Pisarev, conveyed to the public a sense of the intransigence of the government on the questions of political and civil liberty. The greater latitude permitted the press in the early 1860's was progressively curtailed as time went on; and the policies of the Minister of Education, Count Dmitri Tolstoy, appointed in 1866, incurred the hatred of progressive elements of society, including both students and professional people. Sociological researches and two famines toward the end of the decade brought into sharp relief the unfortunate plight of the peasantry under the new regime and reinforced the sympathetic attitude of elements of the educated classes toward the mass of Russian people.

In the later sixties and early seventies the populist movement (*narodnichestvo*)[1] received considerable impetus from the writings of the revolutionary publicists Petr Lavrov and Mikhail Bakunin. Both envisaged a great peasant upheaval against the existing social and political order, to be instigated by the intelligentsia. Both, following in the tradition of Herzen and Chernyshevsky, saw the collectivistic peasant commune as the nucleus of the agrarian socialist order they proposed to erect. The contours of the new society they projected were more than a little vague, for, quite characteristically, they were more concerned with demolition than with construction. Both had definite anarchistic leanings[2] and therefore qualified theirs as a social-revolutionary movement, aimed not at the winning of political rights within the state, not at the reform of the state, nor even at its conquest and utilization for the establishment of their social programs. They wished once and for all to put an end to the state which, in their view, was by its very nature an instrument of coercion.

The prominence of the anarchist ideal in the Narodnik movement requires explanation. One might expect revolutionary movements in a country groaning under the yoke of absolutism to have a positive attitude toward political liberty and constitutional government. That at least was the pattern in the earlier history of West European countries. Just because Russia's development lagged behind, radical movements there took on a different coloration. From the mid-nineteenth century on, such Russian observers of Western Europe as Herzen were persuaded that the liberal revolutions had overthrown one tyranny only to install another. Absolutism had been replaced by the dominance of the bourgeoisie, and the great majority still remained oppressed. In the eyes of Russian radicals who followed this lead—and they prevailed during the seventies—constitutional government and political liberty were merely a deception intended to mask the political supremacy of the exploiters of the people. Failing to grasp the significance of the rule of law, and the potentialities for democratizing the then narrowly based political systems of Western countries, they were inclined to reject liberal political philosophy in toto. The Russians, they resolved, would not be taken in; they would not struggle to overthrow tsarism only to give the people a new set of masters. Instead, the centralized state organization, which seemed inextricably bound up with oppression, would be destroyed; the people could be free only if power were diffused to the numerous communal organizations which should make up the body politic.

Lavrov and Bakunin, though their basic outlook and aims had much in common, differed as to means. Bakunin believed the peasants to be natural revolutionists, always on the verge of eruption, so that the intelligentsia going among them could call forth rebellions immediately by a few inflammatory words. Lavrov, while agreeing that the peasants represented sound revolutionary material, was less hopeful about the ease of arousing them. Therefore, instead of calling for immediate agitation as did Bakunin, he insisted upon a preliminary period of propaganda among the peasantry to ensure and solidify their support for the anarcho-socialist revolution. A third revolutionary strategist, whose ideas were destined to have a considerable vogue some years later, was Petr Tkachev. In contrast to the other two, Tkachev had little faith in the revolutionary propensities of the peasants, and, accordingly, laid the responsibility for making the revolution exclusively upon the intelligentsia. They must conspire to seize the state power and afterwards use it in support of the social revolution. In other words, Tkachev did not share the anarchist views of Lavrov and Ba-kunin but saw in the state a positive weapon for bringing about the estab-lishment of a new socio-political regime.

In conformity more with the ideas of Lavrov than Bakunin in the first instance, circles of the intelligentsia known as the Chaikovskists, after one of their leaders, were secretly organized in the early 1870's. Parallel with these, revolutionary propaganda was carried on with considerable success among the hundreds of Russian students who were attending universities in Switzerland. The aim of these movements was to build a force of propagandists among the intelligentsia to go among the peasants spread-ing the new gospel. The two parallel movements, or more accurately the two branches of the movement, converged in 1874 when the Russian gov-ernment, having got wind of the revolutionary propaganda among Russian students abroad, ordered them all to return home.[3] In the summer of 1874 there occurred the first of the extraordinary pilgrimages "to the people," when hundreds of youths of upper- and middle-class backgrounds, as if under the spell of some apocalyptic vision, forsook their studies and occu-pations, left their homes and families, donned peasant clothing, and set off to the countryside to enlist the collaboration of the peasants in bringing heaven down to earth. The apostles of the new evangel were often rudely awakened by their inability to communicate with the peasants, who were extremely suspicious of the strange visitors, if not downright hostile. Not infrequently, the young enthusiasts were refused shelter for the night—although the inhospitable peasants sometimes notified the police and thus secured for their well-wishers quarters in a district jail.

Between 1874 and 1876, over wide areas of Russia, similar experiences were registered. Everywhere, the Narodniks found the peasants deaf to socialistic propaganda but clearly enthusiastic about a division of the land of the nobles. Wherever they penetrated, dozens and hundreds of the Na-rodnik faithful were arrested and jailed: in two months of 1874 alone, 770 were arrested. Discouraged, their numbers sorely reduced, a few stalwarts who had escaped imprisonment, together with the new recruits who flowed into the movement, organized in 1876 a new sort of activity, more in keeping with the tactical dicta of Bakunin. The new direction taken involved both the creation of a much more conspiratorial and tightly knit organization and the discarding of socialist propaganda among the peasantry in favor of an agitation for immediate uprisings, to culminate in a massive revolution for "land and liberty." Zemlia i Volia (Land and Liberty), the magic words counted upon to galvanize the peasants into action, was the name given to the new organization. At that stage in its development, Georgii Plekhanov's life merged with that of the revolutionary movement.

In St. Petersburg in 1873 and the years immediately following, when revolutionary fervor gripped a significant number of the educated youth, a university student brought up in devotion to principles of justice, altruism, and responsibility to the people could not but have been drawn into the revolutionary whirlpool. The wonder is that Plekhanov remained outside as long as he did, for it was not until late 1875 that he joined the revolutionary cause. Had Plekhanov been an ardent revolutionist in the summer of 1874, he would surely have joined the crusade "to the people" instead of occupying himself in Gudalovka with preparation for the entrance examinations to the Mining Institute. In his first year at the Institute he so distinguished himself as to be awarded a stipend for the following year,[4] which is sufficient proof of his preoccupation with studies. Even so, he was no doubt exposed to revolutionary literature; but he had not yet been caught up in the movement of the young idealists. He could not yet subscribe to their credo (as it was later recalled by one of their number, Pavel Axelrod):

He who wishes to work for the people must abandon the university, forswear his privileged condition, his family, and turn his back even upon science and art. All connections linking him with the upper classes of society must be severed, all of his ships burned behind him; in a word, he must voluntarily cut himself off from any possible retreat. The propagandist must, so to speak, transform his whole inner essence, so as to feel at one with the lowest strata of the people, not only ideologically but also in everyday manner of life.[5]

Axelrod, who was eventually to become Plekhanov's closest collaborator, came from a background very different from that of Plekhanov. He was born in Pochep in the Ukrainian province of Chernigov in 1850 to an impoverished lower-middle-class Jewish family, and during his boyhood suffered want and discrimination.[6] With the aid of some well-to-do members of the community he managed to secure a gymnasium education in a state school. Encounters with the works first of Belinsky and then of Lassalle infused him with an exalted idealism, with a stirring conception of the high calling of man, and he resolved to devote his life to the liberation of all the poor and persecuted of Russia. In the early 1870's, he joined the Narodnik movement and began propagandistic activities among students at the University of Kiev.* By 1874 he had abandoned Lavrism for Bakuninism. Obliged to leave Russia to escape arrest, he spent the greater part of his stay abroad in Switzerland, where he collaborated with some of Bakunin's Russian followers in publishing activities.

Axelrod first met Plekhanov in the winter of 1875–76, when the younger man gave shelter to the returned revolutionist in his room in Petersburg. Since there was some risk involved in playing host to a person wanted by the police—and to a virtual stranger at that—one can certainly assume that Plekhanov was by this time more than a lukewarm sympathizer to the revolutionary cause. From Axelrod's point of view, however, Plekhanov's continued attendance at the Mining Institute put him outside the movement. But he was attracted by Plekhanov's intelligence and self-discipline and attempted to dissuade him from completing his studies: "If you take so long to perfect yourself in chemistry, when will you begin to work for the revolution?" According to O. V. Aptekman, a later associate of Plekhanov, Georgii was deeply impressed by Axelrod's "supreme loyalty to the revolution," although it was not Axelrod's influence which chiefly determined Plekhanov's total commitment. Before his meeting with Axelrod, Plekhanov had already attended clandestine meetings of revolutionary students, and of intelligentsia and factory workers; and it was by way of this channel that he moved into the career of a revolutionist. Early in 1876, he permitted his room to be used for meetings,[7] and more and more of his time went into studies of a social and political nature, less and less into mining engineering.

A few months after Axelrod had left, Plekhanov gave refuge to Lev Deutsch, who also was to become a close collaborator. Deutsch, born in southern Russia in 1855, was one of the boldest and most energetic of all the revolutionists of the seventies. While doing military service in the early 1870's, he became associated with the Bakuninist advocates of rebellion centered in Kiev. Among them were Iakov Stefanovich and Vera Zasulich, with whom he formed very close attachments. He made himself a wanted man by carrying out an assignment that resulted in the liberation of an arrested comrade from prison. He himself was then apprehended and faced the prospect of a military trial. In 1876, he managed to escape, and, subsequently, together with Stefanovich, masterminded the so-called Chigirin Affair. He was arrested again, escaped once more, and afterwards participated in the attempted killing of an *agent provocateur*.

We are indebted to Deutsch for the following description of Plekhanov

* According to one of his later associates, F. Dan, "for subsequent generations of Social Democrats he became the guardian of the best moral traditions of the revolutionary movement." See *Proiskhozhdenie bol'shevizma*, p. 192.

in 1876, which, among other things, gives evidence of the deep impress made upon Plekhanov's personal habits and appearance by his military training:

> In his external appearance and dress, Plekhanov—in contrast to almost all of us revolutionists of that time—didn't resemble a "'nihilist": he dressed cleanly, neatly, but without pretensions of being a dandy; his hair was brushed straight back, and his small dark-red beard was regularly trimmed, whereas many of us rarely encountered a razor and comb, so that our hair was in "picturesque disorder."
>
> In manners, ways, and habits, also, Plekhanov was sharply distinguished from us: he was polite, correct, produced the impression of a "well-bred young person," whereas our "nihilistic manners" had gained a noisy notoriety.
>
> Thinking back now of the twenty-year-old youth I have described, and comparing him with Plekhanov as he was in more mature age, I do not find any especially large difference either in his appearance or in his manners, ways, character: the general type remained almost without change. Until old age, he preserved the swarthy color of face, the military bearing, and the slightly graying hair.
>
> Women found him attractive; but in the entirely regular features of his face there was something Mongolian, which he himself explained by the Tartar origin of his distant ancestors—indicated, in his words, by the name 'Ple-khan-ov.'
>
> He had a very expressive, intelligent face, which attracted attention at once. Especially remarkable were the dark hazel eyes which seemed to penetrate his interlocutor, which looked out sternly from under extraordinarily thick eyebrows and long eyelashes with an ironical smile.[8]

In those early years, Deutsch added, Plekhanov liked to sing "La donna è mobile."

The academic year 1875–76 was decisive for Plekhanov's transformation into a revolutionist. Little by little he was drawn into a full commitment from which there would be no return; and, in proportion as he gave himself to revolutionary activity, his attention to his studies declined. The student whose outstanding work won him a stipend at the end of his first year was expelled for failure to attend classes at the end of the second.[9]

In the summer of 1876 Plekhanov went to visit his mother in the country —for the last time, as events proved. His words and manner gave notice of the new life upon which he was embarking and led to painful and emotional scenes. All his family was distressed, and his mother begged him to forswear his intentions. Georgii tried to explain his decision as an inevitable conclusion from the devotion to truth and justice which she herself had instilled in him. Disarmed by this reply, she could only murmur, "But you will perish." Not wishing to cause her anguish but even more strongly impelled not to turn back, he retorted: "And what would happen if everyone reasoned that way?"[10]

Plekhanov's return to Petersburg in the fall of 1876, and his complete

immersion in the revolutionary movement, coincided with the founding of
Zemlia i Volia, an organization in which he was destined to play a leading
role. In a matter of months, he had already attracted attention among the
students as an outstandingly capable and energetic recruit.[11] Thus he took
a conspicuous part in the Kazan Square demonstration, a well-known event
in the history of the Russian revolutionary movement which Plekhanov
himself later described with clinical objectivity.[12]

The demonstration was the desperate act of a group of revolutionists,
repulsed by the people whose interest they were pledged to uphold and,
in the bargain, mercilessly harassed by a powerful governmental apparatus
they were impotent to cope with. Remnants of the revolutionary forces
filtered back from the country into the urban centers, especially St. Petersburg, where such leaders as Mark Natanson and Sophia Perovskaia re-
formed them into new ranks under the banner of Zemlia i Volia. Those at
liberty were outraged that hundreds of their comrades languished in
prisons, not yet brought to trial; some had even been so harshly handled
that they had died. Having failed in the countryside, the revolutionists
began propaganda in the factories. Inspired by a demonstration staged by
the intelligentsia the previous spring at the funeral of a student who was
said to have been murdered by his jailers, a group of workers proposed a
demonstration of their own, to which they promised to attract as many as
two thousand. The growing sympathy of the leaders of Zemlia i Volia for
militant Bakuninism led them to favor the plan. A demonstration would
serve as a protest against the government for its treatment of their imprisoned comrades and as a device for exciting further public actions.

Plekhanov was one of the organizers of the demonstration, and he did
his best to ensure a large turnout. But as the day fixed for the demonstration neared, it became clear that the rosy promises of the workers were
quite impossible of realization. Nevertheless, to avoid loss of face and demoralization of the movement, it was decided to go ahead anyway. On
December 6, 1876, a crowd numbering more students than workers began
to gather before the Kazan Cathedral. After delaying the proceedings for
some time in hopes that additional demonstrators would turn up—estimates
of the number in attendance vary from 150 to 500—the leaders decided to
act. Suddenly, in the center of the crowd which stood in one corner of the
open space before the cathedral, a young man waved a cap over his head
and cried, "Comrades!" The noise of the crowd subsided and the throng
closed in to listen. The speaker delivered a rapid, impassioned harangue
in which he reminded the assembly that Chernyshevsky, long imprisoned
only because he wished the people well, was now joined by hundreds of
the youth who suffered for the same "crime."[13] The prisoners, in their tor-
ment, were at one with the peasants whose "liberation" had turned out a

sham. When the speaker had finished, a young worker unfurled a red banner on which were inscribed the words "Zemlia i Volia." The crowd shouted in response: "Hail to the socialist revolution! Hail to 'Land and Liberty'!" Hardly had the first syllables of the speech been pronounced when the shrill whistles of the police sounded, summoning the janitors of the neighborhood to their aid. Before the speech was over, the police had begun seizing individuals in the throng. A melee ensued in which some were injured and some arrested, while the rest scattered and fled. Plekhanov was among those who managed to escape, but now his bridges were burned irretrievably. For he was the orator of the Kazan demonstration; he had celebrated entry upon his twenty-first year by irrevocably putting himself outside the law.

Shortly after the demonstration, Plekhanov, thenceforth an object of keen interest in police circles, escaped abroad, where he remained until the middle of 1877. He was accompanied by Natalia Smirnova, whom he had married in October 1876. Little is known about Natalia. She was a medical student, a radical, from Orel, and apparently had children by a former marriage when she became Plekhanov's wife. Prior to their marriage, the two had shared an apartment, along with a third student. Even more obscure than their pre-marital association was the course of their wedded life. We know only that they were separated after two years.*

Aside from a brief stay in Paris, Plekhanov spent his time abroad in Berlin. His judgment of the Social Democrats in the German capital deserves attention for what it reveals of his outlook at the time.[14] As a Bakuninist, Plekhanov abominated established authority and believed in militant opposition. His attitude toward the Social Democrats was on that account supercilious: they seemed to him to partake of that same distasteful "moderation and regularity" many Russians attributed to the German people. In the eyes of a Bakuninist, little could be expected of those who were so utterly lacking in revolutionary spirit that they even "made professions of loyalty to the emperor."

Although it is reported that Plekhanov had read Marx's *Das Kapital* in 1875–76 (it had been translated into Russian in 1872), his impressions of the German Marxists only confirmed him in his Narodnik convictions. Ironically enough, within a few years—in the early phase of his Marxian career—he and his cohorts became the target of some of the same reproaches he earlier directed against the German Social Democracy.

While Plekhanov was abroad, Zemlia i Volia was readied for action. The outlines of a party program were drawn up, a constitution drafted,[15] and new forces added to the old. The new organization bore the strong

---

* But not officially divorced until 1908.

impress of Bakunin's ideas in the realm of organization and method as well as outlook. The charter provided for a strongly centralized, highly conspiratorial organization to be directed by a "basic circle," in the hands of which all the threads of the movement were to lie. Under this coordinating body, a number of divisions were set up to carry out the party's tasks: a section for administration, including the forging of identity papers; sections for propaganda, agitation, and organization among the intelligentsia, the workers, and the peasants; and a "disorganizing" section, the functions of which included the freeing of imprisoned comrades, defense against "government arbitrariness," and the execution of traitors.

Zemlia i Volia was impressively businesslike in organization, but it was a long way from being a mass movement. Its members, most of whom were in their twenties or thirties, were counted by dozens rather than thousands. The organization could, however, draw upon the support of many more sympathizers. Besides, it partly made up for its small numbers by its inner discipline and by the complete dedication of its people to their cause. Decades later, in developing his own organizational conception, Lenin was much influenced by the Zemlia i Volia pattern. The small dimensions of Zemlia i Volia of course limited the scope of its activities, but in addition to the basic circle, centered in St. Petersburg, it had groups of adherents in several other cities, and it occasionally sent out teams of agitators to areas thought to be in a state of ferment.

Plekhanov, in exile, was outside the programmatic and constitutional deliberations, but he had sufficient standing to be elected to the "basic circle."[16] And after his return to Russia in mid-1877 he devoted himself to the cause with tireless energy. His activities underline the fact that the sections established were in no sense water-tight compartments, for in little more than a year's time his work took him among peasants, students, factory workers, and even Cossacks. If he never became an adept of the "disorganizational" section, neither was he alien to the coin in which it dealt. In this period Plekhanov carried brass knuckles, practiced the use of the dagger, and slept with a revolver under his pillow.[17] He had no job other than that of professional revolutionist; then and for some years to come, Zemlia i Volia, financed by a few rich sympathizers and members, defrayed his few expenses.

His first assignment after returning from abroad took him to Saratov on the lower Volga, the scene of popular disturbances in the past, where the revolutionists were establishing bases for action among the peasants. The local groups of Zemlevoltsi patterned the division of labor in their organizations on that prescribed for the entire enterprise in the constitution. But although Plekhanov had the chance in Saratov to prove his talents among the workers and intelligentsia, so fashionable was the desire to go among the peasants—the authentic people—that he insisted on securing a position as a teacher in a village school. He was still wanted by the police, and since there existed no local facilities for fabricating the papers that would be required, he accepted those of Alexander Mikhailov, another member of the "settlement" who as yet had no police record. In the course of an interview with the school council of a neighboring village he was almost unmasked. When the priest who examined his papers recognized the name of the son of an old friend, he plied Plekhanov with a long series of questions about the members of the Mikhailov family. With a coolness and self-possession that he was to reveal more than once, Plekhanov answered to the priest's satisfaction. However, he failed to obtain the post and returned to Saratov. Events seemed to conspire in driving Plekhanov into association with factory workers rather than peasants; when he went "to the people," the people turned out to be city workers, a fact of no little importance for his ideological evolution.

Back in Saratov, Plekhanov succeeded in attracting to Zemlia i Volia a worker group that had been under the influence of the Lavrists and also some of the intelligentsia.[18] According to Aptekman, who was in the Saratov revolutionary group, Plekhanov at the time proved his worth as a writer by sitting down and dashing off a "brilliant" program in twenty or thirty minutes. In the fall of the year (1877), the police, having quietly inquired into the doings of the "settlers," raided one of their centers. A little later, Plekhanov was caught in a trap set by the police at the apartment of one of those who had been arrested. On the way to the police station, he surreptitiously attempted to get rid of one of the two sets of papers he carried, but a kindly gentleman, seeing it fall to the ground, retrieved it and handed it back. Still unsuspecting, the policemen allowed Plekhanov ample time at the police station without surveillance to rid himself for good of the damaging document. It was a lazy Sunday, and the policeman in charge grew bored with Plekhanov, accompanied him to his apartment, where he made a cursory inspection, and then released him after asking him to sign a paper promising to appear at the police station on the following day.[19] Having played to perfection his role in this comic opera incident, Plekhanov conveyed warnings to all the other Saratov revolutionists and then fled to St. Petersburg.

The period from mid-1877 on witnessed a quickening of the tempo of social action, giving reason to believe that "Russian society was beginning to lose its patience," and was "ready seriously to protest the arbitrariness of the government."[20] In July 1877, Bogoliubov, a political prisoner awaiting trial, was publicly whipped at the order of the Governor of St. Petersburg, General F. F. Trepov, for failing to stand when the general came through on a tour of the prison. This brutal act, following rumors that had been filtering out of still worse treatment inflicted upon the prisoners, aroused the resentment of the educated public.* This sentiment was sustained and heightened by the autumn trials of the Narodnik youth, many of whom had been awaiting judgment for more than three years. The defiant speeches some of them made in court found a sympathetic response in one part of the public, which in like manner secretly blessed the attempted assassination of Trepov in January 1878 by Vera Zasulich.

Zasulich, who later was to become one of Plekhanov's most intimate associates, was born in Smolensk in 1852. The daughter of a small landowner, she was educated at a *pension*. Instead of becoming a proper young lady, however, she modeled herself on the nihilists. She paid little attention to her appearance, and the slovenliness of her dress and unconventionality of her way of life were to become proverbial in radical circles. From nihilism to revolutionary activity was but a step; and Vera, full of compassion for the people and too morally earnest to halt in the realm of talk, moved easily from one to the other while still in her teens. At sixteen she was already involved in conspiratorial maneuvers on the fringe of the notorious Nechaev circle.† She was arrested in 1869, and spent the following four years in prison or exile. Upon returning to western Russia, she became associated with the "rebels" operating in the Kiev area. Moving to St. Petersburg in 1877, she was outraged to learn of Trepov's brutal treatment of Bogoliubov and felt impelled to vindicate human dignity. Shy and self-effacing though she was, she mustered the courage to plan and execute the attack on Trepov all by herself. Following the conclusion of the mass trial of the Narodniks, she came to Trepov's office and fired a shot that wounded him gravely but not fatally. She then gave herself up.

At the conclusion of her trial in March 1878, the jury brought in a verdict of Not Guilty; and this public expression of lack of confidence in the government was seconded when the crowd prevented the police from re-arresting Zasulich, thus enabling her to escape abroad. In the same period, dissatisfaction among the factory workers erupted into strikes. And, a little later, in the south, the Don Cossacks engaged in disorders in protest against certain new government regulations which they viewed as an infringement upon their traditional rights. For the partisans of agitation, these manifestations of discontent and willingness to take action were harbingers of the impending success of their movement. Such encouraging portents called forth extraordinarily energetic endeavors on their part. Plekhanov

* The Russian penal system in those days was curiously inconsistent in the application of punishment to political prisoners, being tyrannical and brutal in some cases and relatively lenient in others.

† The creation of Serge Nechaev, a fanatical revolutionist who affirmed that the end justifies the means, and insisted upon blind obedience of his followers to his dictates. It is most doubtful that Zasulich was aware of Nechaev's Machiavellianism.

stood at the very center of things, seizing every opportunity to make capital of the nascent spirit of opposition. His endeavors brought him into conflict with the Lavrists, who, with their insistence on the need for a gradual and extended preparation and their increasing sympathy for the German Social Democrats, seemed to Plekhanov a travesty of a revolutionary party. The "Orator," as Plekhanov had been called since the Kazan demonstration, impressed audiences by his passionate conviction and dialectical skill. The manner in which he could reduce the position of an opponent to absurdity may be illustrated by the account of a witness of one of his early triumphs.[21]

In one of a series of debates between the Lavrists and the Bakuninists which took place in a student apartment, the Lavrists had almost demolished the Bakuninists, but had consented to continue the debate a few nights later. At the second session, the students in attendance seemed ready to acknowledge the superiority of the Lavrist position, which one of its exponents defended persuasively against the Bakuninists:

We are no less revolutionists than you. But a revolution grows naturally out of the whole aggregate of social conditions, and we can only prepare conscious participants for it, while opposing every attempt at a rebellion, uprising, mutiny. . . . A rebellion is not a revolution, but only retards the revolution. An unsuccessful mutiny—and a mutiny cannot, must not, succeed—throws the movement back for whole years, for decades. A premature uprising is a crime against socialism and against the people. The blood of the fighters who perish, the suffering of the anguished masses, the prolonged victory of reaction—all of that must lie upon the conscience of those who are always pushing the people into "continuous revolution," as your Bakunin puts it.

Nonplussed at this line of attack, the Bakuninists sat dejectedly, whispering among themselves and glancing anxiously into the adjoining room. Suddenly animated cries were heard: "Georgii! Georgii! Orator! How late you are! Speak, Georgii!" Plekhanov thereupon burst in on the scene of the debate, and immediately took up the attack against the Lavrists:

I ask the meeting to forgive me, but I could not come earlier. . . . I have just come by the back stairs from a meeting where I was concerned with doing just what the proponents of peaceful progress reproach us buntarists [advocates of rebellion] for doing: pushing toward "continuous revolution." Speaking more plainly, I advised the representatives of the students to organize demonstrations everywhere in the higher schools, and if possible also with our worker groups, in anticipation of the announcement of the verdict in the trial of the 193. . . .

I have come just as one of your orators was feelingly expanding on the theme that he too, you see, is a revolutionist but not a buntarist; that he, of course, with all his soul is for a good, nice, beneficial revolution, but with all his mind and heart against a bad, nasty, pernicious rebellion. . . . I value the nobility of his sentiments but I cannot follow his invitation to love virtue in the form of the revolution and to hate vice in the shape of a rebellion. . . . I cannot because I am in doubt: does the orator possess some sort of invention office where an incipient movement can secure a patent for the correct manufacture of a revolution? Give me such a patent and I am with you! But can you say in advance, at the very beginning of a movement, that this is a revolution and that a rebellion? . . . And what if suddenly we begin to make a nasty rebellion and out of it there begins to emerge a nice revolution? Do we have no right, without your patent, to participate in a spontaneously arising movement? Must we refuse all participation? . . . Perhaps even stand at the side of the government and fight against the movement? And what if suddenly, at some unforeseen hour, out of the rebellion should grow an unpatented revolution? . . . Oh, my God, how awful that would be.

Now it was the turn of the Lavrists to be discomfited, but presently one of them rejoined: "That is a sophism. When a real revolution breaks out, no one will ask if this is a revolution or not." At this point Plekhanov interrupted:

Excuse me, sir peaceful revolutionists! That is not so easy to recognize at the outset. . . . At what hour was the taking of the Bastille transformed into the great French Revolution? On which day did the three-day July uprising of 1830 cease to be an uprising and become a revolution worthy of mention in history? And the Revolution of 1848? Perhaps, in your opinion, it would have been proper to stop with the liberal banquets and not push the workers into the street? That is what the liberal bourgeoisie wanted to do. . . . And today bourgeois liberalism speaks from your mouths.

Amidst the applause of the Bakuninists and the mutterings of the Lavrists, there were protests: "More sophistry. . . . We are not bourgeois but socialists. . . . We will answer you in a minute." But before the Lavrists could reply, Plekhanov, smacking a clenched fist into the palm of his other hand, retorted:

You are socialists? Perhaps—I do not know. But in any case you are Christian theologians. They, too, believe in the Immaculate Conception and the bloodless birth. . . . We revolutionists don't believe in it just as we don't believe in the peaceful progress of humanity, as we don't believe in a revolution with the permission of the officials. Every great historical achievement of humanity was won in battle, was gained only with blood. . . . And in you who pretend to erudition, there is not the slightest understanding of history and not the least bit of revolutionary feeling. . . . That is why the youth is abandoning you. . . . You are a mutual admiration society and nothing more. . . . Stay with your self-blessed patent for a mythical bloodless revolution!

This account was written from memory by N. Rusanov long after the event, but it has the unmistakable ring of truth. In these passages one gets striking evidence of the early development of Plekhanov's polemical method. We see him immediately taking the offensive, in the belief that a good offense is the best defense; driving his opponent from one position to another, affording him no opportunity to recover and counterattack; relentlessly bombarding him until all his defenses appear to have been reduced to a shambles. We witness the self-assured dialectician, taking the antagonist's propositions and disclosing their inadequacy by developing their logical implications; buttressing and embellishing his argument with historical and literary references; employing a merciless wit, as well as caricature, to render the opponent ridiculous; imputing to him subservience to bourgeois ideology; and, finally, denying him any competence whatever in the subject under discussion. These methods made Plekhanov a formidable adversary, but they were better suited for total war than for winning disciples away from other persuasions, a circumstance that would impede Plekhanov's effectiveness as a political figure.

The passages just cited are noteworthy also from another point of view. When, a few years later, Plekhanov abandoned Bakuninism for Marxism, he was actually taking up an ideology which had many of the features he had denounced in Lavrism. In later debates with the opponents of Marxism, he repeatedly affirmed propositions he had earlier seen fit to ridicule. At the center of his later theory, there stood the doctrine of revolution as the culmination of the "natural" development of society in accord with historical laws; like the Lavrists before him, he warned against revolutionary adventurism, attempts at a premature seizure of power which could only damage the popular cause. He himself would produce something very like a formula "for the correct manufacture of a revolution," and would pillory those who dared advance other tactics. Long years after his battles with the Lavrists, he himself would be branded by his opponents as a "bourgeois" masquerading as a socialist. For the moment, he epitomized the revolutionary will to which he later opposed a deterministic historical process. The problem of reconciling will with "nature" or law was to be a central difficulty of the revolutionary system he upheld throughout most of his life.

Plekhanov's stormy debates with the Lavrists represented only one side of his revolutionary activity. In December 1877, he was also agitating among the students in connection with the trial of the 193, and speaking as a representative of the radical youth at the funeral of the poet Nekrasov.[22] A sizable group of Zemlevoltsi turned out for the procession that accompanied Nekrasov's coffin to its final resting place. Carrying a wreath with the words "From the Socialists," an inner group was surrounded by a ring of their fellows armed with revolvers in the event of police interference. When the procession had reached its destination, Dostoevsky, then fifty-six and a famous literary figure, and Plekhanov, the radical youth of twenty-one, delivered eulogies. Dostoevsky was not overfond of Nekrasov, but he rose to the occasion by placing the deceased poet on a plane equal with Pushkin. Plekhanov spoke the mind of the younger generation, nurtured on the radical critic Pisarev's utilitarian views, when he insisted that Nekrasov dwarfed Pushkin. Somewhat ludicrously, there in the cemetery, surrounded by an armed bodyguard, Plekhanov argued the superiority of Nekrasov's poetry to that of Pushkin, in that the latter "limited himself to singing of the toes of ballerinas," whereas Nekrasov brought a social consciousness into his poetry.

In a matter of days, the same energetic agitator helped to organize a demonstration among the workers of a St. Petersburg cartridge factory where several employees had been killed in an explosion. He wrote an inflammatory leaflet for distribution among them; and on the day of the funeral, he and a number of the other Zemlevoltsi accompanied the mourners to the cemetery. After the coffin had been interred, one of the workers, under the influence of Plekhanov's leaflet, began a fiery speech against "the bosses." So outnumbered were the police on the scene that when they tried to interfere they were not only restrained but held captive by the crowd.[23]

The leaflet Plekhanov wrote for the funeral demonstration is the earliest surviving example of his literary endeavor.[24] It is typical of the agitational methods of the Bakuninist Narodniks, who were intoxicated with the spirit of rebellion: Plekhanov chides the workers for their passiveness in the face of every kind of exploitation and provocation; he charges the explosion to the negligence of the factory officials, who, then, with a show of sanctimony, paid a mere pittance to the bereaved families by way of compensation. "The high officials care not a kopek for your interest; for them the life of a worker is cheaper than that of a dog." Then, rising to a shrill pitch, he concludes: "Workers! It is time for you to begin thinking; you can expect help from no one. Don't expect it from the officials! . . . Long have you been patient and waited until they burn you alive and throw your families out into the world! *Are you still going to be patient, working people!?*"

A similar tone infuses the many other manifestoes Plekhanov wrote during 1878: an appeal to the workers of all St. Petersburg factories to render aid to the strikers of the New Textile Company; an enthusiastic paean to Russian society for acquitting Vera Zasulich and preventing her re-arrest; a denunciation of the subsequent government decree depriving persons detained for political reasons of the right of trial by jury; an incitement to the Cossacks "not to give up without a struggle what your grandfathers won with blood"; a declaration of encouragement and support for demonstrating students who, in the latter part of 1878, were subjected to beatings and mass arrests but fought back valiantly; and an open letter to the Minister of Justice on the treatment of imprisoned students, which he likened to the savage behavior of the Turkish Bashi-Bazouks in Bulgaria.[25] These pronunciamentos mark the varied agitations in which Plekhanov was involved in 1878. They may also be regarded as forerunners of the newspaper that was founded by Zemlia i Volia toward the end of that year, of which Plekhanov became one of three editors.

In the spring of 1878, the constitution and program of Zemlia i Volia, as provided by its charter, were due for review and possible amendment. Under the prodding of Aleksandr Mikhailov, one of the most dedicated and rigorous of the leaders, the organization underwent still further centralization; it was now stipulated that, in all things, "the individual is subordinated to the organization." Plekhanov was entrusted with the working out of the definitive form of the party program, which until then had existed only in a sketchy draft. This task did not require the introduction of new concepts—the party leaders were unshaken in their allegiance to the old—but only the inclusion of some amendments on activity among the people and the putting of the whole into finished form.[26]

The same period saw the resumption of the agitation among the workers that had absorbed Plekhanov's attention prior to the Kazan demonstration, in Saratov, and again in connection with the cartridge factory incident. In March 1878 Plekhanov became intimately engaged in the strike of the New Textile Company.[27] When the factory management lowered wages and introduced a new series of severe regulations, the two thousand hands struck the mill. The strike was partly the result of agitation by a small circle of workers within the mill who were linked to Zemlia i Volia; and a number of the regular Zemlevoltsi, led by Plekhanov, quickly sprang to their assistance. They participated in their mass meetings, gave tactical advice, and collected funds to enable the workers to hold out in their struggles with management. According to one of his friends, Plekhanov made so great an impression upon the workers by his courage, intelligence, and dynamism that they took to calling him "Eagle." In Plekhanov's own account, the workers applied the name to all the nonproletarian revolutionists among them.[28]

The strike proved an exceptionally valuable experience for Plekhanov and his co-workers as well as for the factory hands. To Plekhanov, it meant the discovery of the workers' naïveté: with peasant simplicity, they believed that the Tsar was their friend and that an appeal to the authorities would surely set everything right. Plekhanov and his fellows were thus put into the awkward position of having to compose a petition in the workers' behalf to the royal heir—which, as Plekhanov said, was like asking Satan to offer a prayer to God. But they went ahead, convinced that there was no other way to shatter the fantasies of the workers. The calculation worked brilliantly, for not only did the royal heir ignore the petition, but police forces and Cossacks were even sent against the strikers. The strike ended after two weeks, with some concessions to the workers.

In the course of the strike, one incident occurred which might easily have brought Plekhanov's revolutionary career to an untimely end.[29] As the strike wore on, the police were instructed to detain anyone in the vicinity of the mill who looked suspicious, and Plekhanov found himself arrested one day while simply walking in the neighborhood. Fortunately, he carried with him a set of forged identity papers that made him out to be the son of a respected citizen. The lack of any compromising evidence on his person, and his quietness of dress and manner, convinced the police that he was harmless, and after a day he was released. This escape was not his last. Several months later, anti-government disorders began to occur among the Don Cossacks, and Plekhanov, along with a few other Zemle-voltsi, rushed to the scene. Finding the situation there propitious for agitation, he sent to Petersburg for aid. But before Mikhailov, who had been dispatched for the purpose, appeared in the Don region, Plekhanov returned to the capital to hasten the printing of a manifesto he had drawn up with the collaboration of the insurgent Cossacks. He arrived in Petersburg a few days after a police dragnet had captured many of the most experienced and reliable members of the "basic circle"—a development of which he was entirely ignorant. By good luck, on the way from the railroad station to the "conspiratorial quarter" of the party, where the police lay in wait for just such game as he, Plekhanov chanced to meet one of the survivors of the recent raid, who told him of the disaster and warned him off.[30]

The police action had been so disastrous that the Don agitation had to be dropped in order to restore the organization to some semblance of working order. Together, Plekhanov and Mikhailov undertook the task of rebuilding the organization. Their efforts proved more than merely adequate. Indeed, they were so successful that only a few months later they were able to launch the publication of a monthly newspaper. Once again, Plekhanov's intention of leaving the city for work "among the grass roots" had been thwarted. Placed by fortune in an urban milieu again, he now entered upon a sustained period of agitation among the factory workers, relieved only by the literary duties he assumed as one of the editors of Zemlia i volia.

In the last months of 1878, and more especially in the first months of 1879, a wave of labor unrest swept over Petersburg.[31] These new disturbances were clearly linked to those of the previous spring, for one of the first moves of the strikers at the Koenig textile factory, in late November 1878, was to seek out the assistance of the "students." In January 1879 the workers of the New Textile Company struck again, and they were immediately joined by those of the neighboring English-owned Shaw textile factory. In the sequel, the "worker section" of Zemlia i Volia, headed by Plekhanov, assisted in drafting the demands presented to the factory management and was instrumental in spreading the labor unrest in the capital. Plekhanov drew up a manifesto, distributed at the gates of many of the city's factories, calling attention to the strikes that were going on and soliciting monetary aid for the strikers. Not only was such aid given, but the spirit of dissatisfaction communicated itself to the workers of other plants, some of whom then proceeded to make demands on their own employers. Several employers yielded concessions before the strike movement was broken, as it had been before, by arrests and police violence against the workers. But if the rift between the workers on one side and the employers and police on the other grew deeper, the workers themselves were joining together, and, moreover, were closing ranks with the revolutionists.

At the same time Plekhanov was also having the satisfaction of writing his first formal articles. These pieces, all but one of which appeared in the party organ, included a series of reports on some of the popular agitations of which he had first-hand knowledge, and an extremely interesting theoretical essay in amplification of the program of Zemlia i Volia. In December 1878, another of his articles appeared in a journal called *Nedelia* (The Week), at the invitation of one of the editors, Kablitz, who was a Narodnik sympathizer.[32] In this brief article, Plekhanov appears as the defender of Narodnik conceptions against what he represented as the canards of the belletrist Gleb Uspensky, a well-known author of tales about peasant life.

These promising agitational and literary enterprises were soon to be seriously jeopardized, however. For some time, a crisis had been maturing within the party, and in the spring of 1879 it came to a head. In a matter of weeks, Plekhanov's world came tumbling down around him. For the crisis culminated in his abrupt withdrawal from Zemlia i Volia and from its newspaper as well. Into such extreme isolation was he driven that he seriously considered abandoning his revolutionary vocation and returning to a career in science.

3

REVOLUTIONARY SCHISM

Wᴵᴛʜᴵɴ ᴢᴇᴍʟᴵᴀ ᴵ ᴠᴏʟᴵᴀ a tug of war had been going on for some time between the proponents of mass agitation and the proponents of terrorism. A long train of experiences in the life of the revolutionary organization had given rise to these different tactical emphases, which reflected different conceptions as to how the future of the movement could be assured. The crisis that brought the dissolution of Zemlia i Volia involved theoretical as well as tactical considerations. It came to a head in the disagreement over whether or not to assassinate Alexander II. When a majority of the members elected to sanction that campaign, Zemlia i Volia approached its demise. Plekhanov spearheaded the opposition to the expansion of terrorism, and to the war against Alexander in particular. It is no exaggeration to say that his spirited resistance caused the rupture of this remarkable revolutionary organization.

In spite of great improvements in organization and the seemingly more realistic slogans adopted by the populists under the aegis of Zemlia i Volia, the results of their work among the peasants were hardly more encouraging than before. Bakunin's image of the peasant as a natural revolutionist, who could be aroused to action if only the right words were spoken, bore little resemblance to peasants in real life. Occasionally peasants seemed willing to listen to the subversive ideas of the young revolutionists;[1] but these were isolated encounters, usually reported by a populist who settled in a peasant village, took up an occupation, and gradually gained the confidence of the inhabitants and exerted some influence on a few. This sort of activity took years to develop, however; and, in any case, the winning of a limited influence in a handful of Russia's innumerable villages was a far cry from the spectacular successes that Bakunin had promised. Ironically, the one group of revolutionists that managed to enlist some hundreds of peasants, of the Chigirin district in western Ukraine, into a revolutionary plot owed its success to a forged manifesto of the Tsar. The manifesto made it appear that the officials and the landowners were thwarting the Tsar's wish to turn the land over to the peasants. Thus, the revolutionists could invite the peasants to take up arms *in support of* the Tsar. That such a stratagem alone could win a measure of mass backing speaks volumes about the hopelessness of the populist cause at that time. No wonder that Andrei Zheliabov, one of the leading revolutionists, exclaimed in discouragement that the populists were "like fish beating against the ice." No wonder that Zemlia i Volia gradually curtailed its work in the countryside.

But by no means all the revolutionists were so discouraged. Those who had established themselves in rural communities, made contacts among the peasants, and fancied they observed sympathy for their views, were loath to quit the activity they had initiated only with considerable difficulty. Numbers of these so-called Derevenshchiki (country workers) regarded their work as well begun, and nurtured hopes that it would in time bear fruit. For some, inertia was perhaps the chief reason for refusing to give up; loyalty to the spirit of populism and to the program of Zemlia i Volia may have made them unwilling to draw depressing and painful conclusions about the revolutionary character of the peasants. There probably seemed to many to be no alternative. Like Plekhanov, who became a leading spokesman for the faction, they were unable to conceive of a successful revolution that was not a popular revolution. Since the peasants constituted the great mass of the Russian people, to abandon all effort to revolutionize them appeared tantamount to abandoning the revolution itself.

Although this consideration surely weighed most heavily with Plekhanov, it is likely that in the period 1877–79 some fleeting doubts crossed his mind. His own experience among the peasants was slight, to be sure, but he was aware of the absence of conspicuous achievements among them. Some of the Zemlevoltsi were impressed by the apparent success of the methods employed by Deutsch and others in the Chigirin district, failing to recognize the damning implications against the premises of populism that the episode provided; but Plekhanov was not one of them. He vigorously protested any further use of tactics of deception.[2] Here was an early manifestation of his repugnance for nonrational behavior, which he later came to regard as typical of the peasantry.

He must also have been somewhat disturbed by the failure of the youth, even those who freely professed Narodnik views, to proceed from word to action. In particular, he later alluded to the difficulty of securing recruits to continue the agitation among the Cossacks in the autumn of 1878.[3] By contrast, the success of Plekhanov's agitation among the factory workers made its mark on his thinking. In an article published in *Zemlia i volia* in February 1879, he denounced as "a completely mistaken judgment" the view that the city workers would be "without a large role in the future social revolution."[4] Yet, after all this has been said, it must be emphasized that these doubts merely flickered across Plekhanov's consciousness; that in spite of the relatively greater importance he now attached to the city workers, for him the center of gravity of the future revolution still lay in the countryside. Therefore, he could in good conscience act as the spokesman of the Derevenshchiki in the factional struggle within Zemlia i Volia.

The reservations of the Derevenshchiki notwithstanding, the propaganda and agitation in the countryside did in fact shrink in scope in 1878–79. But the slack was not taken up by a corresponding expansion of propaganda and agitation among the students, professional classes, and factory workers of the urban centers. Instead, a combination of circumstances brought about the magnification of "disorganizational" activity. The government's relentless harassment of the Narodniks, and its frequently atrocious treatment of them in prison, so outraged the revolutionists that they were driven to concentrate their fire directly upon the government. Vera Zasulich's attempt on the life of Trepov met with an enthusiastic response among them. Although the act was her own, not a party enterprise, it did much to redress their sense of injury, and it began a long series of terroristic deeds committed thereafter against high government officials. In the following months, several officials, the most important of whom was N. V. Mezentsov, the head of the notorious Third Section,* were slain; A. R. Drenteln, Mezentsov's successor, narrowly escaped the same fate. Early in 1879, a proposal for the assassination of the Tsar himself began to be canvassed.

Terrorism was attractive to many revolutionists who were discouraged by the lack of success among the peasants, but there were diverse views about positive objectives.[5] At one extreme were those who thought little about the significance of what they advocated, and were simply determined to show their hatred of the regime in a direct and forceful way. At the other extreme were a few individuals, under the influence of Tkachev, who believed that terroristic activity might eventually disorganize the government and permit the seizure of power by the revolutionists. Between the two extremes stood others who conceived of terrorism as an effective means of attaining desired ends, but ends considerably more

---

* The government department to which all police operations were subordinated.

modest than those of the Tkachevists. Some, like Zheliabov, without equiv-ocation defined the aim as the winning of a constitution and political and civil liberties. But such aims were disclaimed initially by most of the ter-rorists, who, still under the strong impress of Bakuninism, scorned politics. Such people—and they probably constituted the majority—argued simul-taneously for war against autocracy and against the establishment of a constitutional regime as well. They thought of terrorism as a means of forcing the government to forgo its interference with their agitational activities among the peasants. They were in the absurd position, as one of the Zemlevoltsi later trenchantly put it, of wanting "no freedom but the freedom of rebellion."[6] This position, incongruous though it was, might have a certain appeal for those of the Derevenshchiki who stood ready to underwrite any means whatsoever that promised to facilitate the agrarian agitation they were bent on advancing.

Most of the terroristic acts of 1878 and early 1879 were executed by persons associated with Zemlia i Volia, although the organization itself was not the initiator, nor were the acts done in its name. However, the increasing absorption of many of its members in such activities made it imperative for the party to define its attitude to terrorism. The proposal to assassinate the Tsar, which if adopted would require a concentration of forces and resources, made a stocktaking all the more urgent. Above all, the opposition in the party leadership to the developing line of action had to be contended with. This opposition, at first latent and then increasingly overt, centered in the Derevenshchiki, headed by Plekhanov.

These elements did not flatly reject every kind of terror, let alone all violence. Their attitude on the latter point was typified by Plekhanov's verbal flogging of the "peace-loving" Lavrists. On the narrower issue, neither Plekhanov nor his allies objected to the party constitution, although it provided for a "disorganizing" section, empowered to carry out assaults on enemies of the party. Plekhanov's impassioned participation in the agi-tations connected with the trial and acquittal of Vera Zasulich suggests that he, no less than other revolutionists, greeted her act with enthusiastic approval. Yet he opposed the repetition of such acts and, particularly, the proposal to assassinate the Tsar. To him and his faction, the adoption of such policies would be a distortion, if not simply the out-and-out abandon-ment, of the basic methods and aims of Narodnichestvo. Not called Derevenshchiki for nothing, they understood populism to mean "going to the people," and working among them for a mass revolution against the very foundations of the social order. Consistent with this image of the revolutionary process, Plekhanov favored the promotion of "mass terror-ism" in the factories and countryside. In the spring of 1877, he had advo-cated the training of the peasants for armed combat, and, a year later, he had himself taken part in an attempt to set fire to a plant whose managers were extravagantly exploiting the workers.[7] But what did such operations have in common with a contest, mainly in the capital, of the revolutionary intelligentsia alone against the government? The Derevenshchiki sanctioned armed self-defense and might condone an occasional act of individual terror of a retaliatory nature. But they did not believe in either the efficacy or the suitability of such methods for achieving the goals of populism. A mass upheaval could hardly be touched off by a handful of revolutionists concentrated in St. Petersburg, they reasoned; and without popular support the foes of the established order could never develop the strength essential for its overthrow. Instead of making agitation in the countryside easier, a program of terrorism would undoubtedly result in new and harsher government repressions.

Besides, they argued, in striking directly against the government, the terrorists would be launching a *political* campaign, instead of devoting themselves to what should be their first concern—the urgent social and economic plight of the people. Those who hoped to attain political liberty through individual acts of terror, Plekhanov contended, were certain to be disappointed. As he said: "You cannot establish a house of parliament at the point of a pistol."[8] But feasibility aside, he rejected even the aspiration for constitutional government, finding it irreconcilable with the anarchist premises of his populism. This objection was to prove critical for Plekhanov, and it highlights one of the qualities that set him apart from most of his revolutionary comrades. Already leaning toward theoretical interests and conceptions, he grasped as others did not the true import of terroristic acts against the state, and their incompatibility with the traditional outlook of populism. The unfortunate concomitant of his strength in theory was neatly indicated by Mikhailov, one of the leading proponents of terrorism, who later said, almost certainly with Plekhanov in mind:

Everywhere the majority had only one desire; a bloody fight with the government. But there are people who are more influenced by theory than by the logic of events, and they did not share this state of mind. These people had their representatives in the populist organization.[9]

Among the Derevenshchiki, Plekhanov more than anyone feared that if terroristic activity were not kept in check it would soon command all the funds and personnel of the organization and force the suspension of all other activities. If the terrorists were given free rein, he warned, the organization would be forced "to abandon one after another its old realms of activity, just as Rome abandoned its provinces one after another under the pressure of the barbarians."[10] Not only would such a course be disastrous for the movement, in his view, but it also implied extremely distasteful consequences for him personally. When the proposed assassination of

Alexander II was under discussion, it became clear that its acceptance would entail the temporary suspension of the newspaper and the departure from the capital of those members not directly concerned. Such measures would put an end to Plekhanov's literary work and also to his efforts among the factory workers—the two enterprises to which all his attention was devoted.

Plekhanov's strictures upon terrorism did not emerge fully until the early months of 1879. Earlier, there had seemed to be little reason for alarm, for at the spring conference of the leaders of Zemlia i Volia in 1878, a large majority had voted *against* a resolution calling for the expansion of disorganizational activity.[11] In spite of this decision, however, assassination had followed upon assassination in the summer and fall of 1878. Plekhanov may well have begun to entertain some anxiety, but once again extremely persuasive evidence turned up seeming to indicate that his fears were unwarranted. In the first issue of *Zemlia i volia*, Sergei Kravchinsky, one of the three editors, wrote an article defining the proper relationship between the revolutionists and the masses, and between terrorism and agrarian activity:

Revolutions are the business of the popular masses. History prepares them. The revolutionists haven't the power to control anything. They can be only the instruments of history, the voices of popular aspirations. Their role consists only in organizing the people in the name of these aspirations and demands and in advancing them into the struggle for their realization; to facilitate the hastening of that revolutionary process which, in accordance with the irresistible laws of history, is taking place in the present period. Outside of that role, they are nothing; within its bounds, they are one of the most powerful factors in history.

Therefore, the foundation of any really revolutionary program must be the popular ideals as they have been created by history in a given time and in a given place. Throughout time, whenever and to whatever extent the Russian people rose up, they demanded land and liberty. Land, as the common property of those who work it, and liberty, as the universal right of all people to conduct their own affairs.

[As for terror] we must remember that not by this path will we achieve the emancipation of the working masses. Terrorization has nothing in common with the struggle against the foundations of the existing order. . . . Only the people can destroy the system. Therefore, the chief mass of our forces must work among the people. The terrorists are nothing more than a *security* detachment, designated for the defense of those workers from the treacherous blows of enemies. To direct all our forces into the struggle against State power would mean to abandon our chief, constant goal in order to pursue an incidental, provisional one.[12]

These passages were so close in spirit to Plekhanov's own thinking that he might have written them himself. What made them dramatically convincing was that they were written by the man who had committed one of the most sensational of the terrorist deeds, the very person who had assassinated Mezentsov. With Kravchinsky taking such a stand, it may be inferred that in October 1878, at least, the differences between the Derevenshchiki and the terrorists had not clearly emerged. But in the next few months they rapidly came to a head.

In spite of the disclaimers of people like Kravchinsky, at the end of 1878 and in the first months of 1879 more and more of the resources and efforts of Zemlia i Volia were in fact devoted to terrorism. The increasingly favorable temper of the revolutionists with regard to guerrilla warfare found expression in the killing of a secret police agent, in the attempt on the life of Drenteln, the new head of the Third Section, and, at last, in an attempted assassination of the Tsar himself (April 2, 1879), all in little more than a month. Kravchinsky had by this time gone abroad, and Morozov, the third editor of *Zemlia i volia,* attempted to provide a theoretical rationale for terrorism and for that very struggle against state power which Kravchinsky had termed "an incidental, provisional goal." Morozov's articles did not appear in *Zemlia i volia,* but in a separate series of leaflets issued by the now frankly terrorist Zemlevoltsi group in Petersburg. On March 15, only two days after the attack on Drenteln, Morozov declared:

Political assassination *is the most terrible weapon for our foes,* against which neither a menacing army nor a legion of spies will help. . . . That is why three or four successful political assassinations [have done more to demoralize and disorganize the government] than years of propaganda, a century of discontent in Russia, the agitation of the youth, the curses of thousands of victims tormented by it in penal servitude and exile.[13]

The growing practice of terrorism, now buttressed by theoretical arguments, served to harden the attitudes of Plekhanov and the Derevenshchiki at the party center.

Plekhanov had questioned the wisdom of assassinating Drenteln, suggesting instead a plan of "urban, economic terror" which might grow out of labor strikes. But the vote in favor of assassination was unanimous, with only Plekhanov abstaining.[14] When Morozov's defense of political murder appeared, Plekhanov and his adherents protested—not only because of its message but also because Plekhanov, although an editor of *Zemlia i volia,* had been given no opportunity to read the article before its publication. Deeply disturbed about the direction the party appeared to be taking, Plekhanov insisted that a conference should be held to determine whether Morozov's views or his actually represented the party program.[15] By such means, he hoped to bring the weight of his faction, whose members were scattered over the country, against the terror-minded Petersburg group, which increasingly dominated party affairs.

Factional strife in St. Petersburg rose to a crescendo in March 1879.

At the instance of a certain Solov'ev, who offered to assassinate the Tsar, Mikhailov placed the proposition before a meeting of party leaders. In his rejection of the proposal, Plekhanov, outwardly calm, emphasized the infinite harm terrorism would cause to the movement as a whole by swallowing up all other party activities. One of the Derevenshchiki, M. R. Popov, threatened to warn the intended victim, in order to thwart the terrorists. "That is treason," a terrorist cried; "we will deal with you as we deal with all traitors!" To which Popov replied: "Does that mean you want to murder us? If so, don't forget that we can shoot as well as you."[16]

Just then a bell rang, and Mikhailov exclaimed: "Gentlemen, the police! . . . We shall of course defend ourselves?" "Of course!" was the unanimous reply of both the terrorists and the Derevenshchiki, as they drew revolvers from their pockets. A cautious inquiry proved the ringing of the bell to have been a false alarm. Clearly, the anti-terrorists, though opposed to rampant assassinations, would not turn away from armed conflict. When the discussion was resumed, an uneasy compromise was reached. In order to avoid an open break, which ties of sentiment and experience made it difficult to contemplate, the party officially declined to sponsor Solov'ev's assault on the Tsar, but it gave leave to individual members to assist Solov'ev if they saw fit. "But," Plekhanov reported long afterward, "we Narodniks went home with the conviction that the old, once exemplary unity of Zemlia i Volia had been destroyed and that now each faction would go its separate way, not concerning itself, and indeed not even having the moral possibility of concerning itself, with the interests of the whole."[17]

On April 2, as the Tsar left the palace for his morning walk, Solov'ev fired, but his aim was bad and he missed. He was at once seized by the police. As the Derevenshchiki had warned, the government immediately instituted new repressions: it smashed the recently formed labor organization, the North Russian Workers' Union; it made a large number of arrests; and in the following months it carried through a dozen executions. More urgently than ever, the revolutionists were faced with a grave decision: whether to continue along the same road until Alexander had been killed or to revert to agrarian activity. The question required a definite and authoritative answer, such as could be given only by a party congress. The basic differences between the Derevenshchiki and the terrorists, specifically reflected in the editorial board dispute between Plekhanov and Morozov, constituted the basis for convening in June 1879 the Voronezh congress of Zemlia i Volia, a major event in the annals of the revolutionary movement and in the life of Plekhanov as well.

In urging the congress, Plekhanov probably thought he had a good chance of securing a resolution that would confirm the old program of

Zemlia i Volia, with first priority to mass activity in country and town, and with "disorganizational" work greatly restricted in scope. The minority in St. Petersburg who joined with him against the partisans of terror would be supported by the representatives of those in the field actually engaged in agrarian propaganda and agitation. The terrorists calculated similarly, and to counteract their anticipated minority, as well as to make plans for the future if the congress should indeed end in a rupture, they held a secret caucus at Lipetsk, just before the Voronezh conclave.[18]

At Lipetsk the terrorist faction, led by Mikhailov, Morozov, and Lev Tikhomirov, pledged itself to a brief program for a new revolutionary organization. The key paragraph, as it was recalled much later by Morozov, read:

In observing contemporary social life in Russia, we see that, as a consequence of the prevalence of government arbitrariness and violence, no activity whatever in behalf of the people is possible. There exists neither freedom of speech, nor freedom of the press for action by persuasion. Therefore, for every advanced social activist it is necessary first of all to put an end to the existing method of government; but to fight it is impossible other than with weapons in hands. Therefore, we will fight in the manner of William Tell until the time when we obtain such free institutions under which we will be able without interference to discuss in the press and in public meetings all political and social questions, and decide them through the agency of free people's representatives.[19]

In keeping with the program adopted, the caucus declared the assassination of Alexander II the first order of business. Whatever might happen at Voronezh, they would not be deterred from executing the death penalty upon the Tsar. So that their position might in fact prevail at Voronezh, the Lipetsk group planned to nominate as members of the congress three of their number who were not actual members of Zemlia i Volia. It may be inferred from what eventually took place at the congress that the group further devised a clever stratagem which could lead to victory: they would aim at the isolation of Plekhanov and the "extreme" Derevenshchiki by an apparently conciliatory policy which would commend itself to the moderates.

On June 24, 1879, some two dozen revolutionists, seemingly off on a picnic, rowed out to a wooded island in the river near Voronezh for the first session of the party congress.[20] At the outset, the terrorists disarmed the Derevenshchiki by unanimously supporting one of the agrarian group as chairman of the meetings. Mikhailov then moved the acceptance as delegates to the congress of the three nonmembers whom the Lipetsk group had designated. The congress voted its approval, and it also approved the admission of three candidates proposed by the Derevenshchiki. These latter, however, in contrast to the candidates of the terrorists, had not been smuggled in with the baggage of their sponsors and did not, therefore, participate in the congress. In what followed, it became evident that the terrorists need not have troubled to build up their voting strength by questionable means. For, thanks to their tactical suppleness—although not to that alone—the agrarian faction, with the single exception of Plekhanov, proved far more conciliatory toward them than they had dared expect.

The terrorists quickly established the tone of the meetings on a note favorable to their plans. Morozov read aloud the last letter of Valerian Osinsky, a popular comrade who had recently been executed by the government at Kiev.[21] Then the news of the recent execution at Odessa of Dmitri Lizogub, another well-loved comrade, was announced. The delegates were thus brought to a high pitch of hatred for the government, and were in a mood to agree with the dictum of Osinsky's final testament that revolutionary terrorism was the most effective method—the only method—available to the Zemlevoltsi under present circumstances.

In the discussion of the party program that followed, the terrorists conducted themselves with admirable modesty. They saw no inconsistency in joining with the others in voting for the reaffirmation of the old party program, which defined the goal of party activity as "economic revolution" and declared the center of gravity of its work to lie, as before, among the people. The only amendment to the old program came from the practicing Derevenshchiki and concerned the endorsement of "agrarian terror" in the countryside—the advancing of the discontented peasantry into terroristic action against local authorities, kulaks, and landlords. It was backed with alacrity by the Lipetsk group, in a move which in a sense obligated the Derevenshchiki to throw their support to political terror in the cities, the next point on the agenda and the crucial question at the congress.

In the stormy quarrel on this issue, Plekhanov, who had until now been unable to secure a handle with which to beat his apparently so conciliatory opponents, took the offensive. Seeking to expose what from the point of view of an orthodox Narodnik was the vulnerable flank of the terrorists, he challenged them to say what they expected to gain from political terror. His tactic succeeded; for in the heat of the argument, Mikhailov blurted out an unequivocal answer: "We will obtain a constitution, we will disorganize the government and force it to give us one!" In the uproar that followed this disavowal of a party program the terrorists had just voted to confirm, Plekhanov hotly protested that for a Narodnik revolutionist to strive for a constitution was equivalent to betrayal of the people's cause. Disorganizational activity, in any case, was incapable of achieving such ends. It would only bring in its train intensified government repression, and governmental victory over the revolutionists. The only change that could be counted upon with assurance was the replacement of the two numerals after Alexander's name by three.

Zheliabov met Plekhanov head on, declaring his belief in frankly political action, and the scrapping of "class struggle." Since, in his view, the winning of political liberty should take priority over any other objective, he argued for an agreement with the liberals to that end. Plekhanov was aghast at such heresy and accused Zheliabov of wishing to make the revolutionists subservient to the liberals and their goals, of wanting the revolutionists to pull the chestnuts of the liberals out of the fire.[22] Against Zheliabov's contention that efforts to unleash a class struggle of the masses were for the time being doomed to failure, Plekhanov pointed out the successes scored among the factory workers. Were such activities to be forsaken? Zheliabov, with greater insight than Plekhanov possessed at the time, replied that the strikes of the Russian workers were political acts, and on that account were worthy of continued support.[23] In this angry exchange, the sharp opposition between political struggle and socialist activity in the minds of the revolutionists was clearly apparent.

Tikhomirov intervened in the dispute in an effort to find a middle ground on which the sharply opposed forces could meet. At length, the congress passed a compromise resolution that "political terror as a form of struggle is acknowledged only as an extreme and exceptional measure for certain special circumstances." The resolution merely shifted the ground of the debate, however; it failed to suggest what ought to be done under existing circumstances. Nonetheless, the skirmish could be counted as won by the terrorists, for in agreeing to the classification of political terrorism as "an extreme and exceptional" form of struggle, they reassured the Derevenshchiki in general, if not Plekhanov, that essentially they remained Narodniks.

Having thus secured their position, the terrorists were ready to win the day. They had maneuvered to reduce the apparent divergences between themselves and the majority of the Derevenshchiki to negligible proportions. With few exceptions, that group agreed with the terrorists that the prevailing circumstances *were* sufficiently "extreme and exceptional" to warrant the continuation until victory of the campaign to assassinate the Tsar. Accordingly, a majority of the delegates voted to render aid to the terrorists, who now could celebrate their triumph.

Plekhanov made one last effort to stave off defeat by attempting to reopen the policy debate in a discussion of the party press. Here, too, the majority voted against him, and Morozov was acquitted of any breach of responsibility in having published articles favorable to political assassination before the party had voted on the issue. Plekhanov thereupon flew into a rage and delivered a philippic against the congress, indicting it for having severed all connection with the revolutionary-Narodnik traditions of Zemlia i Volia. Since the congress persisted in such a course,[24] he said, there was nothing more for him to do there. And, turning on his heel, he strode off through the woods. Several of those who had supported his position rose as if to follow him, but after a moment's hesitation resumed their seats. As he walked off alone, Vera Figner, an advocate of terrorism, said anxiously: "We must call him back." But Mikhailov, in a characteristic effort to exclude sentiment from the determination of policy, answered in an agitated voice: "No matter how painful it may be, we must not call him back." The congress then voted to consider Plekhanov as having voluntarily withdrawn from Zemlia i Volia. The next day, Plekhanov sent a more coolly reasoned, written appeal to the congress, begging it to reconsider its stand, but the delegates were in no mood to rescind their action.

The terrorists so completely secured the approbation of the congress for their demands that they saw no need to establish a new organization. Everything they opted for at Lipetsk was legitimized at Voronezh. And, in the bargain, Plekhanov—the chief thorn in their side—had been gotten rid of. His departure also seemed to indicate that thenceforth the party organ could, without hindrance, serve as the mouthpiece for the terrorist point of view. As for the Derevenshchiki, most of them were satisfied that the future of their work had been guaranteed.

Plekhanov's own interpretation of what happened at Voronezh, written almost thirty years after the events, is interesting, but it cannot be accepted at face value.[25] Not only does it contain numerous inconsistencies, but also it misrepresents the behavior of all those concerned.* Plekhanov's claim that he went to Voronezh expecting defeat rather than victory appears to be based upon hindsight. At the congress, but not before, he learned that the Derevenshchiki were bent on compromise, whereas he deemed it mandatory that a clear choice be made between agitation and terror. He rejected compromise for fear that terrorism, if it were given an inch, would end up consuming all the energies and resources of the party. In his account he says that even before the congress convened he had made up his mind to walk out in the event that the Derevenshchiki did not close ranks against terrorism. Such a move, he hoped, would steel their determination for a more vigorous and sustained battle against the disorganizers. At the same time, however, he represents himself as having realized the unlikelihood of carrying a resolution against terror and, accordingly, of having gone to the congress with the more modest aim of persuading the delegates

---

* Misrepresents, that is, when Aptekman's, the most contemporary and complete account, and the one Plekhanov explicitly commended, is taken as the standard. See *Sochineniia*, XXIV, 310.

to limit the expenditures allotted for "disorganizational" activity. Such a line would itself have been a policy of compromise. As events turned out, Plekhanov left the congress before financial appropriations were considered. After his departure, the congress earmarked one-third of its budget for terrorism and two-thirds for agrarian activity. Yet, although Plekhanov remained in Voronezh for the duration of the meetings and was kept informed of the decisions, he made no effort to return. If his behavior may be partly charged to wounded pride, undoubtedly greater weight must be attached to the issues of principle at stake, upon which he took a stand of no compromise.

In portraying himself as willing to compromise, and the terrorists as the victors precisely because of their one-sidedness and intransigence, he really reverses the roles played at Voronezh. The Derevenshchiki deserted their leader just because of his inflexibility, which they feared would provoke a schism. The terrorists, whatever their private thoughts, gave every appearance of wishing to meet the Derevenshchiki halfway. That they stood ready to appropriate two-thirds of the party budget to mass-agitational activity suggests more than lip service to it—unless, as Popov and Aptekman claim, this, too, was a deception, the terrorists knowing that, with the adoption of their program, all the funds and personnel, willy-nilly, would flow to their enterprise.[26] The notable absence of Narodnik phrasing in the Lipetsk program tends to support this view.

Plekhanov's charge that the Derevenshchiki failed to take a stand on principle was justified. But for them the issues of principle were by no means so sharply drawn as they were for him. Practical rather than theoretical considerations largely determined the conduct of the Derevenshchiki. If some of the terrorists envisaged as their goal the winning of political liberty, the Derevenshchiki discerned other good reasons for backing their initiatives. Terrorism was associated in the minds of some of them with the construction of a powerful central organization, essential both for the coordination of the various local activities they were engaged in and for use as a club over the government to keep it from interfering in Narodnik activity. Others felt that the task of executing the Tsar, since it had been undertaken, ought to be completed; after that, the old type of agrarian activity could once again be resumed. Most of the Derevenshchiki, it must be stressed, preferred to compromise with the terrorists rather than witness the breakup of the most effective organization yet developed by the revolutionists, one which would not be easy to replace.[27]

Crushed by his defeat, Plekhanov left Voronezh for Kiev, to join Rosaliia Markovna Bograd, with whom he had been living for some months past. Rosaliia, twenty-three, the daughter of a well-to-do Jewish family of Kherson, in southern Russia, was enrolled as a medical student in

St. Petersburg. She shared Georgii's revolutionary interests, and into her sympathetic ear he poured the whole disagreeable story of his experiences at Voronezh.[28] The movement was doomed, he was sure, if it persisted in its present policy. In particular, he insisted that terrorism would result in the loss of the valuable connections among the people which the revolutionists had so laboriously established. He was particularly scornful of the Derevenshchiki who had agreed with his stand at the congress but had "lacked the manliness" to follow his example in bolting. It was bitter to be alone outside the movement to which he had been devoting his full energy.

Long years afterward, Rosaliia Markovna asserted that, whatever the setbacks, Plekhanov's temperament would never have permitted him to abandon his revolutionary career for the life of a "cabinet scholar."[29] But Deutsch, who became Plekhanov's close collaborator shortly after the Voronezh affair, represents Plekhanov's attitude after the congress quite differently. According to Deutsch, Plekhanov told him, apropos of his feelings at that time:

It was painful. But I have a remedy for whatever ails me—the desire to gain more knowledge: if you had returned from abroad not as adherents [of my views] but . . . as terrorists; and if there had not occurred the breakup of Zemlia i Volia, which I would not have re-entered, then I would have devoted myself entirely to science.[30]

No matter how strong his attachment to the popular cause, he was incapable of working in a movement with whose fundamental principles he could not agree. In the absence of opportunity to work for the people in some way that was consistent with his principles, he might well have devoted his abundant energies to pursuing the intellectual interests that he had been forced to curtail since leaving the Mining Institute.

However, new revolutionary possibilities soon appeared with the return of Deutsch, Stefanovich, and Vera Zasulich—all recently inducted Zemlevoltsi, who had been abroad during the Voronezh congress in June. They arrived in St. Petersburg late that summer, and Plekhanov hastened to meet them there, confident that they would be sympathetic to his position. The four reached a quick understanding, and Deutsch, Stefanovich, and Zasulich, along with a few loyal Derevenshchiki, undertook to keep Plekhanov informed of the inner workings of the organization. They made it clear to the terrorists that they expected them to regard the resolutions of the congress as binding commitments rather than mere verbal camouflage. They insisted that the major emphasis of the party should be on agrarian activity, with funds disbursed accordingly, and they demanded a say in determining the policies of the newspaper. At the same time, instead of helping to carry out the schemes of the "disorganizers," they busied themselves with winning over to their point of view wavering or uncommitted members of the organization. At the congress Plekhanov had been isolated and the terrorists triumphant; but in the sequel Plekhanov's faction was stronger and more importunate than before. The split which many had expected at Voronezh now seemed unavoidable.

At last, in October, a formal agreement to dissolve the organization was concluded. The funds were to be divided between the two groups. Both pledged themselves not to use the name Zemlia i Volia for their organizations or for any publication they might launch. Each side promised to render whatever aid it could to the other. The close and friendly relations among the revolutionists, which had done much to prevent a schism at Voronezh, made it possible thus amicably to divide the organization when its breakup could no longer be averted. The terrorist faction now, in effect, reverted to the plans laid at Lipetsk, and formed a new organization, Narodnaia Volia (The People's Will). The orthodox Narodnik faction chose the name Chernyi Peredel (The General Redivision), in token of its solidarity with the old Narodnik aspiration for an agrarian revolution which would divide the land among the peasant communes and lay the foundation for a Russian agrarian socialism. Instead of becoming a cabinet scholar, Plekhanov re-entered the revolutionary stream as the chief figure in Chernyi Peredel.

From Plekhanov's standpoint, the breakup of Zemlia i Volia represented a triumph, or at least a partial truimph. Instead of the whole corps of active revolutionists and the entire sum of revolutionary energy being given over to terrorist activity, the personnel and means for maintaining the continuity of orthodox populist activity had been salvaged. With the terrorist elements cut away, it would now be possible, Plekhanov thought, to develop a strong mass movement. But these expectations quickly proved but dreams and fancies. Within a few months, the course of events seemed to have established not that the terrorists had deviated unforgivably from the true revolutionary path but that the traditional populists had worked themselves into a cul-de-sac.

O. V. Aptekman, the chronicler of Chernyi Peredel and one of its leading members, begins his account of it with these doleful words: "Not in a fortunate time was the organization Chernyi Peredel born. God did not give it life, and three months later, it expired."[31] He evidently fixes the date of its death as January 22–24, 1880, when a series of police raids resulted in the seizure of the group's printing press and the arrest of nearly all the members who were not out of the country. It could be argued that the expiration of Chernyi Peredel came well before then, however; for, as Aptekman's narrative makes clear, the organization never really got beyond the planning stage into action. Granting that it did begin, one can argue that it lived rather longer than Aptekman says. Aptekman was one of those arrested in January 1880, and it is not strange that he should regard the end of the movement as coinciding with that event. A few members had escaped abroad, however—Plekhanov, Zasulich, Deutsch, and several others—and they managed to keep the organization more or less alive for another year or so. In Russia, Axelrod, who had joined in December and somehow stayed out of the hands of the police, re-formed a few small youth groups and established contact with the Peredeltsi abroad.[32] But aside from a few issues of a newspaper, the group in the end died away leaving but little trace.

It had begun with high hopes. Speaking for the new association in the first issue of its newspaper, Plekhanov affirmed its solidarity with the traditions of populism: "Zemlia i Volia, as before, will remain our practical fighting slogan, since these two words most fully and broadly express the popular demands."[33] But even before these words were in print the impossibility of following through had been demonstrated. It was all too evident that Narodnaia Volia was vastly more attractive to potential recruits than Chernyi Peredel; as agitational methods had once triumphed over Lavrist propagandism, so now terrorism was triumphing over Bakuninism. Now, as before, impatient radicals favored plans of action which promised to engage the foe most directly and forcefully. They were eager to get quick results, and though they gave due respect to the sincerity of the Peredeltsi, they had no desire to spend their own time on activities which seemed by contrast so tame. Moreover, the "to the people" movement had passed its zenith by 1879, and few youths were ready to face the difficulties involved in working among the peasants.

This attitude was not confined simply to convinced terrorists. Plekhanov and other Peredeltsi encountered students enough who said what former Narodniks had said; but few of them were willing to do as former Narodniks had done. Even more discouraging was the fact that a good many older Narodniks had begun to find village life intolerable and were drifting back into the towns. With few recruits, and with seasoned Narodniks themselves losing heart, the ambitious plans for large-scale agrarian agitation never got beyond the discussion stage. Chernyi Peredel failed utterly in the realm where it proposed to make its main effort.

Unless they were to forsake revolutionary activity entirely, it was obvious that these proponents of an agrarian revolution must turn their attention to the urban classes. The oppositional elements of the professional classes, if for different reasons from those of the students, by and large favored the political aims of the Narodovoltsi, although certain reservations about terrorism somewhat inhibited their lending active support. Many secretly hoped, no doubt, to see the government forced by the terrorists to yield significant concessions to the public. The Peredeltsi, then, were no more able to find a point of support here than among the peasants.

Partly in consequence of his earlier successes in their midst, but also in default of any alternative, Plekhanov proposed to the Peredeltsi that they devote themselves to agitation among the factory workers.[34] He argued forcefully that the workers were seeking assistance; that since the workers were essentially peasants in any case, the revolutionists could agitate among them without violating their program; and that if their agitation succeeded the organization should have a stronger chance of attracting recruits from the intelligentsia.

The proposal was adopted. But the prospect of fruitful activity in the worker milieu very soon proved illusory. Plekhanov had re-established connections with former worker friends, including Stepan Khalturin, the organizer of the North Russian Workers' Union, but he could do little in the face of the enormous prestige of Narodnaia Volia. Even as the terrorists' acts brought broader and more intensive government repressions, it grew all but impossible to engage in any form of revolutionary activity except new acts of terror. Advanced workers who had earlier denounced terrorism, but who were known to regard political freedom as essential to the growth of the labor movement, lost little time in joining the terrorists in the emergency.[35]

Eventually, Khalturin, whom Plekhanov had much admired for his dedication to a mutual cause, asked Plekhanov to put him in touch with the terrorists. Plekhanov reluctantly complied. The populist tribune had good reason to despair when this "most talented, most enlightened representative" of the Petersburg proletariat took the path that he "counted harmful for the growth of the revolutionary movement."[36] In the sequel, Khalturin played the leading role in the third unsuccessful attempt to destroy the Tsar, in February 1880. It was he who carried through the dynamiting of the Tsar's dining room in the Winter Palace, an attempt which failed because the Tsar was late for dinner.

The Peredeltsi were beset with additional troubles from the police, who were on the alert for all revolutionists after November 10, 1879, when agents of Narodnaia Volia made an unsuccessful attempt to blow up a train in which the Tsar was traveling. Ironically, the police regarded Plekhanov as the instigator of the first attack upon the Tsar, in the spring of 1879, and were especially eager to apprehend him. Therefore, when Plekhanov and Rosaliia returned to Petersburg in late 1879, they took extraordinary precautions.[37] First of all, it was essential to procure a good set of identity papers. These having been fabricated in a few hours in the name of a respectable provincial nobleman and his wife, Plekhanov and Rosaliia engaged a room at an inn in order to test their reliability.

(The proprietors of hotels and the like were required to turn the papers of their clients over to the police for inspection and certification.) When the time came to reclaim the papers, a crowd of friends accompanied Plekhanov and Rosaliia to the inn in order to rescue them from arrest if necessary. Rosaliia proposed that she go alone to claim the papers, counting herself less valuable than he to the revolutionary movement, and finally she had her way, although Plekhanov's protests were so great that his friends had to hold him back. Much to everyone's relief, Rosaliia returned at once: the papers had been found in order. Subsequently, Plekhanov and Rosaliia rented an apartment in a quiet quarter of the city. Plekhanov not only shaved off his mustache and beard but took the precaution of remaining in the rooms by day, reading and writing, and taking meals from the landlady.

Not long before the end of the year, rumors began to spread that the police intended to scrutinize and verify the papers of all persons in the capital. The central group of Chernyi Peredel therefore voted to send Plekhanov, Zasulich, Deutsch, and Stefanovich abroad until the extraordinary police alert should be relaxed. In January 1880 the four left Russia for the West. Only days after their departure, the first number of the newspaper *Chernyi peredel* was issued, and within days after that the police had seized the secret press, the printers, and virtually all the members of Chernyi Peredel who were still in Russia.

Plekhanov learned of the catastrophe soon after his arrival in Geneva. The failure of Chernyi Peredel signified a crisis for Narodnik orthodoxy. For that group stood squarely upon the principles for which Plekhanov had fought so stoutly at Voronezh and after, thus necessitating the dissolution of Zemlia i Volia. To the challenge to his ideological system he responded with sensitivity and audacity. Not more than two years after the establishment of Chernyi Peredel, Plekhanov shed his Narodnik trappings and emerged in a radically different guise. In the next phase of his development, he became the prophet of Russian Marxism.

4

PRELUDE TO EXILE

IT MUST NOT BE IMAGINED that prior to the early 1880's Marxian ideas were unknown to the Russian literate public. Marx himself had wryly observed to a correspondent: "By some irony of fate, it is just the Russians, whom for twenty years I have incessantly attacked, . . . [who] have always been my well-wishers."[1] In 1848, and for years thereafter, the works of Marx and Engels could legally be imported because, according to the censor, they constituted "an abstract speculation" with no relevance to Russia.[2] Such was Marx's reputation among Russian radicals that when the government later banned further importation of some of his writings, the underground hectographs and presses of the revolutionists labored to fill the gap.

As early as the 1840's, Marx's writings were known to advanced Russian intellectuals such as the members of the Herzen group and Belinsky. The influential journal *Sovremennik* (The Contemporary), while under the editorship of Chernyshevsky, printed an exposition and a defense of Engels's views on "the working class in England." In the 1860's, Tkachev maintained that hardly anyone would contest the basic principles of Marxian historical materialism. Bakunin agreed; and, in spite of his personal antipathy to Marx, it was he who, in 1869, made the first Russian translation of the *Communist Manifesto*. As for *Das Kapital*, it was translated into Russian before any other language (1872), and in six months a thousand copies were sold. Whereas, according to its author, silence met the volume's appearance in Germany,[3] an animated discussion followed its publication in Russia.

In the middle seventies, N. I. Ziber brought out in Russia his study, *David Ricardo and Karl Marx and Their Economic Researches,* in which he expounded with approval the basic economic theory of Marx. Both from his professorial chair at Kiev and in his articles in the journal *Slovo*

(The Word), Ziber propagated Marx's economic ideas. Interest in Marx was further reflected in the political trials of the 1870's, wherein evidence of printing, distribution, and study of Marxian tracts was conspicuous. When, in 1877, a certain Zhukovsky published an attack upon Marx, both Ziber and the Narodnik writer N. K. Mikhailovsky rose to his defense in the widely read journal *Otechestvennye zapiski* (Annals of the Fatherland).

This is not to say, however, that there were in Russia prior to 1880 any genuine Marxists. Until 1882, the attitude of radical Russian thinkers toward Marx varied; but all agreed in failing to accept a thoroughgoing Marxism with its economic, political, sociological, and philosophical implications. Some persons such as Belinsky were acquainted only with fragments of early Marxian thought. Chernyshevsky, although familiar at least with one of Engels's important works, under no circumstances can be made out a Marxist.[4] Tkachev, who sang the praises of historical materialism, propagated political and social views that brought upon him a vitriolic polemic from the pen of Engels. Lavrov incorporated elements of Marxism into his system but found Marxian sociology and philosophy inconsistent. Ziber, while fully accepting the economic theory of Marx, was a liberal in politics. Although Bakunin openly espoused Marxian materialism, he bitterly attacked the Marxian parties and their tactics. In like manner, the revolutionary organization Narodnaia Volia, though it had little in common with Western Social Democratic parties of the time, wrote to Marx: "The class of advanced intelligentsia in Russia, always attentively following the ideological development of Europe and sensitively reacting to it, has met the appearance of your works with enthusiasm.[5]

The striking contrast between the respect and admiration Marx enjoyed among Russian leftists and their failure to base their thinking and action upon his ideas is to be explained by the peculiarities of Russian populism. Russian radicals regarded Marx as a keen analyst who had correctly laid bare the roots and workings of Western capitalist societies. But, like the government authorities, they believed his diagnosis and prognostications to be inapplicable to Russia. That their homeland had not yet entered upon the capitalist phase of development; that it was destined to attain socialism, not according to the prescriptions of Marx, but in a uniquely Russian way—these were articles of faith to the populists.

Years before he avowed himself a Marxist and began campaigning for a Russian Social Democratic party, Plekhanov had felt the influence of Marx. Indeed, one of the most striking features of his first long published article, a defense of populism in the pages of *Zemlia i volia*, was the deference he showed to the founder of "scientific socialism." Deutsch may be right in crediting I. F. Fesenko, a propagandist who gave lectures on political economy to clandestine worker groups, with interesting Plekhanov in political economy in general and in *Das Kapital* in particular.[6] We are unable fully to evaluate this claim, although no doubt exists as to Plekhanov's association with Fesenko.[7] It has been asserted that Plekhanov read Marx's monumental work in 1875–76;[8] if in fact he did, this initial perusal does not seem to have left important traces in his outlook of the time.

On the whole, the early influence of Marx upon Plekhanov seems to have been exerted not directly but through intermediaries. If in the case of Fesenko the facts are not certain, the roles of Bakunin and of Ziber in this connection are incontestable. As an informed populist, Plekhanov was of course familiar with Bakunin's *State and Anarchy*. In that work, the "apostle of pan-destruction" emphasized his support of the materialist interpretation of history in these words:

[Marx] stated and proved that unquestionable truth, confirmed by all the past and contemporary history of human societies, peoples, and states, that the economic fact always preceded and precedes juridical and political right. In the exposition and proof of this truth resides one of the chief scientific services of Marx.[9]

In later years, Plekhanov acknowledged how, from the works of Bakunin, he had acquired "a great respect for the materialist interpretation of history."[10] In his first long article, Plekhanov quoted with approval "one of the most talented students and popularizers of Marx;"[11] although Plekhanov did not give his name, the writer to whom he referred was none other than Ziber. Inasmuch as the populists generally knew Bakunin's work and yet revealed in their writings nothing of the peculiar stamp apparent in Plekhanov's essay, D. Riazanov's argument for the significance of Ziber's influence carries weight.[12]

The essay alluded to, in which he set forth the commonplaces of the populist program in a most uncommon way, is a convenient starting point for an analysis of Plekhanov's ideological evolution in the decisive period, 1878–82. The essay, written in late 1878 and published in January 1879, was entitled, "The Law of the Economic Development of Society and the Problems of Socialism in Russia." The title suggests, and the contents confirm, that Plekhanov had grasped and was skillfully applying that basic postulate of Marxian historical materialism according to which the economic history of society determines the modes of its life and thought; or, stated in its most general form, that being determines consciousness rather than consciousness being. In applying this formula, which later he would repeat with monotonous regularity, Plekhanov aimed to fix upon an unshakable foundation the program that the populists generally upheld. Following in the footsteps of Marx and the Marxists, he ridiculed the "utopian" socialists of the thirties and forties who, he contended, considered the mind all and life nothing; who supposed that a happily conceived plan for a well-proportioned and smoothly functioning society could, by virtue of apt propaganda, be translated into reality irrespective of the stage of economic development existing at a given time and place.[13] As Marx had "scientifically" demonstrated the "inevitability" of socialism's emergence from capitalism, Plekhanov sought to prove the nonutopianism of the anarcho-socialist order the populists projected.

In a manner that left no doubt whatever as to the high regard in which he held the author of *Das Kapital*, Plekhanov forthrightly declared: "Let us see to what the teaching of Marx obligates us . . . in view of the necessity of establishing the starting points of our program."[14] Anticipating the objections of other populists, he insisted that Marxian principles were relevant to all societies, not simply to capitalist societies. Unlike others, he recognized that Marx's analysis of capitalism represented merely the specific application of principles which, in Marx's scheme, were universally operative. But this affirmation, in his view, held no disturbing implications for the populist belief in a unique social evolution for Russia. Marxian principles did not dictate that all peoples must have identical histories; for "weaving and combining variously in various societies, they give entirely different results, just as the same laws of gravity produce in one case the elliptical orbit of the planet, in the other the parabolic orbit of the comet."[15]

If Russia's destiny differed from that of the West, he argued in effect, that corroborated rather than refuted Marxian doctrines; for her peculiar destiny stemmed from the different material conditions of her society. In Russia's overwhelmingly agrarian order, Plekhanov identified as the key feature of the social landscape the myriad peasant communes, those basic units of social organization which he believed had come down from time immemorial. Within the commune, land was held collectively rather than individually. From the field of landholding, so vital to an agrarian people, the principle of collectivism had spread into other realms, until it had become the dominant note in the habits of work and thought of the Russian people. The future of Russia, of necessity, would be determined primarily by the collectivist bias of the mass of the people, but also by their age-long aspiration for liberty from oppression. In the projected revolution, which the intelligentsia would instigate by galvanizing the peasantry into motion, the lands of the state and the nobles would be distributed among the peasant communes. At the same time, the peasant's yearning for freedom would find expression in the destruction of the coercive, centralized state organization and its replacement, from the bottom up, by a "free federation of free [self-governing] communes." In this fashion, the anarcho-socialist order cherished by the Narodniks, and rooted in the existing institutions and values of the people, would become a reality. Although much was left unsaid in this prospectus, Plekhanov clearly anticipated the attainment of socialism in Russia by means of the revolutionary action of the peasantry, and without the necessity of passing through a capitalist stage of development.

Yet, unexpectedly, Plekhanov assigned an important part in this revolution to the urban factory workers,[16] who one would suppose were a product of that very capitalistic production he insisted Russia should avoid. Indeed, he contrasted this group with the rural elements of society to the disadvantage of the latter. Whereas the peasants in the village were under the influence of "the more conservative and timorous members of the peasant family," the "city workers . . . constitute the most mobile, the most susceptible to incitation, the most easily revolutionized stratum of the population." This characterization in no sense altered Plekhanov's conception as to the nature of the coming revolution; it would be an agrarian upheaval, but the urban workers were destined to be invaluable allies of the peasants. At the moment of the revolution, they could engage and neutralize the forces of the government in the towns, and thus enable the rural insurrection to spread and consolidate.

In attempting to smooth over what he may have faintly perceived as awkward contradictions in his position, Plekhanov became entangled in others. The factory workers could be counted on to support the peasant revolution, he argued, because they themselves were really still peasants, sharing the popular sympathy for communal landholding and the aspiration for "land and liberty." Since they worked in the towns only intermittently, he continued, they could render exceedingly important services to the revolutionary cause by acting as intermediaries between the intelligentsia in the cities and the peasants in the villages. Both in the asserted attachment of the workers to the land and in the temporary nature of their factory employment, Plekhanov no doubt saw evidence of the inability of capitalism to make inroads in Russia. But, in the same essay, he urged that the workers possessed an "independent significance"; that they were ardently interested in "the increase or reduction of wages, greater or lesser fines . . . greater or lesser ferocity by the policemen"; and that agitation among the workers must be conducted "daily and hourly [on the basis of] even the most trifling facts of the worker's life." In so far as they possessed independent interests and an independent significance, the conclusion might be drawn that the factory workers were of more than passing importance. In so far as their way of life and modes of thought differed from those of their rural relatives, they could but doubtfully be classified as peasants. But so long as Russia's impregnability to capitalism remained for him a controlling assumption, Plekhanov did not admit to the presence of any difficulties in his argument.

In contrasting Russia to the West, Plekhanov was dispassionate and scientifically analytical. If Russia reached socialism by a different route from that upon which the West appeared to be embarked, that was only because the peasant commune had fallen in the West, and with it the collectivistic instincts of the people. When the one and the other were replaced by individualism, the possibility of socialism in the West vanished until the much later emergence of large-scale factory production. As a result of the socialization of labor it entailed, this new economic basis of society had once again restored the collectivistic spirit which in the West had decayed with the decay of the commune.[17] Once the commune had disintegrated in the West, the peoples there could achieve socialism only by way of the institutions and habits that a well-developed capitalism fostered. In Russia, where the collectivistic commune persisted and where, moreover, it "does not bear within itself the elements of its own doom," this institution could yet serve as the basis of a socialist order.[18] Although Plekhanov in the essay expresses no doubts about the vitality of the commune, everything clearly hinged on that factor. If the commune in Russia should break down, then the social conditions essential for the establishment of socialism would no longer obtain in Russia. In that case, only a utopian could speak of the likelihood of socialism in the near future.

There is in the essay clear evidence of Marxian influence, but it is equally clear that Plekhanov was not at the time of writing a Marxist. Not long before its publication, he had described all of Russian history not as "the history of class struggle," but, in anarchist terms, as "an unbroken struggle of the state against the striving of the commune and the individual for autonomy."[19] So poorly oriented was he in questions of Western socialism in 1879 that he grouped Marx and Engels together with Rodbertus and Dühring as "the brilliant pleiade" of socialism,[20] apparently unaware that only the preceding year Engels had published his famous attack upon Dühring. Plekhanov regarded Marxian principles as an invaluable support for the populist program. But this was, at least in part, an erroneous judgment. He looked for the revolution to destroy the state and open the way to an anarcho-socialist order, whereas the Marxists considered the state, and indeed a strongly centralized state, essential for the transition to socialism.

As we have seen, Plekhanov the exponent of orthodox populism viewed politics and political action with disfavor. To him, as to his mentor Bakunin, politics was the domain of those concerned with the exploitation of the people, and all states were but organizations of power to facilitate that exploitation. Political struggle was no more than the conflict between various groups of exploiters for supremacy in the state. Those who stood on the side of the people, by contrast, took popular socio-economic conditions and needs as the ground of their activity. They sought to fulfill the popular wants by unleashing an "economic" revolution which would, among other objectives, destroy that agency of coercion, the state. In terms more familiar to us, the Bakuninist position emphasized class struggle, leading to a social (and socialist) revolution, instead of political struggle, leading to a political revolution. The two were conceived as incompatible, mutually exclusive forms of activity; political struggle and socialism had nothing in common. Plekhanov's adamant stand against the "politicals" at Voronezh was based on this conviction.

In contrast to this anarchist position, Marxists were deeply concerned with political action, the winning of political rights, and, ultimately, political supremacy. Yet, oddly enough, the hostility of Bakunin to politics, and of Plekhanov after him, derived in some part from an eccentric interpretation of Marx. If, Bakunin reasoned, the economic factor is always determining, and the state accordingly is only part of the superstructure of society, the revolutionizing of society cannot be effected merely by attacking the state or changing its character. Only an "economic" revolution could succeed in altering the foundations of society.[21]

Around the end of 1878, Plekhanov's outlook was Marxian-materialist in form, Bakuninist-populist in content. At one and the same time he could be a good populist and yet be faithful to Marxian precepts, as he then understood them. To him, there seemed no contradiction between the two. Otherwise, he could not in good conscience have advanced these views, for already in his first article in the public press, in *Nedelia* (December 1878) he had demonstrated his demand for rigorous intellectual consistency. There, the neophyte writer had chided the veteran editors of the respected journals *Slovo* and *Otechestvennye zapiski* for printing articles expressing diametrically opposed points of view; striking a contrast, to their disadvantage, with the "rigorously thought-out and rigorously defined tendency" of the periodicals in "the golden age of Russian journalism."[22] His demand for consistency signified that something would have to give when, with the passage of time, he became persuaded of the essential incompatibility between populism and Marxism.

In the first instance, his doubts concerning populism were aroused by the frustration at every turn of the efforts of Chernyi Peredel. He was not disposed to attribute its dismal fate wholly to circumstances beyond its control. Could it be that the principles it espoused, which Plekhanov had so insistently defended, were faulty? Even before he left Russia in January 1880 his doubts were compounded by his encounter with a study that cast new and alarming light upon the status of the peasant commune. The work in question was Orlov's *Communal Property in the Moscow District.* Plekhanov by then knew the sociologist M. M. Kovalevsky's recent survey of the fate of communal institutions in many countries. Kovalevsky intimated that the commune declined everywhere owing to causes internal to itself, and especially because of the growth of a clash of interest between the poorer and more affluent groups within it.[23] Orlov's profoundly unsettling book presented irrefutable data on the existence of these same phenomena in the Russian commune.

As Rosaliia Markovna later recalled:

It was impossible to disagree with the figures. We read the book together, stopping on every fact. I remember Plekhanov's passionate commentaries on these facts, which he did not dispute; but he was fervently convinced that the misfortune might still be avoided. . . . G. V. was completely engrossed in this reading; it seemed that the question of whether the commune were to be or not —if it were to disintegrate or not—was for him a question of life and death.[24]

Indeed, it was a question of life and death—not for Plekhanov personally, of course, but for the populism upon which he had staked all. His unqualified conviction as to the latent strength of the commune, and thus of populism, now yielded to a more conditional assessment. In a learned article which he published about that time in the legal periodical *Russkoe bogatstvo* (Russian Treasure), there is a reflection of the great change in his thinking:

We cannot consider the destruction of the commune as an inevitable historical manifestation. Given a certain combination of negative forces, this destruction really is inevitable . . . ; it does not follow that given another combination of conditions, it would be impossible for the commune to grow and develop.[25]

In this essay, Plekhanov had to admit that the situation of the commune in Russia was not reassuring. Economic differentiation was proceeding among the peasants; the commune "is being divided into two parts, each of which is hostile to the other"; and elements of capitalism were appearing in Russia.[26]

Yet, he insisted, the causes of the decline of the commune were external rather than inherent in the commune itself.[27] He singled out for criticism excessive state levies upon the peasant's meager income and the exploitation of impoverished peasants by usurers. Many peasants were compelled to leave the land for work in urban industrial enterprises, financed by the capital the usurers accumulated at the expense of the peasants. But these destructive factors, Plekhanov suggested, could be neutralized and arrested by a "consciously positive attitude" toward the commune on the part of the peasants and the intelligentsia.[28] Translated into the non-Aesopian language of the clandestine press, this meant that the commune could be saved if the socialists should succeed in igniting a revolution; they must bend their efforts, therefore, to move the peasants "from a passive expectation of a general redivision" to an "active demand for it."[29] In consideration of the extremely dim chances of starting a conflagration at the end of 1879, the prospects of populism all but vanished. It is scarcely to be wondered at that Orlov's work "strongly shook" Plekhanov's populist convictions, as he himself later reported.[30]

Well might he have been reluctant to go abroad just then, as his friends urged him to do. For on his own premises, quitting the agrarian agitation, no matter what difficulties beset it, could only mean writing off the peasant commune and the agrarian socialist society of the future. On the other hand, with all the will in the world, it had proved impossible to launch an agitation of any sizable dimensions. If he remained in Russia, he could scarcely call up a popular revolution singlehandedly. But, as his friends protested, he might very easily fall into the hands of the police.

When Plekhanov left Russia, Rosaliia did not accompany him. She had just given birth to their first child, a daughter named Vera, and may well have thought it unwise to subject the infant to a long journey.* Also, after five long years of medical study, she could not bring herself to give up her final examinations. With the degree in hand, she would never be without the means to support herself and, if necessary, her family. But half a year elapsed from the time of Plekhanov's departure until she yielded to his importunings and joined him in Geneva. Rosaliia was a revolutionist too, and she found it difficult not to feel that somehow, despite the good reasons, Plekhanov had deserted the revolution.[31] At last, on the counsel of a friend, she was able to reconcile her doubts and her desires and to convince herself that she would not be betraying the popular cause if she went into exile with him.†

As for Plekhanov himself, once convinced that the situation in Russia was hopeless for the time being, he began to see the positive aspects of a trip abroad. Perhaps he comforted himself with the thought that the disintegration of the commune could not be encompassed in weeks or months, and he would soon be back. In the meantime, the fixed points of his ideological system had dissolved to such an extent that he felt uncertain of his bearings. Deploring the inadequacy of his knowledge and the difficulty of supplementing it in Russia, with all its restrictions, he welcomed the opportunity to visit the West. There, without harassment, he might seek out the information that would quiet his doubts, verify his views, and make

---

* The baby died within a year. The Plekhanovs had three other children, all girls. One of the three died of meningitis at the age of four.

† It was not until 1908 that Plekhanov legally divorced his first wife and married Rosaliia.

more secure their theoretical foundations. Half in jest, he remarked that he was going abroad "to study and to attain there the scholarly equivalent of a master's or a doctor's degree."[32]

Plekhanov gave succinct expression to the ideas passing through his mind in the first article he wrote after reaching Geneva. In a description of the way of life of the hunted revolutionist in Russia, we recognize his own experience and his response to it:

The incredible strain of the struggle with the government does not permit the socialist-revolutionary quietly to occupy himself with filling the gaps in his education. For that he has neither the time nor the appropriate conditions. Having been caught from his earliest years in the fire of police persecution, he often does not even have a room that he can call his own. Whole months, and sometimes even years, he has no regular dwelling place. He leads a peripatetic way of life and, upon awakening in the morning, does not always know where he will find refuge the following night. Under such conditions, intellectual labors, if not entirely impossible, are extremely difficult.[33]

This passage testifies to Plekhanov's intellectual approach to revolution, his inability to be content with revolutionary activity unless it was grounded upon a solid fundament of knowledge. All the more impressive is this feature of his character in that, his feelings of inadequacy notwithstanding, he unquestionably was far more learned than any of the other revolutionists in Zemlia i Volia or either of its organizational successors. In the first years of his revolutionary activity, he frequently managed to take refuge in a library in order to continue his self-education. Shortly after he went abroad, he astonished by his erudition concerning their respective fields of interest some of his distinguished fellow-émigrés, the historian and former professor Dragomanov and the geographer and anthropologist Mechnikov;[34] soon his qualities were recognized by the celebrated writers Lavrov and Mikhailovsky as well.

In spite of his strong intellectual orientation, the center of gravity of Plekhanov's activity before leaving Russia lay in practical affairs. When he went abroad, the focus of his work shifted sharply and permanently to the area of theory and scholarship. Left behind were the disguises and false papers, the revolvers and brass knuckles, and the rest of the cloak-and-dagger paraphernalia of the perilous existence he had led for three years. Now he moved into a way of life that corresponded more to the basic inclination of his nature. Not without difficulties though his new life turned out to be, they were difficulties of a very different order from those he had known in the revolutionary underground. Now he could drink his fill at the fountains of knowledge which had never ceased to lure him, even in the arduous days when all his senses and energies needed to be fully mobilized simply for the sake of survival.

But the studies Plekhanov undertook in the West did not, as he expected, bolster his populist faith. On the contrary, his system, which had been shaken first by the failures of Chernyi Peredel and then by Orlov's revelations, in the West received a third and final blow. The experience of Western conditions and a rapidly enlarged familiarity with Western socialism endowed him with the perspective for a critique of that "Russian socialism" whose standard-bearer he had been. As Plekhanov recalled in retrospect, "the more we became acquainted with the theories of scientific socialism, the more doubtful became our populism to us from the side of both theory and practice."[35]

5

FROM POPULISM TO MARXISM

PLEKHANOV ARRIVED in Geneva in January 1880 anticipating a stay of some weeks or months. As it turned out, he did not see his native land again for thirty-seven years. The pattern of his life in his first years abroad calls to mind the sequence Toynbee denominates "withdrawal and return." Virtually retiring from the hurly-burly of revolutionary life, Plekhanov devoted himself to study and reflection. Then, renewed by such pursuits, the former standard-bearer of populist orthodoxy returned to the revolutionary stage as the prophet of a creed that deviated far more from the traditions of populism than did the political terrorism against which he had so vehemently contended. The period from 1880 to 1882 proved to be the most decisive in the whole of Plekhanov's intellectual life, for in these few short years his intellectual odyssey carried him all the way from populism to Marxism. To the Marxian position he then worked out he remained attached until the end of his life.

One cannot but be impressed by Plekhanov's audacity in breaking out of his accustomed ideological framework to found a program so strongly at variance with the traditions and the prevailing perspectives of the revolutionary movement. On almost every point, Russian Marxism was to be diametrically opposed to populism. Moreover, it must be emphasized that the economic and social premises for the creation of a Marxian movement were as yet poorly developed in Russia. But we misrepresent Plekhanov's intellectual evolution in the early 1880's if we treat it purely and simply as a shift from one pole to another. As we have seen, even before he left Russia he had demonstrated a high regard for Marxian ideas, in so far as he understood them, his outlook being a blend of populism and Marxism. What occurred subsequently was the sorting out of ideas that he found incompatible. Populist theories, from a better informed Marxian standpoint, he regarded as falsely representing the character and potentiality of Russian society, and therefore unsuitable as the basis of the revolutionary movement.

Although Plekhanov's full conversion to Marxism was certainly not inevitable, a number of reasons clearly predisposed him to it. He left Russia troubled by the failures of Chernyi Peredel and plagued by newly awakened doubts concerning the vitality of the peasant commune. The barren results of years of agitation among the peasants were only too apparent, as was the headlong plunge of the radical intelligentsia into political struggle. At the time of his first trip abroad, four years earlier, Plekhanov had viewed the world with the uncritical eyes of a Bakuninist, and he had found little in the West to attract him or to stimulate his thinking. Now, his dogmatic self-assurance shaken, he came to the West seeking information and ideas that might enable him to clarify and solidify his thinking. This change in attitude allowed him to perceive much that had eluded him before.

Plekhanov's second arrival in the West coincided with the relative expansion of Marxian as against the rival anarchist influence in labor and radical circles. He was unlikely to find in the declining anarchist movement—whatever its affinities to the outlook he himself upheld—support for his sagging populist faith. Moreover, the evidence strongly suggests that Plekhanov went abroad believing he should find in Marxism what he was looking for. If he had become somewhat skeptical of his old populist convictions, the same could not be said of his belief in the necessity of validating the revolutionary program by reference to Marx. If his knowledge of Marx's teachings was as yet quite limited, certain of their qualities had already made a strong appeal to him. Plekhanov's rationalistic bent was already announced in his populist essay of 1879. He was captivated by the idea that a fundamental orderliness underlay social life and human history, no matter how chaotic and meaningless they might appear to a superficial observer. Projecting his rationalistic predilections upon the outer world, he chose to believe that history was law-abiding rather than capricious. Marxism exercised an enormous attraction for him precisely because of its claim to have discovered those "objective laws of history," concerning the existence of which he entertained no doubt. He seems at an early date to have taken at face value these professions of Marxism, with the accompanying implication that a scientific basis had now been placed under modern socialism. His haste in applying himself to the study of Marxism immediately upon his arrival in Geneva followed from these considerations. The mastery of Marxism, he believed, would permit the social activist to harmonize his aims and methods with the tempo and direction of march of the historical process. Thus he should secure guarantees of the success of his enterprise.

Geneva, or its environs, was to be Plekhanov's home for the greater part of his long exile. It was a city that had sheltered many a Russian émigré, and several other Peredeltsi were there also in 1880. Axelrod, who had succeeded in reconstituting a few pro–Chernyi Peredel groups, came to Switzerland in the middle of the year for a discussion of programmatic matters;[1] and when he decided not to return to Russia, the relationship between the Peredeltsi abroad and the remaining fragments of the organization in Russia naturally was terminated. The Geneva group did little more than issue a couple of numbers of *Chernyi peredel*—containing articles by Plekhanov which are interesting as evidence of his growing shift away from populism.

In his first years abroad, Plekhanov entered into one other revolutionary association. In the spring of 1880, he joined several other émigré revolutionists in a publishing enterprise called the Russian Socialist-Revolutionary Library. Although he was not one of the editors and probably devoted little time to the enterprise, the nature of the undertaking and the character of his associates reveals something of his thinking. In the announcement of this new publishing venture, which Plekhanov composed,[2] he emphasized his concern for the theoretical inadequacies of the revolutionary movement. He saw the publication of socialist literature as a helpful contribution to a situation which, if left unattended to, must inevitably be paid for in defeats and frustrations.

Interestingly enough, in this endeavor Plekhanov consented to be yoked with his old Zemlevoltsi opponent Morozov and with L. Gartman, another terrorist, both of whom had fled Russia in late 1879. Evidently his animosity toward Morozov and the terrorists diminished as his ardor for his position at Voronezh cooled. This is not to say that Plekhanov became positively disposed to terrorism; but after coming abroad he did assume an increasingly favorable attitude toward the political struggle waged by the terrorists. No doubt the special character of the enterprise also counted; it proposed to be not a party organ concerned with tactics but rather a publisher of general works on socialism and history. To refuse collaboration in such an important field simply because of past disputes with its sponsors would have been petty and inexcusable. However, it was largely because of Lavrov, the third editor, that Plekhanov was drawn into the enterprise. A friendship between the two men had grown out of a chance encounter. Immediately upon his arrival in Geneva, Plekhanov began attending meetings and discussions of the Russian revolutionist colony, and he quickly earned a place of some eminence, partly because of his erudition and oratorical brilliance, partly because of his record of revolutionary activity.[3] Only a month after coming to Geneva, the twenty-four-year-old Plekhanov was chosen, together with Zhukovsky, the venerable former secretary of the Russian section of the International, to represent the Geneva colony in a delegation of Russians who met Lavrov in Paris for the purpose of intervening in extradition proceedings against Gartman. They were successful in presenting their case to Gambetta, who was then president of the Chamber of Deputies.

Lavrov was the head of the delegation. Thirty-three years Plekhanov's senior, he had spent several decades as a mathematics professor in the Russian College of Artillery before being drawn, in the late 1850's, into radical socio-political activity. In 1866 he was arrested and then exiled to the Vologda region of northern Russia. Four years later, with the assistance of some younger revolutionists, he managed to escape abroad, reaching Paris in time to witness the rise and fall of the Commune. In the following years, he exercised a profound influence on Russia's radical youth, first through his book *Historical Letters*, and subsequently as editor of the populist review *Vpered* (Forward). Lavrov's work was instrumental in diverting elements of the intelligentsia from concern with natural science to ethical and social problems. A man of unusual ethical sensitivity, he did much to instill in the intelligentsia that sense of obligation to serve the people so conspicuous in the populist movement.

Lavrov and Plekhanov took to each other. The younger man, to be sure, had earlier polemicized mercilessly against Lavrov's followers. But the passage of time had brought about a convergence between their views. Thanks to his recent studies Plekhanov was drawing away somewhat from Bakuninism and becoming more sympathetic to Social Democratic ideas. As for Lavrov, his Narodnik inclinations were combined with a sincere respect for Marx and Western Social Democracy.* Lavrov's prestige as a major ideologist of the revolutionary movement was magnified in Plekhanov's eyes by the fact that he personally knew Marx and Engels. Besides, certain traits of character drew the two together. Lavrov shared with Plekhanov a great respect for learning, which both translated into an emphasis on the importance of theory for the revolutionary movement. They had much to talk about. And since Lavrov quickly recognized Plekhanov's gifts and scholarly attainments, their meeting bore fruit in three years of collaboration.

Lavrov contributed articles to the two issues of *Chernyi peredel* which were published in Geneva and actively supported its initiatives. As for Plekhanov, since word had reached the Peredeltsi of the seizure of their press in Russia, he felt free to accede to Lavrov's request that he collaborate in the publication of the Russian Socialist-Revolutionary Library. The friendly contact between the two did not end here. Plekhanov stayed on in Paris for some time after the delegation had completed its work, and

---

* Axelrod later credited Lavrov with having popularized among the Russian revolutionists certain elements of Marxism and Social Democracy. See his "Petr Lavrov," in *Rabochii klass i revoliutsionnoe dvizhenie v Rossii.*

later that same year, after Rosaliia had come from Russia, he returned with her to Paris for a year's stay. When he was not in Paris, he and Lavrov corresponded.* In this time of feverish intellectual searching and growth for Plekhanov, Lavrov's wide knowledge of socialism and socialist literature were extremely helpful. The older man gave suggestions for reading and lent Plekhanov rare items from his own considerable library. The fortunate opportunity to develop and test his ideas in discussions with a learned and much more experienced person than himself undoubtedly contributed to the clarification and crystallization of Plekhanov's own thought.

Over and above these important services, Lavrov proved generous and sympathetic to the material difficulties which beset Plekhanov and his family in their very first year abroad. The virtual collapse of Chernyi Peredel, while freeing Plekhanov from obligations which might have grown annoying, also deprived him of the financial support the organization had undertaken to give him. He possessed no independent means of his own. And from mid-1880 on his requirements mounted steeply.† Soon after Rosaliia joined him in Geneva, they moved to Paris, where their household was enlarged by the addition of one of Rosaliia's close friends, a woman who was destitute and afflicted with consumption. She lived with them until her death in the summer of 1882. The Plekhanovs' baby died in 1880, but a second child was born in 1881, and a third two years later.

Unfortunately, also, Rosaliia's plans for ensuring the support of her family had gone awry. The government authorities, knowing of her association with the "state criminal" Plekhanov, instructed the medical examiners to deny her a passing grade, and thus the medical diploma.[4] She was therefore barred from practicing her profession abroad and bailing the family out of its financial difficulties. Plekhanov's letters in these first years of exile are marked with the accents of desperation, which were to appear again and again in the succeeding decades. He writes of being in "a chronic financial crisis," and of having debts "greater than those of the Russian state treasury." On one occasion, he explained to Lavrov that he had written a postal card rather than a letter for lack of "the purchasing power" to do otherwise.[5]

* See the correspondence in *Dela i dni*, No. 2 (1921), pp. 78–100. These letters show Plekhanov requesting permission to write Lavrov concerning theoretical questions, anxiously awaiting his opinion of an article Plekhanov had written, responding warmly to Lavrov's approval and encouragement. The younger man's gratitude and respect are expressed in his assertion that Lavrov had been one of his "favorite authors"; and in this passage (p. 86): "You gave me materials, advice, references, and recommendations. Thanks to your support, perhaps I will have the opportunity to work and develop without having in prospect starvation or indebtedness without hope of payment."

† Rosaliia's family appears to have promised to support her when she left Russia, but either the funds were not dispatched or they were far too small to meet the family needs.

In these trying circumstances, Lavrov proved a true and openhanded friend. He possessed some resources of his own, and was able to extend substantial loans to Plekhanov. Plekhanov, of course, was obliged to think of how he would maintain his family in the years ahead, and in fact, the sheltering and nurturing of his family persisted as an unsolved problem for a great part of his exile. Besides the direct loans, Lavrov also assisted Plekhanov in developing what was to become one of his principal sources of income. Aware of Plekhanov's intellectual gifts, and having important literary contacts in Russia, Lavrov encouraged Plekhanov to write salable articles for the progressive journals. The occupation was one which not only would be remunerative but would allow Plekhanov to continue his studies. Limited though such an endeavor might be for a revolutionist, it did indeed furnish an opportunity. In 1881, through the good offices of Lavrov, Plekhanov succeeded in publishing a long, scholarly piece on developments in economic theory in the leading radical journal *Otechestvennye zapiski*,[6] edited by N. K. Mikhailovsky.[*] Mikhailovsky inquired of Lavrov who "the apparently young, talented scholar" was,[7] and commissioned him to write for the magazine a study of the German economist Rodbertus.

In spite of the grim prospects that seemed to lie in store for a professional revolutionist without organizational support, Plekhanov never thought of abandoning his calling. The example of Jules Guesde, the leader of the French Marxian movement, with whom he became acquainted in these years, helped him to accept his lot. The two men met at the end of 1880, after Plekhanov's wife volunteered to look after Mme Guesde during a period of illness.[8] The Plekhanovs thus saw at first hand the poverty of Guesde's material circumstances; and from him, at the same time, as Rosaliia makes clear, they received considerable intellectual and moral stimulation.[9] The precise extent and nature of Guesde's ideological influence upon Plekhanov cannot be determined, but, above all, the Russian was deeply impressed by Guesde's willingness to sacrifice his own well-being to socialism and the cause of humanity.

Whatever positive influence Lavrov and Guesde may have exerted in promoting his conversion to a full-blooded Marxism, the chief emphasis must be placed upon Plekhanov's own inquiries and reflections, with which he was principally occupied in his first years abroad. In this period, he seemed bent on acquiring a complete education. Not content with the study of socialist tracts alone, he attended lectures at the universities in

---

[*] In *Mikhailovsky and Russian Populism* (London, 1958), pp. 102–3, James Billington wrongly describes Plekhanov as a contributor to this journal in 1876. To say that he was ever "a protégé of Mikhailovsky" (p. 162) makes little sense.

Paris and Geneva on such diverse subjects as organic chemistry, geology and anthropology, zoology and comparative anatomy. He worked at the Bibliothèque Nationale in Paris and at the University library in Geneva. Further evidence of the great breadth of his interests may be found in his notebooks of this period,[10] which are crammed with titles of books on ancient civilizations, political economy, and European history, especially as related to the French Revolution and the development of socialist thought.

While zealously seeking to fill the gaps in his education, he was of course not unmindful of relating his studies to the requirements of the Russian revolutionary movement. In works on ancient civilizations, it may be surmised, he searched for clues regarding communal forms of life. Books on political economy, by far the most numerous in his notebooks, he very likely expected to assist him as he groped for an understanding of the relationship between economics and politics, and of the impact of economic change upon social institutions. His study of the French Revolution and early socialist writings was clearly meant to shed light on Russia's situation and destiny. Conspicuous in these notebooks of 1880 and 1881 is the paucity of works on Russia or by Russians. In the Western milieu, Plekhanov appeared to be looking for data and ideas that would help him to understand Russia in terms of the development of other countries and civilizations, in terms of some general system of thought. Much less inclined than other Narodniks to consider Russia *sui generis*, he was intent on finding a common measure which would equally illumine Russian and non-Russian development.

Although he did cast his intellectual net very broadly, Plekhanov seems from the first to have relied heavily upon Marx for assistance in restoring some semblance of order and consistency to his battered theoretical position. According to Deutsch, who was with him in Geneva, Plekhanov devoured everything he could get his hands on concerning the First International, in which Marx had figured so prominently. So attentively did he study that organization—no doubt in pursuit of prognostic and strategic guidance—that he soon could recite its statutes by heart.[11] Inasmuch as the Herculean struggle between Marx and Bakunin lay at the very center of the history of the International, these studies must have given him plenty of food for thought. Doubts as to the compatibility of Marxism and Bakuninist-inspired populism came into sharp focus. Probably his heightened awareness of the conflict between anarchism and Marxism in the Western socialist movement led him back to the primary sources of each. At any rate, at an early date, he read Proudhon's *The Philosophy of Misery*. It was not Proudhon's work, however, but Marx's destructive critique of it, *The Poverty of Philosophy*, which excited Plekhanov.[12]

With his admiration of the founder of "scientific socialism" heightened, Plekhanov felt obliged to master German so that he could gain a wider, and firsthand, acquaintance with the works of Marx and Engels. Applying himself with characteristic diligence, in a matter of a few months Plekhanov was reading German Social Democratic pamphlets. By the end of the summer of 1880 he had finished Engels's *Anti-Dühring*, which he described enthusiastically as "a classic work."[13] From there, he went on to other Marxian writings, including not unexpectedly—since it was their only public pronouncement on Russian revolutionary aspirations—Engels's famous polemic against Tkachev (1875).[14] In view of the authority Engels already enjoyed in his eyes, the impact of this article upon Plekhanov must have been stunning. For in it Engels not only gave vent to a blistering attack upon the Russian Blanquist but virtually laid waste the foundation premises upon which the whole populist edifice rested.

Engels's conclusions regarding Russian economic development paralleled those of Orlov, emphasizing the decay of the commune and the intrusions of capitalism in town and countryside as well. Communal property, Engels contended, "long ago passed its high point in Russia, and to all appearances is nearing its doom." Moreover, nothing the Russians themselves could do, but only proletarian revolution in the West, could save it from definitive collapse. He appeared to be saying that the whole activity of the Russian revolutionists had no meaningful relation to their ends. Ridiculing populist affirmations that the peasants were "instinctive revolutionists," and the Russians "the chosen people of socialism," Engels defined the coming Russian upheaval as a bourgeois rather than a socialist revolution. This last theme, with its devastating implications for populism, Plekhanov echoed—if somewhat more tentatively—in one of his own articles, which appeared in *Chernyi peredel* in September 1880.[15] When he came out unequivocally with a Marxian program, his reading of the Russian situation closely followed most of the dicta in Engels's 1875 article; but that did not occur until two years later.

Ironically enough, although it was Engels's five-year-old polemic against Tkachev which gave substantial impetus to Plekhanov's retreat from populism, the views of Marx and Engels themselves had by 1880 evolved in a direction more favorable to the Narodniks. The comments of Marx on this subject from 1877 to his death in 1883,* if conditional and even ambiguous, never shut out the possibility of a Russian historical evo-

---

* *Perepiska K. Marksa i F. Engel'sa s russkimi politicheskimi deiateliami*, pp. 177–80, 242; Marks i Engels, *Sochineniia*, XV, 601. Since the first of his three pronouncements, a letter to Mikhailovsky in 1877, was not made public until considerably later, Marx's views on the Russian situation could not have influenced Plekhanov prior to March 1881, the date of Marx's letter to Vera Zasulich.

lution radically different from the West's.* There may be some validity in the frequently repeated speculation that Marx deliberately refrained from attacking the theoretical position of the Narodniks in order not to demoralize a group that was striving actively to overthrow the Russian despotism he so despised.[16] But evidence has also been adduced that Marx became persuaded—pursuant to his study of Chernyshevsky and Russian social conditions—that under favorable circumstances Russia might indeed go over to a socialism based upon the peasant commune, without passing through a stage of well-developed capitalism.[17] He prescribed as the conditions for such an eventuality the overthrow of Russian tsarism followed by successful socialist revolution in the West.

The irony does not end here. In the early 1880's, Marx and Engels came close to espousing the same Blanquist position that Engels had so roundly denounced a few years before on the basis of orthodox Marxian premises. Consider Marx's acid comment on the appearance in Western Europe of the Peredeltsi. The majority of them, he said, had "abandoned Russia *voluntarily*—in contrast to the terrorists whose heads are at stake— to form a so-called propaganda party. In order to carry on propaganda in Russia, they come to Geneva. How is that for a *quid pro quo*?"[18] In 1881, while castigating the "Genevans" once again, he lauded the terrorists who were on trial in St. Petersburg for the assassination of Tsar Alexander II in March of that year: "They are sterling people through and through, *without a melodramatic pose*, simple, businesslike, heroic. Shouting and dying are irreconcilable opposites. . . . They try to teach Europe that their *modus operandi* is a specifically Russian and historically inevitable method about which there is no more reason to moralize—for or against— than there is about the earthquake of Chios."[19] Even after conceding that Marx may have been poorly informed about the Peredeltsi and their ideas, his denigration of propaganda activities (designed to promote class consciousness) in favor of terrorism ill accords with the professed conviction of Marxism that classes make history, and make it in dependence upon the growth of their organization and class consciousness.

As if this were not enough, when Plekhanov made a Russian translation of the *Communist Manifesto* (1882),† Marx supplied a Foreword from which the populists could easily have taken comfort. Marx conceded that the village commune had been seriously undermined, but he still saw the

---

* It is difficult to see how Gustav Wetter can find Marx's stand "unequivocal," and Plekhanov's insistence on a capitalist phase for Russia a case of being "plus royaliste que le roi." (*Dialectical Materialism*, p. 80). Plekhanov arrived at his position not on a dogmatic basis but as a consequence of his revolutionary experience and his studies of Russian society.

† Bakunin had made the first Russian translation of this work, in 1869.

possibility of a revolution in Russia that might set off a proletarian revolution in Western Europe, thereby permitting "the prevailing form of communal ownership of land in Russia" to "form a starting point for a communist course of development."[20] With Marx seeming to lend the prestige of his name and authority to the populists, Plekhanov had to have great fortitude to declare his own view. For he was to be in the anomalous position of acclaiming Marx and the Marxian method while arguing, in effect, that in judgments concerning Russia Marx was wrong. This opposition found further expression still later in the restrained enthusiasm, not to say coolness, with which Engels greeted the appearance of Plekhanov's Marxian-inspired Emancipation of Labor Group in 1883 and his important book *Our Differences* (1885),[21] which presented a Marxian analysis of Russia and a Marxian program for the revolutionary movement.

Reflecting later upon the early years of the eighties, when his ideas were forming, Plekhanov wrote:

One who did not live through that time with us can with difficulty imagine the fervor with which we pounced upon Social Democratic literature, among which the works of the great German theoreticians of course took first place. . . . The theory of Marx, like Ariadne's thread, led us out of the labyrinth of contradictions into which our thought had been driven under the influence of Bakunin.[22]

If the first part of this statement may be accepted, the second should be taken—to use one of Plekhanov's favorite expressions in later years—*cum grano salis*. In his exploration of Marxian literature which began in 1880, he did indeed discover what he regarded as a rich treasure trove. It seems not unreasonable to assert that months after his arrival abroad, he had obtained a new and clearer grasp of the general principles and approach of Marxism, and that he became confirmed in the belief that this system furnished the concepts for a scientific understanding of society. But if we allow that Plekhanov had arrived at that point by late 1880, we must then note that two more years went by before he developed out of Marxism a revolutionary program for Russia. Only then, in the Preface he wrote for his translation of the *Communist Manifesto*, do we see Plekhanov for the first time as a full-blown Marxist. *Socialism and Political Struggle*, his first long Marxian essay, published in 1883, summarized the results of this era of travail. In tightly compressed form, its title points up the central problem with which he wrestled in the two-year interval, the problem he had to resolve before he could advance from adherence to theoretical Marxism to the propounding of a Social Democratic revolutionary strategy. That problem read: How can a political struggle on behalf of a bourgeois revolution be justified by socialist theory? How can a socialist movement participate in such a struggle without betraying its own principles?

Oddly enough, although Plekhanov's reconciliation of political struggle with socialism was the last step in his elaboration of a Social Democratic strategy, his denial of the importance of political struggle and political liberty was the first element of his populist outlook to give way under the impact of his experiences in the West. The first evidence of an altered view emerged in discussions about Chernyi Peredel between Axelrod and Plekhanov in the summer of 1880.

Axelrod had become acquainted with German Social Democracy during an earlier extended stay in Western Europe, and as a result his views differed in important respects from those of his colleagues. In a program for a worker group which he composed in 1879, he included—albeit in a subordinate position—demands for universal suffrage and civil liberties. His recognition of the value of these liberties found an echo among the youth he recruited to Chernyi Peredel in the first half of 1880. At the request of the younger Peredeltsi in Russia he drew up a new program, the notable feature of which was the inclusion, along with the standard Narodnik planks, of demands for political and civil liberty. The new program, tacitly acknowledging the impossibility of establishing an anarchist order on the morrow of a revolution, provided for a federal political organization embodying political and civil liberties as a transitional step to the ultimate anarchist goals.[23] Axelrod arrived in Geneva in June 1880 with the idea of persuading his colleagues there to accept his program, and to coordinate their efforts with those of the younger groups in Russia.

Expecting to meet resistance, Axelrod discovered that he was trying to force an open door. The opposition of Deutsch and Zasulich to political struggle, even at the time of the flight from Russia, was considerably less adamant than Plekhanov's. After the dynamiting of the Winter Palace in February 1880, they were powerfully attracted to the Narodovoltsi. After all, were the terrorists not achieving some of the success they promised? Had not the Tsar, on the heels of the third attempt on his life, appointed the conciliatory Loris-Melikov to take charge of the government? As for Plekhanov, six months abroad had sufficed to alter his outlook on political liberty, though not on the efficacy of terror in obtaining it. Already, in six months, he had consumed a substantial volume of German Social Democratic literature, as well as a selection of the writings of Marx and Engels. It had not escaped his notice that neither the most conspicuous theorists of Western socialism nor the strongest socialist party shared his distrust and antipathy for political struggle and political liberty.[24] Moreover, if his first experience of Western conditions made little impact upon him, the same could not be said of his second. His flight from Russia after the Kazan Square demonstration came only a short while after he had entered upon the harried life of the illegal revolutionist. On that occasion, he passed most of his sojourn abroad in Bismarck's Germany, which was certainly no citadel of freedom. In 1880 he breathed the free political atmosphere of Switzerland and France after three years in the underground.

The contrast between Russia and the Western countries was startling. The very activities that made him a criminal in Russia here were carried on every day in a matter-of-fact way. People, not even excluding aliens, dwelt in security where they pleased, and came and went freely without government authorities prying into their affairs at every turn. Here no official intervention intruded between the individual person and whatever literature he might desire access to. Men and women gathered at will, spoke their minds and published their ideas without fear of sudden imprisonment. Here, as he himself had seen, not only could a delegation make representations to a government, but it might even be given satisfaction. Although it was true that Bismarck did everything in his power to frustrate the German Social Democrats, in France and Switzerland, at least, as he had personally observed, even the socialists were free to organize and to propagate their views through meetings and publications. A bourgeois state this might be—and Plekhanov would not have been the last to discern its limitations from the point of view of nonpropertied groups—nevertheless, the prevailing conditions made it unmistakably clear that the form of the state was not, as Bakunin had insisted, a matter of indifference.

Plekhanov's altered attitude toward political liberty and political action was given voice in the draft program he drew up for Chernyi Peredel following his discussions with Axelrod. The place allowed the political element is an extremely modest one: the document as a whole is strongly populist in tone, and only at the end is there a laconic allusion to the possibility of "a constitutional movement in Russia"—a movement which might make it feasible for the organization to participate in electoral agitations and campaigns.[25] Probably for tactical reasons, Plekhanov even admitted the necessity of political terror in this program. In his articles of the next year or so, the eclecticism of his orientation is quite apparent. Yet with each new publication he moved further away from populism and closer to a new synthesis.

His article in the second number of *Chernyi peredel* (the first to be published in Geneva), which appeared in September 1880, is hardly recognizable as the work of the author of the main article in the first number, published only nine months before. Instead of projecting an agrarian revolution that would create an anarcho-socialist order, he now considered it more likely that "society" would cut "the Gordian knot"; that the Tsar would be forced to yield a constitution to the upper classes. Accordingly—and in this formulation the influence of Engels's polemic against Tkachev appears—Russia's next historical stage would probably be a bourgeois-constitutional order.[26] Such an evolution clearly implied a capitalist development for Russia and the untenability of a uniquely Russian historical destiny, but Plekhanov as yet shied away from such conclusions.

Within this framework, which he was ready to employ at least on a tentative basis, he strove unsuccessfully to integrate his new attitudes with his old. "We know the value of political liberty," he declared; "we greet every struggle for the rights of man." But having made this large admission, thus repudiating the populist orthodoxy he had defended with such heat only a year before, Plekhanov promptly diluted it, attributing to such struggles "only a secondary significance" for the socialists.[27] This ambivalence expressed Plekhanov's impulse to break away from populism and yet his inability to disengage himself from the key Bakuninist doctrine concerning the incompatibility of socialism and political struggle. Since the impending revolution would put the bourgeoisie in power, he reasoned, the struggle for political liberty was of the utmost importance to that class. But that which constituted the overriding interest of the bourgeoisie could hardly have the same significance for the socialists. True, political liberty might have some value for the people at large, to whose interests the socialists were dedicated; but a value only of a secondary kind as compared with the gains the bourgeoisie would achieve with the overthrow of absolutism. Above all, the impending dominance of the bourgeoisie would signify for the people not the end of exploitation but only the replacement of one exploiting group by another.

If the socialists, therefore, were to make the struggle for political liberty their primary task, they would be serving the interests not of the people but of its future exploiters; they would become, *de facto*, pawns of the bourgeoisie. Still tending to treat politics and economics as mutually exclusive, unrelated spheres, Plekhanov defined as the proper task of the socialists an agitation based upon the *economic* needs of the people, an agitation calculated to arouse, organize, and unite them into a powerful social-revolutionary movement. Only by stressing the economic plight of the people could the socialists secure mass support, he contended. While "everywhere and always" the people are deeply concerned with the "burning" economic question, they are comparatively indifferent to political matters. If the socialists were to devote themselves primarily to the political struggle against absolutism, at the moment of the revolution they would find themselves "a staff without an army." In that case, the bourgeoisie could and would monopolize the fruits of the revolution with complete disregard for the interests of the people. If, on the other hand, the socialists exerted their energies in their proper sphere, at the moment of the revolution they would have behind them massed forces sufficient to ensure consideration of the popular needs.[28]

Acting upon such premises, Plekhanov yielded to others the field of political agitation. Let the bourgeoisie and its representatives do their own work of spreading political propaganda and fighting for political freedom. As for the socialists, they would continue to propagate among the people the idea of the socialist revolution, "the transfer into the hands of the laborers of the means and products of labor." Here we encounter one of the several unresolved difficulties of Plekhanov's position at this time. Whereas he appeared to anticipate the establishment of a bourgeois-constitutional regime upon the overthrow of absolutism, he also seemed to favor the presentation of socialist-revolutionary demands to the bourgeois revolutionists at the moment of their triumph.[29] In other words, he balked at accepting the prospect of an extended period of bourgeois rule; and, like Trotsky at a later date, he envisaged the commencement of an all-out struggle for the socialist revolution immediately after the fall of absolutism. If his study of Western history, and especially of the French Revolution, drove him to think in terms of a bourgeois dominion as Russia's next historical stage, his continuing attachment to the populist ideal of socialism kept him from abandoning belief in its attainability in the near future. For that reason he wished to make the two revolutions more or less coincide in time.

Although much of this discussion had a rather abstract character, ill-suited to Plekhanov's professed enthusiasm for the materialist method, he gave at least one clear hint about his evolving view of Russia's socio-economic foundations. The agrarian question, he asserted, remained the chief concern of the socialists. But, he added, although "the industrial development of Russia is as yet insignificant," it "is not standing still." "Along with this, the center of gravity of economic questions is shifting to the industrial centers." Therefore, to think exclusively in terms of an agrarian socialism would be a mistake. It was impossible "to define in advance from which layers of the laboring population the chief forces of the social-revolutionary army would be recruited."[30]

In this extremely important and fascinating article, it should be observed, Plekhanov dimly perceived the outlines of a different historical evolution for Russia from the one he earlier believed in. The transitional and eclectic character of his thinking at the time is evident in his failure to rationalize conclusions, to reconcile newly acquired views with persisting populist concepts. If his readings in Marxism suggested that a bourgeois rather than a socialist revolution impended for Russia, he continued to think with the populists that Russian industrial development was still unimportant. If, in some unspecified way, he regarded political liberty as having real value, he nevertheless insisted on dissuading the socialists from struggling in its behalf. While still arguing that for the socialists the agrarian question remained paramount, he reported with considerably more warmth on the results of agitation among the industrial workers than among the peasants. If he were to bring consistency and order into his outlook, he needed a surer delineation of the socio-economic development of Russia, a subject on which he apparently had obtained little new data. He also needed to adjust the aims and methods of socialist activity to the evolving material conditions of Russian society.

Plekhanov's third article in *Chernyi peredel,* written for the January 1881 issue, is notable for its forthright statement that Russia's next socio-economic formation would be a bourgeois-constitutional regime.[31] In it Plekhanov took a definite stand for the inclusion in the program of Chernyi Peredel of the demand for political liberty, coupling it with planks for economic amelioration, such as tax reform, factory inspection, and shortened working hours. Here, for the first time, Plekhanov gave—though yet imperfectly—that synthesis of political struggle and socialist activity which was to be one of his major contributions to Russian revolutionary thought. Yet in the same issue he defines as the leading task of the time the working out of a synthesis between agitation for "land and liberty" and "the ideas of contemporary socialism."[32] Having to all appearances moved far toward a Social Democratic program, he was still striving to reconcile populism and Marxism. In spite of the strong appeal Marxism made to his intellect, he could not bring himself to total acceptance because of certain repugnant implications it seemed to carry for the Russian revolutionists.

The dark fear that lurked in his mind was given expression by his friend and colleague Vera Zasulich in a poignant letter of inquiry she addressed to Marx early in 1881:

If . . . the commune is fated to perish, the socialist has no alternative but to devote himself to more or less ill-founded calculations, in order to find out in how many decades the land of the Russian peasant will pass from his hands into those of the bourgeoisie, and in how many centuries Russian capitalism will perhaps attain a development similar to that in Western Europe.[33]

If the commune was indeed doomed, then so also was the contemporary Russian socialist movement, and it would take centuries of economic development before socialism could once again be something more than a utopian dream. In that case, the populists had sacrificed in vain. In that case, no truly fruitful activity was possible for the Russian intelligentsia, and generation after generation of its members could be nothing more than frustrated "superfluous men." Here was a prospect to chill the heart and to make any convinced socialist turn away. The pathos of Plekhanov's particular situation lay in the fact that while he progressively lost faith in the nostrums of populism, he could not bring himself to exchange them entirely for Marxism, which seemed to hold the most grim implications for the Russian socialists.

His uncertainty as to Russia's direction and his sense of the possible futility and impotence of the socialist position are conveyed in an entry in his notebook made in the winter of 1880–81:

Our social relations until now have been in a transitional state, between capitalism and communal natural-economy. On one side, the commune continues to serve as the main type of relationship among the peasantry on the land; agriculture until now continues to be the chief branch of Russian production; and on the other—in this commune, capitalism has already begun to put down its roots. . . . Thus the country is living through a transitional economic stage.[34]

Plekhanov interpreted the dichotomy that had emerged within the revolutionary movement as a reflection of this dualism in Russia's economic situation:

(a) . . . the struggle against absolutism . . . corresponding to the liberal current of capitalism and (b) defense of the form of communal life in and for itself— the populism of '76–'77 . . . which dreamed of the pretenders, cut itself off from socialism, and in the definition of the tasks of its propaganda added nothing to the ideal of Razin and Pugachev [the Cossack leaders of great peasant revolts in the 17th and 18th centuries], the populism that created social-revolutionary organizations with the help of spurious decrees of the Tsar.[35]

Through these lines comes the feeling that perhaps his had been the misfortune to have been born at the wrong time, when the peasant commune had disintegrated beyond the point where it could serve as the nucleus of a socialist society and when capitalism was as yet much too feebly developed to give scope for effective socialist activity. Significantly, he characterized the two revolutionary tendencies, with disdain, as "political opportunism" and "economic old-belief."[36] To make common cause with the bourgeoisie in the struggle against absolutism appeared to him as a betrayal of socialist principles. But to continue operating on the basis of the obsolete dogmas of populism made as little sense as the blind adherence of a portion of the Russians to religious "old-belief."

In the notebook entry quoted above, Plekhanov sees Russian economic development as being in a transitional state between communal agriculture and capitalism. Under no illusions about the possibility of reversing the economic process, in the next months Plekhanov came to the conclusion that the commune was doomed. Toward the end of 1881, he confided to Lavrov his belief that Russia was launched on the capitalist path of development and "that all other routes . . . are closed to her."[37] Moreover, he went on to draw the inference that only from the city workers could something significant be expected by the revolutionary movement.

Once Plekhanov had convinced himself that Russia could no longer avoid a capitalist stage of development, he was struck with greater force than ever by Marx's arguments. Even though he had earlier viewed the world through populist spectacles, he had been deeply impressed by the response of urban workers to the revolutionists and their propaganda. In spite of himself, he had been obliged to recognize the superior revolutionary qualities of the proletarians as compared with the peasants, but he had rationalized this awkward fact by considering the workers as essentially peasants—by denying in effect that Russia had a proletariat. But once he had admitted the presence in Russia of capitalist development, and of its concomitant, a proletarian class, the claims of Marxism in regard to the proletariat seemed confirmed by his own experience.

The last element of his new outlook to fall into place concerned revolutionary strategy. For a long time Plekhanov was at a loss to deduce from the general principles of Marxism a socialist strategy for an economically backward country like Russia. If Russia were destined to undergo capitalist development, then the possibilities of socialist activity would be sorely limited for a long time to come. But this was a limitation he refused to accept, for it meant that all his work had been in vain, and that no fruitful activity was possible to him. His reconciliation of the political struggle against absolutism, which history seemed to have placed on the agenda, with socialist activity came most appropriately in the Preface he wrote for his translation of the *Communist Manifesto*, which was published in the spring of 1882. There for the first time he plainly enunciated a Social Democratic strategy—a strategy suggested, appropriately enough, by the *Manifesto*. To the significance of this work in his ideological development, Plekhanov testified long after: "I can say for myself that the reading of the *Communist Manifesto* constituted an epoch in my life."[38] It seems hardly credible that Plekhanov should not have discovered this most famous work of Marx and Engels until more than a year and a half after he had begun his intensive study of "scientific socialism." More than likely, he reread it then, and found in it the resolution of questions that had become crucial to his thinking.

His study of the *Manifesto* served to break down finally that wall between economics and politics which had been a permanent part of the furniture of his thinking since he entered the revolutionary movement. As a result, he no longer placed political struggle (the fight for political rights and ultimately political hegemony) in opposition to socialist activity (agitation among the masses designed to bring about the destruction of the state and a socio-economic revolution). He now understood that political struggle and socialist activity, so far from being mutually exclusive, were intimately interrelated; that neither could be stressed to the neglect of the other; that only *by way of* political struggle could socialism be attained. He commended the *Manifesto*, therefore, as a corrective to the one-sidedness both of the orthodox Narodniks, who opposed political activity, and of the terrorists, who became so caught up in the political struggle against absolutism that they forgot about the creation of the mass movement, which alone could ensure the future of the socialist party.[39] Having initially adhered to the first position, he subsequently damned both, and in the end united the two in a new combination.

His reasoning now ran as follows: Even though the coming revolution must have a bourgeois rather than a socialist character, the masses still had much at stake. If they were awakened, organized, imbued with class consciousness, then upon the fall of absolutism they would be in a position to demand and obtain the political rights that would help greatly to secure their ultimate achievement of socialism. The tactic Plekhanov recommended to the Russian socialists was the one that Marx in the *Manifesto* had urged upon the German communists. They must fight alongside the bourgeoisie in so far as it proved revolutionary in the struggle against absolutism; but, at the same time, they must endeavor to develop in the minds of the workers the clearest awareness of the antagonism of the interests of proletariat and bourgeoisie. The Russian socialists must draw the workers into the struggle against absolutism as allies of the bourgeoisie, but they must also make plain that proletarian interests dictated the inauguration of a struggle against the ally on the morrow of absolutism's fall.

Well might the *Manifesto* have constituted an epoch in Plekhanov's life, for its pronouncements unified and illumined concepts and experiences which Plekhanov had been unable to reconcile. Now he understood that the Russian workers were not wrongheaded in seeking to win political rights. On the contrary, they were seeking something indispensable to the attainment of socialism. Now he could better appreciate why most of the liberals and radicals after 1879 had been aloof to the apolitical Chernyi Peredel. Now his whole revolutionary experience appeared in a brilliant new light and seemed to provide an astonishing confirmation of the views of Marxism. The workers had proved the most sympathetic to revolutionary propaganda and the most easy to organize because, as Marx pointed out, they were destined by history to be the most revolutionary class of the modern epoch. As for the peasants, Marx's allusions to the "idiocy of rural life" tended to confirm Plekhanov's own impressions of their ignorance and backwardness.

It must also be emphasized that the *Manifesto* was a revelation to Plekhanov because it seemed to affirm, in crisp, clear language, that the Russian socialists had not come too early, that despite the relative backwardness of Russian social and economic conditions important work could be done. Immensely inspiriting were the tidings that the revolutionists need not retire in despair to make "ill-founded calculations," but could carry on their revolutionary work in the conviction that their activity was consistent with the rational movement of the historical process.

Plekhanov's ideological evolution had brought him to a position which represented an innovation in Russian revolutionary thought. It represented as well the triumph in his thinking of a Western approach to the socialist problem. He was now convinced that "in Russian history there are no *essential* differences from the history of Western Europe."[40] Consequently, he maintained that the problems of the Russian socialists could best be elucidated by the study of West European social development and Western socialist teachings. Thus he took his place in the tradition of the Russian "Westernizers." As Peter the Great had introduced Western military and administrative techniques to Russia, as the Decembrists and the men of the thirties and forties had hoped to "Westernize" Russia politically and culturally, now Plekhanov adopted a Western version of socialism, and set out to make it the ruling tendency. As Peter had fought the tradition-bound clergy and boyars, as the Westernizers of the time of Nicholas I had done battle with the Slavophils, so now Plekhanov undertook to demolish Russian populist socialism. Now he announced that he was ready to make of Marx's *Das Kapital* a "Procrustean bed" for Russia's revolutionary leaders,[41] and thus bring the movement into harmony with the march of the historical process. If he long failed in this, his lifework in the end did stamp the imprint of Marx's thinking deep into the texture of Russian life.

6

THE EMANCIPATION OF LABOR GROUP

PLEKHANOV'S CONVERSION to Marxism had no immediate organizational consequences. It was not until the latter part of 1883 that he and a few friends established the Gruppa Osvobozhdenie Truda (Emancipation of Labor Group), the first genuinely Marxian organization in the history of the Russian revolutionary movement. Equally surprising at first glance are the organizational activities of Plekhanov and his comrades in the two preceding years, indicated in a note appended to the September 1883 announcement of the creation of Osvobozhdenie Truda:

In view of the constantly repeated rumors of a union of the old group Chernyi Peredel with Narodnaia Volia, we consider it necessary to say a few words in that regard here. In the last two years, negotiations were in fact conducted between the two groups regarding union. But although two or three of our group even fully adhered to Narodnaia Volia, it was not possible, unfortunately, to effect a complete merger.[1]

Plekhanov not only refrained for a significant interval from launching a Marxian organization but even came close to a rapprochement with the terrorists whom he had berated so severely! How can this apparently inconsistent behavior be accounted for? And what brought on the collapse of the reunion efforts, and the subsequent renewal and intensification of Plekhanov's assault upon Narodnaia Volia—this time under the aegis of the Emancipation of Labor Group?

When Zemlia i Volia split into two, a possible future alignment was not absolutely excluded. To be sure, substantial differences in program and principle existed. Yet sympathetic relationships between members in each faction had made it possible to divide the organization amicably and, thereafter, to maintain cordial and helpful contact. The absence of unrestrained attacks upon the terrorists in the pages of *Chernyi peredel* gave evidence of a desire not to become embroiled in polemics that might deepen divisions and make difficult or impossible a future reconciliation. Of course, reconciliation would be unthinkable unless and until ideological differences might be composed or at least narrowed. But it was not beyond the range of possibility that they might be narrowed or composed, as the revolutionists gained new experience and new insight.

Plekhanov's hopes for Chernyi Peredel, following the breakup of Zemlia i Volia, proved illusory. In contrast to the dwindling Narodnik movement, the boldness and spirit of self-sacrifice displayed by the Narodovoltsi won enormous prestige for their organization. Radically inclined students were swept away by their dashing heroism and their courage; liberal-thinking professional men and workers who favored political liberty contributed moral support, money, and some recruits to the terrorist organization. The distinguished Mikhailovsky secretly collaborated with it. And, in Western Europe, Marx presently expressed unrestrained admiration for the Narodovoltsi, calling Russia "the leading detachment of the revolutionary movement in Europe," and the Tsar "the military prisoner of the revolution."[2] Although it gave him little satisfaction, Plekhanov's prophecy that terrorism would swallow up all the substance of the revolutionary movement appeared well on the way to fulfillment.

The distinct possibility existed that Chernyi Peredel itself might be swallowed up. At the time they left Russia with Plekhanov, Deutsch and Zasulich were at least half convinced that the terrorists and not the Peredeltsi were pointing the way for the Russian movement.[3] Even Plekhanov himself could hardly remain blind to the merits of the terrorists. Whatever their theoretical inadequacies from his point of view, they were incontestably the only force fighting vigorously and bravely against Russian despotism.

Plekhanov's opposition to terrorism at Voronezh and before had been largely a result of his conviction that political goals were alien to popular needs and incompatible with socialism. But one who, after nine months in the West, wrote that he knew "the value of political liberty" and greeted "every struggle for the rights of man" could hardly reject the efforts of the Narodovoltsi to attain them. Slowly, Plekhanov became aware that perhaps they and not he had been right at Voronezh; and with such an awareness an important difference between the groups faded.[*] On the other

---

* *Sochineniia*, XIII, 26. A year or two later, Plekhanov explained the historic role of Narodnaia Volia by reference to Hegel's famous dictum: "The owl of Minerva begins to fly only at twilight." The terrorists did not fully comprehend the significance of the activity they had inaugurated. Although they erred in regarding political assassination as an appropriate strategy for successful revolution, nevertheless they had materially advanced the prospects of the revolutionary movement by pushing political struggle to the fore. *Literaturnoe nasledie G. V. Plekhanova*, I, 141.

hand, some of the Peredeltsi mistakenly believed that the Narodovoltsi, tacitly acknowledging that *they* had been in error, were once again giving proper attention to agitation among workers and peasants.[4] Developments such as these seemed to have narrowed the difference between the two factions sufficiently to give some promise of an alliance. In January 1881 Plekhanov put out a feeler for union of the two factions on the basis of his as yet imperfectly formulated reconciliation and integration of political struggle with socialist activity among the masses.[5] A few months later, Axelrod publicly stated that the two organizations might soon merge.[6]

While such possibilities were being bandied about, the émigré revolutionists heard the electrifying news of Alexander II's assassination. After three unsuccessful attempts, the "Tsar-Liberator" had finally been destroyed by the Narodovoltsi. Opponents of the regime joined in celebrating this "triumph," their joy tempered only by an awareness of what lay in store for the arrested conspirators. Few understood that at the very moment of its greatest success Narodnaia Volia proved its impotence. Behind it stood no force to follow up the initial blow with a decisive assault upon the state. The terrorists who remained at liberty had to content themselves with a letter to the heir to the throne, offering to discontinue their activities in return for certain political reforms.[7] Would an irresistible movement have come as a suppliant asking the Tsar to enact reforms? The letter of the Narodovoltsi was an act of weakness, an acknowledgment that they could disorganize the government but not overthrow it. Fully cognizant of his power and their impotence, Alexander III discarded existing plans for a mild reform and embarked upon a reign notable for its unrelieved reactionary character.

Among the émigré revolutionists the prestige of terrorism now rose to flood tide, threatening to carry away Deutsch, Zasulich, and other Peredeltsi who were already favorably disposed to it. Writing from Geneva on behalf of Zasulich, Stefanovich, and himself, Deutsch declared to Plekhanov in Paris that this was a "grandiose event" and an occasion for joy.[8] He and his friends, he said, anticipating the grant of a constitution in the near future, were anxious to return to Russia and make some contribution to the continuing struggle. Plekhanov replied that he saw no reason to leave Western Europe just then, and he tried to dissuade his friends. Stefanovich traveled to Paris to discuss the situation with Plekhanov, and came away disappointed: far from burning to get into battle, Plekhanov was wholly absorbed in the study of Marxism.[9]

The event that fired so many others left him cold. His reaction sprang from his well-known conviction of the need of a mass force for a successful revolution. While his friends appeared to be losing sight of that consideration, Plekhanov's awareness of it had been reinforced by his studies of

Marxism.* These convinced him of the folly of the methods, if not the goals, of the terrorists. In the absence of a *class* capable of placing limits on the power of the Tsar, the heroic sacrifices of the revolutionists must be wasted. "Yet another Alexander will they kill," he said, "another two or three generals, and with that they will cease to exist."[10] Although he was still uncertain about Russia's future course or the proper tasks for the socialists, he was convinced that the terrorists were on the wrong track.

Plekhanov's position on the question of organization, although it gained in clarity in the year following the assassination of the Tsar in March 1881, remained consistent throughout. He still disapproved the total commitment of the revolutionary forces to political terrorism, but he desired the unification of the revolutionary movement. His friends, he feared, were ready to capitulate unconditionally to the Narodovoltsi. Stefanovich did in fact return to Russia in the summer of 1881 to join the terrorist organization, and only a lack of funds kept Deutsch from accompanying him. Stefanovich wrote Deutsch a stream of letters fervent in praise of the Narodovoltsi, their struggles and prospects. Deutsch responded by assuming for them among the émigrés the role of partisan and aide, seeking to gain them not only favor but financial and other material support. Zasulich, who was Deutsch's common-law wife, shared his views. That Axelrod, who was off by himself in Zurich, tended in the same direction is evident from the appreciative remarks he made about the terrorist organization in a speech to the congress of the German Social Democrats in the spring of 1881.[11]

In the following months, as Plekhanov moved further toward an unqualified Marxian stand, with its attendant Social Democratic political implications, his outlook and that of his friends sharply diverged, a fact forcefully brought home to him when he returned from Paris to Geneva in the fall of 1881. He quarreled violently with Deutsch, and relations between them cooled abruptly. The state of mind of his friends in Geneva, he wrote to Lavrov, was expressed in the words "No matter how much we may bargain, let us unite with Narodnaia Volia at all costs."[12] Much as he wanted unification, he thought that it would do more harm than good if it were carried out on a faulty theoretical and programmatic basis. His policy in the next year and a half rested on the premise that the correction of the ideological line of the revolutionary movement took precedence over premature and indiscriminate merger plans.

A merger in late 1881, as he knew, would have meant the assimilation of the Peredeltsi into Narodnaia Volia, and the virtual loss of any leverage

---

* Deutsch tells us that Plekhanov had endeavored to draw Zasulich and him into the study of Marx. But such study as they had accomplished had not so far affected their basic outlook; see "Kak G. V. Plekhanov stal marksistom."

for switching the movement onto Marxian tracks. If there were to be any hope for Marxian influence, he must first of all bring about a closing of ranks with his colleagues. There could be no hard bargaining with the Narodovoltsi unless his own faction was reunited. Hence his efforts to persuade the others not to return to Russia for the time being; hence his ardor to educate them in Marxian thought. To that task he devoted no little attention in the winter of 1881–82 and thereafter. Nor did he confine his attention to the former Peredeltsi: having experienced a revelation, he burned to make it known. He urged all Russians whom he encountered in Geneva to apply themselves to the study of Marxism, and he also delivered a series of lectures on Marxism and its relevance to the Russian situation. The lectures were a great success, Deutsch says, but made no converts. It proved later to have been a costly mistake—though an unwitting one—not to have made some attempt to educate the Peredeltsi in Russia as well. Owing to their neglect of the ideological development of their comrades at home, those who presently established the first Marxian revolutionary group gratuitously forfeited support, and at the inception of their organization found themselves practically isolated from Russia.[13]

Plekhanov only gradually managed to regain his authority with his friends and to consolidate the group for organizational initiatives. With his return to Geneva, Deutsch and Zasulich were subjected to pulls from opposite directions. Stefanovich in Russia continued to send glowing accounts about the Narodovoltsi, and urged the émigrés to put themselves entirely at the disposal of the terrorist organization. Plekhanov exercised his influence against any such complete commitment, and stressed the necessity of devoting time to the mastery of Marxism. Actually a kind of double-gauge, compromise policy was adopted. Deutsch and Zasulich collaborated with Narodnaia Volia in matters of organizing press facilities and raising money. Through them Plekhanov himself was persuaded to contribute to its literary enterprise; specifically, and significantly, he undertook to provide material for leaflets for workers to be published in Russia.[14] At the same time, Deutsch and Zasulich applied themselves to serious study and gradually came to adopt the Marxian point of view. Axelrod, in Zurich, where the headquarters of the harassed German Social Democrats were maintained and their newspaper published, was able to keep in touch with developments in the European socialist and labor movements, which he reported upon for a Russian liberal newspaper. Thanks to his extensive contacts with the Germans, he, too, was evolving toward a Social Democratic position. But, like the others, he felt gratitude to Narodnaia Volia for its valiant fight and for having awakened the revolutionary movement to the importance of the struggle for political liberty.[15]

In the course of 1882, negotiations for closer collaboration between the two groups and their ultimate amalgamation proceeded by fits and starts.

The situation mirrored the uncertain attitude of the former Peredeltsi to the terrorists. Although sympathetic to those engaged in an uncompromising struggle against the common foe, Plekhanov and his friends were progressively more critical of the Narodovoltsi ideological position. Beginning early in the year, events brought notice of a new and sharp divergence of views. In connection with the negotiations, Plekhanov's circle received in February a letter from the Narodovoltsi in Russia outlining their views in terms that created a sensation.[16] Until then, the stated intentions of Narodnaia Volia had been the overthrow of Tsarism by a popular revolution, to be followed by the convocation of a constituent assembly; or, alternatively, the extortion of political rights from the Tsar. Now Tikhomirov, the writer of the letter, gave a radically different emphasis to the terrorist plans. "A state overturn," the first act of which, he explained, would be a seizure of power by the revolutionists, "is our to be or not to be. . . . To this goal we subordinate *all else*: program, tactics, all interests, all questions. This you must understand in the most profound way if you wish to be with us."[17] The ideology of Tkachev had gained the upper hand in the councils of Narodnaia Volia.

The shift represented a belated response of the surviving terrorists to the fiasco of March 1, 1881. The assassination of the Tsar having changed nothing, the bankruptcy of the politics of assassination stood nakedly revealed. The Narodovoltsi had long since despaired of arousing the people to revolutionary action, and they clearly had no intention of reverting to agitation among the masses. Thus, for those who persisted in working for a revolution, there seemed no alternative to the direct seizure of power by a conspiratorial coup. Men like Tikhomirov, who were most sensitive to the questions and realities of power, drew the indicated conclusions and secured leadership of the organization.

Plekhanov was appalled by the new line, which he termed "unthinkable." More than ever he rebelled against joining forces with the Narodovoltsi, who, he declared, "do not possess an elementary understanding of contemporary socialism and the West European labor movement."[18] Having pursued and acquired theoretical clarity by a study of Marxism, he found mystifying and repellent such passages of the letter as the following:

In order that we may act together as comrades, we must agree on the fundamental point of view and clarify it, which is the most difficult task. Here details and incidentals are not important, not that one is a socialist and the other a political radical, that one acts among the people and the other among the military. . . . All these are incidentals in which we may differ without ceasing to serve the same god. And the essential feature of the Narodovoltsi, which distinguishes them from all other revolutionary tendencies, is just that for the Narodovoltsi all these matters are incidental. From beginning to end Narodovolism was a current of *immediate action, a state overturn*. . . . We are what we are, that is, neither radicals nor socialists, but simply Narodovoltsi.[19]

Perhaps because of his influence, Plekhanov's friends also felt misgivings about this letter from the Narodovoltsi. Nevertheless, they counseled conciliatoriness in the reply, in order not to wreck forever all chances of union. Plekhanov was of two minds. In the matter of theory, he reasoned, the Narodovoltsi were so ignorant and confused that it would be impossible to work with them in the same organization. But tactical considerations suggested the need for caution. If he insisted upon a clean break, as he had at Voronezh, he might find himself isolated once again. To avoid that, he was prepared, for the time being at least, to bow to the dictates of "party discipline." He knew that since his return to Geneva he had made headway in reshaping the views of his friends. Pending a complete meeting of minds, he felt it politic to give some ground to them. Accordingly, he consented to the diplomatic reply Deutsch wrote to the Narodovoltsi.[20] The latter responded favorably, holding the differences between the two inconsequential, and certainly no barrier to the joining of their efforts.

At this time Lavrov and such other well-known revolutionists as Kravchinsky and Kropotkin were associated with Plekhanov's group in the negotiations for unification. For the consolidated organization there was projected the publication abroad of a journal, to be called *Vestnik Narodnoi Voli* (Courier of the People's Will). Along with Kravchinsky and Lavrov, Plekhanov was invited to become an editor. In the spring of 1882, he expressed in a letter to Lavrov his hopes and fears concerning the journal and the prospects for amalgamation. Since Lavrov and Plekhanov's other friends desired it, he stood ready to become an editor; but he emphasized the conditional character of his compliance by drawing attention to the divide that separated the outlook of the Narodovoltsi from his own:

Our disagreements with the Narodovoltsi are already not so inconsequential as might appear from our letter to them. The letter was written more or less diplomatically for various reasons. You know my way of thinking, and I can assure you that it has not changed since I left Paris. If we put in the shade rather than emphasize our differences in the letter, that may be explained by the fact that we hoped and hope still to turn Narodovolism onto the right road. . . . In case of failure on our side, we shall have to go into opposition again: would that be fitting for me, as an editor of *Vestnik Narodnoi Voli?* Furthermore, there exists between me and Serg. Mikh. [Kravchinsky], it seems to me, a significant difference in views: he is some sort of Proudhonist, I don't understand Proudhon; our characters are not alike: he is a person who is extremely tolerant of every variety of socialist thought, I am ready to make of *Capital* a Procrustean bed for all the collaborators of *Vestnik Narodnoi Voli*.[21]

Plekhanov would presently learn that Lavrov stood much closer to Kravchinsky than he did on the question of the tolerable limits of socialist diversity. His own preoccupation with doctrinal orthodoxy was to be salient feature of his political career.

In the ensuing months, Deutsch, Zasulich, and Axelrod came around to full support of Plekhanov's ideas and strategy. Whether or not union of the two groups could be effected thus was to depend ultimately upon whether the Narodovoltsi would agree to accommodate themselves to Plekhanov's Procrustean bed. For some time, the pertinent evidence was ambiguous. As long as it was, the factions continued in uneasy association.

In the summer of 1882 Tikhomirov left Russia for Switzerland after a new and devastating assault upon the terrorist organization. In the meantime, Kravchinsky had withdrawn as an editor of the forthcoming journal, and Tikhomirov was slated to replace him. Tikhomirov seemed as a result of the recent debacle somewhat disenchanted with the latest program of Narodnaia Volia, but the opinions he expressed in conversations with Plekhanov's group appeared at the same time to rule out the possibility of collaboration. He told Deutsch that Marx was a charlatan who did not himself believe the propositions he expounded.[22] He told Axelrod that an illegal organization of several hundred dedicated revolutionists was of more significance than all the electoral successes of the German Social Democrats.[23] To Plekhanov he indicated his tolerance of the anti-Jewish pogroms in southern Russia in 1881, and his lack of interest in establishing contacts with the German socialists.[24] Finding Tikhomirov's views irreconcilable with his own Social Democratic ideas, Plekhanov suggested that the two could scarcely work together as co-editors. But Tikhomirov disarmed him, asserting that he himself really had nothing against Social Democracy; however, he argued, the Russian revolutionists were generally prejudiced against it, and it was therefore necessary to prepare them gradually for the acceptance of a Social Democratic program.[25] Plekhanov then quickly agreed to be an editor, on the understanding that he would be given free rein to "re-educate" the movement. Tikhomirov, it seemed, had fallen in completely with the aims of Plekhanov's group.

Tikhomirov's conduct at the time is difficult to fathom with assurance. He is said to have become disillusioned with the program of Narodnaia Volia after witnessing its many defeats and losses. Perhaps for that reason, and also because of his bland indifference to theory, he was willing to be conciliatory if something stood to be gained. Clearly, he neither understood Social Democracy nor sympathized with it. But he could nonetheless agree with the Social Democrats on some matters: he, too, took a dim view of the surviving Narodniks. Moreover, he was pleasantly surprised to discover that the Marxists were not quietists but, on the contrary, held the most extreme political views.[26] To one who valued revolutionary militancy more highly than any theoretical system, this was a consideration of great weight. Finally, and probably most important, Tikhomirov realized that his organization could be put on its feet again only with the assistance of revolutionists of prestige and talent. Zasulich, Plekhanov, Axelrod—and Lavrov, who seemed to be aligned with them—were names to conjure with. If they could be drawn into the work of Narodnaia Volia, surely that would be worth some theoretical concessions.

So matters rested for about a year. For only in the summer of 1883 did the Narodovoltsi secure the money with which to launch the *Vestnik Narodnoi Voli*. In the meantime Plekhanov had taken Tikhomirov at his word and, with Axelrod, was preparing a powerful lesson in Marxism for the first issue of the new journal. Axelrod contributed an article saturated with the Marxian spirit entitled "Socialism and the Petty Bourgeoisie." In a review of a book on the historian Shchapov, Plekhanov called for a critique of Narodnichestvo. And he proceeded to supply the critique himself in a long article, "Socialism and Political Struggle," which found in Social Democracy the means to overcome the defects of the existing revolutionary programs. As for Narodnaia Volia, he called it "the most revolutionary but also the most unprincipled" of all the opposition parties.[27] Tikhomirov boggled at this but nevertheless agreed to accept the article.

As the actual publication drew nearer, the factions began maneuvering for position and influence. Plekhanov tried to get the name of the journal changed to something less official-sounding. He felt uneasy about working under a masthead suggestive of a tradition and ideas strongly at variance with his own.[28] He also sought to impart a Social Democratic flavor to the announcement of the new journal,[29] in which was set forth the editors' conception of the tasks and goals of the revolutionary party.

It was not these matters, however, but the organizational question which proved the insurmountable barrier. In the spring of 1882 a verbal agreement had evidently been reached on the merger of the two groups. With publication imminent, Plekhanov's faction pressed for a formal announcement of the amalgamation, with an explanation of its basis. They were reluctant to work in the organization if they were not to be extended the rights and privileges of members. But now Tikhomirov reversed himself, maintaining that Narodnaia Volia's constitution forbade the admission of an entire organized group. The faction would have to dissolve, and its members then be voted on individually by the Narodovoltsi.

Plekhanov and his friends were outraged at this unexpected turn, for, as Plekhanov wrote Lavrov, they did not consider it possible "to be smashed into atoms in order to be assimilated to Narodnaia Volia."[30] As much as anything, they resented the raising of a constitutional issue when the terrorist organization had been reduced by successive government blows to little more than a handful of green youths. Must the veteran leaders, who had so much to contribute, submit to such a demeaning procedure for the sake of some absurd legal point? Moreover, some evidence existed of an intention on the part of the Narodovoltsi to exclude at least one of the other faction.[31] The former Peredeltsi absolutely refused these terms. Seeing that he might lose all, Tikhomirov subsequently sought to mollify the group by offering to intercede with his comrades in Russia on behalf of a satisfactory adjustment of the point at issue. However, since a good many months might pass before a decision could be reached, the offended faction was not in fact mollified. Its members showed their displeasure by partially withdrawing their cooperation.

The former Peredeltsi chafed at the situation in which they found themselves. They had hoped to exert a powerful influence in the organization, but now it appeared that their talents were simply to be exploited. They felt that they would be regarded by the public as Narodovoltsi while in fact they were not; that they would be working for the glory of an organization that refused to concede them a voice in its affairs. The prospect was so distasteful that they began to discuss the possibility of forming a new group,[32] and then to act on the premise. Plekhanov began looking for funds with which to back an independent publication.[33] Deutsch tried to persuade Axelrod to withhold from the *Vestnik* the article he had promised, and Plekhanov hoped his long article would be refused, since it would make an effective vehicle with which to launch a Marxian movement.[34] To invite its rejection, Deutsch pointed out to Tikhomirov's wife the all but insulting remarks about Narodnaia Volia in the article.[35] The intrigue worked. Tikhomirov shortly declared that the article could not be published unless it was either altered or he was permitted to append a note to it. He would not consent to Plekhanov's getting the last word with another note, so that the final decision was to reject the article. Plekhanov thereupon resigned his editorial duties, with a promise to continue collaboration on some other basis.[36]

Tikhomirov and his group, of course, were not blind to the efforts of the former Peredeltsi to precipitate a break. To be sure, he tended to overlook the effects of his own behavior, in alienating them and arousing their suspicion. His own *volte face* resulted from his gradual realization that he had gone too far in giving the other faction a free hand. The aggressiveness with which Plekhanov advanced the Marxian outlook in his articles for the new journal may have awakened him to the danger for the Narodovoltsi, and the pressure of his comrades in Russia was important. By letter, they pointed out that Plekhanov's group would add little or nothing to the fighting forces in Russia, or to the financial solidity of the organization, while threatening to secure ideological predominance.[37] There were good reasons for reserve toward the Social Democrats.

Both parties were obviously losing interest in the amalgamation for which they had been preparing for more than a year. Complete collapse of the effort could be only a matter of time. It came in the following way. Deutsch failed to receive a letter his friend Stefanovich had sent him from Russia, and he suspected the Narodovoltsi of having intercepted it. The latter feigned ignorance of the letter but at last, under heavy pressure, delivered it. Tikhomirov maintained that the organization "had a right to take a letter of its member."[38] But Plekhanov declared that the revelation of the methods employed by the Narodovoltsi had taken from him "all respect, not for 'the party' but for the persons who represented it here."[39] Late in August Tikhomirov and Plekhanov had a stormy interview, and on September 12 the break was made complete with the announcement of the formation of the Gruppa Osvobozhdenie Truda and its publishing arm, the Library of Contemporary Socialism.

Thus ended the effort to join the two incompatible groups. The differences between them were too great to permit of a stable union. A conspiracy for the seizure of power by a revolutionary clique, after all, had rather little in common with the principles of Social Democracy as understood in the 1880's. Since the two tendencies could not live in connubial bliss, it was inevitable that each should try to assimilate the other. Failing that, there could be little interest in continued association. Each party could, with some justice, accuse the other of intrigue and bad faith. Both parties considered that the future of the revolutionary movement was at stake. And neither was willing to make an agreement except on condition of predominance of its own views.* The former Peredeltsi were attempting to capitalize on the popularity of the name Narodnaia Volia, while trying to infuse that name and organization with a Social Democratic content. Tikhomirov, it appears, intended to turn the well-known names and the experience and talents of the former Peredeltsi to the advantage of his organization, without, however, allowing them a predominant voice. The Narodovoltsi had determined not to accommodate themselves to Plekhanov's "Procrustean bed." The major consequence of the collapse of negotiations was the birth of Russia's first Marxian revolutionary organization.

---

* In all the cross-fire, Tikhomirov had been careful to impress upon Lavrov an image of himself as the apostle of unity and compromise, while he made his opponents out to be saboteurs and intriguers. In this tactic he succeeded, for Lavrov stayed on as an editor after the others withdrew from collaboration. An incidental result of the break, therefore, was the severance of the intimate ties between Plekhanov and Lavrov. The cardinal sin with which Lavrov reproached his former friend was that he had chosen to fight against other revolutionists rather than against the common enemy. See Lavrov, "Sotsializm i politicheskaia bor'ba," *Vestnik Narodnoi Voli*, No. 2 (1884), Part 2, p. 65.

7

SOCIALISM AND POLITICAL STRUGGLE

In the first two years of the Emancipation of Labor Group Plekhanov laid the foundations of Russian Marxism, thus securing for himself a place in general Russian history. The carefully wrought construction that stands as his important contribution was embodied in his major works of these years, *Socialism and Political Struggle* and *Our Differences.** The first, which had been one of the bones of contention between him and the Narodovoltsi, became in 1883 the initial offering of the newly created Library of Contemporary Socialism. No short pamphlet itself, it was followed a year or so later by the full-length statement, *Our Differences* (1885). The latter served in part as a detailed rebuttal of the adverse criticism his first treatise met in the pages of *Vestnik Narodnoi Voli*. But it was much more than that. The Soviet historian Pokrovsky merely stated the obvious when he remarked that this work contained "practically all the basic ideas that formed the stock-in-trade of Russian Marxism up to the end of the century."[1] After the fateful split in Russian Social Democracy in 1903, we may add, these same ideas continued to exert a large influence upon the thinking and action of the Mensheviks. The Bolshevik faction led by Lenin, although introducing certain major modifications, likewise remained profoundly indebted to Plekhanov for many of its leading ideas. As for Plekhanov himself, he proved extraordinarily faithful throughout the rest of his life to the theoretical system and practical program he worked out in the first half of the eighties.

The form of Plekhanov's first two big Marxian works was determined

---

* He produced a large number of smaller pieces addressed to the same themes in the decade 1883–93. Inasmuch as these articles sometimes elaborated certain points more fully or formulated ideas more succinctly, I shall draw upon them occasionally in the present discussion.

by his own revolutionary past and by the contemporary status of the revolutionary movement, as he envisaged it. To some extent, and especially in *Socialism and Political Struggle*, he set out to give a critical review of his own revolutionary experience, to clarify the circumstances of his ideological development and metamorphosis. Since, in the space of a few years, he had proceeded from Narodnichestvo to Marxism, inevitably much of his attention was devoted to a critique of the former. Moreover the times demanded such a critique, he felt, because the continued attachment of most of the revolutionists to Narodnik premises had created an acute crisis in the revolutionary movement. He was less concerned to justify himself than to provide the movement with a way to overcome the crisis.

Socialism and Political Struggle differed from its successor both in the scope of its coverage and in the relative mildness of its comments on the Narodniks and the Narodovoltsi. In spite of their recent feud, Plekhanov's friends had persuaded him to soften his judgments concerning the terrorists. Nor had he himself entirely lost hope of the conversion of at least some of them. If they were given an opportunity to consider dispassionately a carefully argued statement of the reasons for their failures, perhaps they would see the light. Might they not be impelled to embrace Social Democracy, if shown the promise it gave of revolutionary achievement? Plekhanov wanted less to score off Narodnaia Volia than to win support for his own point of view, and, for once, he allowed the need for tact to take precedence over his polemical ardor.

No prodding was needed to make him pay generous tribute to Narodnaia Volia's past services, which he genuinely valued. To it belonged the great merit of having opened "the epoch of *conscious political struggle* with the government."[2] That step, embodying a break with the Bakuninist apolitism of the Narodniks, had very materially advanced the revolutionary movement toward a proper tactical line. In the pamphlet, he chose to interpret the aim of their political struggle as the conquest of political rights—the goal that stood at the top of his own political agenda. Still, it appeared to him that the terrorists continued to uphold certain other ideas of Bakunin regarding the primitive character of Russian social and economic life, the commune, the peasantry, and the possibility of an immediate socialist revolution. In this, Plekhanov detected a glaring inconsistency: the struggle for political liberty and the drive for a socialist revolution, although not unconnected, were movements of an entirely different order, appropriate to two quite different historical moments. In no case could they be made to coincide.[3] Moreover, if the terrorists had changed their tactics so radically, if Narodovolism represented "an all-round denial of Narodnichestvo" on the tactical level, then surely the theoretical premises of the movement would have to be revised accordingly.[4] For that reason, he urged upon the Narodovoltsi the necessity of "an attentive re-examination of our ideological baggage." As the outcome, he hoped for the complete abandonment of the Bakuninist outlook, and the assimilation in its place of "contemporary scientific socialism"—which alone could validate and make consistent with socialist aspirations the fight for political liberty the revolutionists had launched.

His overtures were paid in different coin by the editors of *Vestnik Narodnoi Voli*. In the second issue of the journal, published in April 1884, Lavrov limited himself to a skeptical estimate of the future of the new group; for, in his view, Plekhanov's position suffered from more inadequacies than the movement he criticized. With some bitterness, Lavrov renounced all desire to debate with a faction that preferred attacking other revolutionists to fighting the oppressive Russian state.[5] But on this point the editors parted company, with Tikhomirov providing a vigorous riposte to Plekhanov's critique.[6]

In his defense, Tikhomirov advanced the same populist arguments Plekhanov had once propagated but now found untenable. Russia's impermeability to capitalism and the universal desire of the Russians for land defined the character of the coming revolution, he argued. This upheaval would be no mere political revolution, giving the bourgeoisie new ways "to discipline the working class"; it would deliver Russia directly into the realm of socialism. Adding his own special ingredient, Tikhomirov foresaw such a social transformation taking place through the seizure of power by the revolutionary party and the subsequent employment of that power to assist the popular revolution expected to break out thereafter.

Going over to the offensive, he charged Plekhanov with wishing to create a class in whose name he could act—the proletariat—while regarding with equanimity, and even with positive approval, the liquidation (by deprivation of their land) of millions of working people already in being— the peasants. The glitter of a system had so enthralled the former Peredeltsi, he charged, that they were even prepared to make an alliance with the hated bourgeoisie. Unable to conceive of socialism except as an outgrowth of capitalism, the Marxists perforce welcomed the victory of capitalism and the bourgeoisie. In effect, he said, the new group proposed to abandon the struggle for socialism, which they now described as a fantastic goal, in order to aid the bourgeoisie in securing political predominance.

Our Differences took up in detail the charges of Lavrov and Tikhomirov, with its polemical edge turned principally against the latter. What angered Plekhanov was not so much Tikhomirov's unregenerate affirmation of "outmoded" Narodnik views as his open and unequivocal support of the doctrine of a conspiratorial "seizure of power"—which Plekhanov considered a step backward as compared with the revolutionary Narodnichestvo of the seventies.[7] Tikhomirov simply refused to accept that very feature of Narodnaia Volia's activity that Plekhanov regarded as its most important contribution. Instead of repudiating Bakunin's conceptions and agreeing to put the struggle for a constitutional regime into a Social Democratic framework, Tikhomirov rejected not only the framework but the struggle for a constitution as well. Moreover, he had also discarded the one element of Narodnichestvo that Plekhanov still cherished—agitation among the people to foment a mass revolutionary movement. Although Tikhomirov had lost faith in the possibility of a peasant revolution, he did not on that account go over to Social Democracy with its promise of a working-class base. Instead, still clinging to the Bakuninist belief in immediate socialist transformation, he fixed his hopes on a conspiratorial coup. Far from disappearing altogether, Bakuninism "described an arc of 180 degrees and was resurrected as a Russian form of Blanquism, basing its revolutionary hopes upon the economic backwardness of Russia."[8] Tikhomirov proposed to lead the revolutionary movement back to the program Tkachev had propounded ten years before, only to be utterly demolished by Engels. To this incredible pass had the leadership of the revolutionary movement come.

Our Differences highlighted the great divide that now separated Plekhanov from those he had imagined might soon become Social Democrats, constituting as it did a full-scale critical analysis of the Russian revolutionary movement, down through what he took to be its latest phase, Narodovolism. It also presented a lengthy and detailed Marxian analysis of Russian social and economic conditions and developments, and derived therefrom a Social Democratic program and a course of action for the revolutionary movement. Plekhanov's ideological construction may be conceived as possessing several different levels of analysis. The outlines of his position, in both its critical and positive aspects, will perhaps be most readily grasped if discussed in terms of these successive levels.

HISTORICO-PHILOSOPHICAL

On the historico-philosophical level, Plekhanov subjected to a trenchant critique the procedures by which his opponents arrived at their conception of Russia's situation and its prospects, and the role and methods of the revolutionary movement. Taking their sincerity for granted, he characteristically attributed their practical failures to their theoretical deficiencies. The program and tactics of the revolutionists naturally were determined by their understanding of existing possibilities of social transformation, and those in turn by their image of contemporary Russian society. If, as he contended, theirs was a distorted image, then inevitably all their calculations must go awry. Ultimately, the success of the revolutionary movement depended upon its acquiring a theoretical instrument adequate for the clear-sighted perception of the nature and dynamics of society. In a striking figure directed against the well-known predilection of the terrorists, he urged: "An idea that is revolutionary in its internal content is a kind of dynamite for which no other explosive in the world may be substituted."[9] And he announced his own key to revolutionary victory with the rhetorical question: "Is it possible to speak seriously today of any other 'analysis of social relations' . . . besides that found in the works of Marx and Engels?"[10]

On the highest level of generality, Plekhanov's most substantial charge against his antagonists was their failure to reckon with historical development and its laws. As a Marxist, he posited the existence of an objective, law-abiding, and, therefore, intelligible historical process—a process independent of human will, which with iron necessity established the limits of rational social action. In his system, the institutions and phenomena of any given society were all interrelated, with material conditions and relations considered antecedent to and determinative of philosophical, juridical, and indeed all spiritual phenomena. In particular, he regarded the economic forces of society as decisive in determining its social structure and ideological superstructure. In the developmental process, alterations in the material basis of society provided the initial impetus to institutional and ideological change. At any given moment in time, certain institutions and tendencies of one and the same social order might be in contradiction, with some in the ascendant, others passing out of existence. Accordingly, institutions and phenomena could be properly understood and evaluated only when examined in social context, and from the developmental point of view. A social movement, if it hoped to attain its goals, must comprehend the true nature of the relationship between the components of society and the dynamics of the historical process that assured the future of certain ideas and groups while condemning others to oblivion. It must recognize the limits placed upon its reforming zeal by the objective conditions of society, and set for itself only such goals as were practicable. It must base itself upon those tendencies, institutions, and groups that the march of history was advancing to the forefront. Plekhanov himself readily acknowledged the binding force of an objectivist determinism and endeavored to shape his goals and methods accordingly. In doing so, he attained a sublime conviction of the ultimate triumph of his views; for he felt in his innermost being that this outlook was scientific, that the principles of historical materialism represented the alpha and omega of the most advanced social theory.

But his antagonists, he maintained, knew nothing of all this. In their ignorance, they violated virtually every one of these precepts. While paying some lip service to the binding force of external circumstances, the Narodniks and the Narodovoltsi in fact took socialist teaching as a kind of geometry, which could at will be adopted and implemented by any people, at any time, without reference to its stage of historical development. Instead of taking the trouble to ascertain accurately the prevailing circumstances, they simply affirmed a whole series of indefensible propositions about the prospects of capitalism, the collectivism of the peasantry, and the ripeness of Russia for socialism. Instead of determining by actual study how history had been and was being made, they invented new paths for history to take,[11] as if a people's destiny could arbitrarily be decided by the whim of a revolutionary group. In effect, they had committed the disastrous error of trying to substitute their own subjective ideals for historical development. Of Tikhomirov, Plekhanov wrote:

He is not concerned with the development of social forces, with the rise of the kind of institutions that make impossible a return to the old regime. . . . He does not reckon with history, does not strive to understand its laws and direct his revolutionary activity in correspondence with them; he simply substitutes his conspiratorial skill for historical development.[12]

Having built their programs upon such flimsy foundations, the revolutionists paid the penalty in a long series of demoralizing fiascos. The "laws of history" could be neither ignored nor violated with impunity.

To Plekhanov's way of thinking, the Narodniks of the seventies and their terrorist successors shared the dubious distinction of demonstrable retrogression. Their much admired predecessor, Chernyshevsky, had popularized the possibility of a direct transition for Russia from primitive communism to "the highest form of communism," without an intervening capitalist phase. But he had striven to understand the peasant commune in a dialectical way—that is, in relation to society as a whole, and in awareness of its changeability. Plekhanov now disputed Chernyshevsky's favorable conclusions about the commune, but he valued Chernyshevsky's method: he had, at least, been sensitive to the possibility that the peasant commune *might* undergo changes that would render it unserviceable as the foundation of socialism. But, Plekhanov argued, the Narodniks, for whom Chernyshevsky figured as an idol, had taken over the letter of his teachings and not their spirit. Heedless of the profound alterations in Russian society since the Emancipation, they continued to think of the commune as immutable.[13]

This failure of the Narodniks, in Plekhanov's view, had been compounded by their inability to identify the crucial areas of social life upon which the further development of society necessarily depended. The "logical fall from grace" of the Narodniks, he asserted, resided in their failure to comprehend "the concept of commodities and exchange value . . . on the basis of which alone a proper conclusion could be made about the mutual relations of producers and the economic organization of the future."[14] The Narodniks had neglected to focus their attention upon the dynamics of Russia's economy, which, in the final analysis, would determine the country's future. According to Plekhanov, the economic movement of Russia since the Emancipation had wrought changes in Russian society that rendered nugatory the dream of a socialist order based upon the peasant commune.

A related item in his bill of particulars taxed the Narodniks with a lack of understanding of the true relation between the component elements of society. They were confident of their predictions concerning the commune because, instead of making a detailed analysis of its actual internal relations, they took the juridical forms to represent the facts of the situation. But, Plekhanov instructed them, in the long run it was not juridical norms that determined the character of the organization of production, but vice versa; one must begin not with juridical norms but with economic facts.[15] For the Marxist, being determined consciousness and not consciousness being.

He further accused Tikhomirov of an inability to grasp the developmental process, in which individual phenomena possessed contradictory sides which had to be taken into account. In Plekhanov's opinion, the leader of Narodnaia Volia could not see how the peasant, at one and the same time, might be both a member of the commune and, in spite of himself, "an irrepressible destroyer of the commune"; how one could recognize the useful activity of capitalism, and still organize the workers for a struggle against it; "how one could defend the principles of collectivism and yet see the victory of progress in the disintegration of one of the most concrete manifestations of that principle, the peasant commune."[16]

Although he never said it in so many words, Plekhanov's mission—as he conceived it—consisted in carrying out in Russia the fundamental task Marx had accomplished some decades earlier in the West: to effect a transformation of socialism, shifting it from a "utopian" to a "scientific" basis. His review of the history of the revolutionary movement in the previous few decades had convinced him of its lack of realism. To what he considered the subjective idealism of the Narodniks, he now opposed the "objectivist materialism" of Marxism. Earlier he had believed populism to be consistent with Marxism, and therefore devoid of utopian taint; now he discerned their incompatibility and opposed the "scientific" quality of one to the "utopianism" of the other. If, at an earlier date, the comparatively undeveloped state of Russian social and economic life made understandable and even inevitable the adoption by radicals of the utopian view-point, economic developments since the Emancipation, on the one hand, and, on the other, the severe defeats the revolutionists had suffered under the aegis of utopianism made it imperative that they scrutinize their ideo-logical heritage with the utmost care. The crisis in the revolutionary move-ment, Plekhanov averred, could not adequately be accounted for by the ferocity of police repression. There existed a tremendous amount of "potential energy" for the Russian revolution; the failure to convert it into "kinetic energy" resulted from the retention by the revolutionists of ideas that were powerless to catalyze the transformation of one to the other.[17]

ECONOMIC

The differences between Plekhanov and his opponents on the substantive side centered around their contrasting answers to that question of "life and death" with which Russian thinkers had been preoccupied for decades: the question of "the fate of capitalism" in Russia, or, alternatively, of the peasant commune. From his point of view, the question could be dealt with only through an investigation of the present condition and vitality of the commune and of the inroads capitalism had made, if any. It would be necessary to show whether conditions in Russia favored the growth and development or the decay and elimination of the commune, the penetration and expansion of capitalism or its exclusion. His own studies persuaded him that "the old forms of Russian national life carried within themselves many germs of disintegration and could not 'develop into the highest communist form,' "[18] under prevailing conditions. On the contrary, he observed, the commune was undergoing disintegration, whereas capitalism "can become and is becoming the all-powerful master of Russia."[19] If he carefully stipulated that capitalism had not yet tri-umphed, he left no doubt of its ultimate success through the working out of irreversible processes which had already been in motion for some time.

Plekhanov acknowledged the remarkable stability of the peasant com-mune in Russia prior to the emancipation of the serfs. That feature he explained as a concomitant of the rather static, not to say stagnant, charac-ter of the pre-reform economic system. The system had featured the pre-dominance of a self-sufficient, *natural economy*,[20] in which exchange, and therefore money, the medium of exchange, were at a minimum. Within that context, the myriad, isolated agricultural communes with the regu-larity of the seasons reproduced themselves and provided subsistence to their members. But they did not possess an internal dynamic of develop-ment nor were they obliged to change basically through contact with external forces. In short, Russia had been what we would today call a traditional, agrarian society.

But the emancipation reforms of Alexander II, whom Plekhanov called "the Tsar of the bourgeoisie,"[21] opened the way for the dissolution of the old order. The reform decrees, he indicated, were followed by a whole series of money speculations, by the establishment of banks and joint stock companies, and by the construction of railroads. These innovations made for a greatly expanded capacity for production and exchange; they inevitably promoted *money economy*, the indispensable basis of capitalism. Moreover, in its quest for ever larger revenues, the State fostered the same tendency by supporting all measures to increase the circulation of money in the country, and to quicken the pulse of social and economic life.[22] Plekhanov found most unconvincing the pleadings of the economist Vorontsov, upon whom Tikhomirov relied, against the possibility of a capitalist development in Russia. Vorontsov argued for the nonviability of capitalism on the basis of the limited markets available to it in Russia, and he saw no possibility of successful competition with more advanced industrial states for foreign markets. Plekhanov resolved the first of these difficulties to his own satisfaction by pointing out that "the transition in any country from natural economy to money economy is accompanied by a tremendous broadening . . . of its internal market," which would no doubt be captured by the Russian bourgeoisie.[23] As to the second, history showed that countries which entered upon capitalist development comparatively late had nevertheless succeeded in acquiring for themselves a part of the international market. Russian entrepreneurs, he maintained, were already seeking to emulate their Western counterparts in this regard.[24] The fact that the Russian government gave aid to Russian capitalism hardly proved the bankruptcy of the latter, for most of the states in the West also supported their capitalist classes with subsidies and protection.

Plekhanov presented evidence which left no room for doubt as to the presence of capitalism in Russia. Yet he made no extravagant claims. For example, he asserted in *Our Differences* that capitalism had penetrated deeply into the textile industry but had hardly begun in other fields. "The main stream of capitalism is as yet small," he admitted, and "there are still few places where the relation of employer to worker would completely correspond to the generally held conception of the relation of capital to labor in capitalist society."[25] Objecting to Tikhomirov's estimate of 800,000 proletarians in Russia as too low, he cited other data which set the figure at a still not very impressive level.[26] But, in any case, he thought, the question of capitalism in Russia was not to be decided by reference to how small or large its stream might be at any given time, by how deeply it had as yet penetrated into this or that industry, by how many workers existed at a given moment. Everything depended upon the general direction of the economic movement.

He himself was certain that in both industry and agriculture capitalism progressed from day to day. Its manner of advance in industry, he illustrated through a description of the fate of the peasant-handicraftsman, whose home manufacture of goods the Narodniks regarded as a bulwark against capitalism. Many of these, he insisted, preserved the appearance of independent farmers when in fact their subjection to capital was "hardly less than that of any homeless factory worker." That he did not go to work in a factory, and maintained the semblance of an agricultural economy, did not prove the handicraftsman's economic independence. The entrepreneur consented to distribute raw materials to the homes of the worker-peasants rather than herd them into a factory because he profited thereby. Where the peasants continued to live on the land, and derived some income from it, the capitalist could pay incredibly low wages for labor. But the peasant-handicraftsman, often unable to give adequate attention to both of his income-earning activities, generally permitted his farm enterprise to run down. When the peasant economy lay in ruins and the wage of the worker had to be raised, the employer found it more advantageous to bring the laborers into the factory, where specialization and division of labor made for an increase in productivity.[27] Thus, the domestic system gave way to factory production, and the peasant-handicraftsman to the proletarian. As for the small entrepreneurs, most of them inevitably would be squeezed out with the introduction of machines. In this fashion, he concluded, "capitalism goes on its way, dislodging the independent producers from their unstable condition and creating an army of workers in Russia by the same tried and true method"[28] that had already been worked out in the West.

Nor were the peasant communes exempt from the effects of capitalist encroachment, he urged. If a natural-economy environment was congenial to the stability of the commune, then its replacement by its opposite—a system of money economy—must have revolutionary consequences for the commune. According to Plekhanov, the development of money economy had created acute contradictions between the ancient peasant institution and its environment which were being resolved by the disintegration of the former. He conceived of money as a dynamic force which constantly extended its influence over new areas, dissolving away natural economy wherever it touched and promoting specialization of production and exchange of products. In the normal course of events, therefore, money economy would inevitably have extended its dominion into the area of communal life. But in fact, he contended, the communal peasantry had been delivered *directly* into the sphere of money economy by the terms of the Emancipation.

The peasants had been allotted lands which they were required to redeem by money payments. To secure these funds, they were obliged to enter upon commodity production, that is, production for exchange.[29] This involved concentration upon the production of one or a few products that could be sold on the market for cash, and also the purchase by the peasant family on the market of certain articles it no longer had the time or space to produce. In this way, the Emancipation settlement forced a shift from self-sufficient, natural economy to commodity-producing, money-based economy. The end result of the process, Plekhanov believed, would be the destruction of the commune and the triumph of capitalism in Russian agriculture.

For the inauguration of commodity production, to his mind, represented but the first step on the road to capitalist production. In time, commodity production, by "an internal, inevitable dialectic," is converted into capitalist production; "at a certain stage of its development, commodity production leads to the exploitation of the producer, creates the capitalist-entrepreneur and the proletarian-worker."[30] The dialectical process he referred to was the progressive differentiation in economic status over a period of time of the separate producers who compete in the market. As he depicted the process, the differentiation at last becomes so marked that some producers become capitalists while others become proletarians. Such would be the fate of the communal peasantry in the long run, Plekhanov believed;[31] and, already, he could present persuasive evidence which appeared to foreshadow that conclusion. These data consisted largely of signs of the growth of inequality and individualism among the communal peasantry, developments Plekhanov understood as the negation of the traditional equalitarianism and collectivism of the commune. On the one hand, significant numbers of peasants had lost or were in the process of losing the capacity to till their land allotments and surrendered their use to others, while resorting to wage-work to meet their own needs; on the other hand, a well-to-do class of peasants was emerging, which cultivated the allotments of one or more peasants in addition to their own, purchased and/or rented additional lands, and hired labor.[32]

It mattered not, in Plekhanov's scheme of things, that juridically the land belonged to the commune and was supposed to be repartitioned periodically among its members. He pointed to the decline, and often cessation, of periodic repartition of the land as unmistakable proof of the rise of individualism within the commune, as a portent of the ultimate conversion of communal land into individual private property. In a money economy, land itself tended to become a commodity, and it could only be a question of time until the juridical forms came into correspondence with economic realities; until ability to pay—a tenet of money economy and capitalism—became the basis of land ownership and control.

The conflict between traditional communal principles and the dynamics of post-Emancipation development had become so sharp, Plekhanov thought, that already the interests of a large proportion of the peasantry were incompatible with the perpetuation of the commune. The poor peasant who was unable to cultivate his plot for lack of means was equally unable to rid himself of it because of the difficulty of alienation. If he left the commune to find wage-work, he was still required to pay communal taxes. The well-to-do, under the communal principle of "joint responsibility," were obliged to pay the taxes of those who could not muster their own. The principle of periodic repartition worked against the security of land tenure, which was essential for planned capital improvement. Further, they were hindered in introducing improved agricultural techniques, for when these required different schedules of planting, cultivating, and so on, the more affluent peasants once again might be at odds with communal habits.[33]

Only the middle peasant showed an unqualified sympathy for the commune, Plekhanov thought. Yet he conceded that all the peasants were somewhat ambivalent toward it. It was true that actual conversions of communal property to individual, hereditary holdings were so far relatively infrequent: the peasants, "by force of habit, loyalty, and partly by conscious conviction," were inclined "to preserve the old *collective* principle of *ownership* of land after the means of *acquiring* land had come to be based entirely upon a new, monetary, *individualistic* principle."[34] But, he argued, such subjective elements could only delay the fall of the commune and the growth of capitalism; they could no more prevent its eventual triumph than had the guilds in the West.

In *Socialism and Political Struggle,* while asserting propositions which pointed to the doom of the commune, Plekhanov contrarily had also quoted with apparent approval Marx's rather favorable opinion regarding the use of that institution as the basis of a socialist agriculture. His citing of Marx should probably be taken as a tactical feint, meant to disarm populist sympathizers, whom he still had hopes of winning over. In *Our Differences* there is scarcely any equivocation at all.[35] What feeble chances he saw for the survival of the commune came to practically nothing as compared with his numerous strong predictions of its demise. The Emancipation had "dislodged the commune from the stable equilibrium of natural economy and delivered it over to the power of all the laws of commodity production and capitalist accumulation."[36] Since "all the principles of contemporary economy" were in "irreconcilable hostility to the commune," "to hope for its further independent 'development'" was like hoping for "the multiplication of a fish that had been pulled up on the shore."[37]

For the future, he predicted the dissolution of the commune, the gravitation of landed property into the hands of a class of well-to-do farmers, and the progressive concentration of most agricultural operations in large mechanized, capitalistic enterprises. Parallel with this, he foresaw the emergence of a numerous class of landless peasants, rural proletarians, who would be forced to sell their labor to the capitalists in agriculture or industry. And as for the industrial sector of the economy, he anticipated the continued growth of productive forces, the squeezing out of the small entrepreneurs, and again the concentration of production in a comparatively small number of large-scale enterprises.

The implications for the Narodniks of such an image of Russia's present and future were clear. They comforted themselves with visions of a unique evolution for Russia, bypassing capitalist development, but, Plekhanov declared, they had only to open their eyes to see that capitalism had already arrived, was making new conquests every month, and could not be halted or wished out of existence. To ignore this obvious aspect of Russian development and to ground one's socialist aspirations upon the disintegrating village commune and the patriarchal peasantry was the height of folly. If it hoped to succeed, the revolutionary movement must rely instead upon the progressive socialization of production and labor in town and country, and upon the multiplying numbers of the proletariat, the revolutionary class of the capitalist epoch.

SOCIAL AND POLITICAL: THE SOCIALIST REVOLUTION

Plekhanov conceived of the socialist revolution as both the culmination of a long evolutionary economic development and the last stage of a class struggle that arose in the course of that economic movement, and was fought to a finish in the political arena. Since the socialist revolution presupposed an antecedent evolutionary development of considerable duration, it made absolutely no sense to think of attaining socialism by skipping a whole historical stage. He would have concurred with the view that the social history of a people resembled the natural history of an individual in that a comparatively backward society could no more adopt the most advanced type of social organization than a child could assume at will the role of an adult. The "objective conditions" for a "socialist organization of production," far from obtaining in a pre-capitalist system such as the populists judged Russia to be, were laid down in the very process of capitalist development they were so anxious to avoid.

The economic precondition for socialist reconstruction, in Plekhanov's scheme of things, was nothing else than a highly developed industrial, capitalistic system. An economy ripe for socialist transformation should possess a tremendous quantity of productive forces, organized into massive and interdependent enterprises, thus embodying a large-scale socialization of production and of labor. Such patterns of organization, both in industry and in agriculture, set the stage for the major move in the socialist program, the socialization of the means of production.[38] As we have seen, Plekhanov thought the dynamic of Russia's economic development was working toward that end.

We have had intimations, too, of the radical transformation of Russia's social structure that he understood to be integral to this economic process. In a petty-bourgeois country, he once remarked, the economic emancipation of the masses must await the replacement of the majority group of small producers by two clearly defined antagonistic classes.[39] The forward march of capitalism in Russia gradually accomplished that task, elevating some to bourgeois status and destroying the independence of countless other peasants and artisans, compelling them to enroll in that army of proletarians whose battalions would man the great industrial and agricultural enterprises of the future. Thus, in the very process of its natural development, capitalism approached its end; for it inescapably augmented the numbers of the proletariat, the class destined by history to overthrow it. In employing the term "proletariat," Plekhanov had in mind primarily full-time, *bona fide* factory workers, who had severed all connection with the land. But, from time to time, he also designated the rural proletariat (landless agricultural workers) and the poorest peasantry (i.e., semi-proletarians) as allies of the industrial workers in the socialist revolution.

Ample evidence exists for stating that Plekhanov expected this coalition, in the normal course of events, to constitute a majority at the time of the socialist revolution. This proposition accords with the image he projected of Russia's economic order at the moment of the revolution. Should such an order materialize, the proletariat and its allies would inevitably constitute a majority. But such a majority could not in itself be considered a sufficient guarantee of the revolution. A cardinal tenet of Plekhanov's outlook was that "the liberation of the working class must be the task of the working class itself"; but the working class must first comprehend the reasons for its exploitation and the steps necessary for its liberation. Only as it became instilled with class consciousness and united in an effective political organization would it be equal to its historic task. In this regard, too, according to Plekhanov, capitalism promoted the conditions of its own ultimate extinction; for "parallel with the development of productive forces and with the [social] organization of production corresponding to it" proceeds the mental preparation of the proletariat for the socialist revolution.[40] The principles of scientific socialism, he maintained, were nothing but the generalization of conditions met with daily by the workers, the explanation of the laws which determine their role and share in production. Therefore, the workers would experience little difficulty in recognizing the validity of these principles.

At this point, a major inconsistency entered into Plekhanov's system. His outlook thus far unmistakably pointed to the rise of proletarian consciousness as a "natural" and inevitable accompaniment of capitalist development. But he refused to draw the indicated conclusion. He did not contend that the workers on their own were capable of awakening fully to socialist consciousness, of deducing socialist conclusions from their experience of capitalist production. Rather, he assigned a crucial role to the socialist intelligentsia. Upon it devolved the task of guiding the revolutionary feelings engendered among the workers by the capitalist system into socialist channels. The socialist intelligentsia, he wrote,

must become the leader of the working class in the projected liberation movement, must explain to it its political and economic interests as well as the connection between these interests, must prepare it for an independent role in the social life of Russia. It must with all its forces strive so that in the first period of constitutional life in Russia, our working class can come forth as a special party with a definite social-political program.[41]

Plekhanov confidently expected the workers to respond positively to the promise of emancipation to be realized with the establishment of a socialist organization of production.[42] But it required the activity of the socialist intelligentsia to evoke such a response, to arouse the class consciousness of the proletariat. Its activity was therefore an indispensable link in the chain of conditions essential for the socialist revolution.[*]

The conception of proletarian consciousness as a necessary consequence of proletarian experience under capitalism corresponded to what Plekhanov regarded as the central thesis of Marxism: "being determines consciousness." That thesis could hardly be sustained, however, if proletarian consciousness had to be aroused by the socialist intelligentsia. The activity of the latter posed a further difficulty. How could the intelligentsia rise to socialist consciousness when the circumstances of its life were utterly different from those of the proletariat under capitalism? Plekhanov's system counted on the awakening of proletarian consciousness in the proletariat by a nonproletarian element! The problems inherent in his formulation were never laid to rest. Again and again they cropped out in the ideological controversies and political conflicts that marked Plekhanov's career.

In acquiring class consciousness with the aid of the intelligentsia, the

[*] Despite the importance of this idea to Plekhanov's thought, Alfred Meyer contends that Lenin's emphasis on consciousness was noteworthy because "the concept had been neglected more and more by European and Russian Marxists in the late nineteenth century." See *Leninism,* pp. 28–29.

proletariat prepared for a class struggle with its capitalist oppressors, who could not be expected to surrender their stake in the existing order without a fight. But, declared Plekhanov, "every class struggle is a political struggle."[43] It mattered not that the differences between the proletariat and the bourgeoisie arose in the economic realm. The proletariat, and indeed any class that hoped to achieve its social aspirations, must strive for political hegemony. Political power was the indispensable means to social reconstruction. Far from being a matter of indifference to the proletariat, political struggle constituted its most effective means of social self-help. For that reason, the class struggle of the proletariat became *conscious—* that is, rationally directed to its ends—to the extent that it became *political* in character. By contrast, blind revolts, uninformed by political and social realities, would not further the cause of socialism by a single step. No mere coincidence led Plekhanov, at the very opening of the Marxist phase of his career, to couple the propaganda of Marxism with the formation of elements of a Russian workers' party as the two aims of the Emancipation of Labor Group. By means of political action, the proletariat was to assist in the overthrow of absolutism; and, in the sequel, again by political struggle, this time against the bourgeoisie, the proletariat would at last emancipate itself.

It was in the light of such a conception of the socialist revolution that Plekhanov found the dreams of the populists and the terrorists utterly fantastic. They were full of assurances of the possibility of an immediate socialist revolution, but by his criteria the "objective social conditions of production" were far from sufficiently "matured" for the establishment of a socialist economy. He agreed that Russia, in this respect, stood in advance of such countries as India, Persia, and Egypt; but it was not to be placed on a par with, much less ahead of, the well-developed societies in the West.[44] The decay of the commune precluded the erection of socialism on that foundation stone. And capitalism in Russia had not yet succeeded in creating the economic conditions or the social forces for a socialist revolution.

Although Plekhanov was certain that neither a peasant revolution nor a seizure of power by a revolutionary clique enjoyed any chance of success, he was willing to grant the opposite in order to prove his case once again. Suppose that one or the other had occurred, then what steps, he asked, would be taken to bring about the social and political reorganization of Russia? In answer, he affirmed that policy ineluctably was determined by the *social* character of the revolution; whether the peasants themselves or a revolutionary clique in their behalf made the revolution, the only conceivable result would be a peasant program. All, then, hinged upon the actual aspirations of the peasantry. But such solidarity as existed among them, Plekhanov maintained, was based not upon a common conviction concerning the necessity of a socialist organization of production, but on the desire for a distribution of land. Such a "general repartition" of the land, he emphasized, could not qualify as a socialist program. Among other things, this reform left untouched the vital area of commodity production, which ensured renewed economic differentiation and the sending down of new roots by capitalism.[45] In fact, he insisted, "the economic emancipation of the working class can be attained only by the transfer into the collective property of the toilers of *all* the means *and products* of production *and the organization of all the functions of social and economic life in conformity with the needs of society.*"[46] Since the rural population felt no sympathy for such goals—and, indeed, could not in the absence of a highly social organization of production—it was fruitless to speak of a peasant socialist revolution.

Plekhanov considered the revolutionary intelligentsia no more aware than the peasants for whom they claimed to speak of the need to abolish commodity production. But even if they did grasp this all-important consideration, they could do nothing about it. As he put it: "You cannot create, by decrees, conditions alien to the very character of existing economic relations."[47] The revolutionary committee alone, he implied, would be powerless to overcome the vast opposition the peasants would offer to schemes of socialist reconstruction which had little or no support in the objective conditions of social and economic life. In an extraordinarily prophetic moment, he projected the possibility that a revolutionary committee, having seized power, and recognizing the divergence between the people's aims and its own socialist objectives, might nevertheless choose to retain control in its own hands. But if it were to attempt to organize national production in the absence of both the objective conditions for and popular approval of socialization, then "it would have to seek salvation in the ideals of 'patriarchal and authoritarian communism,' introducing into those ideals only the change that a socialist caste would manage national production instead of the Peruvian 'Children of the Sun'* and their officials."[48]

At some future time, a part of the rural population—the proletarian by-products of the breakdown of the patriarchal peasantry—might well play a positive role in a socialist revolution. But, under existing circumstances, Plekhanov tended to view the peasantry as a negative factor in relation not only to socialism but to progressive aims in general. In his mind, economic progress took the form of advances from petty-bourgeois to large-scale bourgeois production, and thence to socialist production. The senti-

---

* An allusion to the despotism of the Incas. For a recent study, see Alfred Métraux, "The Inca Empire—Despotism or Socialism," *Diogenes*, No. 35 (Fall, 1961).

ments of the peasants, however, did not extend beyond the petty-bourgeois horizon. They had no quarrel with commodity production and the profit system; yet, at the same time, they opposed the movement toward large-scale capitalist production inherent in a system of commodity production. When and where they combated the big bourgeoisie, they did so not for the sake of socialism but rather to preserve their own unstable system of small production, threatened by the forward march of capitalism. For Plekhanov, the petty-bourgeois ideal constituted a reactionary utopia. It required the arresting of economic development, upon which all progress ultimately depended. And it sought to combine incompatibles—commodity production and the perpetuation of the small producer. The very irrationality of their aspirations disqualified the peasantry as a reliable revolutionary force.[49]

Plekhanov considered the latter conclusion to be irrefutable in the light of the peasant orientation to political questions. An effective revolutionary class, by his definition, possessed a high degree of political consciousness and organization. But not "a ray of political consciousness" existed among the peasant masses. To be sure, in this regard the Russian proletariat also left a good deal to be desired. But Plekhanov's own experience as a Narodnik among the industrial workers had impressed upon him their "greater susceptibility to revolutionary propaganda." And, indeed, some of the advanced proletarians had raised political demands even while most of the revolutionary intelligentsia still expressed a strong aversion for politics. Among the peasantry, on the other hand, "political indifference and mental backwardness" were so prevalent, Plekhanov thought, that he considered this one of the principal historical buttresses of Tsarist despotism. So isolated were they from political realities that they sometimes attributed the actions of the revolutionists in their midst to the intrigues of nobles and officials. Given such conditions, it was possible that the peasants might be goaded by counterrevolutionists into overthrowing a provisional revolutionary government established by a conspiratorial coup.[50]

Plekhanov's severe judgment upon the peasantry undoubtedly owed much to his reflections upon the Chigirin Affair. His suspicion of, not to say hostility to, this group received powerful reinforcement in the teachings of Marx, especially in Marx's castigation of "the idiocy of rural life." Yet, even though he regarded it as doomed by economic evolution, Plekhanov could hardly dismiss summarily a class comprising four-fifths of Russia's population. Instead, he reached an uneasy and unsatisfactory compromise, neither writing off the peasantry entirely nor conceding to it a significance and role commensurate with its numbers. Now and again, he called attention to its importance for the revolutionists and the revolution. But it was all too clear that, whether treating of either the first or the second revolution, the peasantry did not figure as one of Plekhanov's constant and primary concerns.

SOCIAL AND POLITICAL: THE BOURGEOIS REVOLUTION

If Russia could not vault over capitalism and bourgeois democracy into the socialist realm, Plekhanov reasoned, then the much discussed differences between Russia and the West had no really significant basis. In the Western nations, the development of capitalism paved the way for the overthrow of absolutism and the establishment of constitutional and representative government, dominated by the bourgeoisie. Since Russia, too, had embarked upon the capitalist path, there existed every likelihood that she would experience such a revolution in the first instance, rather than a socialist upheaval. The "Europeanization of Russian social life"—the phrase Plekhanov devised to describe Russia's capitalist development and attendant social transformation—had proceeded sufficiently far to make feasible the "Europeanization" of Russia's political system. Realistic revolutionists would make no mistake in putting the overthrow of absolutism high on their agenda.

In taking such a position Plekhanov clearly believed the foundations of Russian autocracy to be in a state of decay. Those foundations consisted of the static system of agrarian, natural economy, the fragmentation of society into a multitude of self-sufficient and isolated communes, the predominantly peasant make-up of the population, and the passivity and immobility that characterized the peasantry in a traditional society. The intrusion of capitalism signaled the erosion and ultimate dissolution of the foundations of the old order. Capitalist industrial production gave greater weight to the urban center. In the city, and in the village as a result of the breakdown of the commune, there appeared bourgeois and proletarian classes which, in contrast to the peasantry, historically had striven for civil and political liberty. Corresponding to the displacement of a static by a dynamic economy, the immobile peasantry was replaced by more conscious, articulate, and active groups. These changes were making an anachronism of Russia's political system, which corresponded less and less to the emergent socio-economic order.

The impending downfall of absolutism Plekhanov saw prefigured in what he held to be an almost universal antagonism to the existing order. Even most of the upper classes, he maintained, were at odds with the Tsar, and power rested now in the hands of a clique of "serfowners [sic], hypocrites, and mercenaries."[51] He was referring here to the "objective" conflict between the interests of various social groups and the perpetuation of autocracy. In terms of active forces for its destruction, however, he counted very largely upon only two classes, the bourgeoisie and the proletariat. Even though it stood to gain from the coming revolution, the peasantry, because of its mental narrowness and divorce from political realities, could not be inscribed on the muster of revolutionary forces. On the other hand, although Plekhanov recognized that the inertia of the peasants had facilitated absolutist rule, he did not expect the peasants to come to the Tsar's defense in a revolutionary crisis. As for the emergent middle class:

Our bourgeoisie is now undergoing an important metamorphosis; it has developed lungs which require the clean air . . . of self-government, but at the same time it has not yet atrophied its gills, with the help of which it continues to breathe in the turbid water of decaying absolutism. Its roots still rest in the soil of the old regime, but its top has already reached such development as points to the necessity and inevitability of replanting.[52]

He acknowledged in *Our Differences*, and even more emphatically in later years, the favor Russia's government bestowed on various capitalistic groups. Nevertheless he insisted upon the fundamental incompatibility of the interests of the bourgeoisie with the continued rule of absolutism. The growing conflict had already forced important segments of this class to recognize that "the acquisition of political rights" was "indispensable for their welfare."

Although he gave little supporting evidence, Plekhanov viewed an unlimited state power as an incubus upon the bourgeoisie. It maintained in force regulations that were detrimental to business enterprise. It purportedly wished to restore certain aspects of the outlawed system of serfdom, which could not but harm bourgeois interests. Most important, however, was the adverse effect of state fiscal policies on the bourgeoisie.[53] The unrelenting pressure of the government, he contended, so impoverished the peasantry that they were less and less able to provide the needs of the exchequer. With the treasury empty, with debts growing, and with no possibility of meeting them under existing fiscal arrangements, the government would have no alternative but to appeal to "society" in order to avoid bankruptcy. At that point the members of the bourgeoisie would become, as Plekhanov later put it, champions "of justice and the rights of man."[54] Obviously, the sequence of events leading up to the French Revolution had powerfully shaped his thinking. As in France in 1789, he believed that the bourgeoisie would demand as the price of its financial succor the sharing of power with the monarch through a legislative assembly.

While predicting a bourgeois revolution and the passing of political predominance to the bourgeoisie, Plekhanov's writings were not without reservations concerning its revolutionary qualities. It could be counted upon to make a revolutionary contribution, he thought, but the bourgeoisie was incapable of taking the initiative; nor could it be relied upon for sustained revolutionary action.[55] Its submissiveness and apparent cowardice he explained by its relatively undeveloped condition—reflecting the backwardness of Russian economy—which inspired in it a sense of impotence vis-à-vis the powerful State apparatus. On that account, it could be expected to throw down the gauntlet to absolutism only if and when there had already been collected a massive opposition, ready to fight and seemingly possessing good prospects of victory. Even in the successful "bourgeois" revolutions in the West, he remarked, the decisive blows were struck not by the bourgeoisie but by the "people." If in 1830 and 1848 the French bourgeoisie had dared to come out openly for the revolution only after the workers had mounted the barricades, then the overthrow of Russian absolutism was unthinkable without the active participation of the proletariat. Again and again he declared, "political freedom will be won by the working class or not at all."[56]

In his mind, there existed no question about the desirability of lending proletarian support to the campaign against absolutism. Since a bourgeois-democratic regime indubitably would be a progressive step for Russia, any group that came out against the liberation movement of the bourgeoisie would, by that act, become *a tool of political and social reaction.*[57] This, the proletariat must not be. But Plekhanov showed equal concern that it not be "a blind tool of the liberals." Though classifying the coming Russian revolution as a "bourgeois" revolution of the Western type, he set out to ensure a somewhat different result in his native land. There, things must be so contrived as to guarantee that the working class—unlike its Western counterpart—receive suitable compensation for its services. To that end, his revolutionary strategy was deeply concerned with the question of the mutual relations between the bourgeoisie and the proletariat in the struggle against absolutism.

In the West European revolutions of the first half of the nineteenth century, the workers had entered the lists under bourgeois-liberal leadership. They had supposed that the liberal program expressed their own interests and that, if carried out, it would eliminate from the existing order the sources of their own misfortunes. With one party to the revolutionary coalition clearly conscious of its interests, whereas more or less muddled thinking characterized the other, the outcome was a foregone conclusion. Even though in terms of forces the workers had made the decisive contribution, the bourgeoisie pre-empted the spoils, leaving the workers nothing. If the Russian workers were to avoid the fate of the Western proletarians, they must fight under Social Democratic leadership, and as an *independent self-interested* force.[58] It was the mission of the revolutionary intelligentsia to carry socialist propaganda and organization to the workers, so that they could fight against absolutism in full awareness of their real interests and how best to promote them. For just as the winning of political freedom was unthinkable without the active participation of the proletarians, so the defense and advancement of proletarian interests was unthinkable in the absence of class consciousness on their part.

Only such a class-conscious force could avoid the numerous pitfalls that lay ahead. The workers must reject the absurd proposals of those who, like the Narodovoltsi, sought to make the two separate revolutions, bourgeois and socialist, coincide in time. They must resist efforts of liberals to lead them into the struggle for political liberty, while deliberately concealing from them the relevance of "the burning economic question." In the event that a government should appear that guaranteed their material welfare while denying them political rights, they must refuse to accept the status of *"satiated slaves, well-fed working cattle."*[59] They must equally guard against overemphasis upon either political or economic struggle, recognizing the interdependence of the two, and steering "between Charybdis and Scylla, between the political reaction of state socialism and the economic charlatanism of the liberal bourgeoisie."[60]

Much of the tactical wisdom Plekhanov pressed upon the proletariat was embodied in Marx's injunction to the German communists in 1848. The workers must support the bourgeoisie to the extent it proved revolutionary; at the same time, they must harbor no illusions concerning the relation of their interests to those of the bourgeoisie. Then the proletariat would be safeguarded against utopian expectations about the first revolution, would understand that the ultimate goal of socialism could come only in the sequel. Comprehending the relation between the bourgeois revolution and socialism, the workers should strive to secure in the former the rights which would enable them, on the morrow of the revolution, to defend their interests, and the more freely and effectively to pursue their ultimate objective.

If the overthrow of absolutism took place in conformity with his construction, Plekhanov maintained, the Russian proletarians would reap a rich harvest of economic and political advantages. He refused to admit Tikhomirov's imputation that the Social Democrats were subservient to the interests of the bourgeoisie. If the Marxists stood ready to fight alongside the bourgeoisie, it was for the sake of the proletarians rather than the capitalists. The achievement of political freedom would benefit not only the bourgeoisie but the workers as well. Moreover, the form of support the Social Democrats proposed to render to the bourgeoisie, while beneficial to its present interests, was inimical to its future interests. It involved the instilling into the working class of that class consciousness upon which the future of Russian socialism depended. The support to be given involved the organization of the working class, not merely for the political struggle against absolutism but for political struggle *and* socialism. In that formula resided the most efficacious means of serving the interests of the working class.

In the bourgeois-constitutional regime, the socialist workers would enjoy the civil rights requisite to their organization, without fear of persecution, and to the propagation of their views by the spoken and printed word. Under a democratic constitution, they could openly establish a workers' socialist party, expressing their interests and promoting them through propaganda, political pressure, and legislative action. Plekhanov undoubtedly envisaged the creation of trade unions, capable of securing improved conditions of work and compensation for the factory operatives. In this fashion, as well as through legislative enactments, the workers might count upon the amelioration of their lot. Looked at from the more general point of view, the great advantage the proletariat would gain from the bourgeois revolution would be "the possibility of political development and education." And for Plekhanov, "political education" was the "indispensable preliminary condition of the proletariat's economic emancipation." With the overthrow of absolutism, the working class, to be sure, should organize itself not as a governing but as an opposition class. Yet, if the bourgeoisie were to enjoy political dominance, the proletariat should secure the means to develop into a force that was sufficiently large, educated, and capable to become itself a governing class.

In this connection, it may be noted, Plekhanov projected the extension of socialist propaganda to the rural areas as well, under the conditions of political freedom. He excused the Social Democrats from such propaganda in connection with the battle against autocracy on the ground that the limited forces at their disposal dictated the necessity of deploying them where they would be most effective—among the industrial workers. But later, under a constitutional regime which allowed freedom of agitation, the socialists should turn their attention to systematic propaganda among the peasantry. Plekhanov envisaged the class-conscious worker as the ideal link between the intelligentsia and the peasant: "cast out of the village as the most impoverished member of the commune," the proletarian would return to it "a Social Democratic agitator."[61]

Such agitators might expect to win a sympathetic hearing as a result of the campaigns in behalf of the peasantry which the Social Democratic representatives would make in the legislative assembly. The socialist legislators, Plekhanov suggested, must work for a "radical revision" of the conditions of land redemption, and might even go so far as to press for the "nationalization of land." Further planks of his agrarian program called for the peasant right of free movement and of alienation of land. With such a program, he reasoned, the Social Democrats could count on expanding socialist strength by drawing into their ranks at least some of the poorer elements of the peasantry. In this fashion, additional momentum would be gathered for the transition from the bourgeois-democratic to the socialist order.

PECULIARITIES OF PLEKHANOV'S MARXISM

Even after having embraced the general outlook of Marxism, Plekhanov only slowly and with difficulty had managed to work out its application to Russia. One cannot emphasize too strongly the special character of the problem he confronted: his was the first attempt to devise a Marxian socialist program for an underdeveloped country. He fully recognized that Marxism first arose in a social context very different from contemporary Russia's. Yet, in time, he saw no difficulty in adjusting it to the Russian scene. For, while acknowledging that West European and Russian society had long differed in fundamental respects, he believed that the gap between the two was closing. With the penetration of capitalism, Russian society was becoming "Europeanized." This conviction he underlined by basing his model for the future historical development of Russia upon the French Revolution of 1789 and the subsequent experience of the Social Democratic Party of Germany. Anticipating that Russia would follow patterns already traced in the West, Plekhanov came to consider Marxism no less applicable to Russia than to the West.

Still, an assertion of the general applicability of Marxism to Russia did not automatically yield a political program. Cognizant that Marxian politics dealt with the transition from the bourgeois to the socialist state, Plekhanov for a time was uncertain as to whether a Marxian party had a role to play in a country so backward that it had not yet carried out its bourgeois revolution. If socialism was unthinkable for Russia other than in the more or less distant future, then was it not premature to proceed with the formation of a Russian Marxian party? He was inclined to answer affirmatively until he found the basis for an opposite position in the closing pages of the *Communist Manifesto*. There, in a few, brief strokes, Marx and Engels sketched a tactical line appropriate to a socialist party in a country (Germany) still under the rule of absolutism. What was for them little more than an aside became the central theme of Plekhanov's political strategy.*

---

* It should be apparent that neither in 1883–85 nor in 1892, as Leonard Schapiro would have it, did Plekhanov consider it "unthinkable" that the Social Democrats, during the period of cooperation with the bourgeoisie, should at the same time endeavor to explain to the proletariat the ultimate antagonism of their interests to those of the bourgeoisie. The contrary view was the leitmotiv of Plekhanov's tactics. For Schapiro's view, see *The Communist Party of the Soviet Union*, p. 13.

Whereas formerly he deemed it something of an anomaly, now he took as axiomatic the legitimacy of a Marxian party's existence in an underdeveloped country, for there were abundant opportunities for fruitful work. More than any other group, the Social Democrats could hasten the end of absolutism, for they were best equipped to arouse the working class to political action. In the campaign against absolutism, the Social Democrats would help the workers achieve an awareness of their true interests, so that at the moment of the fall of the old regime, the proletariat would be in a position to demand and secure civil and political rights. The activity of the Marxists among the workers would have laid the basis for the establishment of a Social Democratic party at the very beginning of the new regime. Its organizational work and political initiatives not only would assist in the day-to-day defense of the workers' interests, but would facilitate the transition from bourgeois-constitutionalism to socialism. In short, a Marxian party in a relatively backward country had it within its power to hasten significantly the political process that was to culminate with the establishment of socialism.

In effect, Plekhanov affirmed that backwardness was not after all an unmitigated liability. Anticipating Trotsky's "law of uneven development," he discerned for a backward country certain peculiar advantages not possible for the more advanced. Russia, for example, would not need to repeat in detail the history of industrialization in the West but could at once adopt the latest and best methods. This would hasten economic development, bringing Russian capitalism to maturity more quickly than in the West, and would reduce its span of life correspondingly.[62] Russia's economic backwardness, Plekhanov believed, was also responsible for the belated emergence of the movement against absolutism. But owing to the diffusion of ideas from the more advanced West to the East, socialists already were active in Russia before that movement was well under way. The Russian socialists, appearing on the scene when "capitalism was still in embryo," would not have to proceed by trial and error as had the socialists in the West. Instead, they might directly appropriate the experience of the labor movement and the teachings of Marx and Engels, and in that way bring about the transition to socialism with the least waste of time and effort.

The general advantage enjoyed by the socialists of a backward country, Plekhanov thought, consisted in their ability to grasp the line of march of the historical process through study of the more advanced countries. By such study, the Russian socialists could avoid the pitfalls revealed in the history of the West European labor and socialist movements. Above all, they could intervene in the political life of the country, laying the basis for the emergence at an early date of an *independent* movement of the working class.* Plekhanov strove to introduce an amendment advantageous to the socialists into a Russian historical evolution he believed would be basically similar to that of the West. He could hardly have done otherwise once he decided upon a Marxian program for an underdeveloped country such as Russia. But he failed to understand that his amendment might create new pitfalls that could throw off his calculations completely.

The position on which he took his stand bore a curious resemblance to that of the Narodniks he so roundly castigated. The Narodniks, and Plekhanov as long as he was one of them, saw in Russia's retarded development the opportunity to build upon surviving collectivist structures; it might thus pass directly into socialism, the destination toward which Western capitalist society seemed headed, without the intervention of the capitalist phase. In other words, they believed that Russia's backwardness would enable it to skip a whole historical stage and move directly to socialism. As a Marxist, Plekhanov rejected such a position, because, as he said, it left out of account historical development, substituting for that the will of the revolutionists. It is clear, however, that he was prepared to countenance the shortening if not the elimination of the capitalist stage of development. And this would be achieved by a modification of the historical process through the political activity of the revolutionary party. Of course, Plekhanov sharply delimited his outlook and strategy from that of the Narodniks, on the ground that the voluntaristic activity of his revolutionary party must always be kept within confines determined by the prevailing level of economic development. In his estimation, recognition of those limits set Marxism off from the assorted utopianisms. It subordinated revolutionary will to the historical process and its laws, thus guaranteeing the rationality of Marxian revolutionary policy. For all that, it is apparent that Plekhanov's system embraced elements both of voluntarism and determinism, which he did not succeed in reconciling.

Plekhanov's inability to make such a reconciliation had a personal as well as a philosophical basis. As a leading member of Zemlia i Volia, he seemed to exemplify the qualities of militancy, revolutionary passion, and determination generally associated with Bakunin. He threw himself unreservedly into the struggle, determined to ignite the revolution with all possible haste. He almost epitomized revolutionary will. In the latter

---

* There has been a good deal of misunderstanding about Plekhanov's revolutionary strategy. John Plamenatz, in *German Marxism and Russian Communism*, pp. 222–24, erroneously makes it appear that it was Lenin who first argued for bringing the Russian working class as an independent force into the political struggle against autocracy. Another British writer, J. L. H. Keep, takes Axelrod to be the author of Russian Marxism's two-stage revolutionary scheme. See his unpublished University of London thesis, "The Development of Social Democracy in Russia, 1898–1907," p. 477. In spite of such lapses, both works are eminently worthwhile.

part of his career in Zemlia i Volia, apparently under the influence of Marx, he had already brought the concept of historical determinism into play as a check upon revolutionary fantasies that had no relevance for the real world. When he became a full-blown Marxist, the deterministic cast of his thought of course was greatly strengthened. Yet, though he himself was unaware of it, he had not quite succeeded in subordinating his revolutionary will to the dictates of the historical process as he apprehended it. An element of Jacobinism in his make-up kept cropping out from time to time. This is apparent, above all, in the manner in which he proposed to modify the historical process by means of the political activity of the revolutionary intelligentsia; and one discerns additional evidence of it elsewhere in his discussions of the mode of transition from capitalism to socialism.

On that transition, in contrast to his delineation of the transition from absolutism to a constitutional regime, his stand was ambiguous. In the presence of an intransigent autocratic power, he had no doubt that force would be required for the acquisition of political liberty. Thereafter, internal economic and social developments would gradually prepare the way for the socialist revolution. The process he envisaged embraced the gradual swelling of the ranks of the proletariat, corresponding to the continued expansion of capitalist enterprise; the gathering of this evergrowing force into a class-conscious community which would steadily acquire greater power in the legislative organ of the state; and, at last, the winning of majority status and political predominance. Whereas on one hand he seemed to envisage an evolutionary, and possibly a peaceful, transition to socialism, on the other, his pamphlets bristled with such terms as "revolution," "seizure of power," and "dictatorship of the proletariat."* Undoubtedly, the French Revolution with its stirring episodes, violent clashes, and popular demonstrations strongly influenced his thinking, furnishing him with a sort of model of how the revolution might be carried out. Be that as it may, there existed an incongruity between the evolutionary process he limned and his revolutionary passion.

Further evidence of a Jacobin tendency emerged in Plekhanov's occasional remarks concerning the possible international setting of the Russian revolution. It seemed to him that victory of the proletarian revolution in the West might shorten the capitalist phase of Russia's history. Although he gave no precise indications, it may be conjectured that this might come about in three ways: (a) if one or more successful revolutionary regimes directly intervened in a war for socialism; (b) if the proletariat, inspired by the news of socialist victory abroad, launched a revolutionary

* Such highly charged terms occurred neither in the Gotha nor even in the more militant Erfurt Program of the German Social Democratic Party.

offensive at home; or (c) if there were a combination of the preceding two. Any of these cases would have represented a striking departure from the approach to socialism Plekhanov almost invariably prescribed. We may suppose that he saw the possibility of a socialist revolution where capitalism had progressed sufficiently to create a proletariat of considerable proportions, although not yet a majority, and where the workers were keenly aware of their class goals and eager to reach them. In that case, what would be wanting in proletarian strength might be compensated for by assistance from a foreign socialist power. At the congress of the International in 1893, Plekhanov brought such a possibility into the open, seeing an analogy in the extension of the ideals of 1789 into Germany by the revolutionary armies of the French Convention.

Taking his Marxian writings as a whole, one sees that Plekhanov's account of the movement to socialism unmistakably depended upon a "natural" evolutionary process, in conformity with law. But what he designated the economic and social preconditions of socialism were evidently capable of modification, especially in the sense of becoming less stringent and binding, in certain circumstances. Few indeed were the Marxists who were so attentive to the demands of economic determinism as Plekhanov. Yet even he did not quite manage to bring voluntarism into a perfect balance with determinism—even at the level of logical argument. How much more likely it was that imbalances might arise at the level of practice. How much more likely that others, less fastidious than he, might be incapable of holding the balance. This was to be a critical difficulty in Plekhanov's system and a recurring problem in Russian Social Democracy. Ever and again Plekhanov had to grapple with it. In a way, his whole career was engaged in struggles centering around such themes as utopianism *vs.* science, revolutionary will *vs.* determinism, and subjectivism *vs.* historical law.

8

A DECADE OF ISOLATION

In the decade following the publication of *Socialism and Political Struggle*, Plekhanov's political and intellectual life centered in the Emancipation of Labor Group. This organization, created in 1883, lasted twenty years, until its dissolution at the Second Congress of the Russian Social Democratic Labor Party. In the second decade of its existence, the Group was a prominent element in the Social Democratic movement. But in the span between 1883 and 1893, it was not only prominent in the movement; it was the movement. For the history of Russian Marxism in that period virtually coincided with that of the Emancipation of Labor Group.* In the following decade, the pioneer Marxists blended into the larger Social Democratic current which their efforts had done so much to set aflow. Before that welcome opportunity arrived, however, they had suffered isolation, frustration, and physical hardship enough to have daunted any but the totally committed.

The misfortunes of Plekhanov and his friends may be traced in part to the inauspiciousness of the times for revolutionary activity in Russia. The wave of opposition that had begun in 1873 was inspired by the idealism, dedication, and optimism of the revolutionary youth. Moreover, the revolutionists gained a significance all out of proportion to their numbers, because they were buoyed up by the coincidence of dissatisfaction and unrest in the ranks of society at large.

* For a recent Soviet account of this period, see Chapter 2 in Polevoi, *Zarozhdenie marksizma v Rossii,* which gives details on the publications of the Emancipation of Labor Group and on Plekhanov's activities in the international socialist movement. More than half of this large volume is devoted to the few groups in Russia in the period 1883–94 that leaned toward Marxism. This study should be used with caution with reference to the orientation of Marx and Engels to the Russian revolutionary movement in general and to the Emancipation of Labor Group in particular.

Government officials were kept on tenterhooks for fear that rumors among the peasantry of an impending land division might spark a rash of uprisings. An industrial crisis, bringing with it unemployment and wage cuts, resulted in an eruption of strike activity in 1878–79. The universities became centers of radical propaganda and recruiting grounds for the revolutionary army. Among the educated classes, not only the mistreatment of captive revolutionists but also the bungling that characterized the campaign against the Turks in 1877–78 heightened anti-government tendencies. Some even wished that Russia would be defeated in the war, for a trouncing like that of 1856 might again bring reforms. At the conclusion of the war, when the Tsar permitted the installation of a constitutional government in Bulgaria, the Kharkov zemstvo had the temerity to ask Alexander II "to give to your loyal people that which you gave to the Bulgars." In the following year or so, the zemstvos repeatedly advised the Tsar they could not assist in the fight against the revolutionists as long as the rights of all the people were being trampled. In short, the mood of the country in those years—particularly 1876–80—was such that the revolutionary movement could secure ample material and moral support, as well as a continuous stream of recruits to take the place of those exiled or imprisoned.

The élan of the revolutionists remained high, in spite of their heavy losses, when the draconic measures decreed by the government from 1878 on failed to halt their activities. Indeed, in 1880 the opposition-minded in Russia had some reason to believe that the government was being forced to make important concessions to the public. For Loris-Melikov, whom the Tsar called to office in February of that year, not only eased pressures against the zemstvos and the press and dismissed the hated Count Tolstoy from the Ministry of Education, but also drafted a project for a modicum of public participation in government work. This project, which would hardly have satisfied the demands of the revolutionists, was to have been made law upon the very day the Narodovoltsi assassinated Alexander II. Although, in the immediate aftermath, the opposition celebrated a "glorious triumph," presently the import of what they had done was seen in its true light. The revolutionists had played their trump card but had failed to vanquish the enemy. By force of habit, they might carry on as before, but the old optimism could not be recaptured. Russian autocracy, in fact, had won the contest, for the revolutionists possessed no weapon capable of striking it down. In a series of arrests between 1881 and 1884, the government removed from the field almost all the veteran terrorist leaders. Owing to the consistent record of revolutionary failures, the apparent discrediting of the ideas upon which the movement had been based, and the harsh punishments imposed upon the apprehended, the stream of reinforcements to the movement was reduced to the merest trickle. The disillusionment of the terrorists themselves, of the educated youth whence had come the bulk of their reinforcements, and of those elements of society which had hoped for much from their revolutionary initiatives, together constituted one principal factor in the depression of enthusiasm for revolutionary activity in the eighties.

The other major factor was the harshly reactionary and repressive regime inflicted upon the country by the government of Alexander III. The new Tsar looked upon his father's tragic end as the logical if deplorable consequence of catering to liberalism, and of irresolution in dealing with "subversive" forces. As if to guarantee himself against any such lamentable breaches of statesmanship, he designated as his chief adviser and collaborator Constantine Pobedonostsev, the archadvocate of a militant policy of "autocracy, orthodoxy, and nationalism." Before long, Pobedonostsev succeeded in bringing Count Tolstoy back into the government, this time as Minister of Interior—a move which symbolized Alexander's autocratic intentions and was in flagrant disregard of public opinion. In concert with the Tsar, men of this stripe devised a policy compounded of support for "reliable" groups, tighter controls upon the "unreliable," and suppression of the hostile. With such singlemindedness and energy did they implement this policy that they contributed notably to the drastic curtailment of revolutionary activity for eight or nine years and to a conspicuous change in the temper of society.

Considering the nobles the most dependable and loyal social class, the government endeavored to bail them out of their financial difficulties by the creation in 1885 of a special Nobles' Land Bank, empowered to extend loans on terms much more advantageous than those made available to the peasants. The position of the nobles was markedly strengthened by a decree in 1890 which reduced peasant representation in the zemstvos, and by the establishment in 1889 of the office of *zemskii nachalnik* (land captain). The holders of these posts, in whom were vested both administrative and judicial authority over the peasants, were to be appointed exclusively from the local nobility. In an apparent bid to buttress its position further, the government erected tariff barriers for Russian businessmen and supported this class in other ways as well. No doubt it expected the Russian bourgeoisie, as a *quid pro quo*, to reconcile itself to its lack of a voice in policymaking.

As for the peasants, so many new indignities and burdens were heaped upon them during the reign of Alexander III that many thought serfdom was to be restored. Laws of 1886 strengthened the patriarchal structure of the peasant family and established onerous conditions of contract between peasant laborers and their employers. To the villager, the institution of the land captaincy must indeed have recalled the old order. The regime no doubt hoped by means of this device to nip any incipient peasant disorder in the bud, and, parenthetically, to root out any revolutionist who might have infiltrated a country district. Lest the peasantry attempt to employ the zemstvo to right their grievances, the nobles were given a comfortable majority in those bodies. Conditions of industrial depression and the violent resistance of factory workers to the cutting of their living standards resulted in the enactment of the first factory legislation in 1882 and 1886. But this apparent departure from the general pattern of reaction soon lost much of its significance owing to the resistance of factory owners to the enforcement of the legislation.

In an effort to choke off the sources of free discussion and thought, the government brought out well-tried repressive measures for the press and schools, and invented several new ones. Censorship was made more rigorous, and any journal with the slightest liberal taint was forced to discontinue publication. Secular peasant schools were placed under the control of the Holy Synod; middle schools were directed not to enroll students of lower-class backgrounds; and the universities were deprived of their autonomy and placed under control of the Ministry of Education. In the institutions of higher education, tuition was raised steeply, students were ordered to don uniforms, and women were all but excluded. The regimentation of the universities also took the form of de-emphasis of scientific studies, sociology, and philosophy, and the dismissal of such outstanding and controversial professors as Kovalevsky and Semevsky. Any students who, in spite of all these precautionary measures, developed radical attitudes might well have been discouraged from deeds; for, leaving no stone unturned, the government had strengthened the police organization, further curtailed the independence of the courts, and made conditions in the penal settlements more severe.

The mutually reinforcing effects of the decline of social protest and the government's repressive policy determined the peculiarly stultifying character of the eighties. According to the historian of Russian social thought, Ivanov-Razumnik, most of the intelligentsia betrayed their great tradition by failing to offer serious and sustained resistance to the onslaught of reaction.[1] There was little social idealism, and on the infrequent occasions when groups dared to declare themselves on social questions, their action took defensive forms. Students now and again demonstrated against the imposition of new obscurantist regulations. Labor disturbances grew out of wage cuts and fines. As for the zemstvos, petitions for a constitution gave way to a struggle for existence. The desire for political and social change apparently so widespread in the seventies had now, it was clear, given way to a desire to be reconciled with reality. Belief in the all-powerfulness of the intelligentsia yielded to belief in the all-powerfulness of the police. "Liberals" acted and spoke as though all would be well with Russia if only the bureaucrats were honest teetotalers and did their work conscientiously. Self-improvement, earlier regarded as a means of the liberation of the people, now became an end in itself. "Small works" were said to be more efficacious in building a better society than daring but bootless deeds. Men tended to avoid the larger questions of life, concentrating instead on the immediate and excusing themselves from social responsibility by referring to their modest endowments. Mediocrity, vulgarity, and boredom were now the hallmarks of society. As for the rule of life, it approximated to the dictum: "Better to be a satisfied swine than a miserable human being."

So pervasive did this atmosphere become that it even penetrated deeply those historic hotbeds of revolutionary ferment, the universities. The changed situation was reported by a student at St. Petersburg in the late eighties:

There were few self-sacrificing participants who completely consecrated themselves to the cause. I almost never met a professional revolutionist and did not meet illegals. . . . Scarcely anyone thought to abandon the university . . . to give himself entirely to the revolution. All wanted to finish the course as soon as possible and then to live entirely within the law.[2]

Obviously, the Russian social climate in the eighties boded ill for the progress of any revolutionary movement, no matter what its outlook. But the times were especially unpropitious for the followers of Marx. After all, the proletariat, to which they pinned their hopes, was still so small as to be almost negligible. But more than that, history lay heavily upon the minds of those Russians who still regarded themselves as revolutionary socialists. Even though populism and terrorism may have ceased to give inspiration, the radically inclined were reluctant to break with ideas and ideals which had called forth such heroic actions and created such a rich tradition. There existed a particular disinclination to discard the ideological baggage cherished for years for the sake of Social Democracy, a creed widely distrusted and disdained. If Plekhanov and his friends had altered their opinions in this respect, Russian radicals in general continued to regard Social Democracy as a peculiarly German and unrevolutionary ideology. It is highly revealing of the predicament they faced that the Russian Marxists chose so innocuous a title for their organization on the ground that if they were to call themselves Russian Social Democrats their movement might be blighted at the outset.[*]

[*] Deutsch, Gruppa "Osvobozhdenie Truda," I, 169–70. As late as 1889, Engels pointed out to the members of the Group the disadvantages of calling themselves Social Democrats; see Sochineniia, XXIV, 174.

This tactic of caution, however, did not reduce the skepticism and coolness with which the new group was greeted. Lavrov voiced the sentiment of others besides himself when he described Plekhanov's efforts as disruptive of the revolutionary movement rather than a positive service. He and Tikhomirov advised their colleagues in Russia that they had no relations with the Group because of its reprehensible assault upon the terrorists in *Our Differences*.[3] It need hardly be added that those sympathetic to the Narodovoltsi followed their lead. Shortly after the Group's inception, the old Bakuninist émigré Zhukovsky passed upon it the sardonic judgment: "You are not revolutionists but students of sociology."[4] The oppositional journal *Obshchee delo* (The Common Cause), arguing for the inapplicability of Marx's ideas to Russia, derisively suggested that Plekhanov's second work might more appropriately have been called *Our Misunderstandings*.[5] Even several years later another critic remarked—and not without some justification—that the program of the Group was "conscientiously translated from the German."[6]

The founders of the Emancipation of Labor had anticipated that their group would be assailed by rival Russian revolutionary factions. They were quite unprepared for the negative response elicited from the Western Social Democrats. Supposing that they could count upon the warm support of those in the West who shared their Marxian point of view, they discovered that their initiative was viewed with disfavor in that quarter also. Axelrod, who was in close touch with the German Social Democrats at Zurich, bitterly complained to his friends:

I am convinced that even the warmest opponents of Bakuninism and Blanquism among the [Western] Social Democrats are ready to reconcile themselves with the one and the other in Russia and triumphantly to greet the devil himself, if only he should succeed in making them believe in his power to deal with Russian absolutism, and to rid the civilized world of this bulwark of reaction.[7]

He had accurately fathomed the reason for the chilly reception given the new group by their Western confreres. If Marx himself had still been alive, his reaction would probably have been the same. He had taught his followers in the West to regard Russian autocracy as the greatest impediment to progress in Europe. Neither he nor his supporters was overfastidious about the ideological orientations of those who fought energetically against Tsarism. Narodnaia Volia appeared to be the most potent force to have engaged the enemy in battle in Marx's lifetime, and he spoke in the most admiring terms of the terrorists.[8] So deeply did he wish for their success that he persuaded himself and others that they actually possessed the power to triumph over the autocratic regime. Such a great overestimation of the capabilities of Narodnaia Volia led the Western Marxists to regard any word or deed directed against it as disruptive of the Russian revolutionary movement, and as a disservice to Western socialism as well. Hence, whatever their intentions, when Plekhanov and his friends created a rival revolutionary organization and inaugurated a polemic against the terrorists, they could hardly be given the blessing of the Western socialists.

To their chagrin, Engels himself advised the group that he doubted their wisdom. In a letter to Vera Zasulich, notable for its ambivalence,[9] he first expressed pride and gratitude at the appearance of a Marxian trend in Russia and then spoke critically of the strategy Plekhanov had laid out in *Our Differences.** Forgetting his own strictures against Tkachev a decade or so earlier—a critique which had done much to shape Plekhanov's own views—he affirmed that if ever a Blanquist coup had a chance to succeed it was then in St. Petersburg. Russia was approaching her 1789, he predicted, and it mattered not under what banner the revolution began. Clearly, he saw Narodnaia Volia as the vanguard of the revolutionary movement. It would be far better for all revolutionary elements to join forces with it against autocracy than to dissipate energy in internecine warfare.

Faced with indifference, suspicion, and in some quarters with outright hostility, the Emancipation of Labor Group resolutely set out to give a new direction to the Russian revolutionary movement. It proposed to advance toward that end through the distribution in Russia of Marxian literature— translations of the works of Marx and Engels as well as specially written analyses of Russian social and economic life, which formed the basis of their Social Democratic program. The distribution of such literature was intended to deprive populist ideology of whatever credit it still enjoyed among the radical intelligentsia and to convert numbers of them to their own program. It was essential, the Group believed, to win a solid base among the intelligentsia, for upon the intelligentsia devolved the task of initiating agitation among the proletariat, of gathering workers into units of a future Social Democratic party, of preparing these forces for a vigorous struggle for political liberty.

In a vein reminiscent of the old Lavrist position which Plekhanov had so ridiculed, the Group now envisaged propaganda as the indispensable preliminary to revolutionary action. Inasmuch as Plekhanov attributed the failings of the movement to its theoretical shortcomings, and since he considered the way of life of the underground revolutionist incompatible with sustained theoretical work, he and his associates decided to establish their organization abroad. There, secure against violent interruption, they could work in freedom and tranquillity at their task of laying the foundations of Russian Marxism. They could carry on a continuing theoretical

---

* To Kautsky, he spoke more plainly, asserting that Russia needed "a revolution rather than a program." Cited in Keep, "The Development of Social Democracy in Russia," p. 19.

endeavor, keeping abreast and making use of the most advanced ideas to illumine Russia's evolving situation, and, through their publications, rendering invaluable leadership and guidance to the revolutionists in the field. The Group, in fact, was intended to be a kind of revolutionary brain trust. As such, it could not be exposed to the hazards prevalent in Russia.

If this stratagem made sense and brought real advantages, it carried weighty disadvantages as well. There were extraordinary difficulties in maintaining immediate and vital contact with events and people at home. Over long periods when they had no reliable connections, the Osvobozhdentsi felt that theirs was a voice crying in the wilderness. They were obliged to devote much time and energy simply to finding ways and means of getting their publications into Russia—an intention not infrequently frustrated by the interception of their shipments by border guards or other police officials. Most serious of all, perhaps, the Marxists were hardly in a position to respond quickly and deftly to day-to-day developments in Russia, and to that extent they were divorced from the immediate activities and concerns of the revolutionists at home. A small group that proposed to act as the head of a movement, although separated from its body by a great distance, was bound to experience difficulties.

A larger organization might, of course, have been able to build a more substantial and effective base in Russia and to bridge more adequately the gap between the émigrés and their homeland. But at the outset the Emancipation of Labor Group numbered just five persons: Plekhanov, Axelrod, Deutsch, Vera Zasulich, and V. I. Ignatov; very soon it was reduced to three. Ignatov, who had provided a sizable amount of money to back the new organization, died in 1885 of tuberculosis, which had from the start prevented him from taking any very active part in the work. Deutsch was arrested in mid-1884 in Germany, where he had gone to make arrangements for sending a shipment of illegal literature into Russia. The nets set out by Bismarck for the German Social Democrats based in Switzerland had caught an unexpected quarry. After extradition to Russia, Deutsch was sent to Siberia for a long term of penal servitude.[10]

His arrest was a crippling blow to the Group; as Axelrod later wrote:

On the shoulders of Deutsch lay all the material and administrative tasks connected with the Group. With inexhaustible energy, he made acquaintances that might, by any chance whatever, be useful to us, sought out financial sources, managed the press, carried on correspondence with different cities where there existed revolutionary-minded youth, arranged distribution of our publications—in general, executed all the administrative and organizational work of the Group.[11]

No one was ever found who could fill his shoes. Whatever their virtues, the other members of the Group showed little capacity for practical management. Plekhanov's interest lay in the realm of theory, and, so far as possible, he left organizational duties to others; and neither Axelrod nor Zasulich possessed Deutsch's administrative skills. In the absence of a capable organizer, the tasks the Group set itself were unlikely to be accomplished.

It need hardly be said that the strengths and weaknesses of the Group were the strengths and weaknesses of its members. Plekhanov was a man of outstanding intellect and theoretical power, as well as a gifted writer, and his presence in the Group made it virtually certain that its ideas, if given a hearing, would attract attention and evoke interest. For them in fact to receive a hearing, for sympathizers to be brought together for concerted action, for reliable connections among such groups and among the émigrés to be maintained—all this and much more required the kind of attentive management and effective organization that no one in the Group could provide. It is not difficult then to understand why its influence was exerted in rather tortuous and devious ways, and why, although it ultimately did make an ideological impact, its organizational endeavors almost invariably ended in failure.

The first efforts to establish and maintain connections with revolutionists active at home set the pattern for a decade of frustration and near-isolation. In the last months of 1883 and in early 1884, they dispatched many letters to individual revolutionists and to groups in Russia. These communications sketched the aims and hopes of the new group, and requested an exchange of ideas, the sending of representatives abroad to confer with the émigré Marxists, organizational connections, and material support. The Osvobozhdentsi expressed their willingness to discuss and, if advisable, to modify their program and to furnish to the activists such literature as they might require. On a more general level, they pointed out the advantages to the revolutionists in Russia of a center abroad that could maintain the continuity of the movement and ensure its operation in conformity with a clear and consistent line. One of the surviving letters,[12] written by Axelrod, demonstrates the surprisingly modest expectations of the Group. As a minimum goal, it hoped to have recruited a force of 300 to 400 propagandists in three or four years, an objective hardly consistent with Plekhanov's plan of winning political liberty in the near future. Axelrod's more realistic aim forcibly reminds us of the smallness of the forces actively engaged at the time in the struggle against Tsarism.

The first appeals of the Group, which had been made not without some trepidation, yielded a few favorable replies*—enough to encourage the sending of an emissary to Russia. The emissary, Saul Grinfest, was in-

---

* Arkhiva P. B. Aksel'rod, pp. 91–92. Deutsch mistakenly reported many years later that no replies had been received; see Gruppa, I, 19.

structed to reconnoiter the situation, and to seek to promote the interests of the Group in every possible way. This was a large assignment for a youth who had little more experience than working in the press of Chernyi Peredel. Nevertheless, Grinfest did contrive to penetrate Russia and made contacts at the border and in Vilna, St. Petersburg, and Moscow. He wrote to the Group in Switzerland of the confusion and disorganization that prevailed in Russian revolutionary circles, but he also saw hope of progress. Various individuals, he said, had shown interest in the new group, and a circle in Moscow proved its willingness to collaborate by hectographing for distribution Axelrod's appeal for support. Grinfest suggested that a shipment of pamphlets of the Library of Contemporary Socialism was the best way, for the moment, to advance the views and objectives of the Group.[13] It was this shipment that led to the arrest of Deutsch. The pamphlets were intercepted by the police at Königsberg, and Deutsch was arrested when he went to Germany to dispatch a second shipment. Shortly thereafter, the intended recipients in Moscow were also arrested.

Almost a year went by before new contacts could be established. Then, from a Petersburg revolutionary circle calling itself the Party of Russian Social Democrats, the Osvobozhdentsi received an encouraging communication. This group of intellectuals and workers was headed by the Bulgarian student Blagoev, later the founder of the Bulgarian Communist Party. He and his circle, often referred to as the Blagoevtsi,[14] told the émigré Marxists, after becoming acquainted with their program, "We have come to the conclusion that there is much in common between our views and those of the Emancipation of Labor Group."[15] Deferring to their "foreign comrades, who have much more literary preparation and greater revolutionary experience," the Blagoevtsi requested the establishment of regular relations, the shipment of literature, and a discussion of points of the program, and they promised to provide funds. No wonder that Plekhanov cried with relief to Axelrod, "We are not suffering in vain."[16] Thus began a period of about a year of collaboration that ended only in the winter of 1885–86, when the Blagoev group, like others before it, was raided out of existence.

Echoing Plekhanov's own thought, the Blagoevtsi acknowledged the great confusion and loss of direction among the revolutionists in Russia, and the need for theoretical work to help them find their way. The Petersburg group, although labeling itself Social Democratic, affirmed a set of propositions which, in their crudity and inconsistency, must have made Plekhanov cringe. But the Blagoevtsi did acknowledge the importance of agitation among the working class, and since they were ready to be instructed by the Osvobozhdentsi, the latter had little of which to complain. Indeed, their reaction to Our Differences, once they had read it, must have sent Plekhanov's spirits soaring. They described it as "the radical instrument" for "clearing up the mental confusion" of the younger Narodovoltsi in Russia: "If this book does not completely force them to adhere fully to the ideas of our group . . . then undoubtedly it will provide a mass of material for the criticism of the program of Narodnaia Volia, and the reworking of this program is absolutely necessary in the interests of the struggle."[17]

The months of cooperation between the two groups resulted in some positive achievements. A sizable shipment of Marxian literature was successfully smuggled into Russia, and distributed by the Blagoev circle. The promised financial aid was forthcoming, and the Petersburg organization also managed to publish a couple of numbers of a newspaper for workers, to which both Plekhanov and Axelrod contributed. In this fashion, they made their first contact with Russian workers since becoming Marxists. The two sides also exchanged views on a program, discussions which led to the scrapping of the 1884 draft of the Emancipation of Labor Group in favor of a modified version. The alterations involved detail rather than the main outlines of the program Plekhanov had drawn up earlier.

With the sudden end of the Blagoev circle, the Osvobozhdentsi lost virtually all organizational contact with Russia for almost six years. An occasional bit of correspondence with one or another circle was the sole exception. Not only did the Group not directly initiate activities in Russia in these years, but it often was ignorant of labor and socialist developments that occurred independently. They did not even hear of the massive strike at the Morozov textile works in 1885 until some time after it took place. A "Social Democratic" organization called the Tochiisky circle, formed after the demise of the Blagoevtsi and itself destroyed in 1888, was unknown to the Group until it received in 1891 a letter giving a list of the members who had fallen into the hands of the police. Their joy knew no bounds when they learned of the May Day celebration staged by Petersburg workers in 1891, and of the Social Democratic tenor of several of the speeches. But the rally had taken place without their participation or knowledge.

It was only toward the end of 1891 that the émigrés made their first significant contact with revolutionists in Russia since the collapse of the Blagoev circle. Sensing a quickening of the pulse of social life at home, the Group sent an agent to establish relations with any circles he might encounter that professed Social Democratic sympathies. The agent, Raichin, got in touch with a group in Warsaw, and in Petersburg he met members of the important Brusnev circle.[18] His negotiations with the latter led to agreement for mutual aid and to plans for building an all-Russian movement.[19] Here again, however, the police intervened. In the process of developing a considerable activity among industrial workers, the Brus-

nevstsi had come under police surveillance, and just when the revolutionists appeared to be readying an expansion of their work, the police arrested
Raichin and the Brusnev Group was wiped out.

The sudden extinguishing of this spark of hope almost as soon as it had
appeared must have been terribly discouraging to Plekhanov and his
associates. Would the Group be forced to wait another five or six years
before new links could be established? And might a similar plight not
befall it then as had just occurred? In their published writings, the émigré
Marxists put up a brave front. They professed to see in Russia's social
development portents of an inevitable revolutionary upswing. Yet they
could hardly avoid wondering on such occasions whether their whole
enterprise was not in fact a failure; whether they might not remain isolated,
their message falling on deaf ears, until the end of their years. They had
little way of knowing that 1891–92 marked the end of the epoch of social
indifference, and the threshold of an unprecedented era of oppositional
activity. They could hardly have imagined, even in their most sanguine
moments, the great successes Marxism was destined to score before the
close of the nineteenth century.

The minute size of the Group materially hindered the realization of its
projects; but despite ample opportunities, the Group was not enlarged. At
an early date, and especially once the difficulty of maintaining contact with
Russia was brought home to them, the Osvobozhdentsi endeavored to
promote their objectives by propaganda among the Russian students in
Switzerland. As in the early seventies, the Swiss Republic might be made
a training ground for revolutionists who subsequently would go to work in
Russia. In the meantime, the circle of those committed to Marxian views
might be expanded through lectures and individual propaganda, and those
who came under the Group's influence perhaps could assist in its work.
The émigrés in fact succeeded in organizing Marxist circles of Russian
students in several of the Swiss university towns,[20] but they persistently
failed to expand the Group itself.

If they were to perform the function of a brain trust, it would not do to
admit to their select circle everyone who claimed to share their views.
Membership would be by invitation only. The Osvobozhdentsi balked at
amalgamation with those whom Plekhanov superciliously referred to as
"veterans who have never seen a battlefield." At one time or another, membership was offered to Lavrov, to Kravchinsky, and to Aptekman, suggesting that the Group desired as colleagues only seasoned revolutionists, men
of real stature. Still, it was not experience alone that counted with the
Osvobozhdentsi. They were committed to the maintenance of high-caliber
publications, marked by consistency and purity of ideological content. It
is inconceivable that Lavrov or Kravchinsky could have worked with them

in the same organization without first having become Marxists. But if they should admit numbers of youths relatively unschooled either in revolutionary activity or theoretical endeavor, they ran the risk of losing their leadership position and of seeing their ideological line shifted, distorted, or abandoned. This they were unprepared to chance in the early phase of Russian Marxism, when, in their view, everything depended upon theoretical clarity. In essence, they mistrusted numbers and insisted upon a kind of elite leadership of the Marxian movement. But their young followers could hardly be other than perplexed and offended first to be courted and then kept at arm's length. The stand of the Osvobozhdentsi alienated many of their young sympathizers, who, time and again, drifted away from collaboration, thus confirming their isolation and weakness. In a sense, the Group followed a policy of self-isolation little suited to the creation of a broad social movement.

Of the members of the Group, Plekhanov in all likelihood was mainly responsible for the elitist emphasis. His intense preoccupation with ideological purity was not matched by his colleagues, yet the authority he enjoyed with them would have permitted him to have his way. From time to time, it would appear, he felt uneasy and remorseful about his elitist bias. In a revealing letter to Axelrod, which foreshadowed by fifteen years the break between the two in 1903, he wrote: "And my Jacobinism? It is essential that you should restrain me. You have every right to check my centralist and Jacobin tendencies. For it is true that I have sinned on that score."[21] There is in these remarks a foretaste of the elitism which Lenin emphasized in his conception of the party; but one should be cautious about drawing too close a parallel between Plekhanov's elitism and Lenin's later stand. Although Plekhanov insisted upon elite leadership in the embryonic stage of the movement, he expected this principle to give way in the future Social Democratic Party. Thus, he stipulated that the workers themselves would formulate the details of the party program.[22]

Besides its attempts to spur organization in Russia and to recruit and train cadres in Switzerland, the Group from time to time sought to join forces with émigré representatives of other oppositional tendencies. These efforts almost invariably failed, partly because of the legacy of ill will left by attacks upon other groups. Plekhanov, whose pen was the principal weapon in its arsenal, paid scant attention to the sensitivities of the radicals. If he was generous in his praise of the past services of the Narodniks and the Narodovoltsi, his caustic treatment of their epigones brought him the enmity of those who retained some sympathy for populism or terrorism. His sharply polemical style, replete with pejoratives, penetrating thrusts, and merciless mockery, undoubtedly made even many uncommitted readers recoil. On the other hand, his categorical certitude in regard to his own position struck many as intolerable arrogance. The wounds he inflicted upon his adversaries tended to repel the many radicals who believed in fraternal relations among all revolutionary factions. His polemicism erected almost insurmountable barriers to collaboration with other groups when the Osvobozhdentsi themselves, later on, sought it. Even Plekhanov's friends now and again urged him, for the sake of the Marxian movement, to use his rapier more sparingly. But he would never consent. When reproached for his sharpness, he retorted that Christ himself had been harsh with his opponents.[23]

Many of the problems that beset the Group were closely interlinked. The leaders' desire for security meant that they were cut off from Russia; and that isolation, compounded by their policy of exclusiveness in Geneva, made for acute organizational weakness. But the material existence of the Group depended upon its connections and the support given by others. Lacking such connections, the Group was beset with financial difficulties throughout its first decade, which not only inhibited the expansion of its activities but jeopardized its very existence. Theirs was a triple adversity: a time of stagnation for the revolutionary movement in general, of apparent rejection of the new ideology they sought to propagate, and of personal privation and grief.

Owing to the almost constant shortage of funds, the Osvobozhdentsi were forced to experience at first hand the harrowing poverty and care so familiar to the proletariat for which they claimed to speak.[24] Other than Ignatov, whose contribution helped the Group to purchase a press, the émigré Marxists possessed no resources of their own. Receipts from the sale of publications scarcely covered the printing costs, so that little or no income came to Plekhanov and Axelrod from this source. The two, as co-editors of the Library of Contemporary Socialism, had arranged a scale of honoraria to be paid for writings published. Where they themselves were concerned, however, the rule was honored more in the breach than in the observance. Meanwhile, the muzzling of progressive journals and newspapers in Russia shut off a source of income that both had formerly exploited. Except for occasional windfalls, contributions to the Group were not nearly adequate to satisfy the simple needs of Plekhanov and his friends.

For such reasons, they frequently were obliged to turn to tasks quite out of keeping with their main pursuits but indispensable to physical survival. In the early eighties, Plekhanov acted as tutor to the children of wealthy Russians who resided in or near Geneva, although later he was able to earn something by writing for socialist journals in Germany and elsewhere. Axelrod and his wife set up an enterprise for the production of *kefir*, a fermented milk product, which they sold to the Russian colony in Zurich. The opponents of the Marxists were not slow to comment ironically on the incongruity of a socialist leader operating a commercial enterprise. Vera Zasulich, who had no family, eked out a meager existence by doing copy work.

Despite these extraneous occupations, the members of the Group and their families suffered extreme want over long periods of time, and for Plekhanov the troubles were aggravated by poor health. As a result of his years in the revolutionary underground, eating inadequately and irregularly, sleeping little and fitfully, driving himself relentlessly, his system became seriously weakened. In Switzerland, continued overwork and undernourishment, and self-deprivation for the sake of providing more of his family's needs, led to his becoming dangerously ill with tuberculosis. Between 1885 and 1888 he hovered near death. His devoted comrade Zasulich and his wife at last nursed him back to health, but he never made a complete recovery.* From then on, he suffered periodic attacks, and it was of tuberculosis that he ultimately died. After 1889, Zasulich, too, was plagued by the same debilitating malady.

Under the circumstances, Rosaliia Markovna revived her plan to become a doctor. As a convinced socialist, she saw good sense in a division of labor within the family which would allow Plekhanov to devote himself entirely to the revolutionary cause. Unfortunately, she was obliged to repeat in Geneva much of the work she had already completed in Russia, and perhaps also the requirements of Switzerland were more extensive. At any rate, it was not until 1895 that she won her degree and began to practice. Her husband was conscience-stricken over the fate of his family. His letters to Axelrod in the eighties were punctuated with desperate and pitiful cries for assistance. During his illness he pleaded: "I cannot be healed while my family is *literally* starving . . . send what you can, but for God's sake, send."[25] In the following year, he dejectedly informed his colleague that the family was threatened with eviction; besides, for six days there had been no food in the house but milk, and that only because it could be obtained on credit.†

In this chronicle of misfortune, there is inscribed many another entry. In 1889, in an ironical trick of fate, Plekhanov was ordered to leave Switzerland. At Zurich, some Russian terrorists experimenting with combustible materials caused an explosion that killed several people. Plekhanov, who

---

* Plekhanov helped to save his life by a new demonstration of self-discipline. Advised by a doctor that smoking was harmful for him, he quit immediately and never resumed.

† *Perepiska Plekhanova i Aksel'roda*, I, 57. Some of Plekhanov's anguished cries repeat almost word for word the pleas to Engels made from time to time by Marx. Plekhanov's family seemed to experience in detail much of the material want suffered by his mentor's family in earlier years. See Isaiah Berlin, *Karl Marx*, pp. 181–83.

had polemicized incessantly against the Narodovoltsi, was now made to pay for their follies. He moved across the border into the small village of Mornex in the Haute-Savoie, accompanied by the ever faithful Zasulich. For the next five years he remained in France, separated from his family except for occasional brief visits which he was permitted to make to Geneva. Needless to say, he hoped to be reunited with them in some place where he could carry on his life's work and still earn a reasonable livelihood. With this in mind, some of his admirers among the Bulgarian students in Switzerland inquired into the possibility of his being offered a professorial chair at the recently opened university in Sofia. But the persecution of the Bulgarian Marxist students by Prime Minister Stambulov shortly undeceived them concerning their well-intentioned plan.[26]

Plekhanov was expelled from France in 1894, as the result of a campaign mounted against him in the French press following the Zurich Congress of the International in 1893. At the Congress, Plekhanov had denounced the French government for betraying its republican principles by entering into a rapprochement with Russian autocracy. Dynamitings carried out by certain anarchists in France provided a further pretext for the increase of pressure upon the Russian exile who had become *persona non grata*. As the storm clouds gathered, Plekhanov once again began to look for a place of refuge. Concerning his plight and the prospects that lay before him, he wrote to Karl Liebknecht, the German Social Democratic leader with whom he had become friends in the preceding few years:

Thanks to the activities of our dear anarchists, my residence in France is becoming more and more precarious. . . . The Commissioner at Annemasse has confidentially advised me that it would be better for me to leave Mornex for a little while, since my expulsion is entirely possible and once I have been exiled it would be difficult for me to return to France. That is why I am in Geneva. But since I do not have permission to live here, I do not go out of the house at all; it is practically a prison. And I ask myself, how will this end? It is very likely that I shall have to go to England. That is very unfortunate. A Russian living in England is incomparably farther from his country than if he were in any other state on the continent. My Russian friends in the United States invite me to come there to become the head of a Russian magazine. Since I may have to resort to this expedient, in order to be rid of the persecutions of the European police, I ask you not to refuse me "a glance at the New World," which you know so well.

A Russian magazine in America is likely to be rather undependable; one must think of other means of existence. If one does not take into account that my wife and I might work as correspondents for Russian newspapers (appearing in Russia), since that also cannot be depended upon, would I be able to find work in American newspapers? My wife is a surgeon; perhaps, on that account, she could get work at least as an *accoucheur*. But how is such work paid in America? Is an American diploma necessary? Would it be possible to find work in German newspapers appearing in America?

I beg you, my dear citizen, not to refuse to give me this information and generally to advise me in this matter. To go to America means to be separated by a great distance from Russia, but, on the other hand, this means to see and become acquainted with the new world, and if one could at the same time not die of hunger, that is sufficiently alluring.[27]

Liebknecht's reply about the prospects in the United States was more encouraging than what Plekhanov learned about prospects in England; but probably because he could not bear the thought of emigrating to the other end of the earth from his native land, where he might lose all possibility of keeping in touch with the Russian situation, Plekhanov fled from France to England in the fall of 1894. His wife remained behind in Geneva.

While the harassment of Plekhanov in France had been increasing, he had suffered a personal tragedy. A third daughter had been born to his wife in 1889, but at the age of four the child became gravely ill with meningitis. Grief-stricken, Plekhanov wrote to Liebknecht on New Year's Eve, 1893: "I wish you happiness. For me that is no longer possible: my youngest daughter is dying, hopelessly; she has in all a few more days to live. From this, one can lose his mind. And for good measure, they want to exile me from France. However, this is not certain yet. But my daughter, my daughter!"[28] A few days later the child died. Although Plekhanov managed to maintain his composure and a degree of confidence and optimism through most adversities, this loss plunged him into despondency. The accumulation of woes through the years broke his spirit for a time and led him to despair of anything coming of all his labors. To Axelrod, who tried to comfort him, he replied:

Your expression "chosen one of history" makes me laugh. How can any person be persuaded that he was chosen by history? That is possible only with reference to the *past*, but with reference to the present it is senseless, and only braggarts and swindlers can look at themselves through such flattering spectacles. And I, I probably am simply a failure, fit now only for the dusthole [à la voirie]. I am ill, I know not from what—it must be despair, and it is true that such as I am now, I am not suited for anything, so what is there to talk about? A squeezed-out lemon should be thrown away into the dusthole and forgotten the sooner, that is all. Your belief in me does honor to your idealism . . . but if it is prolonged, it will be funny: who idealizes squeezed-out lemons! Now, I am sick, and, in general, my condition is wretched, and what is to come—unknown.[29]

Nonetheless, Plekhanov was touched by Axelrod's consolation and encouragement. Indeed, this episode throws into relief the kind of close and sympathetic support the members of the Group gave one another in the crises they confronted so often. Zasulich had not hesitated to jeopardize her own health in endeavoring to restore that of Plekhanov, and later she followed him into exile in France in order to continue looking after him. A sensitive woman of no inconsiderable gifts,* Zasulich lived a withdrawn, almost solitary existence after Deutsch's arrest. Her principal link with the world was her comrade Plekhanov, whom she worshiped, though well aware of his faults. According to one observer, she even pronounced his name in a special way, as if her soul turned to him as a plant to the sun. Although his many political and literary concerns sometimes forced him to neglect her, he not infrequently showed her tender solicitude. During a period she spent in England, for example, through friends he contrived to see that she got medical attention, when she herself would have let nature take its course. On another occasion, he and Axelrod saw to the financing of a trip to Italy that might mend her health.[30]

Whatever funds any of the Group possessed were freely shared with the others. Axelrod not only gave willingly to Plekhanov and his family whatever he could spare, but behind his friend's back sought assistance for him wherever there was any hope of getting it. Though listed as co-editor of the Library of Contemporary Socialism, Axelrod wrote far less than Plekhanov. His articles, all of which cost him untold travail, were concerned largely with the European labor movement and the tactics of Russian Social Democracy rather than with the abstract, theoretical considerations which interested Plekhanov. Plekhanov genuinely valued Axelrod's work, however, encouraged his efforts, and often deferred to him in the matter of tactics. In a letter of 1892 exceptional for its intimate tone, Plekhanov expressed his appreciation of Axelrod's support and collaboration: "Your praises and approval are the best reward for my work." As for Axelrod's qualities: "Ah, dear Pavel, how I would like to see you, to speak with you. How much more intelligent, elevated, clean, and revolutionary you are than our 'young comrades'!"[31] When somewhat later Axelrod's morale sagged dangerously, Plekhanov came to his rescue, buoying up his spirits and helping to restore the will to carry on.†

The relationships touched on in these paragraphs call attention to the human qualities that lay behind the severe and cold exterior which so put

---

* Always self-effacing, she restricted her work for the Library of Contemporary Socialism mainly to translations. Yet her few original pieces were both lucidly written and unusually perceptive. See, for example, "Revolutionists of Bourgeois Background," Sotsial-Demokrat, No. I (1890). Petr Struve later called her "the cleverest and subtlest woman I have ever met in my life." Slavonic and East European Review, XII (1954), 591.

† To a letter from Axelrod in 1896, full of despair and self-depreciation, Plekhanov replied: "I ask myself how the person who wrote such an intelligent article [an allusion to Axelrod's discussion of the piece Ob agitatsii] can consider himself superfluous, unnecessary, incompetent, etc. . . . In your enormous political wisdom I have always believed. . . . I have always believed that what you approve must surely be good. . . . You are more necessary to us now than ever." Perepiska Plekhanova i Aksel'roda, I, 137–38.

off many who knew Plekhanov. There can be no doubt as to his extraordinary reserve and his difficulty in unbending and in showing any sentiment.* It is significant that through all the years of their association up to 1894, Plekhanov employed the polite rather than the familiar form of address in his letters to Axelrod. Only in the letter just quoted did he for the first time shift to the familiar.

A case could be made—and indeed it was made by a Soviet writer in the 1920's[32]—that the Emancipation of Labor Group was an unqualified failure, that it exercised virtually no influence upon the rise of Marxism in Russia. Such a thesis seems plausible when it is recalled that the Group was isolated from Russia for much of the first decade of its existence, that it could not claim to have founded a party or even any significant number of revolutionary circles in Russia, and that its successes in recruiting students in Switzerland were limited. In the decade 1883–93, the few organizations in Russia that sought to mobilize industrial workers arose independently of the émigré Marxists. The Group's publications did not penetrate Russia in large quantities, and meanwhile other revolutionary organizations both at home and abroad also printed and distributed writings of Marx and Engels. Clearly, in the first decade of its existence Russian Marxism had no swift and stunning successes to its credit.

The numerous obstacles to the Group help to explain the halting and indirect manner in which Social Democratic ideas filtered into the Russian revolutionary consciousness. Yet the eighties were not merely an "ideological void" between the populism of the seventies and the Marxism of the nineties, as Ivanov-Razumnik judged.[33] The breakthrough of the nineties would hardly have been possible had it not been for the patient, devoted, and solid preparatory work of the Group. Part of the Group's historic mission lay in the creation of the atmosphere that would make Marxian ideas acceptable to Russian revolutionists. By its tireless critique of the older revolutionary philosophies, it eroded away some of the foundations of populism and helped facilitate the abandonment of cherished but thus far unfruitful notions. By his pitiless exposure of what he believed to be the unrealistic features and the distasteful implications of the populist outlook, Plekhanov rendered it unpalatable to many of the younger generation. Through the persistent propagation of a Marxian analysis of Russian conditions, the Group furnished materials for a new orientation. As various elements of the older views were gradually abandoned, Social

---

* In an 1898 letter, Axelrod refers to this aloofness. Writing apropos of an article Plekhanov had just published, he says: "Although you do not like tendernesses, I will risk . . . embracing and kissing you most robustly." *Perepiska Plekhanova i Aksel'roda,* I, 196.

Democratic ideas often moved in to fill the vacuum. The émigré Marxists made familiar, and therefore more acceptable, views which at first glance many rejected out of hand.

The logic of events seemed to drive revolutionists remaining in the field toward Social Democracy. Efforts to find in the peasantry a mass base for the revolution had been bitterly frustrated in the seventies. The results of the terrorist offensive from 1879 on demonstrated the futility of attempts by a conspiratorial clique, no matter how heroic, to destroy autocracy or to exact from it significant concessions. Recognition dawned that the revolutionists by themselves could not impose their will upon the government. Police reports of the eighties show that a good deal of illegal activity was then carried on among the working classes,[34] and undoubtedly much of it was initiated by persons who considered themselves Narodovoltsi. Even outspoken foes of the Emancipation of Labor willy-nilly took the path Plekhanov indicated. Lavrov and Tikhomirov, while still favoring terror and the "seizure of power," advised their Petersburg comrades to seek relations with the Social Democrats in the capital and to develop activity among the workers there.[35] A memoirist active in oppositional endeavors in western Russia in the eighties recalls that Plekhanov's works met with disfavor and in some places were even burned. But while heaping opprobrium on Plekhanov, the revolutionists in Vilna did his bidding in effect by concentrating upon the factory hands and distributing appropriate propaganda among them.[36] The Gruppa Narodovoltsev, which functioned in Petersburg in the early nineties, made energetic efforts to organize and influence the workers.[37] Such activities favored the Emancipation of Labor Group and its objectives. Efforts by the Narodovoltsi to arouse the industrial workers clearly helped pave the way for the signal success of Social Democratic propaganda in the nineties. At the same time, the specific character of the revolutionary activity in which they were engaged undoubtedly made these representatives of the radical intelligentsia more susceptible to the arguments with which Plekhanov and his comrades plied them.

There were numerous signs, many of them unknown to the Group at the time, that its efforts were bearing fruit. In 1885 the Petersburg Narodovoltsi notified their leaders abroad that *Our Differences* had made a strong impression on the revolutionary milieu, and there were few capable of refuting Plekhanov's analysis.[38] According to the Blagoevtsi, revolutionists of all parties asked for the work.[39] A police agent in 1885 and an emissary of Lavrov in 1887 both reported that *Our Differences* was widely distributed in Russia and that it had been well received.[40] Unmistakable traces of Marxian influence are evident in the program of the group that plotted the 1887 attempt on the Tsar's life, although the act itself was out of harmony with Marxian thought.[41] Significantly, the younger Narodovoltsi who participated in revolutionary work in Russia under the conditions of the eighties repeatedly sought an alliance with the émigré Social Democrats.[42] The program of the journal *Sotsialist*, published by some of these younger elements with the collaboration of the Group, caused Plekhanov to proclaim exultantly to Axelrod: "We can say that we have triumphed."[43] If the ideas of the Group were making headway with many radicals hitherto firmly attached to the Narodovoltsi, their influence was even greater on oppositional elements who rejected terror.

Plekhanov's works provided the indispensable theoretical underpinnings for individuals and groups in Russia that were moving empirically toward Social Democracy. Admittedly, various tracts of Marx and Engels were published in Russia before the debut of the Emancipation of Labor Group and contemporaneous with it, but none before Plekhanov had incisively and persuasively applied the Marxian system to Russian reality. In the absence of such a presentation, the idea prevailed that Marx's schemes were irrelevant to Russia. That view no longer seemed tenable to some. The Blagoevtsi were not alone in seeing *Our Differences* as "the radical means" to "clear away the fog" and to force a re-evaluation of the old ideals. A Kiev activist declared that the numbers of the quarterly *Social-Democrat*, published by the Group in the early nineties, answered the crying question: "How adapt Marxism to concrete Russian reality?"[44]

In 1893 Plekhanov stated, with considerable justification, that the doctrines of the Group had gained wide currency among the revolutionists.[45] A few years earlier, references to the minuscule size of the Marxian party were both frequent and justified.[46] These apparently contradictory remarks each represented a facet of the truth. The decade after 1883 was a transitional one, featuring a good deal of eclecticism. If Marxian ideas had won a place, many of those who accepted them did not entirely break with their Narodnik views. Ideological clarity was rare during these years, and there were few completely consistent Marxists. Within the heads of individual revolutionists, remnants of old theories peacefully cohabited with recently acquired Social Democratic concepts, as even Blagoev and one of the leaders of the Brusnev circle frankly admitted.[47] It was often noted that individual Narodovoltsi frequently stood closer ideologically to the Emancipation of Labor Group than did some of the self-proclaimed Social Democrats.[48] In the early nineties, terror was no longer a hotly debated question, and both the Social Democrats and their rivals agreed on the necessity and desirability of activity among the industrial workers. But, at that time, the Narodovoltsi showed greater sensitivity to the need for that energetic struggle for political liberty the Group was eager to promote. Meanwhile, the Social Democrats in Russia concentrated on educational work.

In spite of a good deal of confusion in the revolutionary milieu, there is no room for doubt that by the end of a decade of activity, the Emancipation of Labor Group had breached the ideological ramparts which in 1883 had seemed so impregnable.

9

BREAKTHROUGH

Such gains as russian Marxism made in its first eight or ten years were largely subterranean in character. Neither the public nor even the Group itself was fully aware of what was occurring. Toward the mid-nineties, however, matters took an extraordinarily favorable turn for the Marxists. Whereas earlier the émigrés virtually constituted the movement, an impressive force was now active in Russia. That force consisted in the first place of cadres drawn from the intelligentsia into the Social Democratic camp. These cadres, through agitation among the industrial workers of the larger cities, were spurring labor unrest and promoting a large-scale strike movement. Their successes demonstrated that Social Democratic influence was rapidly gaining among the Russian proletariat. Meanwhile, the bridgehead Marxism had established among the intelligentsia was itself expanding markedly. This gain owed a good deal to the easing of government restrictions on the publication of Marxian literature in the period 1894–99. An era of "legal Marxism" gave Marxists inside Russia, and also the émigré founders of the movement, an opportunity to reach a wide audience. Social Democratic circles sprang up in many cities, and an attempt to merge them into an all-Russian movement was clearly in the offing. Not the least remarkable feature of this success story was the attraction Marxism exerted during this period on a galaxy of outstanding Russians.*

The breakthrough of Russian Marxism came about not as the work of the Emancipation of Labor Group alone. It was one of a number of ele-

---

* They included such diverse and talented people as Maxim Gorky, whose literary work would soon receive international acclaim; Petr Struve, the future liberal leader; Nikolai Berdiaev and S. N. Bulgakov, a pair destined to become prominent theologians and philosophers; M. I. Tugan-Baranovsky, an outstanding economist; as well as Lenin, Trotsky, and Martov.

ments which together gave the nineties a character very different from that of the eighties. The most essential change was the return of the intelligentsia to the field of social activism after a decade of all but complete quietism. The impetus for this reversal came in the first instance from the shocking revelations brought to light during the great famine of 1891–92. Drought and consequent bad harvest were misfortunes that might befall any country. The intelligentsia were profoundly disturbed not so much by the natural disasters as by the barbarous reaction to them in a Russia they took to be a modern, civilized country. Millions of people were threatened with starvation, and yet the government made no move to curtail grain exports. Reserves sufficient to tide over the needy were available, but the government proved too indifferent or too inept, or both, to carry out an adequate distribution. Even its efforts to conceal the scale of the disaster from the public failed, and the horrifying spectacle of the government's ineffectuality and callousness in the face of the disaster shocked the intelligentsia into a new sense of social responsibility. "Small deeds," they learned to their sorrow, could breed "great poverty."[1] The reactivation of the intelligentsia, their rededication to the progress and welfare of the country and its people, was a key factor in the political upsurge of the nineties.

In response to the famine crisis, a good many of the intelligentsia and professional people joined with the zemstvos or with private organizations to provide whatever relief and assistance they could to the suffering peasants. These outside efforts put the record of the central government to shame, and pressures began to mount for the government to yield to the public some measure of authority in the formulation and execution of policy. Among those averse to the perpetuation of autocracy, two main currents existed. One, numbering among its adherents so-called Slavophil liberals and moderate liberals, hoped through strictly legal activity, through persuasion, reason, and good behavior, to secure a modification of the political system.[2] Men of this stripe in particular had joined in the public relief effort during the famine. Others, including the left-wing liberals and the revolutionary socialists, believed that the people could not be significantly aided in that way. They held official Russia responsible for the plight of the peasants, and in the famine crisis they saw an opportunity to mount an offensive against the Tsarist government. Only by its overthrow could any substantial improvement in the living conditions of the masses be achieved.[3]

As had happened before in Russian history, the ruling power played into the hands of the revolutionists by refusing to make any concessions whatever. In the last years of his reign, Alexander III gave no sign of having altered his views on what constitutional arrangements best suited

Russia. His successor, Nicholas II, who ascended the throne in 1894, forthwith laid to rest all hopes for even the most modest degree of liberalization through imperial initiative. In a famous speech delivered to an assembly of notables at the beginning of 1895, Nicholas referred to the wish of zemstvo representatives for participation in the affairs of internal administration of the state as "senseless dreams," and went on to pledge unflinching support to the principle of autocracy. He made it amply clear that peaceful and legal representations for modification of the political system would get nowhere. Ardent critics of the regime—and as a result of the famine there were many—were left no alternative but revolutionary action.

The Marxists were the principal beneficiaries of these events of the 1890's. The meekness of the main faction of liberals (principally gentry) in the face of overbearing insolence and provocation, their continued reliance upon a handsome gesture from the throne, could hardly excite the enthusiasm of those whose alienation from the existing order was far advanced. As for the populists, their cause was also adversely affected by the famine episode. Through reports in the press as well as firsthand observations by the intelligentsia, many of whom volunteered for relief work in the country, the miserable state to which the average peasant had been reduced came to public notice. What was revealed had little in common with the rather idyllic image some of the populists evoked—of a peasantry whose material and psychological needs were admirably cared for within the sheltering confines of the harmonious village commune. The foundations of Russian rural life appeared to be something less than ideal. Besides, those who continued to think of peasant insurgency as the engine for the destruction of tsarism found little room for comfort in the events of the famine. In spite of palpable desperation, the peasantry had not spilled over into *Jacquerie*; it seemed that the rebellions of Razin and Pugachev were to have no successors in modern Russia. Reflections such as these sapped the faith of the populists still further; and, happily for the Marxists, they appeared to confirm Plekhanov's judgments on the fate of the commune and the revolutionary potentialities of the peasants.

Meanwhile, Russia was caught up in an industrial revolution which appeared to corroborate another major element of the Marxian analysis. Three decades after the emancipation of the serfs, the build-up of transportation facilities and credit institutions, the enactment of tariff protectionism, and other such measures had laid the basis for industrial expansion. In certain lines of production, large increases in output had already been attained. In the later eighties and in the nineties, particularly under the aegis of the able and dynamic Minister of Finance, Sergei Witte, a vigorous and successful drive for industrialization was in motion. On the

Russian landscape factories mushroomed, many of them employing large labor forces. It was becoming well-nigh impossible to deny that Russia possessed a proletariat or to affirm that capitalism could not send down roots. The famine, among other factors, contributed to the rash of strike action that began in 1892 and picked up momentum thereafter.[4] Intolerable conditions in the countryside brought a great influx of labor to the industrial centers, presenting the entrepreneurs with an opportunity to depress working conditions. When a little later a spurt of railroad building increased the tempo of industrial activity generally, the workers launched a fight for the improvement of their conditions. Labor strikes called to the attention of the intelligentsia a new potential force for revolution in the proletariat. If the peasantry had to be written off, here was another mass force rising in the country which might more than compensate for the loss.

In the early nineties the Emancipation of Labor Group was still smarting from its failure to achieve a concerted drive against autocracy during the famine period and the equally discouraging end of its brief association with the Brusnev Group. Plekhanov and his cohorts were elated by the 1891 May Day celebration of the Petersburg workers, but their elation was tempered by the knowledge that the event had been planned and carried out without their participation. Unable, in Europe, to perceive the Russian situation in all its detail, they did not yet realize that in these very years there was forming a new generation of Marxist leaders, to whom Plekhanov was a prophet who had correctly foretold the course of Russian evolution. His prestige rose quickly, and with it the prestige of the Marxian method which he gave credit for his insight.

Looking back many years later, Petr Struve, soon to become an outstanding leader of "legal Marxism," wrote:

At that time (I mean the period 1890–94) the Russian Social-Democratic doctrine, in its main lines, had been firmly laid down in the writings of the émigré Social Democrats, namely Paul Axelrod, George Plekhanov, and Vera Zasulich. We greedily swallowed their writings, and they exercised a great influence on us. . . . Particularly great had been the influence and charm of Plekhanov's writings . . . as the author of *Our Differences,* he played a very great part in laying down the basis of Russian orthodox Marxism."[5]

Iurii Martov, the future leader of the Mensheviks, describes in his memoirs how he, too, was drawn to Marxism in the same period. Together with a circle of young friends, he had resolved to devote his life to the revolutionary movement. They had made some tentative moves of a not very promising kind when in 1892 they first encountered and were conquered by Plekhanov's writings. One of their number, A. N. Potresov, had smuggled in from abroad a supply of illegal literature. Among these works were the issues of the periodical *Sotsial-Demokrat,* published by the Emancipation of Labor Group, containing Plekhanov's "brilliant 'domestic reviews.' " Quick to accept the validity of his arguments, Martov and his friends soon pronounced themselves Social Democrats.[6]

In the course of the same years, Lenin, then practicing law in the provincial town of Samara, also became a Marxist. To the great role of Plekhanov's writings in his conversion, as well as in the shaping of the movement in general, he freely testified. In his first extended political essay (1893), an attack upon the Narodniks, Lenin made plain that he considered *Our Differences* the classic statement of the Marxian position, the book to be refuted if the Narodniks hoped to remain in the field. How, he asked, could Mikhailovsky—then the leading spokesman for the Narodniks —undertake a polemic against the Marxists and yet not deal with Plekhanov and his circle?[7] Plekhanov's first Marxian treatise, *Socialism and Political Struggle*, according to Lenin, had a significance for Russia comparable to that of the *Communist Manifesto* for the West.[8] For years Lenin regarded himself as a disciple of Plekhanov, and the impress of the latter's influence is stamped indelibly upon all of Lenin's early writings.

Needless to say, not only figures of this caliber but also growing numbers of more modestly endowed men and women of the younger generation were drawn in the same direction. The beginning of the swing to Marxism explains a phenomenon of these years that otherwise would be inexplicable: the drawing up of the big guns of populism for a cannonade against the foe.* To no small degree, Russian Marxism carved out a place for itself in the process of cutting down what its proponents dubbed the "illusions" of populism. In the eighties, when Marxism seemed to make scant headway, Narodnik leaders felt little need to take notice of it. In the first half of the nineties, Marxism's growing strength and aggressiveness were evident in many letters to the editors of journals and in pronouncements at public and private meetings of students and intelligentsia. Populist spokesmen, dispirited by the negative implications of the famine experience for their doctrine, now began to be hard pressed by young Marxists in Russia who harried them much as a guerrilla band does a retreating and disorganized military contingent. The burst of Narodnik journalistic activity in the nineties represented not a confident offensive of a fresh force but a desperate rear-guard action. Thus the stage was set for the great public debate between the populists and Social Democrats in the era of "legal Marxism."

The authorities permitted the debate on the basis of a series of misconceptions and miscalculations concerning the opposition. The Narodniks of the nineties, for example, in the main had forsworn revolution. Bril-

* The populists controlled two important magazines, *Russkoe bogatstvo* and *Russkaia mysl'*. For examples of the sort of anti-Marxist writings they published, see the articles by Mikhailovsky and Kareev in *Russkoe bogatstvo*, No. 1 (1894), and Mikhailovsky, "Literatura i zhizn," *Russkaia mysl'*, No. 6 (1892).

liantly confirming Plekhanov's dictum laid down a few years before, they were now endeavoring to persuade the Tsarist government to use its power for the preservation of those foundations of rural life they cherished, yet felt impotent to save by a revolution. While important Narodnik elements sought an alliance of a kind with the very regime they or their forebears had earlier fought tooth and nail, the government continued to see in populism the irreconcilable enemy of earlier times. Like the generals who can fight only the last war, Russia's police officials were too fixed in their way of thinking to know whence the greatest danger threatened. Even in the eighties, a secret police agent had advised his superiors to allow the build-up of Marxian forces in Russia as a counter to the much more aggressive and malevolent Narodovoltsi.[9] The Narodniks of the nineties were quite a different breed, of course, but the government deliberately followed a policy of allowing considerable latitude for the publication of Marxian literature. Since most Marxian writing in some way discredited populism, officials supposed it would help to kill off the major oppositional ideology. From the Marxists themselves, the government anticipated no trouble. Typically, a Nizhni Novgorod police colonel expressed the opinion that they "are not dangerous at present"; and a Petersburg procurator considered them to be "as yet only theoreticians."[10] The Narodniks were not particularly successful in securing government support for the institutions they valued, but their opponents the Marxists were materially aided by government relaxation of the censorship in carrying on their battle against the Narodniks.

To a situation generally advantageous to the Marxists, then, even the government added a specific contribution of major import, which was effectively exploited by the outstanding new leaders who emerged in Russia in the nineties. An era of legal Marxism might conceivably have commenced even in the eighties—although because of other factors it would probably have been much less conspicuous and successful—if someone like Petr Struve had had the audacity and the imagination to do what he attempted in 1894. Struve boldly submitted for publication a work clearly Marxian in orientation;* and yet he was also sensitive enough to gauge the likely limits the government would tolerate in such a treatise. His book was accepted, and its publication in September 1894 marked the opening of the campaign of legal Marxism that continued for the next five years. In an unprecedented situation, the Russian autocracy gave leave to the Marxists publicly to propagate their subversive views. To be sure, they were obliged to mask the revolutionary political aspect of their outlook, but they were not hampered in the assault they now launched against populism.

* It was called *Critical Notes on the Problem of the Economic Development of Russia.*

With the aid of their legal publications, which soon included periodicals and newspapers, the Russian Marxists enormously enlarged the influence of their doctrine among the intelligentsia. This was the blossomtime of Russian Marxism.

In these developments Plekhanov had a notable part, a fact that calls attention to another aspect of the changing situation in the nineties—the bringing of Plekhanov and the Group into close, continuing, and fruitful contact with the Social Democratic movement in Russia. Within days of the publication of Struve's book, a special messenger was hurrying to Western Europe to announce the glad tidings to the acknowledged master theoretician of Russian Marxism. Sensible of the new vistas opening before the Social Democrats, the emissary, Potresov, sought to win Plekhanov's agreement to legal publication of his own work. Potresov found Plekhanov in London, deeply absorbed in the composition of a book against Mikhailovsky and the populists, whose recent broadsides against Marxism in *Russkoe bogatstvo* (Russian Wealth) and *Russkaia mysl'* (Russian Thought) had stung this stern upholder of Marx and Marxian orthodoxy into preparing a thunderous reply. Apropos of the new populist initiative, he had written Engels in the same year: "You see that if in Marx's time our Russian revolutionaries could draw a certain energy from the idea that Russia would bypass capitalism, in our time this idea is a dangerous utopia. Now it is indispensable to fight it."[11]

Plekhanov reacted favorably to Potresov's proposal that he publish the volume legally in Petersburg rather than in the Geneva press and relished the task of slipping through the toils of the censors.[12] As part of the strategy, it was decided to change the title from the straightforward *In Defense of Materialism* to the formidable and almost impenetrable *On the Question of the Development of the Monistic View of History*. Knowing full well that a work avowedly written by Plekhanov, no matter how abstruse its title, would never pass the censors, the plotters substituted the *nom de plume* Bel'tov. This was the first in a long series of pseudonyms affixed to Plekhanov's many works in the era of legal Marxism. Carrying part of the manuscript with him, Potresov returned to Russia in October, and Bel'tov's book saw the light in December. The edition was sold out in less than three weeks.

The furor it created at the time and its continuing impact have been widely attested. F. I. Dan, one of the leaders of Menshevism, spoke of its "colossal role in the political-ideological development of the Russian intelligentsia."[13] According to Lenin, the book "reared a whole generation of Russian Marxists."[14] To Martov, the great *theoretical* success it scored for Marxism foreshadowed the bright future of the Russian Social Democratic *political* orientation.[15] Why the work enjoyed such acclaim is perhaps best explained by Angelica Balabanoff, later a leading figure of international socialism:

I found it exactly what I needed at the time, a philosophy of method that gave continuity and logic to the processes of history and that endowed my own ethical aspirations, as well as the revolutionary movement itself, with the force and dignity of an historical imperative. In Marx's materialist conception of history [as expounded by Plekhanov], I found a light which illuminated every corner of my intellectual life.[16]

This encomium recalls and appears to confirm Berdiaev's observations on the religious character of the mind of the Russian intelligentsia, with its predilections for grand systems purporting to encompass and explain the whole world and all its component phenomena.[17] The radicals were immensely inspirited by Plekhanov's "revelation" that history unfolds in accordance with objective, immutable laws; that these laws had been discovered by Marx and gave to his followers the master key to the understanding of past and present; and (implicitly) that the process of historical development guaranteed the attainment in the future of the goals of the revolutionists.

The Bel'tov work was a study of the century of intellectual history that terminated with the work of Marx.[18] It traced the development of philosophical thought, and especially social analysis, from the French materialist philosophers of the eighteenth century through the French historians of the Restoration, the utopian socialists, and the German idealist philosophers, particularly Hegel, down to the dialectical materialism of Marx and Engels. These were seen as successive phases in the evolution of thought toward higher and more perfect forms, an evolution reflecting and made possible by the progress of social and economic life. Plekhanov treated the consecutive spokesmen sympathetically, for in his view each represented a necessary stage in the development, each made a contribution to the general advance. However, with great perspicacity and erudition, he also disclosed what he took to be the inadequacies of each outlook and showed how these were overcome one after another by succeeding thinkers. At last, in the historical materialism of Marx, Plekhanov saw a system that had surmounted all visible obstacles to scientific social analysis. In the course of his exposition, Plekhanov subjected the exponents of populism to many a rapier thrust, and toward the end of the book he unleashed the full force of his polemical fury. He castigated them as representatives of antiquated modes of thought replete with contradictions—contradictions that had been resolved by that same Marx and his followers whom the Narodniks denigrated.

In the next several years, a steady stream of material left Plekhanov's desk for publication in Russia's legal press. The oft-mentioned collective

Plekhanov as a young man.

Vera Zasulich at the age of seventeen.

P. B. Axelrod as a young man.

Plekhanov (date unknown).

Lev Deutsch in prison dress.

Rosaliia Markovna at eighteen.

Plekhanov with his wife and daughters,
Lydia and Eugenia; taken in the 1890's.

The Amsterdam Congress of the Socialist International, 1904. *Front row:* Cipriani, Troelstra, Hyndman, Belfort Bax, Kringen, Katayama, Plekhanov, Knudsen, Hillquit, Navroji, Anseele, Ferri. *Back row:* Van Kol, Ugarte, Nemec, Vaillant, Soucup, Rosa Luxemburg, Adler, Bracke, Kautsky, Walecki, Vandervelde, Cambier, Longuet.

Above, Lenin in 1897, aged twenty-seven.
Left, Iurii Martov in 1921.

Plekhanov in Geneva in 1907, with Rosaliia, his daughters, Lydia (on the left) and Eugenia, and his friend Lev Deutsch.

Plekhanov in late years.

Plekhanov's funeral procession making its way down the Nevsky Prospect in Petrograd, June 1918.

volume of 1895, all but one hundred copies of which were confiscated by the police, contained in addition to articles by Lenin, Struve, and Potresov, two by Plekhanov. In the same year, Plekhanov invaded the camp of the enemy when, under the name Ushakov, he published in *Russkaia mysl'* a defense of "economic materialism." In that article, he found a basis for at least limited collaboration with some of the Narodniks. But in 1896, now rebaptized Vol'gin, Plekhanov re-entered the lists with another full-length book against the more extreme Narodniks, with V. Vorontsov bearing the brunt of the assault this time.[19] The irrepressible propagandist also contributed numerous articles—virtually all of them containing anti-Narodnik arguments—to such periodicals of legal Marxism as *Novoe slovo* (The New Word), *Nauchnoe obozrenie* (Scientific Review), *Nachalo* (The Beginning), *Zhizn* (Life), and the newspaper *Samarskii vestnik* (The Samara Courier). Plekhanov's prestige reached great heights during this time. Never before had he enjoyed such a wide audience; never before and perhaps never again in his lifetime were circumstances so favorable for the propagation of the doctrines of Marx.

Conquests among the intelligentsia gratified Plekhanov, and, in fact, he considered them prerequisite to all else. But, as he never tired of pointing out, the intelligentsia by themselves were nothing more than a staff without an army. It so happened, however, that the successes registered among the intelligentsia in the nineties were paralleled by a big breakthrough of Social Democratic propaganda in the working-class milieu. In the latter case as in the former, new leadership vigorously and imaginatively exploited a promising situation, thereby harnessing mass forces to the movement. Again, Plekhanov and the Emancipation of Labor Group were intimately associated with these initiatives.

Beginning as early as 1892, the objective conditions for fruitful activity among the Russian proletariat seemed at hand: a rapid increase of labor forces in the industrial centers, a dissatisfaction created by the worsening of already miserable working conditions, and the presence of at least small numbers of convinced Marxists among the intelligentsia. The Marxists were eager to try their spurs, to "go to the people" as had a former generation of revolutionists, but this time to the proletarians of the industrial centers rather than to the peasants. The first stage of what ensued was strongly reminiscent of the Lavrist phase of the populism of the seventies. The young Marxists understood their task to be the education of the workers. Only recently smitten with "scientific socialism" themselves, they were eager to transmit their new learning to that proletariat which they believed history had cast as the creator of socialism. The desire to establish contact with representatives of the working class led a good many of them to participate in the work of the legal and respectable Committees of

Literacy, which provided basic education for workers. Whether in this way or by a more direct approach, numbers of factory operatives were attracted into secret and illegal Social Democratic circles where education —although of a less innocent sort—continued to be the main business. As the saying went, the Social Democrats were attempting to rear the Russian Bebels* of the future.

This phase in the development of Russian Social Democracy is generally referred to as the era of *kruzhkovshchina*—circle work. In effect, it involved the repetition among the workers of much the same type of activity employed for the recruitment and indoctrination of members of the intelligentsia. On this and other scores *kruzhkovshchina* came in for severe criticism toward the mid-nineties. Circle work, the critics contended, failed to fulfill the essential aim of Social Democracy among the workers—the creation of a mass movement. Experience demonstrated that abstract ideas of socialism, even when imbedded in such a rousing work as the *Communist Manifesto*, had little meaning to the average worker. In circle work, the Social Democrats contrived to narrow rather than broaden the scope of the movement. Instead of addressing themselves to the mass, the Marxists were simply drawing from it the most intelligent and able of the literate workers. In concentrating upon the education of a minority, the propagandists left the mass of workers untouched. Such tactics militated against the building of a mass movement, without which aspirations for political liberty and the ultimate triumph of socialism were chimerical.

Perhaps the Social Democrats vaguely envisaged a time when their protégés would themselves undertake to lead the mass of the workers in a struggle for Social Democratic goals. But in actual practice, the critics argued, the circle workers were so preoccupied with their pedagogical duties that they lost sight of what their real ends should be. Even assuming that they retained a vision of those ends, at what point would they or could they break out of the limits imposed by circle work and go over to mass activity? Circle work was likely to be self-perpetuating, inasmuch as the selected workmen who were raised to the intellectual levels of the radical intelligentsia showed a bias for continuation of the same methods. The Social Democrats, instead of calling into life an irresistible working-class movement, might wind up with nothing more to show for their efforts than a handful of worker-intelligentsia who, because of their education, were separated by a wide gulf from those they ought to be leading. If they persisted in such endeavors, the Social Democrats at least should be under no illusions as to the significance of what they were doing; the service they

* August Bebel, an outstanding leader of the German Social Democratic Party, was himself a worker.

performed was hardly of greater moment than that of the Committees of Literacy.

A critical diagnosis such as this was propounded in an influential pamphlet written in 1894 entitled *Ob agitatsii* (On Agitation). It was based upon the firsthand experience of A. Kremer, a propagandist among the Jewish workers of Vilna. To break out of the enchanted circle, Kremer urged a shift in emphasis from the propagandizing of individuals to agitation among the masses. Theoretical instruction for the most capable workers need not be abandoned, for that would introduce an equally one-sided and false situation. But the chief efforts and forces of the Social Democrats should be directed to the mass of the workers, and this required a different approach. Agitation must rest upon an intimate knowledge of conditions prevailing in the factories. Social Democratic agitators must catch the pulse of the proletarians and attune their appeals to the keenly felt grievances and immediate needs of the workers in the mass. Conducting themselves in this way, the Marxists could mobilize masses of workers in defense of their interests, win their confidence in the course of joint struggles, by stages introduce them to the broader ideas and aims of Social Democracy, and finally organize them into Social Democratic battalions to be advanced into the political struggle. Apart from its other patent advantages, Kremer argued, agitation required only a small expenditure of forces for large gains. A relatively small number of agitators could launch a movement of dimensions that the government would find difficult to control, whereas the circles with their high ratio of intelligentsia to workingmen were easily and repeatedly wrecked by the police.

In the seventies, pedagogical Lavrism which sought to implant abstract socialist ideals in the minds of the peasants had proved unrealistic and had yielded to Bakuninist agitation for what were presumed to be the real peasant ideals of land and liberty. Now history seemed to repeat itself as a bid was made for a shift from the propaganda of theoretical Marxism to broad agitation on the basis of the immediate needs of the working masses. Social Democratic ideas, it was now held, would become timely and meaningful to the workingmen in the mass only as they battled for their clearly perceived interests and not before.

Here was a program apparently well suited to the promotion of a Social Democratic mass movement. Sensitive to the force of the arguments against *kruzhkovshchina*, to the disparity between its attainments and the goals of the movement, active propagandists presently were won to the new strategy. Martov, and a little later Lenin, were particularly conspicuous in its popularization and translation into action. The former, during a period of exile in Vilna, became persuaded of the bankruptcy of *kruzhkovshchina*. Like Kremer, he experienced a sense of frustration in witnessing at first hand how the circle workers, overlooking the very real potential for mobilizing the forces of labor, blundered into a *cul-de-sac*. Martov, in fact, assisted Kremer in getting his tract into shape for duplication and distribution. When he returned to St. Petersburg in 1895, he pressed upon the Social Democrats with whom he was acquainted the desirability of going over to agitation. Lenin, then still known by his family name Ulianov, had come to the capital in 1893. Very quickly, he established a reputation as a profoundly serious revolutionist, an effective organizer of illegal activity, and a polemical writer of bulldog tenacity and force. Under the influence of Plekhanov and Axelrod, he, too, had recently come round to the necessity for a transition from *kruzhkovshchina* to agitation. Martov and his friends presently merged with Lenin's group to form the Petersburg League for the Emancipation of Labor.[20]

The relationship of Plekhanov and the Geneva Emancipation of Labor to the *kruzhkovshchina*-agitation controversy was somewhat ambiguous. In a way, their own endeavors fostered and encouraged circle work, something that Plekhanov appeared to admit when he remarked that they had at first indulged somewhat one-sidedly in propaganda.[21] In their preoccupation with theory and the necessity of Marxian propaganda among the intelligentsia, the Group had tended to slight the Russian working class—at least in the area of publications. That was one of the charges brought against it by those who in 1888 and again in the early nineties formed oppositions. The younger Marxists found it incongruous that a self-styled Social Democratic center should publish abstruse theoretical tracts which would be unintelligible to workers. As one of them objected to Plekhanov in 1888, "If you had your way, you would still expound and publish Hegel."[22] In truth, Plekhanov did not believe that one and the same literature would serve the needs of both workers and intelligentsia; a comparison of the pamphlets he wrote for these different audiences makes this perfectly clear. His emphasis on theory stemmed from the conviction that elements from among the intelligentsia were needed to initiate Social Democratic activity among the working class. Intellectual recruits to Marxism in the early nineties no doubt regarded circle work as the fulfillment of the injunctions of their mentors. Were they not, after all, extending into the working class the style of activity of the elder statesmen themselves? Where they erred, the critics would have rejoined, was in the uncritical adoption of the same methods for carrying Social Democracy to the workers as had been employed for winning the intelligentsia.

As for Plekhanov, if his activity and that of the Group in some ways set the pattern for *kruzhkovshchina*, his conception of the development of the movement as expressed in his writings gave little basis for it. If the younger

Marxists had done as he had said rather than as he had done, they probably would have avoided the pitfalls of circle work. The ideas of *On Agitation,* which appeared novel to many in the mid-nineties, may be found in his earliest Marxian writings, and indeed they go back even further. Even as a Narodnik, he always envisaged the task of the revolutionists to be the creation of a mass movement: "The emancipation of the people can be accomplished only by the people themselves." But since emancipation fundamentally meant the throwing off of the yoke of economic exploitation, he who hoped to mobilize the people for the act of self-liberation must take their economic grievances as the ground of agitation. When he crossed over to Marxism, Plekhanov retained this conception of his Narodnik days, modifying it to emphasize that a class striving for emancipation must perforce give battle in the political arena. To suit his new perspective, he also changed the wording of the key slogan cited above back to the form in which Marx had originally framed it, substituting "the working class" for the "people."

Although he had dealt with the matter as far back as 1880, while still a Narodnik, it was during the famine crisis that Plekhanov propounded his classic discussion of propaganda and agitation and their mutual relations.* Admitting that the line between them is sometimes difficult to draw, he laid down certain distinctions which still enjoy official endorsement in the U.S.S.R. He defined propaganda as an activity carried on in the normal day-to-day life of a country; agitation as propaganda for those special occasions that call forth a certain sensitizing of social feeling, that compel the attention even of those who ordinarily would not listen to the propagandist. Besides, the propagandist conveys many ideas to only one or several persons, whereas the agitator presents only one or several ideas to a whole mass of people. In this last difference, according to Plekhanov, lay the fundamental contrast. Propaganda, in the final analysis, could have little historical significance unless it was joined to agitation. It reached only tens, hundreds, or thousands of people; "but influence on the social life of contemporary civilized countries is unthinkable without influence upon the mass, that is, without agitation. . . . Consequently, agitation is indispensable to every party that wishes to have historical significance. A sect may be content with propaganda in the narrow sense of the word. A political party never."[23] By these definitions, circle work was the format of the sect, whereas Plekhanov from the first strove to create a party. He

---

* Meyer (*Leninism,* p. 50) gives the impression that Lenin originated the distinction between propaganda and agitation characteristic of Russian Marxism. Although Meyer frequently takes ideas of Plekhanov to have been developed by Lenin (and he is by no means the only one to do this), his book is admirable in many respects.

had already condemned *kruzhkovshchina* before it was well born. Later in the same essay, he presented a whole series of precepts for successful agitation.

In discussing this subject, Plekhanov had no need to remain in the rarefied realm of theory. In 1890, he published a vivid memoir of his own firsthand experience among the Petersburg workers in the latter seventies.[24] It lent support to his fervently expressed conviction that the Russian worker would respond positively to carefully planned and skillfully executed agitation. Coming before the spate of labor activity of the nineties and to a generation few of whom had the slightest inkling of the earlier labor ventures, his brief was calculated to encourage the radical intelligentsia to initiate agitation in Russia's industrial centers. Just as Herzen had once cried, "To the people!" so Plekhanov in effect called, "To the workers!" A few years later, the movement to the workers was in full swing, and Martov has recorded how Plekhanov's prescriptions aided the Petersburg Social Democrats in the mid-nineties to effect the transition from circle work to agitation.[25] It may be added that *On Agitation*, which had been available in Russia only in hectographed copies, was published by the Emancipation of Labor Group in 1896.

The growing influence of Marxism in the nineties made almost inevitable the termination of the Emancipation of Labor's long-endured organizational isolation. Young Russians sympathetic to Social Democracy made pilgrimages to Geneva in increasing numbers to see and confer with the "grand old men" of Russian Marxism. Plekhanov and Axelrod eagerly plied them with questions; and some of those who made extended visits completed their Marxian education in part by assisting the older men in their work. In the same period, Marxism gained a more substantial following among the Russian students at Swiss universities. Gradually, communication with the movement in Russia became more frequent and more reliable. One of the early events of the closer association was the receipt by Plekhanov in 1893 of a mandate from Martov's group of Petersburg Social Democrats to represent them at the Congress of the International in Zurich that year. Although he and Axelrod had attended the founding congress in 1889, this was the first occasion upon which he represented an active Social Democratic organization in Russia.

The year 1894 ushered in the era of legal Marxism. It brought Potresov's mission to Plekhanov and the publication of the latter's work in Petersburg. In the same year, one of the Petersburg group who had just visited Plekhanov and Axelrod advised his coworkers upon his return that the "old men" judged the time ripe for Social Democracy to come out as a party.[26] Their urging perhaps was responsible for the conference of representatives of the Social Democratic organizations of several cities at the end of 1894, out of which came a decision to coordinate action on the basis of agitation.[27] To assist the agitational campaign, the representatives pledged to work for the establishment abroad of a center for the publication of a literature specifically for workers. Lenin and E. I. Sponti, representing, respectively, the Petersburg and Moscow organizations, were commissioned to journey abroad to secure the agreement and cooperation of the Emancipation of Labor Group in such an enterprise. Even before their arrival, however, a step had been taken to knit together the dispersed elements of nascent Russian Social Democracy.

On several occasions, efforts had been made to merge the Emancipation of Labor with groups of younger Russian Social Democrats in Switzerland. For a variety of reasons, some of which have been alluded to, they failed of their aim. In 1892–93, particularly strained relations developed between the Group and the younger Marxist émigrés. A certain Polish socialist named Iogiches (Grozovskii), who possessed a considerable personal fortune, came to Switzerland and sought to enter into relations with the Group. Inasmuch as they were perpetually in financial need, the Osvobozhdentsi invited Iogiches to become a member. Apparently not satisfied with that, he endeavored to exact terms which they regarded as demeaning in return for financial backing of the Group's publications. A trial period of association proved intolerable to both sides and ended with mutual recriminations. Meanwhile, Iogiches had gathered around himself a sizable number of the younger Social Democrats in Switzerland, many of whom were dissatisfied with the Group's *modus operandi*. After breaking with Plekhanov and Axelrod, he organized a rival enterprise for the publication of Social Democratic literature in the Russian language, with his friend B. N. Krichevsky in charge. This new Russian Social Democratic Library even sought to compete with the Emancipation of Labor for the good graces of Engels.* In the course of 1894, however, Iogiches withdrew from the Library in order to devote himself wholly to the Polish Social Democratic movement. His departure helped clear the way for the establishment of harmonious relations between the rival groups, whose differences were organizational rather than ideological. Once the socialist movement at home began to burgeon, there existed a particular urgency to call a halt to the rivalry and discord among the émigrés. Fruitless bickering had to be stopped if the movement were to be given the energetic

---

* For references to the differences between Iogiches and the Group, see *Perepiska Plekhanova i Aksel'roda,* Vol. I, *passim.* Plekhanov summarized the Group's side of the controversy in a letter to Engels, printed in Deutsch, *Gruppa "Osvobozhdenie Truda,"* II, 317–22. A defense of Iogiches was offered by his friend Varskii in *Proletarskaia revoliutsiia,* 1928, Nos. 11–12.

support it deserved. Toward the end of 1894 the Group, while still maintaining its own identity, joined with the younger Marxists abroad to form
the Russian Social Democratic Union. The Group agreed to put its press
at the disposal of the Union if Plekhanov and Axelrod were left as editors.

Whatever importance the Group attached to this accord, it was far
more heartened by the encounter in May 1895 with Lenin and Sponti.
Axelrod, who has left a memoir of these meetings, referred to them as "a
tremendous event in the life of the Emancipation of Labor Group."[28] It
was practically the first time in twelve long years that emissaries from
active Social Democratic organizations in Russia had been sent to negotiate
with them. Moreover, the two delegates, although markedly unalike,
commanded the respect of the émigrés. They were living witness to the
seriousness and solidity of the Social Democratic movement coming to life
in Russia. In contrast to the young Social Democrats abroad, most of
whom Plekhanov and Axelrod regarded as frivolous chatterers, here at
last were men whose air of competence and devotion to the cause seemed
comparable to that of the revolutionary heroes of the seventies. Sponti and
Lenin each in turn spent about a week with Axelrod in Zurich and presumably a similar period with Plekhanov, who was living again in Geneva
with official permission. The warmth of the welcome extended to the
visitors was exceeded only by the unquenchable thirst of the émigrés in
eliciting information about every aspect of the movement at home.

In Sponti, Axelrod saw a "Social Democratic Narodnik," one who combined Social Democratic convictions with the spiritual idealism and
revolutionary temperament of the Narodniks of the seventies. His rather
naïve reverence for the workers recalled the attitude of the Narodniks
toward the peasants in another day. From Axelrod's point of view, whatever Sponti lacked in theoretical sensitivity he made up in revolutionary
devotion. Nevertheless the veteran revolutionist was piqued to be taken
to task by Sponti for the failure of the Group to produce a worker literature.
Echoing the charges of the Group's critics in the emigration, Sponti threw
at Axelrod the reproach: "You are developing scientific, philosophical
theories. But this is hardly accessible to the working masses." Even Marx
was not spared: he, too, had written nothing directly for the workers.
Axelrod attempted, not entirely successfully, to justify the Group's position by reference to its divorce through most of its life from elements
active in Russia. Now that that situation was coming to an end, he promised, the Emancipation of Labor would without fail produce the pamphlets
for workers that were required. Thus mollified, Sponti transferred to the
Group funds collected by the comrades in Russia and arranged for the
receipt of literature, an exchange of communications in the future, and
so on.

A few days after Sponti's departure a short, pale young man bearing greetings from Plekhanov, whom he had just visited, turned up at Axelrod's home. He presented to Axelrod a Marxian symposium recently published in Russia, one of the few copies which had not been confiscated by the police. After a brief chat, he asked permission to return on the following day and then left. Axelrod was delighted with the spirit of Social Democracy that shone through the contents of the volume. In particular, an article signed "Tulin," criticizing both populism and Struve, made "an excellent impression" upon him. He felt in the piece "the temperament of a fighting flame, a sense that for the author Marxism was not an abstract doctrine but a weapon of revolutionary struggle." The next day, Axelrod learned that his visitor was that very Tulin, an early pseudonym of Ulianov, who is better known by his later *nom de guerre*, Lenin. The young man made a good personal impression, too. Although obviously talented, he showed deference to Axelrod and Plekhanov, whom he revered as his mentors. He carried himself in a serious, businesslike way, but without a trace of vanity. Above all, Axelrod discerned in the newcomer someone who, infinitely more than any of the younger generation whom he knew, was intensely interested in the same questions as the Group.

Lenin and the émigrés did not see eye to eye on all matters, however. Both Axelrod and Plekhanov made the same criticism of the estimate of the liberals he sketched in his article. The younger man made no distinction between Russian liberals and the liberals of the West, who had already played their revolutionary role in the struggle against absolutism and were now aligned with the forces of the status quo against the challenge of socialism. In the opinion of Plekhanov and Axelrod, by contrast, the revolutionary role of Russian liberalism had yet to be played, inasmuch as Russia still lay oppressed under the yoke of absolutism. Accordingly, possibilities for collaboration with the liberals indubitably existed in Russia even if nothing of the kind was conceivable for socialists living in the bourgeois democracies. Plekhanov neatly summed up the difference in points of view when he told Lenin, "You turn your back to the liberals and we our face." In extended conversations with Axelrod, Lenin eventually admitted to error and endorsed the view of his mentors. His change of heart was to prove temporary, however, for this debate in 1895 foreshadowed a major point of conflict between the Bolsheviks and Mensheviks.

Axelrod took pains to elucidate to Lenin both the relation of the Group to the younger Social Democrats in the emigration and what it considered its legitimate and vital role with reference to the movement in Russia. With Social Democracy growing so rapidly, he urged, it was more than ever necessary to preserve the organizational integrity of the Group. Eminently qualified to stand guard over the revolutionary traditions and theoretical stability of the movement, it could provide a needed counterweight to the potential for deviation implicit in the entry of newer forces, only superficially acquainted with Social Democracy. In effect, Axelrod was presenting a brief to the newer leadership of Russian Social Democracy, symbolized by Lenin, in behalf of the perpetuation of the Group as such, the recognition of its authority in the movement, and also the maintenance abroad rather than in Russia of the general headquarters of the movement. He described the desired relationship between the Group and the Social Democrats at home in these terms:

We are a small detachment of an army that is on a high mountain, in a safe place, while at the same time in the valley a battle is going on. From the height, we follow the battle, and thanks to the superiority of our position we can easily observe the whole field and evaluate the whole situation. But the details of the struggle and the situation in the valley escape our view. These details may be mastered only by our comrades directly participating in the struggle. In the interests of the cause, it is essential that there be the closest connection and mutual control between the army and its detachment up on the height of the mountain.[29]

Axelrod's simplicity and sincerity, as well as the force of his arguments, deeply affected Lenin, increasing his admiration for the émigré Marxists. He agreed to practically everything Axelrod requested, which of course heightened Axelrod's opinion of his judgment. The émigré Marxists had convinced him of the need to expand the movement by going over to agitation. He also had taken to heart their plea that the Marxian forces ought immediately to begin acting as a political party, taking a stand on all important social questions and striving to become the center of the growing oppositional mood.[30] There can be no doubt of Lenin's deference for the Group and acquiescence in its own conception of the function it should perform in the projected operations. He willingly accepted Axelrod's suggestion that his organization in Russia take as its name the League for the Emancipation of Labor, thus acknowledging its debt to and connections with the founders of Russian Marxism.

A major project agreed upon was the publication under the auspices of the Russian Social Democratic Union of an agitational literature appropriate for carrying the Social Democratic campaign to the industrial workers. In addition to pamphlets, the RSDU undertook to publish a journal called *Rabotnik* (The Worker). It was to contain news and articles from the comrades in Russia and was to be distributed by them; Plekhanov and Axelrod would serve as editors. By giving technical aid (money, printing services, etc.), by arranging clandestine transport routes, and by submitting occasional articles, the younger members of the RSDU could make a substantial contribution. Thus for the first time the Group, the younger Social Democrats abroad, and the activists in Russia were brought together in a joint endeavor. The Marxists in Russia, Lenin vowed, would do everything necessary to maintain the connections established and to carry out the decisions mutually agreed upon. He proved as good as his word, and even after his arrest in Russia the following December, relations between the émigrés and Russia were not disturbed. A regular traffic in funds, correspondence, emissaries, and illegal literature now became an integral feature of the life of Russian Social Democracy. The reaffirmation of the vital role of the Group was a source of immense gratification to Plekhanov and to Axelrod, who, even after he had come to detest Lenin, described these first meetings with him as "one of the happiest and most luminous moments in the life of the Emancipation of Labor Group."

The Petersburg League for the Emancipation of Labor proved to be the most effective revolutionary organization in Russia since the demise of Zemlia i Volia and the original Narodnaia Volia. Like the old groups, it divided its forces into functional sections, some of which were given agitational jurisdiction in the city's various districts, while others provided technical services. The direction of the League was entrusted to a central bureau, of which both Lenin and Martov were members. Concurrent with the shaping of the organization, a spontaneous wave of strike action rolled through Petersburg, giving the Social Democrats a splendid opportunity. They seized it, and, following the injunctions of On Agitation, gathered from worker contacts exact information on conditions in the various factories and on the grievances that had touched off the strikes. They exploited this information in speeches and leaflets, with a view to uniting the workers, clarifying their objectives, and helping them to formulate tactics.[31] With increasing frequency, the Social Democrats were a dominant voice in the councils of striking workers, and they drew up the workers' demands upon the employers. At the same time, in every possible way, the Social Democrats strove to convey to the workers a sense of the larger issues involved in their struggle: these were not merely battles between the workers of a given plant and its management but episodes in an extensive campaign of the working class as a whole against the capitalist system, with its built-in devices for exploitation. They lost no opportunity to emphasize the role of the state as protector of the bourgeoisie, and the consequent necessity of political struggle if the workers' interests were genuinely to be advanced.

Encouraging evidence that they were sounding the right note began to accumulate. Often the workers' demands were met by the employers, although after work was resumed the ringleaders were sometimes sent into exile. Punitive action did not halt the strike movement; and, according to one report, the appearance of agitational leaflets in the hands of workers frequently was enough to bring concessions from the industrialists. Perhaps under the influence of these events, the so-called Group of Narodovoltsi, also active in the capital during 1895, rapidly shifted to a position identical to that of the Social Democrats. Believing that the swift pace of events made it inadvisable to await the appearance of *Rabotnik,* the Marxists joined with the Narodovoltsi Group in the publication of a newspaper for proletarians. Unfortunately for them, in December a police raid netted the entire first issue of the paper along with a ring of the revolutionists, including Lenin. In January 1896 Martov and others were arrested. Two closely timed roundups had carried off around one hundred persons, including the most seasoned leaders of the St. Petersburg movement.[32] Yet in spite of these serious losses, the movement gained momentum in 1896. Leaflets continued to be turned out by the illegal presses, more and more industrial plants were touched by agitation, and the number of worker circles grew. Whereas in 1895 some forty to fifty thousand workers struck in all of Russia, in 1896 Petersburg alone witnessed a single strike of thirty-five thousand textile hands.

The textile workers' strike had its origin in the complaint of one factory group that it had lost wages, through no fault of its own, when work had been suspended on account of the coronation festivities of Nicholas II.[33] Demonstrating a notable degree of class consciousness, the group sent representatives to call out the city's other textile plants. When their plea was sympathetically received, they followed up with an extraordinary open-air meeting, attended by one hundred representatives of various factories, who together drew up a series of demands for all the textile workers. The demands, including a reduction of the working day from twelve to ten and one-half hours, were printed in leaflet form by the Petersburg League and scattered all over the city. The police were incapable of dealing with the huge throng let out onto the streets by a strike which now embraced thirteen plants. The arrest and exile of a thousand workers did not bring the stoppage to a halt; nor did the appeals and promises of Finance Minister Witte. The workers, who had exhibited remarkable discipline and order during the month-long strike, consented to return to work only after the government had agreed to call a conference of officials and industrialists to consider the reduction of working hours. When the government seemed slow in coming to a favorable decision, a new strike in January 1897 brought fresh pressure to bear. At last, a decree was handed down limiting the working day to eleven and one-half hours. The workers had not secured their full demands, but they had succeeded in forcing the government into a measure of concession. They could exult in having proved their strength, and the Social Democrats could congratulate themselves on their effective leadership during the whole sequence of events.

The Russian labor movement had come to stay, and from that time forward the government was obliged to reckon with it. Despite its sympathy with the employers, from time to time, for the sake of its own security and stability, the government enacted measures designed to appease a turbulent laboring force. For their part, the Social Democrats had won a substantial influence among the Petersburg proletarians and thus enormously expanded their power and potentialities. Agitational strategy was vindicating the promises made for it by its advocates. In addition to other gains, once the Social Democrats were immersed in the labor struggles, their movement lost its former, highly tenuous character and became self-perpetuating. Police repressions might carry off agitators, but replacements were easily found. Having established communication with broad strata of the working class, they now had a chain of relationships which made it possible to move up people from lower levels to fill vacated places. Besides, the successes of the labor movement and the promise it held ensured a continuous lateral flow of members of the radical intelligentsia into the ranks of Social Democracy. Legal Marxism, which was in full swing, facilitated the flow. By way of the Social Democrats, at long last a junction was being effected between a section of the intelligentsia and some part of "'the people" that earlier generations of radicals had despaired of reaching.

Nor was the movement restricted to the capital. As the influence of Marxism spread, Social Democratic organizations sprang up in industrial centers all over the country. Such acts as the exile of the thousand strikers from Petersburg in 1896 gave a fillip to the advance of the movement in many another area. In the course of 1896–97, Social Democratic groups were active in Moscow, Kiev, Odessa, Kharkov, Ekaterinoslav, Tiflis, Riga, Nizhni Novgorod, Rostov, Samara, Ivanovo-Voznesensk, Voronezh, and other cities.[34] The Petersburg League for the Emancipation of Labor, with its clear record of achievement, served as the model for practically all the newly developing organizations. The agitational campaign in general and the Petersburg strike in particular transformed Russian Social Democracy from an inconsequential sect into an oppositional force more potent than any that had existed in Russia in the entire nineteenth century.

In the spring of 1896 Plekhanov wrote to the German Social Democrat Karl Kautsky of his inability to get started on a certain literary project in which both were interested because of his preoccupation with the labor movement, which "is assuming unexpected proportions in Russia."[35] With the beginning of the Petersburg strike, once again emissaries sped their way to the Marxian veterans in Switzerland. This time it was Struve and

Potresov, calling upon the Group to rally the moral and material support of Western socialism for the strikers.[36] Plekhanov and his associates were in a good position to fulfill the request. In some fifteen years, they had built up a close working relationship with the Western socialist movements and could call many of the leaders their personal friends. Even in the earliest years of exile, they, as distinct from their political initiatives, enjoyed the esteem and good will of important socialists. Axelrod had warm relations with Kautsky and Bernstein at Zurich, where the two Germans edited a Social Democratic newspaper in the eighties. Engels composed gracious letters to Vera Zasulich and gladly agreed to have her translate his and Marx's works into Russian.[37] And Kautsky paid Plekhanov an ungrudging tribute as early as 1884, when he wrote to Engels: "He makes a very good impression. Simple, without ostentation, he is very active and so well-read that sometimes I feel ashamed of myself."[38]

Plekhanov first met Engels in 1889, through the good offices of Kravchinsky, with whom he remained on friendly terms in spite of their political differences. Kravchinsky had settled in London and there become acquainted with Engels and other resident radicals. At the conclusion of the founding congress of the Second International at Paris, he invited Plekhanov and Axelrod to visit him in London and meet Engels. They readily accepted, and Plekhanov had the great satisfaction of spending almost a week closeted with his revered master, discussing a wide range of subjects of mutual interest. These were, he later said, "the happiest days of my life." Plekhanov, who had the reputation of being haughty and aloof, was reverent and humble with Engels. When, several years after this meeting, he plucked up his courage to write, he addressed the older man as "Dear and Greatly Respected Teacher," until asked to stop. Thereafter, despite Engels's plea to address him as "simply Engels," Plekhanov more often substituted "My General." His diffidence was evident again when he took refuge in London after his expulsion from France. Wishing to consult Engels's library, which was rich in rare materials, he turned aside on his way several times for fear of being a nuisance. Eventually the two drew somewhat closer, and it was with regret that Plekhanov left his master when he was permitted to rejoin his family in Geneva at the end of 1894. He wrote to Kautsky: "I will not find anywhere a library like the British Museum, nor anywhere will I meet a man like Friedrich Engels."[*]

---

[*] See Plekhanov, *Sochineniia*, XI, 21–22; *Perepiska Marksa i Engel'sa*, pp. 265ff; *Literaturnoe nasledie Plekhanova*, VIII, 257, 265–66; and the letter from Plekhanov to Kautsky dated December 20, 1894, now in the Institute of Social History in Amsterdam. When Engels died nine months later, Plekhanov wrote to Kautsky: "It is needless to tell you how grieved I am. He was a great man and also an amiable man at the same time." This letter is also at the Institute of Social History.

The suspicion and distrust with which the Group had at first been regarded had gradually broken down. The change in attitude was partly the result of the waning hopes for a populist revolution. As the eighties wore on, the Western socialists were obliged to concede that their confidence in the Narodovoltsi had been sorely misplaced. Accordingly, they took a more sympathetic view of those who were attempting to create a working-class movement. Even at that, an occasional slight betrayed to the Group that its acceptance in some quarters at least was something less than complete. No doubt a lingering suspicion in Liebknecht's mind that the Narodovoltsi were still the most serious revolutionary force led him, in 1890, when he was seeking Russian correspondence for his paper *Vorwärts*, to invite the collaboration of Lavrov rather than Plekhanov.[39] It was probably in an attempt to scotch another lingering suspicion that Plekhanov told an international socialist congress in 1891: "We are not doctrinaires who are ready to forgo practical successes of the revolutionary movement for the sake of theory."[40] The undeniable absence of practical successes until that time may well have led some of the Western socialists to suspect the Group of doctrinal fastidiousness. Yet when at last impressive practical successes were registered in the Petersburg strike of 1896, Liebknecht, though not others, reacted coolly. He told the baffled Russian Marxists that labor strikes were an inappropriate method of struggle in Russia, that student disturbances were more significant.*

These were rather unusual incidents, however. They paled in significance when set against the much greater burden of evidence of growing favor to the Russian Marxists among their Western colleagues. Plekhanov no doubt regarded Liebknecht's actions as incomprehensible lapses at best, as evidence of abysmal ignorance of Russian affairs at worst.[41] So far as he was concerned, the vindication of his group and its stance came in 1894. In that year Engels consented to the publication by the Emancipation of Labor of a new edition of his polemic against Tkachev. In agreeing to bring to public attention once again his trenchant critique of populist schemes and his scornful denial of the possibility of a conspiratorial coup, Engels threw the weight of his authority behind the Russian Marxists. He admitted, in effect, that his hesitancy about the launching of the Russian movement was a regrettable error, that Plekhanov had been right in *Our Differences* and Engels wrong in his critique of it. Thus the aid and com-

---

* For all that, Plekhanov's relations with Liebknecht were on the whole cordial. The two had become acquainted in 1889, and Liebknecht visited Plekhanov in 1892, during the latter's exile in Mornex. In the following year, Liebknecht advised Plekhanov that anything he wrote would be welcome in *Vorwärts*. And it will be recalled that in 1894, during a time of adversity and profound despair, Plekhanov appealed to Liebknecht for advice and assistance.

fort Marx and Engels had given the populists, to the great embarrassment of the Russian Marxists, was belatedly redressed.

Paradoxically, the Emancipation of Labor Group secured a place for Russia in the ranks of international socialism years before the Russian labor movement sprang to life. This peculiar situation came about, above all, thanks to the international recognition accorded Plekhanov as Marxist theoretician, scholar, and writer. From the early nineties on, his work attracted the admiring attention of the chief socialist thinkers of Europe. In a letter to Kautsky, Engels pronounced "excellent" a series of articles on Hegel which Plekhanov had written for the German press. Kautsky replied: "It made me very happy that Plekhanov's article pleased you so well. It also interested me extraordinarily. . . . I regard Plekhanov as the most important of the younger Marxists."[42] A year or so later, by way of a response to an article Plekhanov submitted to *Vorwärts*, Liebknecht wrote to the Russian: "Whatever you write we will take with pleasure."[43] Plekhanov did in fact become a frequent contributor to Kautsky's *Die Neue Zeit* as well as to Liebknecht's paper. Soon he was involved in an ever more complex network of literary relations with the most active and powerful of the socialist parties of Europe. Several of his books and articles were translated, and repeatedly he was invited to offer original works on various themes for publication by the German socialist press. His important study *Essays on the History of Materialism,* for example, was written for publication in German in the first instance. Kautsky and Liebknecht each solicited from him polemical essays against the anarchists when the latter became conspicuous once again toward the mid-nineties. Following the German lead, French, English, Italian, and Polish socialists translated Plekhanov's writings into their respective languages. Leaders of all these parties were pleased in turn to render what aid they could to Plekhanov and the Group.

Responding with alacrity to the plea of Potresov and Struve, the émigré Russian Marxists set in motion machinery for obtaining the aid of Western socialism for the striking Petersburg workers. Through their efforts, many European newspapers, socialist and nonsocialist alike, were persuaded to give coverage to the exciting events in Petersburg. In London, Vera Zasulich worked closely with English labor leaders and secured both resolutions of solidarity with the Petersburg workers and a certain amount of monetary help. She also attempted, with modest success, to tap liberal middle-class sources opposed to Russian autocracy.[44] Some response came to appeals published in the Vienna *Arbeiter-Zeitung*, which described the strike as "an event of historic significance."[45] In contrast, Liebknecht depreciated the importance of the strike in his notice of it, with the result that little aid came from the German Social Democratic Party.

Hard on the heels of the strike, the Fourth Congress of the International convened in London. It was a triumphant occasion for Plekhanov and the Russian Marxists. Plekhanov had been reluctant to attend the founding congress in 1889, knowing that he represented no one but his own tiny group. On that account, he and Axelrod declined to participate in the 1891 Brussels Congress, contenting themselves instead with submitting a written report for circulation to the delegates. On the occasion of the Fourth Congress in 1896, however, a large Russian delegation, including Plekhanov, Axelrod, Zasulich, Struve, and Potresov, was seated. They represented Social Democratic groups of ten different cities, including the Petersburg organization which had recently led the textile strike. In 1889, after having been prevailed upon by Paul Lafargue to attend, Plekhanov had delivered to the Congress a brief speech that concluded with the prophecy: "The revolution in Russia will triumph as a working-class movement or not at all."[46] His words, which undoubtedly had appeared far-fetched to most of the delegates, in 1896 seemed to have some basis. If the young labor movement could force the Tsar to attend to its economic demands, it might in time be capable of imposing political conditions too. The significance of the occasion was not missed by the delegates, who passed the following resolution:

The Congress considers it necessary to point out the extraordinarily important and unprecedented fact of the presence of representatives of Russian worker organizations at the International Congress. It greets the awakening of the Russian proletariat to self-active life and in the name of the struggling workers of all countries wishes the Russian brothers manliness and unwavering courage in their difficult struggle against political and economic tyranny. *In the organization of the Russian proletariat, the Congress sees the best guarantee against Tsarist power, one of the last bulwarks of European reaction.* [Italics mine.][47]

Henceforth, the Russian Marxists could hold up their heads among their Western colleagues. Against great odds, they had brought to life a Social Democratic movement that promised to achieve what no other force in Russia had done. The place in the International, until then offered to Russia by courtesy, could now be occupied by right.

10

DEFENDER OF THE FAITH: REVISIONISM

As RUSSIAN SOCIAL DEMOCRACY began to assume seri-
ous proportions, it entered a new phase in its history. Its leaders could
look back with satisfaction upon a series of difficult hurdles successfully
surmounted. An ample corps of "officers" had been recruited from the
radical intelligentsia. These cadres in turn had established contact and
gained influence with a segment of the intended rank and file of the Social
Democratic army, the industrial workers. The movement had managed
to extricate itself from the blind alley of circle work and to move into the
broader and more significant field of mass agitation. While signal successes were being registered there, the scope of activity was still further
widened by the emergence of Social Democratic organizations in many
different cities of the Russian Empire. Axelrod's conversations with Lenin
in 1895 gave some hint as to what the chiefs of Russian Marxism regarded
as the next logical step. Plekhanov stated it openly and clearly when he
concluded his address to the London Congress of the International with
these words:

Between the secret Social Democratic organizations active in various Russian
localities, there are as yet no strong links, and in their activities sometimes not
the requisite unity. The creation of such links and such unity, the building in
Russia of a united and indivisible Social Democratic organization, must be the
chief aim of our efforts in the immediate future.[1]

The other Russian delegates assented to the priority given this goal,
and during and after the Congress the delegation met in caucus to lay
plans for securing a united party. The general principles arrived at, if
rather sketchy, were nevertheless instructive.[2] The two main areas of
concern were program and organization. As regards the first, nothing definite emerged from the caucus itself, although it did call attention to the

necessity of working out an acceptable statement of objectives in concert with the activists in Russia. Very likely, the elder statesmen subscribed to this principle *pro forma*, without attaching much importance to it. After all, had they not long since laid the foundations of Russian Marxism? Would not the program of the Russian Social Democratic Party inevitably be a summary of the gospel they had been preaching for a dozen years, and in harmony with which the movement had, by and large, evolved? They had already expressed their views explicitly in the draft programs of 1884 and 1885. Perhaps the draft of 1885 would need to be reviewed and refurbished, and some details might be altered in response to the wishes of the younger Marxists; but, essentially, there was only needed the formal ratification of what already existed. The founding fathers of the movement did not detect even a wisp of a cloud on the horizon—much less suspect that they stood on the threshold of a major ideological controversy.

On the organizational side, the caucus affirmed the principles of unity, discipline, and orthodoxy dear to the Group. In a move to avoid a repetition of the confusing and disruptive Iogiches situation, the Russian Social Democratic Union (rather than the Group, which was now part of the Union) was designated the sole representative abroad of Russia's organized workers. To make sure that the Union could fulfill the important role assigned it, groups in Russia were to be asked to make regular contributions to its treasury, and to establish definite and safe channels of communication with it. In this manner, the publication and distribution of clandestine literature could be placed on a secure footing, and the coordination of the various activities of the movement could be more nearly realized. Emphasizing the desire to mark off the Social Democratic movement as a distinct force with its own special orientation, a further decision stipulated that groups not in the Union could use its services only if they broke connections with individuals and organizations alien to Social Democracy. Although they obviously tended toward organizational centralism and rigor, these few rules of thumb were apparently adopted without any vigorous dissent. No hint in the discussions of 1896 foreshadowed the furious battles over organizational principles that marked the 1903 party congress.

Whether the decisions of the caucus were communicated to the Petersburg League and other groups in Russia is not known. Potresov, Struve, and other delegates from Russia in all likelihood strove in their respective organizations to popularize and implement the scheme for bringing a united party into being, but little progress seems to have been made in the following year, and a new conference was therefore held in Switzerland in May and June of 1897. This time the veteran Marxists representing the Union joined the spokesmen for a number of organizations in Russia in opting for a somewhat more modest proposal.[3] They agreed to go ahead with the founding of a party, even though it would at first embrace only several rather than all of the existing Social Democratic units. Specifically, they resolved to unite into a single party the Petersburg, Vilna, and Kiev organizations, together with the Union. Among the conferees was Kremer, who had written the well-known pamphlet *On Agitation*. Kremer returned shortly to Vilna, the locus of his endeavors, and in the same year succeeded in gathering together a number of Jewish worker organizations into a single association, the Bund. This achievement lent impetus to the drive for a party, inasmuch as the Bund itself subsequently became the most active proponent.

Largely through its efforts, the founding congress of the Russian Social Democratic Labor Party was convened in March 1898. Although delegates not only from Petersburg, Kiev, and the Bund, but also Moscow and Ekaterinoslav were on hand, the conclave was hardly awe-inspiring. The congress assembled within Russia (at Minsk) rather than abroad, a circumstance that betrays the ineptitude of its organizers. Meeting, of necessity, under rigorously conspiratorial conditions, it attracted only nine participants in all. Among them were none of the leading lights of the movement. Lenin, Martov, and Potresov were all in Siberian exile. The founders of Russian Marxism would not risk a trip to Russia; hence, neither their glamor and prestige nor their experience and talent were brought to the inauguration of the party.* Not surprisingly, the meeting failed to produce either a constitution or a program. Instead of framing a formal charter, it set forth a few loose organizational principles; in place of a constitution, it issued a manifesto by Struve.† A number of writers have called attention, as though it were novel, to Struve's dictum therein that the bourgeoisie of Eastern Europe was weaker than that of Western Europe, a circumstance that pushed the proletariat to the forefront in the struggle for political liberty. Plekhanov had emphasized the point for years.[4]

* Quite probably the Group, or a representative, was not even invited, owing to the disagreeable impression Plekhanov had earlier made upon several of the organizers of the congress. See V. P. Akimov-Makhnovets, "Pervyi s'ezd R.S.D.R. Partii," *Minuvshie gody*, 1908, No. 2, pp. 133–49.

† The manifesto, which was written after the conclusion of the congress, met with the disfavor of several of the delegates who had an opportunity to see it. Although the reason is not clear, Akimov speculates that it was the manifesto's designation of the winning of political liberty as the first task of the Social Democratic movement. See Akimov, pp. 149, 157–63. This was precisely the feature that won Plekhanov's support for the manifesto, when he learned of it. Akimov, who was himself associated with the Economist opposition, implies in his article that something like the Economist point of view was strongly represented, perhaps even predominant, at the first RSDLP congress. By no means unalterably hostile to Plekhanov, the congress voted to send him its greetings on the occasion of the fifteenth anniversary of the publication of *Socialism and Political Struggle*.

A few days after the first congress of the RSDLP adjourned, most of the delegates—including two of the three members of the elected Central Committee—were apprehended by the police. The cause of a united party had been advanced little if at all by the deliberations and decisions of Minsk. The work would have to be done again, more carefully, before it could truly be said that a Russian Social Democratic Party existed. The fact that five years were to pass until that time makes plain that the intrusion of the police could not have been the only, or even the chief, cause of the setback. Formal unity was not achieved, and could not be achieved, because the Social Democratic movement had *de facto* fallen into a set of warring factions.

What divided the factions was Economism, a doctrine which precipitated the first great ideological controversy within Russian Marxism. At first glance, one might be inclined to call the quarrel over Economism merely a tempest in a teapot. Closer inspection makes clear that a struggle for supremacy was being waged between two basically different conceptions of what Russian Social Democracy should be and do. Indeed, the Economist controversy arose coincident with, and was related to, the general crisis in international socialism which commenced with the demand of the German Social Democrat Eduard Bernstein for a revision of the basic precepts of Marxism. The Russian movement was hardly well launched when a crisis of faith in the foundations of Marxism broke on the international scene. In some respects Economism resembled Bernstein's doctrine, and its proponents also received intellectual and moral support from Revisionism. To Plekhanov it appeared as a Russian variant of the Revisionist deviation, the danger of which he was one of the first to scent. He rose to the challenge with a sustained barrage against the threatening heresies, proving himself a very paragon of orthodoxy, a militant defender of the faith second to none.

As early as 1891, he took note of an incident in German Social Democracy that foreshadowed the appearance of Bernstein's Revisionism seven years later. In the preceding year, the Erfurt congress of the party adopted for the first time a thoroughly Marxian program, but not before a minority brief for a change in party tactics had been beaten down. As Plekhanov described the episode, the minority spokesman Vollmar believed the party had achieved sufficient strength to make possible "an advantageous armistice with the ruling classes. And in order to dispose these classes to conciliatoriness, he is ready if not to cut himself off entirely from the ultimate aim of the party—*the socialist organization of production*—then at least to recognize and declare it to be a matter of the distant future, a matter for the sake of which Social Democracy must not refuse advantageous deals with the enemies: a bird in the hand is worth two in the bush."[5] Willingness to soft-pedal or entirely abandon class struggle, to subordinate the ultimate aims of the movement to the realization of immediate gains that might be attained by class collaboration—these were to be leading features of Bernstein's outlook. Plekhanov took satisfaction in Vollmar's defeat but emphasized that it might be only temporary.

Evidence accumulated in succeeding years that Vollmar's bid had not been an isolated, passing phenomenon. In the mid-nineties Vera Zasulich, then living in London, tremulously communicated to her colleagues in the Emancipation of Labor certain doubts that assailed her. A perceptive observer, little given to self-delusion, she saw in England a situation most disheartening for the socialists. If Vollmar's policy were to win, she remarked, it would signify "the dragging down of the Germans to the level of the English." "The authentic 'opportunists' in the labor world are the English: they pay no attention whatsoever to principles but press only for material advantages."[6] Consequently, she stood ready to affirm that England "is not at all going toward socialism. . . . The psychology of the English proletariat has already succeeded in accommodating itself to capitalism. . . . The complete lack of success of socialist propaganda here speaks for the same." Lest her friends suppose that she had been carried away by morbid anxieties which had no foundation, she pointedly advised them that Engels, with whom she had frequent contact, shared her views. Besides, the recently issued third volume of Das Kapital, she found, supported rather than controverted the dismal conclusions that so dismayed her.[7]

Plekhanov evidently refused to be drawn into a discussion of the questions at issue. Did he dread to face up to the plain implication that perhaps socialism was not historically inevitable, that perhaps it was not rooted in a law-abiding historical process? Did he flinch from examining in his usual rational and detached way evidence in conflict with views he stoutly maintained were scientifically grounded? One can scarcely imagine him withholding reassuring answers if he had had them to offer. Axelrod, to whom Zasulich confided her worst fears, could give her no comfort either. Profoundly disturbed himself by her observations, he endeavored to quiet their mutual alarm with an argument neither of them could possibly have believed: that the direction of historical movement lay from capitalism to socialism independently of the state of socialist consciousness of the workers.[8] Some tremors foretelling the future crisis of faith were felt in the Emancipation of Labor Group years before the emergence of Revisionism. Plekhanov and Axelrod were apparently able to suppress their doubts and fears, but Zasulich was permanently affected. However, like Engels, none of the three publicly revealed that his belief had faltered. Wavering in the ranks was not to be encouraged.

Plekhanov surely drew the conclusion that no effort must be spared to prevent the infection of European socialism in general with the malignant disease that had afflicted the English labor movement. The source of the disease obviously lay in the absence of socialist leadership. That explained why the English workers paid no attention to principles, as Zasulich complained, but pressed only for material advantages. Where there was no guiding socialist hand, the workers did not rise to an understanding and critique of the capitalist system as a whole. Failing to appreciate that their liberation was inseparable from its overthrow, they embarked upon the road of trade unionism, led by men who took the existing organization of society for granted and sought the amelioration of the workers' conditions within a capitalist framework. In England, the propaganda of Marxian socialism began long after proletarian consciousness had fallen into the mold of "opportunism." That accounted for its lack of success, for the pitiful weakness of the Marxian party in England, a country which in virtue of its highly developed economy ought to have had the strongest socialist party in the world.

It was hardly likely that the English pattern would be reproduced elsewhere, for it was the result of peculiar historical conditions. With a headstart in industrialization, England already had a mature proletariat by the time Marxian socialism was born. In the more economically retarded states of Europe, Marxian parties appeared soon after the emergence of industrial capitalism. Under such circumstances, it was hardly possible that the proletariats of these countries would fall victim to the malady of the English workers. And yet Vollmar, a prominent figure in the leading socialist party of Europe, was deliberately proposing a course of action like the one the English workers had followed because they lacked the guidance of socialist theory. Surely, there was no room for complacency. It was necessary to fight relentlessly for the constant heightening of the socialist consciousness of labor movements everywhere, and for the preservation of that theoretical purity and orthodoxy among the socialist parties which would render impossible any further sliding down the treacherous path of opportunism.

If Plekhanov figuratively donned his sword and buckler, other socialists reacted differently to the same circumstances. Zasulich, always a sensitive weather vane, reported from London in 1896 a growing interest in Fabianism among non-English socialists there. She herself regarded it with the hostility that revolutionists instinctively felt to the doctrine of the "inevitability of gradualness." Yet one cannot but wonder whether her hope that her illness would end her life did not bespeak despondency over the fear that gradualism indeed was inevitable, and that the revolutionary outlook to which she was dedicated had lost its force. However, as she advised

Plekhanov, Bernstein had committed himself to Fabianism, and Struve was somewhat captivated by it.[9] Fabianism represented an adaptation of socialism to the special circumstances and experience of the English labor movement, or, conversely, the generalization of that experience into an evolutionary theory of socialism that eschewed class struggle. The possibility that the English pattern might be reproduced elsewhere became distinctly more threatening when leading socialists of other countries were attracted to Fabianism. The influence of English example might yet be channeled into the Continental socialist parties. Those admirers of Fabianism to whom Vera Zasulich drew attention were destined, in fact, to become the leaders of German and Russian Revisionism. So long as they refrained from public profession of their second thoughts about Marxism, they were not fair game. Still, it is plain enough that the gathering clouds made Plekhanov increasingly touchy on the subject of orthodoxy. To Kautsky, he revealed his astonishment that Viktor Adler, the Austrian socialist leader, had seen fit to publish a review by A. Lange, a German critic of Marx, and even referred to him as "one of ours." "I am beginning to think," he wistfully commented, "that Marxists are very rare birds in the socialist parties of the West."[10]

The storm broke in 1898. In January of that year, Bernstein began a series of articles in *Die Neue Zeit,* expounding his criticism of certain of Marx's theses. Initially, he subjected to destructive analysis the theory of catastrophe, according to which the life of capitalism could be brought to a close only by a violent and dramatic overthrow. In later articles, he broadened the scope of attack to include virtually all the foundations of Marxism. Kautsky, the chief theoretician of German Social Democracy and the editor of *Die Neue Zeit,* published the articles without editorial comment. His apparent tolerance of radical deviation was not atypical, for, on the whole, articulate opposition to Bernstein developed rather slowly in the German party. It was perhaps symptomatic that none of the three who reacted most swiftly and most violently—Rosa Luxemburg, A. L. Parvus, and Plekhanov—was German. The first two, though then active in the German movement, had, like Plekhanov, come to socialism in the Russian setting. When dissatisfaction gradually mounted, Kautsky discontinued Bernstein's articles, proposing that he set out his views systematically for consideration by a party congress. The result was Bernstein's important book of early 1899, *The Preconditions of Socialism and the Tasks of Social Democracy,*[11] which called for the drastic revision of the theoretical foundations of socialism. With the gauntlet thrown down, for years thereafter not only German but international socialism was rocked by bitter conflicts between the advocates and foes of Revisionism.

Bernstein claimed to be continuing and perfecting the work of Marx and Engels—continuing, in that he remained devoted to the interests of the working class and to socialism; perfecting, in that he called for the jettisoning of those elements of their outlook which historical evolution since the writing of the *Communist Manifesto* had proved to be "utopian" or simply erroneous. He showed that Marx and Engels, true to the scientific spirit to which they paid homage, had themselves been cognizant of a good many developments that ran athwart their system. Bernstein proposed to do what they, departing from that spirit, had failed to do: sum up the damaging evidence and carry through the revision essential to bring theory into correspondence with realities.

Striking directly at the central proposition of Marxian socialism, Bernstein forthrightly asserted that the so-called objective conditions for the transition from capitalism to socialism had not in fact been engendered by historical evolution. Concentration of production in industry proceeded far less rapidly than anticipated, with large numbers of small enterprises managing to hold their own. The same observation held even more for commercial establishments; and, in agriculture, no tendency whatever to concentration was discernible. Instead of becoming polarized into two opposed classes, the few extremely rich and the multitude of poor, society was in fact more complex than before, with an extended scale of social gradations. Middle-income groups, instead of disappearing, had grown in number both absolutely and relatively. As for those presumed to be the "gravediggers" of capitalism, not only were they everywhere a minority, but the horizons of only a minority of that minority actually extended beyond the desire for amelioration of their conditions. Contrary to Marx's forecast, under capitalism the workers had been able to secure rights which brought them meaningful improvements in status and material welfare. Last but not least, the "anarchy of production," upon which the socialists counted so heavily, was being brought under control, so that economic crises occurred less frequently and were less severe.

The catastrophic fall of capitalism, Bernstein therefore argued, could only be an article of faith, for the extrapolation of past and present tendencies did not yield that result. If the forceful overthrow of the feudal structure was unavoidable because of its inflexibility, the liberal society of modern times had demonstrated its capacity for change and development. Disturbing though such argument might be, according to Bernstein, it did not require the abjuration of socialism but rather a new understanding of it. On the philosophical side, it necessitated the frank recognition that socialism was a rationally chosen ethical ideal and not the historically inevitable and scientifically validated society of the future. Kant, with his emphasis on striving to attain a high ideal, suited the socialist movement better than did the determinism and dialectics of Hegel. On the tactical side, everything pointed to the need to gear conduct to the premise of evolutionary development rather than revolution. Parliamentary activity and trade unionism had made for measurable democratization of society to the advantage of the workers. It was ludicrous to suppose that they would leave the tried and proven paths of progress in order to resort to a violent revolution, the outcome of which could not be foretold. To set up an opposition between the established forms of activity and the attainment of socialism simply made no sense, for every gain achieved for the workers by these methods represented a step in a long-range process that brought about the gradual transformation of capitalist into socialist society.

The proper work of the socialists, then, was the struggle to complete the democratization of political and economic life and the raising of the intellectual and moral levels of the working class. The tactics of the German party in fact were so oriented, Bernstein observed, although the true nature of the organization was masked by revolutionary phrase-making. The latter, since it served no useful purpose and indeed was positively harmful, ought to be scrapped. The Social Democrats should openly declare that theirs was "a democratic, socialistic party of reform." If they did, they would disarm their critics and be much more advantageously placed for winning sympathy for their objectives. To act otherwise, to permit the lead to be taken by those who thundered ominously of the coming violent revolution, would not merely militate against the party but would indeed make impossible the realization of its goals. In the unlikely event that a revolution could be successfully engineered, without an extended period of prior positive and creative labors, the destruction of the existing regime would usher in not the government of the workers but "the dictatorship of the club orators." Bernstein, in short, proposed a pragmatic kind of socialism based on the experience and psychology of the workers; for him such data took precedence over the abstract reckonings of the ideologues. The method of the latter he relegated to limbo when he characterized dialectics as a metaphysical speculation having no basis in reality.

Though there had been no dearth of warning signals, the appearance of Bernstein's article in *Die Neue Zeit* struck both Plekhanov and Axelrod like a thunderbolt. Both experienced a physical revulsion. The magnitude of the impact made stands forth in the self-revelatory letters they exchanged. Plekhanov wrote:

Surely this is a complete break with revolutionary tactics and with communism. . . . I almost took sick from these articles; what is most vexing of all is that Bernstein is partly right: for instance, it is impossible to count upon the realization of the socialist ideal in the near future. But truth may be employed for different ends; Bernstein uses it the sooner to filch the Philistine nightcap. Or is the Philistine to be the *Normalmensch* of the future? With this question, a shudder runs through me and I want to say with Gogol: How tedious is this world, sirs![12]

Axelrod's reply was a moving confession of faith:

The inner motivation of my idealism, of all my social activity, has been and is the concept of infinite progress of human nature. . . . And strange to say: the more insignificant present-day human nature appears, the more passionately I dream of its perfection in the future—in a thousand years. . . . And yet, this infinitely far-off perspective with its "supermen" is for me the impulse, the source, or you might say the inspiration. . . . I think the psychological root of this strangeness . . . lies in a kind of religious feeling, which I do not know how to characterize otherwise than in the words: worship of wisdom; consciousness of spirit reaches in me the stage of fanaticism or enthusiasm. . . . If there is no God who has created the universe—and glory be to him there is none—then we are preparing for the appearance upon earth of divine men, possessed of the essence of all-powerful reason and will, appealing to consciousness and self-consciousness, capable through wisdom of changing the world and directing it—there is the psychological basis of all my spiritual and social striving, ideas and actions. . . .

And here, in the last years, this very idea of the infinite perfectibility of man is beginning to become a subject of supercilious irony on the part of decadents, not only among the bourgeois intelligentsia but among our own. . . . I look upon the articles of Bernstein as one of the manifestations and logical or psychological consequences of this lack of faith in the progressive movement of humanity. . . . If you can understand the depressing effect of this upon me you will understand why the last of Bernstein's articles could leave me wounded almost unto death. . . .

However, if one already takes that point of view, relegating humanity to the eternal condition of cattle, not admitting his elevation to the state of full rationality, then the Philistine-tortoise movement recommended by Bernstein has at least a certain superiority over the methods of *Sturm und Drang*, in that less blood will be spilled and there will be less reason for whole nations to attempt the impossible to the degree that happened with the French.

The road will be boring no doubt, but only for separate individuals, and it will lead eventually to what more revolutionary methods might bring.[13]

In these letters, it should be noted, Bernstein's argument is not challenged. The Russians conceded, Plekhanov explicitly and Axelrod implicitly, that there was substance to it. But whatever truth it contained, Plekhanov deemed it reprehensible in the extreme for a socialist leader to bring to the surface and give public expression to ideas which could only damage the socialist movement and give comfort to its enemies. Such a leader, he no doubt believed, ought, instead of acquiescing sheeplike in a tendency subversive of his aspirations, to mobilize against it every conceivable countervailing force. At any rate, his own conduct in the years of the Revisionist crisis conformed to that principle. In his polemics, he condemned Bernstein for accepting "uncritically" the economic analysis of "bourgeois" writers like Schulze-Gaevernitz instead of seeking the data that would refute him. To forestall the spread of Revisionist influence, he led a hard-hitting offensive against it in the German Socialist press and in the International.

Bernstein's attack had a traumatic effect upon the two men because, in their view, it robbed socialism of its heroic and idealistic character. He stripped it of those grandiose perspectives that inspired their activity and gave meaning and worth to their lives. As against their vision of a society rationally organized and directed toward the attainment of ever higher levels of human perfection, Bernstein appeared to put his stamp of approval on the humdrum and unedifying pursuit of immediate self-interest. The perception that fifty years before had led Herzen to renounce his belief in the saving virtue of the West, Bernstein now appeared to sanctify as the normal and the good. The have-nots, instead of fighting passionately for a society founded upon the high ideals of brotherhood and justice, would strive only to join the ranks of the haves. Instead of playing the hero's role in bringing a brave new world out of the wreckage of a depraved capitalism, the working class was becoming infected with the Philistine values of the bourgeoisie. Not by a swift and dramatic march but by a "Philistine-tortoise" pace would society move toward the future. But if all that were true, then the ennobling passion for human progress and for the fulfillment of man's rational potentiality had no *raison d'être*. All their affirmations to the contrary notwithstanding, socialists like Plekhanov and Axelrod were really "superfluous men." The image of a world that condemned men of ideals and passion to futility was to Plekhanov unbearably tedious and depressing. Temperamentally incapable of accepting it, he was of necessity driven to deny its reality.

But there is another major dimension of meaning to Plekhanov's attitude toward Revisionism. By drawing on concrete socio-economic data, Bernstein demonstrated that European society had changed significantly in the last half of the nineteenth century, but not along lines that led to the socialist revolution Marx had projected. This he showed empirically, while the followers of Marx neglected to notice the widening breach between their leading ideas and the course of historical movement those ideas were supposed to describe. History, the high court to which Marxism appealed, rejected its claims. Together with other major precepts of Marxism, the inevitability of the socialist revolution was turning out to be more a dogma than a scientifically validated proposition.

Bernstein stood in relation to Marxism somewhat as Marx and Engels had stood in relation to utopian socialism—or, what is more to the point, as Plekhanov had stood in relation to populism. He who had disposed of the populists by labeling them utopian was now confronted with a historically based argument that his own aspirations were utopian. He who claimed to have put Russian socialism on a scientific footing was compelled to face the possibility that the outlook upon which he so prided himself was more akin to a religious faith. From the perspective of the Russian revolutionary movement, Bernstein's Revisionism tended to diminish the significance of the shift from populism to Marxism for which Plekhanov was largely responsible. Moreover, it threatened to undermine the confidence of the young generation of Russian Marxists in the ultimate triumph of their cause. To a man of his temper and intellectual predilections, no greater blow could have been struck.

Axelrod initially showed a greater degree of tolerance to the expression of Revisionist views than did Plekhanov, and he even perceived that the line of march they indicated might have some advantages. Yet he supported Plekhanov throughout the Revisionist controversy, merely attempting from time to time to moderate the ferocity of his comrade's polemics. As for Vera Zasulich, because of her earlier inner struggle, she was able to view Bernstein's innovations more dispassionately. She already "had developed an unshakeable conviction that, 'economically,' capitalism does not get worse but is gradually freed of crisis and, generally, of the 'anarchy of production.' " Although she hoped that the new ideas would not gain a foothold in German Social Democracy, she saw little hope of controverting them. "You may defend against Webb, Bernstein, etc., may bite away at their figures, but no real and significant blow can be struck, in my opinion."[14]

This may have been one of several considerations that kept Plekhanov, while he raged against Bernstein in private, from striking at him publicly at once. Other factors also contributed. Luxemburg and Parvus, who unleashed polemics against Bernstein immediately after the appearance of his first articles, could respond easily because they were on the editorial staffs, respectively, of the Leipzig and Dresden organs of the German Social Democrats. Besides, as members of the German party, they had every reason to raise their voices against what they viewed as a pernicious deviation in their ranks. Plekhanov's reluctance to intervene in the affairs of an organization to which he did not belong was seconded by Axelrod, who urged caution lest the leaders of the German party take offense. Next to Engels, there was no one in the international socialist movement whom Plekhanov admired and respected more than Karl Kautsky. Kautsky's willingness to publish, and his failure to rebut, Bernstein's articles troubled Plekhanov deeply. He hesitated to intrude, upon learning that Kautsky was indeed provoked with Bernstein but practiced forbearance in the hope that his old comrade might yet be won back. But Plekhanov's patience ran out when he read a new Bernstein article in *Die Neue Zeit* directed at the philosophical foundations of Marxism. Unable to contain himself any longer, he wrote to Kautsky on May 20, 1898:

In the last number of *Neue Zeit*, Bernstein published an article on the two "moments" of socialism. This article is a continuation of that he published in the month of January, and in which he criticized the "catastrophe-theory." Bernstein is now trying to do on the *philosophical* terrain what he thinks he has done on the *economic* terrain. His criticism of materialism is very weak. But as weak as it is, it is launched directly against the ideas of F. Engels. . . . If Bernstein is right in his critical endeavors, one may ask what remains of the philosophical and socialist ideas of our teachers? What remains of socialism? And in truth, one would have to reply: not very much! Or more than that: *nothing at all*. I don't know if you are of my opinion, but I believe you will allow me to answer Bernstein in *Neue Zeit*. All I want is to defend the ideas of F. Engels, which our "philosophers" like K. Schmidt have declared to be old and untenable. I will confess to you that the writings of these philosophers anger me much and my reply will be not entirely amiable. But for me it is a question of very serious matters and I am unable to maintain an academic cold-bloodedness. . . .

Can you be in agreement with Bernstein? It would be too painful for me to believe that. If not, why do you not answer? It is you who are attacked, it is your Erfurt program which these gentlemen envisage in their "critique.". . .

Oh yes, we are going through a crisis, and this crisis is making me suffer very much.[15]

Sensible of his own dereliction of duty, yet psychologically unprepared to combat a comrade-in-arms of eighteen years' standing, Kautsky gladly agreed to have Plekhanov take on the task. Thus it came about that the first polemic against Revisionism in the chief organ of German Social Democracy was that of the Russian Marxist Plekhanov. His first piece appeared in August 1898, but only after Kautsky had pruned out certain passages he considered personally abusive to Bernstein. Plekhanov regarded Bernstein as an out-and-out enemy who should be fought to the death, but Kautsky was far less severe. The differences between the two widened appreciably before the publication of Plekhanov's second article. At the Stuttgart Congress of the German party in 1898, Kautsky, despite his association with the orthodox in the defeat of the Revisionists, was himself attacked by the Left for having published Bernstein's articles without editorial comment. In a defense that aroused Plekhanov's ire, he replied: "Bernstein has forced us to think again, and we must be thankful to him for that." Aligning himself with the Left, Plekhanov published in the Leipzig and Dresden papers a fiery open letter to Kautsky entitled "For What Shall We Be Thankful to Him?" The gravity Plekhanov attached to the Revisionist threat he revealed in the question that he insisted it posed for the socialists: Nothing less was at stake than the matter of "who will bury whom, Bernstein Social Democracy, or Social Democracy Bernstein?"[16]

Although Plekhanov's intransigence nettled a good many socialists, and even dismayed Axelrod, he was encouraged by approving letters from Bebel and Liebknecht to press his campaign with undiminished ardor.[17] The merciless verbal pummeling he gave to Konrad Schmidt, an academician who gave philosophical support to Bernstein, brought such a wave of protests that Kautsky advised him to temper his attacks. To this reproach, Plekhanov responded: "I . . . cannot understand why I do not have the right to abuse these gentlemen who dare to slander our teachers while not understanding a word of their philosophy. Ah, dear Kautsky, if only Engels were alive today, he would not condemn me for my sharpness."[18] Plekhanov's eagerness to impale his foe increased after the appearance of Bernstein's book, which belittled Plekhanov's significance in the Russian movement. The theoretician of Revisionism claimed that the majority of the Russian Social Democrats stood close to his own views, a charge he substantiated elsewhere by reference to the recent "ouster" of Plekhanov as editor of the RSDU's publications.[19]

The chieftains of German Social Democracy (Kautsky as well as Bebel and Liebknecht), while they remained friendly to Plekhanov, never adopted his uncompromising approach. They were unwilling to go beyond letting the issues be debated and the passage of mildly condemnatory resolutions against Revisionism, as in 1899 and 1900. Their differences carried over into the International, too, when in 1900 at Paris the issues of participation of socialists in bourgeois cabinets and the conditions of proletarian conquest of power were discussed. In a clever play on words, Plekhanov chided Kautsky for offering a "rubbery" (kauchokovaia) resolution that lent itself to interpretations acceptable to the opportunists. The German party congress in 1903 pronounced Revisionism dead, and the Amsterdam Congress of the International in 1904 condemned it unequivocally, but neither consented to go as far as Plekhanov would have liked. The socialist leaders recoiled from reading the Revisionists out of the ranks of socialism, as Plekhanov demanded, for they dreaded the consequence that would inexorably follow—a split. To them, organizational unity took precedence over agreement on principles. Plekhanov's own definition of a party, in the given case, would have made a schism inevitable. "Freedom of opinion in a party can and must be limited," he argued, "precisely because a party is a union, freely made up of people with common ideas: once unanimity disappears, a split becomes inevitable."[20] It should be added in fairness to him that he had in view differences not on secondary matters but on the fundamental positions and aims of the organization. Unconvinced that

Revisionism was indeed dead, and not having changed his mind as to its complete incompatibility with Social Democracy, Plekhanov lost no opportunity even after 1904 to hammer away at it.

It was in the philosophical realm that he made his first as well as his strongest attack upon Revisionism. Probably, as a result of the original and extensive philosophical studies he made during the nineties, he felt most competent to wage war on this ground without prolonged preparatory research. If he was less well versed in the economic side of the question, in any case Luxemburg and Parvus were carrying the battle to the Revisionists on that front. Besides, as Plekhanov had revealed before, especially in the Bel'tov work against the Narodniks, his strategy for demolishing an opponent involved the discrediting of his premises and methodology. Be that as it may, his arraignment on philosophical grounds must have left the great majority of his readers wondering what possible relation it could have to the central issues raised by Revisionism. As Axelrod, who admitted his own lack of qualifications, remarked: "In the whole of international Social Democracy, there are scarcely a handful of people capable of even seriously following—not to speak of participating in—these debates."[21] When Kautsky pleaded this reason for wishing to print only a limited amount of this kind of material, Plekhanov replied firmly: "It is essential to *force* the readers to interest themselves in philosophy . . . *it is the science of sciences.*"[22] To the readers of *Die Neue Zeit* he himself addressed these forceful words:

I am defending and always will defend the outlook of Marx and Engels with passion and with conviction. And if some readers shrug their shoulders over the fact that I am so heated in a polemic, which concerns the most important questions of human knowledge and at the same time touches upon the most essential interests of the working class . . . then I say, shrugging my shoulders in turn: *so much the worse for such readers.*[23]

Plekhanov's target was the Neo-Kantian philosophy, which, according to Bernstein and Schmidt, gave a more accurate representation of man's cognitive relation to the external world than did Marxian materialism. The critics, relying upon Kant's brief for the unknowability of "things-in-themselves," maintained that the external world is not truly knowable. Plekhanov declined to go "back to Kant," asserting that it rather behooved the critics to refresh their knowledge of philosophy. For, in his view, Bernstein and Schmidt were so ill-versed in Kant that they were unaware of the central inconsistency in his theory of knowledge. Kant's conviction as to the unknowability of the noumenal world (things-in-themselves, or the essential nature of things) was counterbalanced by his belief in the knowability of the phenomenal world (the objects that exist outside of us and of which we become aware through their action upon our consciousness).

He stood midway between idealism and materialism, never succeeding in resolving the subject-object relationship.* As Plekhanov saw it, the resolution lay in going over either to a consistent subjective idealism—which abounded in absurdities—or to the consistent materialism of which Marx and Engels were the exponents. He emphasized what he took to be the alternative choices by a witty and wicked thrust at his opponent:

If M. Konrad Schmidt did not exist as *a thing in himself*; if he were only an appearance, that is, a representation existing only in my consciousness, then I would never forgive myself that my consciousness produced a doctor so inept in philosophical speculation. But if my representation corresponds to the real M. Konrad Schmidt, then I am not responsible for his logical errors, my conscience is clear, and that means much in this vale of tears.[24]

It is important to note that Plekhanov associated the Kantian idealism he rejected with Hume's skepticism. Indeed, the main objective of his crusade against Neo-Kantianism was to throw up a barricade against the infiltration of skepticism into the socialist movement. If the external world were indeed unknowable, how pitiful and ludicrous would be the pretensions of those who claimed to have founded a scientific socialism. Once the deadly poison of skepticism was within the gates, it would surely sap the élan of the movement. As Axelrod keenly observed at the first blush of the Revisionist crisis, skepticism and pessimism were alien to Plekhanov's spirit and nature.[25] More than that, counting passion a significant factor in the making of history, Plekhanov feared that the spread of skepticism might blight the enthusiasm essential for the realization of the goals of the movement.[26]

By reference rather than by close analysis, Plekhanov also took Neo-Kantianism to task in the area of moral philosophy. In an earlier consideration of Kant,[27] he had taken serious issue with the morality of the "categorical imperative." Kant represented his ethics as "the inviolable commands of 'practical reason.' " His *abstractly* derived morality pertained in particular to the individual and his happiness. But, Plekhanov objected, morality in fact is always *socially* determined and invariably is to be referred to some larger entity such as the tribe, class, or nation. As for Kant's own specific moral norms, according to Plekhanov, they actually conformed to the ideals of bourgeois society. The Marxist took Kantianism to be particularly well suited to the Philistine (read: bourgeois), who defines an ideal as something too high to be realized and yet toward which we are morally obligated to strive. Plekhanov failed to see in this relationship a

---

* In a letter to Kautsky a few years before, Plekhanov said: "The philosophy of Kant for me signifies nothing else but an armistice between the discoveries of natural science and the ancient religious tradition." Undated letter (probably late 1895) at the International Institute of Social History, Amsterdam.

tension that might ennoble and give a sense of direction to life. It is clear enough that the socialist ideal performed precisely that function in his own life. But he would have denied that, insisting that his passion was rationally related to the lawful historical process rather than derived from "abstract" speculation about ethics. The Kantian orientation, in his mind, was merely a warrant for hypocrisy. It offered the self-satisfaction of belief in a high ideal and at the same time the justification of conduct having nothing in common with that ideal.

With sure instinct, Plekhanov asserted, the bourgeoisie associated the growth of materialism and atheism among the workers with a radicalism that boded ill for their interests. In Kantianism, the propertied classes recognized "a powerful spiritual weapon" for countering such tendencies and lulling the workers into a more pacifically minded and amenable state. It left room for the "religious superstition" of the bourgeoisie, which might help to curb the "extremism" of the workers. And it might be employed to persuade the workers to entrust themselves to the moral conscience of their employers instead of relying upon their own efforts.[28] Perhaps he also feared that Kantianism could provide the rationalization for combining lip service to the high but unattainable ideal of socialism with the practice of "opportunism." Could such a philosophy be anything but inimical to a class with the historic mission of overthrowing the bourgeoisie and founding a new social order with its own appropriate morality? Wittingly or not, by smuggling Neo-Kantian ideas into the proletarian movement Schmidt and Bernstein acted as stalking horses for the class enemy.[29]

Although the best of Plekhanov's philosophical sallies against Revisionism sparkled with wit and erudition, it is not clear—as he himself claimed—that he demolished his opponents. These essays, in any case, did nothing to refute those aspects of the Revisionist critique most damaging to orthodox Marxism, the socio-historical and the economic. In regard to the latter, Plekhanov was forced to concede certain points. He admitted, for example, that the number of middle peasants was tending to remain constant rather than diminishing; that middle-income groups had grown faster than the population as a whole; and that the conditions of the working class had in certain respects improved.[30] But in various ways he disputed the significance of these facts, which appeared to undercut important Marxian postulates concerning the dynamics of capitalism. For one thing, he "bit away at the figures" of the Revisionist critics,[31] hoping thereby to reduce the force of their case. More successfully, he cast doubt upon their contention that economic depressions were becoming less frequent and less disruptive. Most essential was his affirmation that those developments, the reality of which he conceded, were quite compatible with continued and even growing social inequality.

Whether true or not, this affirmation involved data relevant to but not adequate for resolving the most crucial question. Marx's projection of a proletarian revolution had as its socio-economic basis not merely the inferior economic status of the working class but its progressive impoverishment under capitalism. In the *Communist Manifesto* he had noted with hearty approval the recent winning of the ten-hour day by the English working class—although, oddly enough, this circumstance, suggestive of the possibility of improvement for the worker under capitalism, did not cause him to qualify his prediction of its violent overthrow. Fifty years later, an orthodox Marxist had to take account of the substantial record of advances that appeared to have made untenable the doctrine of progressive impoverishment. Without a doubt, a large measure of social inequality existed. That it constituted an adequate basis upon which to build and carry through a socialist revolution still remained to be proved. Would the existing social inequality be a spur sharp enough to maintain and augment that class consciousness of the proletariat, without which the attainment of socialism was unthinkable?

Plekhanov well knew that this was the question that insistently demanded attention, and, with little hesitation, he answered it affirmatively. In order to do so, he was obliged to shift his ground, to rely upon the theory of relative impoverishment which was the standard reply of the Marxists to Revisionism. In proportion as capitalism develops, he argued, "the position of the worker worsens relatively, even though his material condition improves in the absolute sense." Even if, as a consequence of militant struggle, the proletarian worked shorter hours and received higher pay, he was exploited more heavily than before, since the gains he made were less than proportional to the increase in his productivity.

The proletarian is in the position of a person who is swimming against a powerful current. If he submits without resistance to the force of the water, he will be carried *very* far back. But he does resist; he tries to move forward and therefore the current pushes him back *not so far* as it *might*; but it *nevertheless moves him back,* because *all the same it is much stronger.*[32]

Viewing the matter in this light, Plekhanov could persist in an unimpaired belief in the inevitability of the socialist revolution. So long as society remained divided into classes, the proletarian would be impelled to fight against the bourgeoisie to keep from being utterly impoverished. So long as he wrested every improvement by class struggle rather than class collaboration, there could be no diminution of class antagonism. So long as the socialist conscientiously fulfilled his task of keeping before the exploited workers the ultimate end of the movement, which brought fresh hope into cheerless lives, their class consciousness would not flag.

As in Plekhanov's revolutionary prognosis for Russia, so in his evaluation of this critical problem of Western socialism, the difficulty lay in his inflated expectations regarding proletarian class consciousness. These, in turn, were premised upon a view of the social world somewhat wanting in realism. So long as society remained divided into classes, the proletariat might well find it necessary to fight against the bourgeoisie. But in the West methods had been devised for fighting against the bourgeoisie without overthrowing the existing framework of society. Trade-union activities and parliamentary struggles could be carried on within the bounds of capitalist society, and yet they indubitably brought material and social betterment for the working class. In so far as the workers experienced improvement in their status and well-being, such forms of combat might well result in a reduction of class antagonism. For the proletarian, it mattered little whether the improvement of his conditions was relative as well as absolute. Plekhanov's dramatic figure of the man swimming against the current could make little impression upon people who knew, from direct experience, that they had gained ground.

Where gains were real and palpable, the lives of the workers became more tolerable and cheerful. Socialist leaders might then find the workers gravitating toward opportunism.* Having gained ground by tried and proven methods, they were reluctant to leave the known and successful for the unknown. As a matter of fact, the trade unions, with their bureaucratic organization and substantial funds and property, became the particular strongholds of opportunism and reformism. Changes in the socio-economic situation of the workers were reflected in their psychology. As Peter Gay has pointed out, "the virtue of Bernstein's optimistic Revisionism . . . lay in the fact that it seemed to give a coherent theoretical explanation of the situation in which the German worker found himself around the year 1900."[33] Plekhanov's assurances to the contrary notwithstanding, it was well-nigh impossible to maintain and augment the class consciousness of the proletariat in the presence of the gradual democratization of society, the amelioration of the conditions of the working class, and, not least, the accompanying popularization of nationalism. Exhortations of party leaders about the ultimate ends of the movement evoked less and less response among the rank and file. Immediate improvements spoke louder than distant utopia.

Plekhanov himself was not unaware of the existence of opportunism in the German labor movement, and he occasionally even displayed a degree of tolerance of it. But he never tired of abusing the Revisionist intellectuals for having "betrayed Marxism."[34] Indeed, he virtually blamed the opportunism of the workers on the "renegades"—a charge that emphasized once again the great significance he attached to the intelligentsia in

---

* As Peter Gay puts it, "the road to opportunism is paved with parliamentary successes." *The Dilemma of Democratic Socialism*, p. 100.

the socialist movement. He might himself have penned the wide-eyed observation one of his disciples made in 1898 concerning the rise of Revisionism: "It is astonishing: the bourgeoisie, frightened by the growth of class consciousness of the proletariat, made some concessions. The representatives of the latter, seeing signs of the weakness of the bourgeoisie, instead of being emboldened and becoming more revolutionary, on the contrary, began themselves to yield."[35] This is an apt enough statement of a changing social relation, but it errs, as Plekhanov erred, in overemphasizing the role of socialist leadership. Plekhanov refused to understand that Revisionism was a consequence and a reflection of the mentality of the proletariat rather than its cause.

Plekhanov dared not confront squarely the circumstances that gave rise to Revisionism. It represented, as did Fabianism, an accommodation of socialist intellectuals to the mood and perspectives of the working class. But infinitely more disturbing was the clear implication that the working class harbored an inherent tendency to opportunism. Both in England, where socialist leadership had been lacking, and in Germany, which boasted the strongest and most able socialist leadership to be found anywhere, the same phenomena appeared. The image of the proletarian as the bearer of socialism—as the unconscious socialist who needed only to be enlightened by the intelligentsia to become conscious—that image evidently did not correspond to reality. Plekhanov was psychologically incapable of facing up to this discovery, for it involved the discrediting of one of the major premises in the argument for the inevitability of socialism.

This consideration perhaps explains why he held the shortcomings of intellectual leaders accountable for the rise of Revisionism. Yet, paradoxically, the emergence in England and Germany of what he considered deplorable tendencies led Plekhanov to shift a greater burden of responsibility to the shoulders of the socialist intellectuals. Having perceived that the working class was less steadfast than he had supposed, he enlarged the role of the intelligentsia, as it were, to redress the balance. As guardians of socialist consciousness, they must never waver in their attachment to the ends of the movement, lest, by insinuating to the ranks a loss of confidence, they open the floodgates of opportunism. He now gave relatively greater weight to the will of the intelligentsia as a requisite for socialism than to the "natural" development of socialist inclinations among the proletarians. The Revisionist controversy made for a shift in his sense of revolutionary dynamics, reinforcing the Jacobin tendency which had been part of his make-up from the first. Nor was this a merely personal consequence of the conflict. If Plekhanov's campaign against Revisionism made little apparent impact upon the German party, it left permanent marks upon his own, as the subsequent history of the Russian movement showed.

For the rest, Plekhanov evaded the issues Revisionism raised by asserting that basically nothing had changed. The leaders of the German party could not follow suit because of the pressure of the trade unions, which bulked increasingly large in the party.

To be sure, the orthodox faction appeared for a time to have retained the upper hand, but even then it prevailed only in the realm of theory. The practice of the party, however, accorded much more closely with the spirit of Revisionism than of orthodoxy.[36] After the repeal of the anti-Socialist laws in 1890, German Social Democracy without important deviations followed the legal and peaceful path of parliamentary activities and trade unionism, securing whatever advantages it could for the workers without excessive fastidiousness as to means. How far it strayed from revolutionism becomes evident when one recalls the nature of the Imperial German constitution. Reserving as it did the greater share of power to the emperor, it sanctioned what was in fact a pseudo-parliamentary regime. Power could not be secured through parliamentary means by the Social Democrats or any other party so long as that constitution stood. Germany had not as yet accomplished its democratic revolution. The Social Democrats, far from making preparations for a socialist revolution, were not even seriously readying themselves for the installation through revolution of a democratic constitution. It seems quite inexplicable that Plekhanov did not press against the Revisionists—not to mention the orthodox—the meaningful charge that they were forswearing revolution while still operating in the framework of a quasi-absolutist regime.

It is not impertinent to wonder how Plekhanov's tactics for the Russian Social Democratic Party, after the winning of a constitutional regime, would have differed from those of the German party. Plekhanov of course expected tsarism to give way to a genuinely democratic political order, rather than to a spurious one of the German type. Accordingly, the Russian socialists could go about their business in greater security and freedom than their German counterparts. He clearly envisaged a Social Democratic Party embracing the largest possible number of workers, engaging in political campaigns and parliamentary activities, fostering the growth of trade unions, and maintaining close contact between party and labor organizations. Frankly stating the desirability of social reforms, he definitely recognized the possibility of securing improvements for the proletariat under conditions of political democracy. While countenancing such tactics, Plekhanov surely would have insisted that the party maintain a revolutionary stance, keeping to the fore the ultimate end of the movement. In short, under his aegis, the Russian party would have emulated the German example of revolutionary orthodoxy in words and evolutionary Revisionism in deeds. If Revisionism arose and ultimately triumphed in the

German setting, the likelihood of the same occurring in Russia would have been all the greater if political democracy had existed there. There is no reason to believe that Plekhanov or others would have been more successful than the Germans in combating Revisionism. Plekhanov had confronted the socialist world with the stark alternatives: "Who will bury whom, Bernstein Social Democracy, or Social Democracy Bernstein?" How erroneous was this posing of the question is ironically evident from the fact that Bernstein's Revisionism presently was to become synonymous with Social Democracy.

The crisis of Marxian orthodoxy that began around the turn of the century had its source not in "treachery" or "ignorance of Marxism" by certain intellectuals. It stemmed rather from the circumstance that that orthodoxy was becoming less and less appropriate to the changing societies of Europe. Marx's system was getting out of joint with the times. The rise of Revisionism in Western socialism represented one of the major symptoms. Its triumph spelled a mighty defeat for orthodox Marxism and for the Russian defender of the faith.

11

DEFENDER OF THE FAITH: ECONOMISM

Economism made its appearance on the Russian
Social Democratic scene simultaneously with the rise of Revisionism in
the German party. Plekhanov, thinking the latter deviation the more
dangerous of the two, concentrated his fire upon it almost immediately.
His first salvos against Economism did not come until more than two years
later. Yet his orientation to Economism must be seen against the background of his struggle with Revisionism. Bernstein challenged the validity
of basic Marxian principles just when it seemed that Plekhanov's efforts to
found a party on those same principles were to be successful. Economism
he saw as a device for channeling Bernstein's heretical doctrines into the
Russian movement. His battle against Revisionism made him more sensitive than ever to ideological deviations, particularly to deviations that
sought a reduction of the role of the intelligentsia in the socialist party,
and he attacked Economism ferociously because he believed it shared
with Revisionism that intention.

However, it was not these associations alone that determined the nature
and intensity of his assault. Of considerable import also was the prolonged
record of embittered conflict between the Emancipation of Labor Group
and those who subsequently became the advocates of Economism. The
campaign against a tendency regarded as subversive of Social Democracy
was doubly vituperative in that it also involved the discharge of personal
animosities which had envenomed Plekhanov and Axelrod for years.

The locus of discord was the emigration where, from the mid-nineties
on, the Group, though affiliated with the Russian Social Democratic Union,
continued to maintain its separate identity. Except for the members of the
Emancipation of Labor, the Union included younger people more or less
recently converted to Marxism. The organizational relationship between

the Group and the Union in the main was patterned upon earlier collaborative efforts of the founders of the movement with the younger Social Democrats. In order to preserve its ideological leadership, the Group reserved the right to edit the publications of the Union, including the journal *Rabotnik*. In addition, the Group enjoyed the right to undertake any independent ventures it might deem useful to the movement. To the younger comrades were left such tasks as fund raising, the operation of the press, the arrangement of transport routes for illegal literature, and the maintenance of contact with revolutionary groups in Russia. The distribution of powers and responsibilities tacitly implied that the Group was the High Command and the other members the noncommissioned officers and rank and file. Nevertheless, the younger Social Democrats possessed greater authority now than in earlier collaborative efforts. The elected officers of the Union might in significant respects influence the organizational life of the Social Democratic emigration. Besides, had not the Group now committed itself to the publication of that "indispensable" worker literature which it had formerly "neglected"? Also, the younger people with literary aspirations would have an opportunity to contribute to *Rabotnik* or to other Union publications.

What can be made out of the constitution of the RSDU suggests that it represented an effort of mutually distrustful forces to suppress—or adjust —differences for the sake of the progress of the movement as a whole. The Group yielded on a number of points to the younger faction, which for some years had viewed its *modus operandi* with a critical eye. At the same time, the veterans showed no disposition to permit the general direction of the movement to fall into the hands of relatively inexperienced recent recruits. On both sides there may have existed the desire to make the relationship work, but in practice things turned out abominably. Troubles commenced early in 1896, not long after the Union was reorganized to facilitate support to the movement in Russia. Beginning with occasional friction over separate and seemingly unrelated matters, clashes grew more frequent, finally coalescing into a pattern of continual conflict which engaged more and more of the energies of both sides. The unedifying record of bickering, sniping, and vilification is too tedious to bear repeating in detail.[1] Yet the story cannot be ignored, for, despite the apparent triviality of many of the skirmishes, they were related to a vital stake. They were, in fact, episodes in a running battle concerned with the constitutional issue of the distribution of power, an issue the importance of which was by no means restricted to the emigration alone.

In the first instance, Axelrod was most immediately involved in these quarrels. In the course of his conversations with Lenin in the summer of 1895, the two had agreed to the desirability of freeing Plekhanov from organizational and editorial duties in order to preserve his time for literary-theoretical work.[2] Consequently, the responsibility for editing *Rabotnik* and other publications of the Union fell upon Axelrod. He would have been a logical choice in any case, since *Rabotnik* was intended to serve the labor movement and inevitably would devote much space to tactics—the very matters in which he had long specialized. Be that as it may, it was he who worked most intimately with the Union people, and it was between him and them that sharp differences first developed. Illustrative of the kind of thing that occurred was a disagreement over financial matters which arose early in 1896.

The administrators of the Union wished to place its affairs upon a businesslike basis, involving, among other things, the keeping of financial records. Axelrod drew upon the Union treasury for expenses incidental to its publishing activities. But when the Union officials asked him to render an account of funds expended, he was thrown into confusion, for he had kept no records. It was typical of the Emancipation of Labor Group that little care was taken with that kind of thing. Its members trusted each other implicitly, and those who contributed to their efforts rarely expected an accounting. The new order the Union was attempting to devise appeared to Axelrod as a lot of unnecessary fuss. The humiliation and indignation he felt at having to produce some sort of record oppressed him, and he cried out to Plekhanov about the "stingy-commercial" attitude of the Union people. His problem was further complicated by his failure to distinguish adequately between funds donated specifically to the Group by its friends and those put at its disposal from the Union treasury.[3]

This incident illustrates several aspects of the fight that gradually took shape between the two elements of the Union. There was, for one thing, the matter of organizational style, with the Group accustomed to an informal, almost familylike pattern based upon mutual respect and confidence, whereas the Union stood for a more impersonal and bureaucratic type of management. The younger comrades had no doubts of Axelrod's honesty, but they took it as axiomatic that an organization could not properly function otherwise than in accord with prescribed rules. Yet Axelrod felt personally affronted when called to account—or thought, at the very least, that he was being subjected to a gratuitous annoyance. The sensitivity of the elder statesmen at being criticized by their juniors was certainly another reason for the strained relations. Axelrod's failure to distinguish between the funds of the Group and the funds of the Union gives some indication of problems that repeatedly came up in consequence of the peculiar organizational relationship that made the Group, at one and the same time, a part of the Union and an independent entity. From the point of view of the younger Marxists in the emigration, Axelrod's maladroitness seemed clear evidence of unforgivably slipshod management. A reasonable desire to bring order and rationality into the operation of the RSDU had aroused intense irritation on one side and, on the other, grave doubts as to the competence of the older leaders.

The situation would have been less serious had it not been for the fact that Axelrod gave his younger collaborators many additional grounds for complaint. Writing slowly and painfully, he not infrequently failed to complete on time work he had contracted to do. Ill-health further interfered with his literary productivity and with the discharge of his editorial function as well. Perhaps it was such circumstances, augmented by the distress they caused him, that explain why well over half a year went by between the decision to publish *Rabotnik* and the appearance of the first number. What must have seemed to the younger comrades like intolerable dilatoriness became more and more vexing as Axelrod consistently rebuffed every effort to take from his shoulders some share of the responsibility that he himself could not fulfill.

Nor was Plekhanov exempt from attack. Inasmuch as he generally stood shoulder to shoulder with Axelrod against his critics, he shared the reproaches hurled at his comrade. Moreover, Plekhanov served as the particular butt of another accusation brought against the Group. The most influential of the younger Social Democrats had come from Russia but recently, after participating in agitational activities there. On that ground, they claimed a more accurate knowledge of the character and needs of the movement than the older men. In particular, they believed the Group to be indifferent still to the publication of that literature for workers which they themselves regarded as the most efficacious means of carrying the movement forward. Was not the Group's deployment of its major talent, Plekhanov, in the field of abstract theoretical and philosophical writing a patent demonstration of its remoteness from Russian realities? No doubt the Group merited undying glory for having laid the foundations of Russian Marxism. But why did Plekhanov persist in whipping that dead dog, populism, when there were new worlds to be won, when all effort ought to be devoted to supplying the wherewithal to develop the enormous potentialities of the labor movement?

In summary, the opponents of the Group prepared a formidable indictment. On the score that they were out of touch with the situation in Russia, and ill-informed of its needs, the veteran Marxists were disqualified from providing leadership. Even if the Group entertained a more realistic conception of what the times called for, its sluggishness and inefficiency made it ill-suited for the directing role it claimed. So long as the reins of control lay in its hands, the accomplishment of essential tasks could not be achieved. Those who had founded and initially given a great impetus to the movement had become a fetter on its further development. Yet they refused to yield place to those who were better qualified, who possessed both a clear sense of needs and the energy essential to their fulfillment. A related charge had it that the Group's hypercritical attitude and intolerance of diversity of viewpoint stunted the growth of fresh literary forces which the movement badly needed. If more sharply drawn than before, the grievances of the younger faction were not dissimilar in kind from those that marked earlier strife between the veteran Marxists and their followers in the emigration. In the new trial of strength, however, the attackers were more self-assured, more insistent, and more aggressive than their predecessors. By organizing opposition to the older men, by invading their prerogatives, by disregarding existing lines of authority, the critics carried on a kind of guerrilla warfare against the Group. They clearly intended to reduce the power of the veterans, and perhaps they dreamed of dislodging them altogether and taking over the guidance of the movement themselves. The Group confronted a rebellion of unprecedented dimensions and vigor against its authority.

Plekhanov and Axelrod reciprocated the hostility of the younger Social Democrats. Certain that the case against them had no substantial foundation, they attributed the complaints of their juniors to ignorance, to wounded *amour-propre,* to malevolence—in short, to anything but real faults of the Group. Their opponents' more recent contact with the movement in Russia gave no particular warrant for superior wisdom; indeed, it was more than offset by their disdain for theory, without which the correct interpretation and evaluation of experience was impossible. Their preoccupation with practical administrative concerns marked them as mere bureaucrats, men lacking in revolutionary passion, and too small in spirit to respond to the grandiose perspectives of the movement. In day-to-day contacts, the older men became convinced of the triviality and ineptitude of the younger Social Democrats. The latter violated organizational discipline, thus creating conditions of anarchy; they could not be relied upon; their relationships with one another too often showed lack of dignity and mutual respect; and among those with literary pretensions there existed little of the requisite talent. The claims of the younger Social Democrats to greater authority and power seemed to Plekhanov and Axelrod a bad joke. They could not contemplate the transfer of leadership of the movement they had brought to life with such travail to an ignorant, incompetent, and mean-spirited crew who could only undo what they had wrought.

The images the Group and the opposition held of each other, though not wholly inaccurate, were strongly colored by emotion. As parties to a conflict that inflamed feelings, neither camp had the perspective to understand its true nature. Logically enough, it was Vera Zasulich, who was away from the heat of the fight in England, who most perceptively characterized what was happening. Urging that the younger people be looked at "historically," she inquired of Plekhanov: "Is it not clear to you that we cannot work with this kind of person in one organization? And not because he is bad! It is simply a difference in years, understanding, and mood."[4] A few weeks later, returning to the diagnosis of the crisis, she wrote:

I know that I possess a much greater grasp of reality than do you. . . . With you, it is confounded (and sometimes to madness) by a conception of what ought to be, but which is not, and for which means to make it so are not available. You are mistaken when you think there are only two fools against us, who need to be blasted out. Against us is practically the entire younger emigration in union with those elements of the students who have already acted or are getting ready to act seriously. They are full of energy, feel that Russia is behind them. . . . We might be able to win a formal victory over our opponents in the Union in one way or another, but it would be our greatest defeat.

We cannot carry out the function of the Union, to create a worker literature. You say we cannot throw up the cause in which we worked for 15 years. Yet in the last three years we have been doing an entirely different work from that which we did in the preceding 12. That we could continue. I propose that we do it. We cannot publish a literature for the workers that would satisfy the demands of the Russians. And it seems to everyone that we are hampering those who can. . . . They will not attain their ideal either, but they possess such an ideal and we do not. They are thirsting for activity of that kind but not under our direction. . . .

I am for a simple avowal that we ourselves have not found the results of our editing of worker literature brilliant and that we give to our critics the opportunity to try their hand.[5]

For the moment, her advice was not taken. But when, in effect, she designated this a quarrel between fathers and sons she surely touched upon one of the main sources of the differences. The crisis in the relations between the Group and the younger Marxists in the emigration was one instance of the trauma that attended the growth of the Russian Social Democratic movement. For a decade and more, the Emancipation of Labor Group had virtually constituted the movement. It had placed upon it a well-defined stamp, expressive of the orientations and characteristics of its founders. Whereas they were inclined, whether from inertia or deliberate choice, to maintain the mold they had created, newer forces entering the movement saw the need for adjustments that would take account of changed circumstances. Whatever their own shortcomings, the younger men were undoubtedly justified in many of their criticisms. If in 1896 or 1897 populism was not exactly dead, evidently greater dividends for the Social Democrats were to be obtained from supporting the nascent labor movement than from polemics against the Narodniks. New times set new tasks. Yet, as Zasulich noted, although the Group was incapable of fulfilling these new tasks itself, it would not permit others to try their hand. Formed in the struggle against populism and in the putting down of the theoretical foundations of Russian Marxism, the Group apparently could not easily adapt to the changing needs of the movement.

The veterans had admitted more than once the shortcomings of the practical side of the Group's activity, but they were at the same time rather contemptuous of those who sought to build a stronger organization. The loose inner organization of the Group, adequate though it may have been when Russian Marxism was a-borning, had to give way to a constitutional order and a well-defined administrative procedure as the movement grew in size and complexity. But the older men, fixed in their ways, did not take kindly to pressures to accommodate themselves to new organizational patterns. At the root of all the difficulties lay the Group's insistence that it continue to enjoy the status of an exclusive center of leadership. So long as it maintained that position, it could effectively hamstring the efforts of those who keenly felt the need of innovations. Just as surely as Russia's changing socio-economic conditions made the situation of Russian autocracy increasingly insecure, so the changing character of the Social Democratic movement was making untenable the virtual autocracy of the Emancipation of Labor.

With relations between the Group and the Union opposition strained almost to the limit by the end of 1897, Economism emerged to complicate the picture. This new tendency first gained expression in the clandestine periodical *Rabochaia mysl'* (Workers' Thought), which began to appear in Petersburg in the latter months of 1897.* Shortly afterwards it was echoed in the emigration by S. N. Prokopovich and his wife Kuskova, who had recently arrived in Switzerland. At first quite close to Plekhanov and Axelrod,[6] the Prokopoviches early in 1898 brought under critical scrutiny a number of fundamental propositions of Russian Social Democracy that had never been questioned before. Until this time, the differences between the Group and the Union related to organizational rather than ideological matters. Now some of the members of the Union came under the influence of Prokopovich and his wife and for the first time confronted the founders of Russian Social Democracy with an ideological opposition. A rather highhanded attempt by Plekhanov to oust the troublesome pair from the Union failed of its aim and instead brought about a closing of ranks against the veterans. Thinking to bring the weight of the Petersburg League into the scales on their side, the Group was staggered to learn that *Rabochaia mysl'* had become the official organ of the League. With the arrest successively of Lenin, Martov, and Potresov, that organization had passed

* It was published at different times in Petersburg, Berlin, and Warsaw.

from the control of faithful adherents of the Group to the Economist opposition. Emphasizing the seriousness of the cleavage in Russian Social Democracy, the League and, a little later, the Union refused to endorse the RSDLP Manifesto which designated the winning of political liberty the first task of the Russian labor movement.

With dramatic swiftness, the dominance of the Group and its position had been thoroughly undercut. Just as the movement was getting on its feet, it appeared to be repudiating the men who had founded it. This unexpected turn was unspeakably painful for Plekhanov and Axelrod. The full magnitude of the disaster can be grasped only if it is recalled that all this happened in 1898, the year that Bernstein's heresy emerged upon the international socialist scene. Bitter though the cup was, the pioneer Marxists were obliged to drink it. When it became clear at a congress of the Union in November 1898 that they were heavily outnumbered, there was no alternative but to resign their editorial role in the Union. Decisions were taken to terminate the publication of *Rabotnik* and to issue in its stead a new paper, *Rabochee delo* (The Workers' Cause). The editors of the new organ, B. N. Krichevsky, V. P. Ivan'shin, and Teplova, imparted to it a moderate Economist orientation.* Perhaps to prevent themselves from being completely isolated, the members of the Group remained associated with the Union. But in the next year or so, the situation grew worse rather than better. The Union people had in their hands all the threads connecting the emigration to Social Democratic groups in Russia, and they utilized these to spread far and wide an account of the differences in the emigration exceedingly unfavorable to their adversaries. Not only had the former pilots of the movement been forced to surrender the helm, but it appeared that they were being given no chance of recovering it.

In the months following the Union congress, there was no letup in the sniping and intrigues. Neither side missed an opportunity to discredit the other or to increase its own numbers and power at the expense of the other. In these varied maneuvers, the Group generally came off second best. This discouraging situation brought on in the internal relations of the Group a crisis that threatened to end its life.[7] The wall of hostility surrounding the initiators of Russian Marxism, and their inability either to breach it or to bring against it significant countervailing forces, brought a severe crack in morale. For years, Axelrod had been rankled by the necessity of working with people whom he considered beneath contempt. He felt degraded by the tedium and sordidness of it all, and again and again in his letters expressed his utter revulsion and weariness. It was "intellectually killing" for him; he felt "nauseated" at the thought of his relations with the

---

* The editors evidently were among those in the Union who refused to subscribe to the RSDLP Manifesto. *Perepiska Plekhanova i Aksel'roda*, II, 86.

Union people; he was in the grip of a "moral stupor."[8] In May 1898, when convulsions in southern Europe commanded attention, he wrote angrily: "In Italy a revolutionary situation, in Spain almost one, in Russia a famine unprecedented in scope, etc., and with what are the Russian Social Democrats busy? With nonsense only! Cretins! To break with them—there seems to be no other way out."[9]

Axelrod had canvassed the idea of a break as early as 1896 and more than once thereafter. In the spring of 1899 he broached the matter more insistently than ever. Zasulich concurred. With her greater tolerance of the younger people, she could see reason for giving them their head. If it served no other purpose, the experience thus given the insurgents might teach them that they did, after all, need the guidance of their more seasoned elders. In any case, she refused to play the role of "enemy within" in the Union. Meanwhile, having divested itself of editorial duties for the Union, the Group had no publishing plans of its own. In April, Axelrod asked whether the Group had any *raison d'être* at all. "Vera says of herself: 'I am sick and under present circumstances cannot take an active part in any group whatsoever.' As for me, I am too little productive in a literary way. And you are engaged in other affairs."[10] Thus laconically he expressed his dissatisfaction with Plekhanov for having neglected to devote three or four months in 1898, as Axelrod had suggested, to literary endeavors which might help to restore the falling prestige of the Group. Now, if it were not "resurrected" for some worthy purpose, he was prepared to countenance its "liquidation" and to cede the leadership of the movement to the Union.

Plekhanov replied in a coldly businesslike manner. On the matter of continued association with the Union, he declared: "I shall not leave the Union so long as I am not driven out or so long as I have not driven out my enemies." Rather than surrender, he proposed to fight for the overturn of the existing balance of power. He underlined his determination with a cutting remark: "If you wish to participate in the present struggle—fine. If not, I alone will follow the road along which my duty as a revolutionary takes me."[11] The hurt he inflicted caused Axelrod to cry out against his "surprisingly incorrigible relation toward our right and freedom to speak our minds"[12]—thus voicing also his chagrin at Plekhanov's summary intervention in Group-Union quarrels on several occasions without consulting his colleagues. Although personal relations momentarily suffered, the questions Axelrod posed proved a stimulus to the resurrection of the Group rather than its liquidation. For, in his reply, Plekhanov laid out a plan of action which satisfied Axelrod that the Group still had an important function to perform. A "categorical imperative" commanded it to fight against Bernsteinism, which, hydra-like, had raised its head in many sectors of the Russian movement.

In view of Plekhanov's commitment to theoretical purity, it is surprising that he was so slow to take up arms against the opposition. Preoccupied during 1898 with the campaign against Bernstein in the German movement, he had been in some measure detached from the vicissitudes of Russian Social Democracy. At the least, he seems to have underestimated the seriousness of the developing opposition, and to have viewed the interminable sparring in the Union as a lot of meaningless sound and fury. Where he recognized a real ideological challenge, as in the case of Prokopovich, he was ready to act, and he proposed to unleash Axelrod against the "upstart."[13] But when Prokopovich failed to publish his manuscript article inveighing against the Group, which had circulated in the emigration, Axelrod was deprived of a target. As for *Rabochaia mysl'* and the Petersburg League, Plekhanov may have seen their deviation as a passing phase of no great moment. Or perhaps he considered it inappropriate to step in, fearing that it might be thought impertinent and dictatorial for him to call to order those who were in the vanguard of the fighting forces.

However, the outcome of the congress and subsequent developments made it obvious that the situation was serious. The opposition in the Union had overpowered the Group. In his full-length statement of the Revisionist case in early 1899, Bernstein himself had taunted Plekhanov with the claim that the majority of the Russian Social Democrats stood closer to him than to his assailant. The prominent legal Marxists Struve, Bulgakov, and Berdiaev, and the legal Marxist periodical *Nachalo* had openly aligned themselves with Revisionism. From Potresov (in exile) came word of the alarming situation in the Petersburg organization, the dominant forces of which aimed at the "utopia" of a functioning "trade unionism under absolutism." By way of corrective action, he called upon the Group to clean out "the Augean stable of Russian Social Democracy."[14] Axelrod's outburst swept aside the last vestiges of hesitancy and crystallized Plekhanov's decision to attack.

As for the ground on which he chose to fight, it has been argued that, for tactical reasons, he strove to tar with the brush of Revisionism an opposition actually composed of quite diverse elements. There is less substance to this charge than would appear at first glance. Certainly evidence existed of the penetration of Bernstein's influence into the Russian movement. Nor was it restricted to the legal Marxists who became the spokesmen for Revisionism in Russia. Not only Prokopovich but also Ivan'shin, now one of the editors of *Rabochee delo,* had declared to Zasulich his solidarity with Bernstein.[15] The opposition also included the Economists of one shade or another. For a while, Plekhanov saw no close connection between the Revisionist controversy and the conflict within Russian Social Democracy. He said as much by way of refuting Bernstein's taunt.[16] Not long after, however, he changed his opinion and chose to subsume Economism as a variety of Revisionism. Nonetheless, it does not follow that this change of attitude was made simply for tactical reasons. Indeed, Plekhanov went on to establish a persuasive case for the kinship of Economism to Revisionism.

Once having decided to counterattack, the Group began to mobilize. The editors of *Rabochee delo* furnished a target by publishing in the spring of 1899 an article criticizing Axelrod's prefatory remarks to a pamphlet by Lenin which the Group had recently issued. They denied Axelrod's assertion that some of the younger comrades unfortunately did not share Lenin's orthodox views as to the tasks of Russian Social Democracy. Exclaiming "this effrontery deserves punishment," Plekhanov in May proposed that Axelrod submit an open letter to the newspaper citing chapter and verse on the opposition to ideological orthodoxy.[17] (The plan he sketched foreshadowed his own *Vademecum,* issued in the spring of 1900, with which he sought to demolish the opposition.) His fighting spirit in the ascendant, he was prepared to vent his rage even though it might lead to a break. In the months following, his bellicosity was kept at high pitch by the "unforgivable" behavior of the editors of *Rabochee delo* on the one hand, and on the other by the unanticipated support thrown to the Group from Russia.

The latter came in the form of a "Protest" of seventeen Social Democratic exiles in Siberia against the so-called "Credo." Jotted down by Kuskova, the wife of Prokopovich, with no thought of publication, the "Credo" was seized upon by the author of the "Protest" as the excuse for a blast at deviations from orthodoxy in general. The author was Lenin, who was still in exile in Siberia. While working on his big volume, *The Development of Capitalism in Russia,* he managed to keep himself informed of the fortunes of the movement, following with special attention the activities of Plekhanov, for him the lodestar of Russian Social Democracy. He received and "read and re-read with real pleasure" Plekhanov's *Beiträge zur Geschichte des Materialismus.* He took an avid interest in Plekhanov's campaign against Revisionism, declaring himself on "the same side as the Monist," who was "perfectly right in pronouncing Neo-Kantianism to be a reactionary theory of the reactionary bourgeoisie and in revolting against Bernstein." It is not surprising that Lenin was "greatly oppressed" to learn of the strife within the RSDU and the "exit" of Plekhanov and his friends from it.[18] Even before being sent to Siberia he had glimpsed the beginnings of Economism and was now dismayed to find that it had apparently triumphed over the Group.

In so far as Lenin was at all critical of his mentor, it was because of Plekhanov's failure to strike back. He longed to throw his weight into the balance on the side of the pioneer Marxists and orthodoxy, and to spur them to counterattack. The article he smuggled to the Group on "The

Tasks of the Russian Social Democrats" constituted support to the be-leaguered orthodox. And Potresov's plea to the Group to raise its voice may have been inspired by Lenin. The opportunity for a dramatic move came when a copy of the "Credo" fell into Lenin's hands. He wrote a smashing rebuttal to its amalgam of Revisionist and Economist doctrines, secured the approving signatures of sixteen other Social Democratic exiles, and forwarded the whole for publication in Switzerland. Thus, from far-off Siberia, the dynamic revolutionist launched the first direct attack upon Economism, spurring Plekhanov and Axelrod to proceed with their own war plans.

The pioneer Marxists, deeply distrustful of two of the three editors of *Rabochee delo,* were ready to cry out at the slightest hint of duplicity. After all, had not Ivan'shin spoken approvingly of Bernstein? Had he not refused to subscribe to the Manifesto of the First Party Congress? As for Krichevsky, he had been closely associated with Iogiches in one of the earlier oppositions to the Group. To Engels, Plekhanov had conveyed the unflattering opinion that Krichevsky was "one of those Talmudists of the newest socialism who succeeds in grasping its *letter* but never its *spirit.* He is the kind of 'true' socialist who is agitated by anything that in the slightest contradicts the formulas impressed upon his memory."[19] The actions of the two editors confirmed the Group's suspicions of them. After promising to publish Axelrod's critical Open Letter, the editors delayed publication interminably, evoking Plekhanov's remark that he and his comrade were being led by the nose.* Lenin had sent a copy of the "Pro-test" to the editors of *Rabochee delo,* as well as to the Group. The editors not only stole a march on the older men by publishing it first; they also appended to it a disparaging editorial comment that once again infuriated Plekhanov and Axelrod.[20]

With access to the public under the control of the enemy, Plekhanov became more determined than ever either to wrest control for the Group or to break with the Union in order to win freedom for an all-out attack. Having little hope of achieving the former, he quietly prepared a bomb-shell for his adversaries. He also asked Axelrod to draw up an announce-ment of the resumption of publication by the Emancipation of Labor Group. The pioneer Marxist organization, Plekhanov exclaimed, "must come out once again more militant, more brilliant than ever."[21] Laying themselves open to charges of Machiavellianism, they concealed their in-tentions and sought in the meantime to secure whatever advantages they

---

* *Perepiska Plekhanova i Aksel'roda,* II, 110. The editors later contended that Axelrod's letter never reached them. *Otvet redaktsii "Rabochego dela" na "Pis'mo" P. Aksel'roda i "Vademecum" G. Plekhanova,* p. 1.

might from their continued association with the Union. The bombshell, Plekhanov's *Vademecum,* was thrown into the camp of the unsuspecting enemy in March 1900. In the following month, at a stormy Second Congress, the Group severed its last remaining ties with the Union. Just as, seventeen years before, Plekhanov, Axelrod, and Zasulich had broken violently with Narodnaia Volia in order to propagate a new revolutionary outlook, now they broke with what was ostensibly the majority of their own Social Democratic movement in order to defend the fundamental line they had earlier laid down. Whatever grief Plekhanov and Axelrod may have felt about the schism was offset by the relish with which they returned to ideological combat, the task closest to their hearts. No doubt they also anticipated with pleasure the impaling of the "dear comrades" who, they thought, had in countless ways demeaned and harassed them.

The onset of Economism was an almost inevitable result of the changing character and composition of Russian Social Democracy. In the space of a few years, it was transformed from an insignificant sect, a mere claque of a few intellectuals, into a dynamic movement that embraced an important segment of the intelligentsia and had wide and steady contact with the workers. The latter factor was crucial. As long as the Marxist intelligentsia restricted themselves to circle work, their ideas concerning the needs of the movement and its proper course went unchallenged. Once they plunged into agitational activity, they discovered a whole new dimension of social thought and aspiration. Having assumed that the workers would readily fall in with their schemes for the liberation of labor, the Social Democrats found that the proletarians had predilections of their own. They bridled at doing the bidding of the intellectuals, and sought to take charge themselves, in order to steer the labor movement on a course more compatible with their own sense of needs. Thus agitational activity, while greatly expanding Social Democracy, also altered its composition and engendered a tension of a kind between its intelligentsia and worker components.

In *On Agitation* the agitators had been urged to base their appeals upon the keenly felt needs of the workers. Specifically, economic grievances had been pointed out as the issues to which the workers would most readily respond. In practice, such agitation proved strikingly successful. Success bore with it new difficulties, however, owing to conflicting views on the meaning and significance of the economic struggle. To the workers, economic struggle, since it gave promise of better wages, shorter hours, and other material benefits, possessed a high value in and of itself. Such a victory as that which came out of the great Petersburg strike of 1896 persuaded them they had hit upon an effective means to better their conditions. In short, they wished to work for amelioration, and, to that end, favored a sort of trade unionism. This preoccupation went together with an indifference to political struggle. Most of the workers saw no relation between the fight for material welfare and a war against the government, which would involve great risks and yet appeared to hold out few if any tangible rewards. They could not see how the displacement of the Tsar by a government beholden to the "bosses" who exploited them could possibly enhance their own welfare. Characteristically, according to one report, an issue of *Rabochaia mysl'* concerned with the details of the labor struggle was met with enthusiasm, while copies of the politically oriented Manifesto of the RSDLP Congress were indignantly flung out of the factory windows.[22] The workers balked at being led by members of the intelligentsia who valued the economic struggle less for itself than as a springboard for a political revolution.

Confronted with a worker psychology of this kind, a majority of the Social Democratic intelligentsia capitulated. In taking the existing level of worker consciousness as the touchstone, they demonstrated their willingness to yield to the workers themselves the ultimate determination of the direction of the movement. The relationship which resulted mirrored the altered composition of Russian Social Democracy, with the working class increasingly dominant and the intelligentsia less and less in control. The latter, instead of trying to direct the movement into channels chosen on the basis of Marxian theory, allowed themselves to be guided by the spontaneously arising demands of proletarian consciousness. Instead of serving as the general staff of a revolutionary army the troops of which were furnished by the labor movement, the intelligentsia would act as an adjutant or administrative auxiliary to the labor movement.

The consent of the intelligentsia to limit its influence in the movement was a result of several circumstances. The arrest of Lenin, Martov, and Potresov meant the loss of an authoritative group of Social Democrats who were strongly committed to the political orientation. With their departure, younger and less experienced persons, whose revolutionary apprenticeship had predisposed them in favor of such a current as Economism, were advanced into positions of leadership. They had obtained their baptism of fire in the agitations among the factory workers which succeeded both in securing gains for the workers and in extending the influence of the movement. Living experience with the working class made a greater impact upon their thinking than abstract theory. They were content to "learn from life," to take their cues from the workers, who, after all, were totally immersed in the relationships peculiar to capitalism. What could be more reasonable, they thought, than to yield control of the labor movement to the workers themselves? Relatively innocent in the area of theory, they did not consider their conduct a serious deviation from Social Democratic orthodoxy. On the contrary, how could a tactic be faulty when it accorded with the aspirations of the workers and at the same time vastly expanded the scope of the movement? Without a doubt, these people were unaware of all the implications of their tactical line. It remained for a third rank of persons—over and beyond the workers and the intelligentsia-agitators—to dot the i's and cross the t's, to generalize the tactics of Economism into theories more or less sharply at variance with orthodox Marxism.

The extreme form of Economism, variously expressed by Prokopovich, Kuskova, and *Rabochaia mysl'*, viewed political struggle as a pet scheme of the socialist intelligentsia that had to be fought. It corresponded, they thought, neither to actual wishes of the workers nor to their true needs, for the overthrow of absolutism would leave their situation basically unchanged. If they wished, the socialist intelligentsia might assist the liberal opposition to the government, but the designation of the fight for political liberty as the first task of the labor movement represented nothing more or less than an "arbitrary" importation from abroad. Rather than be diverted by the intelligentsia from the economic struggle that effectively advanced their interests, the proletariat would fare much better if it were guided by the slogan, "The workers for the workers." A more moderate variety of Economism was elaborated in articles of *Rabochee delo*, which did not deny the value of political freedom for the workers. According to this view, the posing of political aims was senseless until such time as the workers, through their own experience, had arrived at political consciousness. Until the proletariat itself felt the need of political liberty, the Social Democrats ought to concern themselves chiefly with massing the workers into strong labor organizations which would struggle to secure improvements in their conditions.*

---

* In *The Communist Party of the Soviet Union*, Chapter 1, Leonard Schapiro sees the RSDU giving little or no support to Revisionism and Economism and, in general, discounts their significance in the Russian movement. He speaks of Kuskova's "Credo" as "the first, if not the only documentary evidence of the existence of 'economism' as a doctrine." Economism, he continues, "was largely an invention, as far as *Rabochee delo* was concerned," and Plekhanov unjustly attributed to that publication the views of Prokopovich and Kuskova. It is difficult to see how these contentions can be squared with the evidence of sympathy for Prokopovich in the Union and the refusal of the RSDU to support the RSDLP Manifesto. Besides, in their private letters, where they would have had no reason to dissemble, not only Plekhanov and Axelrod but also Zasulich repeatedly allude to new revelations concerning the ideological deviations of the "young comrades" (*Gruppa*, VI, 194, 213, 226; *Perepiska Plekhanova i Aksel'roda*, I, 204, and II, 86). On the other hand, the Program of *Rabochee delo*, as well as its solidarity with the "Protest" of the seventeen Social Democratic exiles in their condemnation of the "Credo," seems to corroborate Schapiro's position. The apparent contradiction may be resolved when the data are seen in the time dimension. The year 1898 was probably the high-water mark of Revisionist-Economist influence in the Union. In the next year or two it gradually receded, as is evident in the line of *Ra-*

Plekhanov's offensive against Economism overflowed with rancor expressive of the chagrin and frustration he felt at the defeats inflicted upon the Group by people he despised. In the Introduction to the *Vademecum*, he lamented, "I never thought that I should be fated to live through such shame!"[23] The division of the movement he had founded into factions that dissipated their energy in internecine strife outraged him. Soon, he commented bitterly, one would have only to meet two Social Democrats to find three parties.[24] The cat-and-mouse game he believed his opponents in the RSDU were playing further infuriated him. In spite of all the evidence to the contrary, including their own complicity, they denied the existence of an Economist tendency in Russian Social Democracy. Whatever the provocation, real or fancied, Plekhanov went to shocking lengths against his adversaries, so much so that many who agreed with his views had grave misgivings about his attack. With highly questionable taste, he published in the *Vademecum* private letters not addressed to him which he thought would serve his purposes. Certain of his foes he denominated "political castrates"; others he dismissed as persons who had not yet emerged from their diapers when he was already an established revolutionist.[25] His case also lost some of its force by virtue of the fact that Prokopovich and Kuskova, against whom a fair share of it was directed, had by then withdrawn from the RSDU.

As may be deduced from the arguments of principle he pressed against his opponents, Plekhanov's indignation stemmed above all from the fear that the Economists threatened to nullify everything he had labored for since he embraced Marxism. In an article entitled "Once More Socialism and Political Struggle,"[26] he recognized that the current controversy paralleled an earlier one. The Narodniks—and Plekhanov himself so long as he was one of them—regarded economic agitation as the sole means of advancing socialism, and shunned politics as an activity irrelevant to that end. That one-sidedness, as well as the opposite error which the Narodovoltsi committed, Plekhanov had "corrected" by showing the inseparability of socialism and political struggle. The Economists prided themselves upon

---

bochee delo as well as in the severance of relations between Prokopovich and the Union. The differences between the Group and the Union were not, as the latter's spokesmen insisted in their reply to Plekhanov's *Vademecum*, solely organizational and practical. But the reply was correct, in a sense, in charging Plekhanov with bringing the ideological issue before the public two years too late. (See *Otvet redaktsii "Rabochego dela" na "Pis'mo" P. Aksel'roda i "Vademecum" G. Plekhanova*, pp. 49–50, 68). A residual difference of no little consequence to the Group was *Rabochee delo*'s refusal to view the ideological deviations of *Rabochaia mysl'* and the "Credo" as the serious threat to the movement the older men made them out. (*Otvet*, pp. 47–48). To Plekhanov, this refusal no doubt seemed damning evidence of disregard for the importance of theory. It also did not reckon with the gains Economism had made in the Russian labor movement.

being the most genuine spokesmen for working-class interests, but they were unmindful of the fundamental truth that "every class struggle is a political struggle." Ironically enough, in the guise of "perfecting" and "advancing" the strategy of the working-class movement, they reverted to that Narodnik error the correction of which constituted one of the major services of Russian Marxism to the revolutionary movement. Yet they dared to call themselves Social Democrats!

Plekhanov professed to believe that, in spite of the Economists, sooner or later the workers would be drawn into political struggle; yet to the extent that Economist ideas pervaded the proletarian milieu, that political activity would be hampered from achieving its proper ends. At issue was another question of central concern to Plekhanov from the moment of his conversion to Marxism—the matter of ideological leadership of the proletariat. Put differently, it was the question of whether the Russian labor movement would follow in detail the example of its Western counterparts or would profit from their experience. Years before, he had posed the alternatives with great trenchancy: "Will the workers fight against absolutism as the blind tools of the liberals, or is their struggle destined to be the first political step of an independent labor party?" Plekhanov had deemed it the mission of Russian Social Democracy to see that the workers fought for political liberty as a self-conscious and self-interested force, as their brothers in the West had not. But if the Economist tendency were to prevail, then the question would be resolved in the opposite sense: in the absence of Social Democratic political leadership, the workers would fight as "blind tools of the liberals," and would be cheated of their just rewards. Furthermore, they would be ill-prepared for the defense of their interests under the new bourgeois-constitutional regime. Those who failed to learn the lessons implicit in the history of the European labor movements would be doomed to repeat their mistakes.

Underlying these familiar arguments was another, which formed the bedrock of Plekhanov's case against the Economists. They were oblivious to the pre-eminent responsibility of the Social Democrats—the promotion of the class consciousness of the proletariat. Not only was a high degree of class consciousness indispensable for the attainment of socialism, but its level among the workers at any given moment largely determined whether they could carry out whatever tasks lay before them. The class-conscious worker understood the implications of his struggle with his own employer, knowing it to be but part of a general war he and his fellow-workers were bound to wage against capital. He nursed no illusions as to the possibility of winning an acceptable level of welfare and status within the framework of bourgeois society, and therefore he was deeply committed to a future socialist revolution. He had learned that the political system in innumerable ways buttressed and sustained the existing social order; that his emancipation was inseparable from the conquest of political liberty; and that the overthrow of absolutism and the winning of political liberty would immensely facilitate both the defense of his immediate interests and his final liberation. In short, the worker who had reached a high level of class consciousness was a Social Democrat.

Early in his Marxian career, Plekhanov had seen as the greatest potential dangers to the timely growth of worker class consciousness "the political reaction of state socialism" and "the economic charlatanism of the bourgeoisie." The first represented a paternalistic state policy which offered the workers a crust of bread in return for their renunciation of political aspirations; the second, the deceitful tactics of the bourgeoisie, who sought to use the workers as pawns in the struggle for political liberty while concealing the existence of conflicting class (economic) interests. But now, to Plekhanov's consternation, danger threatened from an entirely unexpected quarter. Within the socialist movement itself, a faction was striving for supremacy which in every sense but one tended to stifle rather than promote the class consciousness of the proletariat. In so far as the Economist helped to arouse in backward workers of a given factory an active resentment against their exploitation and got them to join in organized measures of defense, he made a positive contribution. Beyond that, however, the Economist emphasis had the effect of arresting the growth of worker class consciousness.

Typically, the Economist-dominated organizations were local in character, concerned with the problems of the workers of a single factory or, at the most, the factories of a single town. With their energies focused upon the day-to-day fight for the betterment of the workers' conditions, the Economists ignored the opportunities of conveying to the workers any awareness of the larger perspectives of the movement. As early as the summer of 1897, Plekhanov identified "the predominance of a narrow group spirit," to the detriment of the general, class, point of view, as "one of the greatest inadequacies of our contemporary Social Democratic movement."[27] Not only the "parochialism" but also the "one-sidedness" of the Economists prevented the growth of class consciousness and rationality among the workers. "We rebel," wrote Plekhanov, "not against *agitation* on an economic basis, but against those agitators who do not know how to take advantage of economic clashes of the workers with the entrepreneurs for the development of the political consciousness of the workers."[28] A proletariat blind to the power of political weapons was still at a primitive level, and it would pay dearly for its incapacity to defend its own interests. Needless to say, Plekhanov blamed the Economists for their "shortsightedness" as well—for forgetting the ultimate end in their concern with immediate tasks.

It cannot be overemphasized that Plekhanov invariably judged the appropriateness of Social Democratic tactics by the degree to which they brought about class consciousness in the proletariat. In his view, the Economists not merely failed in this obligation—they did not even recognize it as one. Instead they eagerly sought to determine what the aspirations of the workers were and to work for their realization. They were content to take the worker as they found him, to operate in terms of his own definition of his interests, no matter how elementary, instead of trying to educate him to his "true" interests, of which he was not yet aware. The responsibility of the Social Democrat consisted precisely in bringing the worker to consciousness of his "true" interests. But the Economists, rather than acting as teachers and guides, chose instead to gaze in awe upon the posterior of the proletarian. So far as Plekhanov was concerned, in failing to exploit the plentiful opportunities for extending the horizons of the workers, the Economists abdicated their responsibility as Social Democrats.

In fact, Plekhanov denounced the whole tendency of Economism as tantamount to the abandonment of Social Democracy and the "scientific socialism" upon which it was based. In what, after all, did the "science" of Marxian socialism consist? Plekhanov would have answered unhesitatingly: "In the general laws of social development deduced from study of the history of society, the projection of which proves the inevitability of socialism." Knowledge of these laws and, with that, the power to understand truly the phenomena of contemporary society and the tendency of its development were obtained through mastery of theory. And the intelligentsia were the bearers of theory to the working-class movement. Yet the Economists insisted that the intelligentsia renounce the role of teacher and guide in order to become a mere auxiliary of the labor movement. If the socialist intelligentsia heeded this advice, it would mean the end of Social Democracy. Theory, distilled from historical experience, marked out the course of advance of the labor movement. Theory pointed up the socialist direction of historical movement; and considerations of theory compelled the Social Democrats everywhere and always to strive for proletarian consciousness, without which socialism could not be realized. It was no mere coincidence that those who ignored and denigrated theory committed such egregious errors.

While acknowledging a difference between extreme and moderate Economism, Plekhanov saw little distinction between their practical effects. The first, in blandly writing off political struggle and declining to concern itself with the ultimate end of the movement, was left with nothing more than trade unionism. The second counted upon the gradual and organic development of political and socialist consciousness among the workers, as they became more mature and accumulated greater experience. But, although he did not hammer the point home as forcefully as did Lenin somewhat later, Plekhanov had at least some latent reservations about the likelihood of the proletariat's being able to achieve socialist consciousness without the aid of the socialist intelligentsia. From the beginning of his Marxian career, he had seen the intelligentsia as an indispensable link in the chain of conditions essential for socialism. Nor was its role restricted to instigating the workers to local struggles, with the rest following "naturally." In consequence of his struggle with Revisionism, the role of the intelligentsia in the socialist movement had become magnified in his mind. Plekhanov was inflexible in his stand against the Economists because at the very time when he, more than ever, saw the need for vigilant Social Democratic leadership to prevent the spread of opportunism in the labor movement, they appeared to want to dispense with it.

Did not the English case demonstrate that in the absence of socialist leadership the proletariat would not go beyond the opportunism of trade unionism? What reason was there to believe that the Russian workers would do otherwise? Of course, he had in mind the German situation as well. Conceding that Economism might have been forgivable as an infantile phase of the movement, through which it would quickly pass, he indicated that no forbearance could be shown once the Economists endeavored to ground their orientation in theoretical concepts drawn from Revisionism.[29] Here he was thinking of the sympathy that Prokopovich, Ivan'shin, and others had expressed for Bernstein's outlook. But he was surely impressed even more by the apparent parallelism of views of the two "heresies," whether direct borrowing could be proved or not. Did not both criticize or depart from the prescriptions of Marx in various ways? Did not both, in effect, set aside the ultimate end of the movement for the sake of absorption in "immediate tasks"? Did not both pander to the opportunistic instincts of the proletarians instead of working to counteract them with the power of Social Democratic leadership guided by theory? Wherever he turned, Plekhanov saw a creeping paralysis affecting the labor movements of Europe. He faced what seemed to be a concerted action aimed at robbing Social Democracy of its vital force. In retrospect, even the dismal record of relations between the Group and the Union took on a new meaning. Did not what had long appeared to be trivial differences in fact mask serious ideological divergences which came into the open only later? The indifference of the younger elements to theory; their partiality to practical organizational activity; their nagging insistence upon an agitational literature for workers, as though that were the sum and substance of the movement; and their hostility to the rigorously orthodox founders of Russian Marxism—did not all this bear the earmarks of Economism, of bureaucratic trade unionism, of opposition to genuine Social Democracy?

Finally, Plekhanov feared that the practical results of a victory of Economism would be similar in kind to, and as deplorable as, the triumph of Revisionism. The logic of Bernstein's position led him to advocate the commitment of the German party to gradualism and reform; and should Economism gain the upper hand in the Russian labor movement, it would mean the abandonment of revolution. From this side, too, it would signify the demise of Social Democracy, for, as Plekhanov put it, "Anti-revolutionary Social Democracy is as unthinkable as a wet flame or dry water."[30] Economism must be fought relentlessly because *de facto* it constituted an enemy both of the true interests of the working class and of Russian progress in general, which depended upon the revolutionary overthrow of tsarism.

The significance and implications of the controversy over Economism were not entirely clear to the principals involved. As in his relation to Revisionism, Plekhanov did not give due weight to the social circumstances which accounted for the rise of Economism. He tended to lay the blame primarily upon the perversity of the intelligentsia while sparing the proletariat, an approach which left out of account the impact of proletarian pressures upon the socialist intelligentsia in the field. In the one case as in the other, it was easier for him to demand conduct rigorously in accord with doctrine than for those he criticized to conform to his demands. Living in exile, out of touch with the Russian labor movement, he could easily disregard the pressures exerted against the orthodoxy he made it his business to uphold. Purity is more easily preserved in a vacuum than in the rough and tumble of life.

Plekhanov also overestimated the possibility that Economism could really succeed in the Russian setting. In view of the public embrace that the extreme Economists conferred upon Bernstein, he could hardly have been tender with them. But in lumping them and the moderate Economists together, and in dealing with the lot most immoderately, he damaged his own cause. The stand he took, especially in the *Vademecum,* could only deepen the organizational split, and in the bargain might drive the extremists and the moderates together. Given Russian conditions, there existed little likelihood that the tactics of the moderate Economists could do other than spill over presently into political struggle. Something approximating to trade unions under absolutism was indeed a utopia. Plekhanov well knew that the dedicated endeavors of the Economists in behalf of the economic welfare of the workers involved both them and the workers in illegal activity. The government could not look on impassively as illegal organizations and activities took shape, and continually intervened to curb and smash them. This kind of thing gave every reason to expect the "natural" development of political consciousness among the workers that the moderates envisaged.

In his polemic, Plekhanov failed to distinguish adequately between political consciousness and socialist consciousness. Yet the most meaningful difference between him and the Economists would seem to lie here. The tactics of the Economists almost inevitably would lead to the awakening of the workers to political consciousness; but Plekhanov would not be content with that. In his view, it was not enough that the workers should merely become involved in the struggle for political liberty. Although admitting that that struggle and the drive for socialism necessarily were separated in time by an extended interval, he insisted on linking them together in his grand strategy. His link between the two was the never ending effort to arouse, maintain, and heighten the class consciousness of the proletariat. The process must begin even as the struggle against absolutism began, and it must continue without relaxation up through the socialist revolution. Economism had the effect of severing the relationship between the two revolutions. Some of the Economists were willing to take the winning of political liberty into their range of vision. But they considered fanciful the shaping of current tactics with reference to a far-off ideal. On the whole, they were inclined to lean toward the maxim: Sufficient to the day is the evil thereof.

If the Economists had triumphed, the chances of liberal leadership in the struggle against absolutism—which Plekhanov warned against—might have been strengthened. The outcome might have approximated to something like the so-called bourgeois revolutions in the West, with the attendant implications which Plekhanov strove so hard to avoid. Whatever faults such an eventuality might have had from Plekhanov's point of view, it would have had the merit of sweeping aside the irreconcilable contradictions that arose in his own revolutionary prognosis from his attempt to connect organically the struggle for political liberty with the long-range movement toward socialism. Of all this he had no inkling.

In reaction to the apparent willingness of the Economists to forgo the role of tutor to the working class, Plekhanov went to extremes in overemphasizing the importance of Social Democratic leadership in the labor movement. As events turned out, Economism was overcome, but that did not mean that Plekhanov's brand of orthodoxy triumphed. Just as the "correction" of the "one-sidedness" of *kruzhkovshchina* (an excess of theoretical propaganda) led to an opposite "one-sidedness" in Economism, so, on another plane, reaction to the "one-sidedness" of Economism (the curtailment of the role of Social Democratic leadership) led to a new one-sidedness which exaggerated such leadership. All unwittingly, Plekhanov helped to pave the way for the ascendancy of Lenin.

12

IN HARNESS WITH LENIN

ON THE THRESHOLD OF the twentieth century, the Marxian movement stood in danger of losing the momentum it had gained in the last half of the nineties. The attempt of the 1898 Congress to bring about a united party had no sequel in the next few years. Energies that might have been employed to enlarge Social Democratic influence in the labor movement were diverted into ideological struggles between factions of the intelligentsia. The civil war within the Social Democratic movement disqualified it from exploiting to the full the increasingly widespread manifestations of discontent in Russia. Another circumstance rendered the situation even more alarming. The Social Democrats, who had had the field largely to themselves in the preceding several years, now were challenged by strong liberal and socialist revolutionary contenders.

The response of Russian Social Democracy to the challenge was embodied in *Iskra-Zaria,* an enterprise around which centered the main developments in the movement between 1900 and the outbreak of the Revolution of 1905. *Iskra** represented a remarkable effort by a handful of self-selected intellectuals to give ideological leadership and organizational coherence to the Russian labor movement. Although Plekhanov and his long-time associates were deeply involved in this enterprise, it is doubtful that they could have initiated and carried it through on their own. Their fortunes for some time had been bound up with those of the talented group of younger Marxists who emerged in Russia in the mid-nineties. It was Lenin, Martov, Potresov, and Struve who got the movement off the ground in Russia. They had made it possible for the pioneer Marxists, whose influence had formerly been indirect and sporadic, to make a more palpable impact.

* *Iskra* will be used frequently hereafter as shorthand for the *Iskra-Zaria* enterprise.

If the breakthrough of the mid-nineties owed much to the successful collaboration between the younger men in the field and their mentors in the emigration, the ideological crisis of the succeeding years is explicable in part at least by the interruption of that cooperation. The arrest of Lenin, Martov, and Potresov removed the politically oriented leadership and enabled the Economists to achieve dominance. Struve, meanwhile, drew away from revolutionary Marxism to Revisionism. Having lost their main supporters in Russia, the Osvobozhdentsi suffered a long series of defeats and rebuffs. Their rally for a counterattack, when it finally came, clearly owed something to the promptings and initiatives of Lenin, Potresov, and Martov (the latter was among those signing Lenin's "Protest"). The release of the three from exile almost coincided with the publication of Plekhanov's *Vademecum.* Shortly, they and the pioneer Marxists were to be united as never before in the *Iskra-Zaria* enterprise. Their renewed collaboration once again provided a powerful impetus to the Social Democratic movement.

Even in Siberia, Lenin had followed the ideological struggle with intense interest. To Martov and Potresov, whose identity of viewpoint with his own became apparent in their exchanges of letters, he proposed a "triple alliance" "for struggle with Revisionism and Economism." Lenin urged that "this alliance must before all else unite forces with the Emancipation of Labor Group."[1] In an article he prepared for an underground newspaper, he outlined his plan.[2] As an effective first step toward the realization of the ambitious goals he sketched, Lenin called for the creation of a Social Democratic periodical, which, through an unrelenting campaign against Economism, could win the field for Marxian orthodoxy. With the ideological basis firmly established, it would become possible to bring the dispersed organizations of Social Democracy together into a united party. Here, in germ, was the organizational scheme behind the newspaper *Iskra* (The Spark). It involved the merger of the *troika* (Lenin, Martov, and Potresov) with the Emancipation of Labor Group for an all-Russian Social Democratic newspaper dedicated to the extirpation of Economism and to organizational preparation for the uniting of the party.

Before this plan was advanced much beyond the drafting board, *The Spark* was almost extinguished in an explosive encounter between Plekhanov and Lenin in late August 1900. Lenin's absorbing account of this episode, written almost immediately after it occurred, but published only posthumously, has attracted considerable attention.[3] Without studying it in conjunction with developments that preceded and followed it, however, one cannot grasp its real significance. Most writers, taking Lenin's remarks more or less uncritically, have failed to see that the quarrel was not so much a personal one as an early instance of disagreement on the nature of the party—on the limits of diversity admissible within its bounds, and on how it should stand with reference to other parties.

For several months after their return from exile, the members of the *troika* busied themselves with negotiations and arrangements for the forthcoming enterprise. Lenin and his collaborators were surprised to learn that they had formed an imperfect impression of the situation in the movement. Expecting to find the Economists everywhere in the saddle, and themselves out of favor, they discovered that they enjoyed greater confidence among groups active in Russia than did the Emancipation of Labor Group.[4] Promises of support came from all sides, both in Russia and abroad. In meetings with Vera Zasulich, who made a clandestine visit to St. Petersburg early in 1900, the *troika* secured what it took to be the approval of the Emancipation of Labor.[5] Then, in the spring, the *troika* was sought out by representatives of the RSDU who had come to Russia to canvass the possibility of convening a second party congress. These delegates insisted that the dictatorial tendencies of Plekhanov and Axelrod and not differences of principle were responsible for the dissension in the emigration, and they disarmed the recently returned exiles by appearing to fall in with their plans. They not only subscribed to the need for party unity, to be solidified by a party organ, but they willingly conceded the editorship to the *troika*, who made no secret of their Plekhanovist sympathies. To Lenin, it no doubt appeared that the differences among the Social Democrats had been grossly exaggerated after all. With a little more tolerance and flexibility than the Emancipation of Labor had shown, he and his allies might form a bridge between the warring factions and facilitate party consolidation.

Meanwhile, negotiations also got under way with the "legal Marxists," Struve and Tugan-Baranovskii, who, like the Union people, appeared ready to recognize the *troika* as the party center.[6] Lenin knew perfectly well that these men had affiliations with Bernstein, and that they had criticized various tenets of Marxism. Nevertheless, they maintained that they stood close to the Social Democrats. Lenin may have been dubious about that. But he believed in the genuineness of their interest in the struggle for political liberty, and, realizing that they were in a position to bring needed financial resources to *Iskra*, he was prepared to accept them as useful allies and to make at least some concessions to gain their support.

As it happened, damaging police raids prevented the conclusion of Lenin's talks with the RSDU representatives. The *troika* then decided to shelve the Union's proposals and to proceed with the publication abroad of an independent organ, in collaboration with the Emancipation of Labor Group and with the support of Struve's group. However, the conversations with the Union representatives and the "legal Marxists" left their mark on Lenin. His draft statement on the editorial policy of *Iskra* was surprisingly conciliatory in tone.[7] Although it attacked Revisionism and both the "Credo" and *Rabochaia mysl'*, it never mentioned by name Economism, the Union organ, *Rabochee delo,* or Struve. "Maintaining the continuity and unity of the movement" was much to be desired, Lenin wrote; but that "does not by any means exclude diversity." He admitted that there were limits to what might be permitted, but he maintained that it was as yet too early to determine how deep was the cleavage among the Social Democrats: he, at any rate, still hoped it would be possible to close the breach and work together. In a remarkably tolerant vein, he declared:

We do not claim that our views in their entirety are the views of all Russian Social Democrats, we do not deny that differences exist, nor shall we attempt to gloss over or obliterate these differences. On the contrary, we desire our publications to become organs of *discussion* of all questions by all Russian Social Democrats of the most diverse shades of opinion.[8]

More than that, the draft even envisaged *Iskra* as an organ of "general democracy," opening its columns to all who were oppressed under the prevailing political system.

Bearing the draft with him, Lenin went abroad toward the end of July 1900. (Potresov had preceded him, and Martov remained in Russia until the following spring.) In the brief interval between his departure from Russia and his first interviews with Plekhanov and his collaborators, Lenin had the opportunity to learn more about the struggle in the emigration. The information he imparted to his wife demonstrated unmistakably that he had read the *Vademecum* and that, in his mind, right lay completely with the Group.

Quite a wrong idea about the *Vademecum* prevails in Russia through the influence of tales made up by those on the side of *Rabochee delo*. To listen to them, it is nothing more than an attack on personalities, nothing but generalities and an exaggeration of trivialities because of the slandering of personalities; nothing but the use of inadmissible methods, etc. Actually, the *doctrinal* side predominates. . . . Attacks on personalities are only by the way. . . .
. . . As for Economism, the young people waged a systematic, persistent, and dishonest struggle against the Emancipation of Labor Group throughout 1898. It was "dishonest" because they did not *openly* show their banner, because they blamed everything on "Russia,". . . because they made use of their connections and practical resources to attack the Emancipation of Labor Group. . . . This struggle with the Emancipation of Labor Group, this attack upon it, was effected in silence, on the sly, privately, by means of "private" letters and "private" conversations—or to put it bluntly: by means of *intrigues*, because the question of the role of the Emancipation of Labor Group in Russian Social Democracy never was, never will be, and never can be a *private* matter. . . .
At issue is *the radical difference between the two ways of understanding the immediate tasks and the vital demands of Russian Social Democracy.* The first

can be expressed by the words laissez-faire, laissez-passer with regard to Economism . . . tactics of . . . free criticism of Marxism on the part of all sorts
of direct and disguised ideologues of the bourgeoisie. The other demanded a
definite struggle with Economism, an open protest against the threatening be-
littlement and narrowing-down of Marxism, an irrevocable breach with bourgeois
"criticism."[9]

One can hardly imagine a more fervent testimonial by a devoted follower than this of Lenin to the Emancipation of Labor Group, and, one
infers, to Plekhanov, its guiding spirit. Yet he evidently saw no need, on
the basis of his revised understanding of the differences in the Social
Democratic emigration, to alter the draft editorial statement. He remained
committed to flexibility, to conciliatoriness, and, by implication, to a broad
movement, tolerant of a considerable range of internal diversity. Organizational unity, broadly based, clearly was more important to him then than
ideological uniformity. He wished at once to mediate between contending
factions and to throw his weight into the balance in support of one of them.
That this was an impossible feat he learned in his encounter with Plekhanov.

The conversations at the end of August had as object the definition of
the organizational forms of the association between the *troika* and the
Emancipation of Labor. Lenin anticipated no difficulty in working out
amicably what appeared to be merely a mechanical problem. Much less
was he prepared for the "degrading" moral ordeal he afterwards described
so feelingly. According to him, Plekhanov behaved reprehensibly, creating an intolerable atmosphere. Disparaging Lenin's literary competence,
making threats and impossible demands, he revealed his utter lack of consideration for the sensitivities and capabilities of the younger man. By
turns, he remained haughtily aloof from the conversations; darkly threatened to retire from political activity; and, in the next moment, by a ruse,
sought to establish his personal domination over the publishing venture.
Lenin was inexpressibly shocked to "discover" such "repellent qualities"
in the man whom, more than any other, he regarded with "such sincere
respect and veneration." So great was the wrench that he could convey it
only by resorting to the language of love. He had cherished an "infatua-
tion" for Plekhanov; was so "enamored" with him that he had closed his
eyes to his imperfections. And then the "beloved," heedless of the un-
selfish love and unbounded devotion offered him, "brutally spurned" the
suitor. In the process, he revealed himself as "a bad man, inspired by petty
motives of personal vanity and conceit—an insincere man." With this discovery, "our indignation knew no bounds. Our ideal was destroyed; gloat-
ingly we crumpled it up and trampled it under our feet." It was "the complete abandonment of the thing which for years we had tended like a

favored child and with which we had inseparably linked up the whole of our life's work." At that point, it looked as though *Iskra* had been "extinguished."

As Lenin describes the clash, one sees an obstinate, egotistical, and power-hungry man outrageously humiliating and exploiting a younger comrade who came to him in a spirit of reverence and devotion. Of vanity Plekhanov possessed an ample measure, and he may well have felt offended that a grand plan for Social Democracy had been devised by others and presented to him only afterwards. Perhaps he thought it pretentious of the *troika* to give itself equality of status with the three members of the Emancipation of Labor in the new venture. Never before had the pioneer Marxists been put in such a position. Plekhanov perhaps sensed that in Lenin he had met a serious rival for leadership of the movement, and he may have treated the younger man condescendingly, and even worse. When he resolved to be disagreeable, Plekhanov had few equals. Not only was he an expert at cutting remarks but, in Trotsky's memorable phrase, he was *"maître de toutes les nuances de froideur."*[10]

When all this has been said, differences of principle and not Plekhanov's "repellent" qualities still must be seen as the chief source of the conflict. Although Plekhanov, in truth, was at the time in an extraordinarily irritable and suspicious mood, his condition cannot be understood apart from the circumstances that caused it. The publication of the *Vademecum* in March 1900 had brought a torrent of abuse upon the "father of Russian Marxism." A congress of the RSDU in the following month was the scene of an acrimonious exchange which culminated with the withdrawal of the pro-Plekhanov faction from the Union. In May this minority constituted itself the Russian Revolutionary Organization "Social Democrat," as if to read its adversaries out of revolutionary Social Democracy. There was no letup in recriminations thereafter. The two groups struggled for control of the press they had formerly used together, and the Emancipation of Labor members suspected their foes of using their lines of communication with Russia to isolate and blacken the reputations of the old-timers.[11] Nor should it be forgotten that Plekhanov's campaign against Revisionism was then in full cry. It was as though he and his little band of followers stood virtually alone, a last outpost against the rising tide of opportunism.

The desperate defense of the cause to which he had dedicated his life made Plekhanov more than ever an intransigent. To Axelrod he had written earlier in the year: "As a member of Emancipation of Labor, *you are infallible and must not and cannot err* (you know I am beginning to lean toward Jacobinism)."[12] In fact, in 1900 and in the next few years, Plekhanov was precisely a Jacobin in spirit. As one of the principal consequences of his protracted and bitter struggle against Revisionism and

Economism, the Jacobin tendency that had always been part of his make-up was powerfully reinforced. More than ever, he was prone to insist that his views and those of the comrades who supported him were holy writ. There could be no compromise with those who, whatever rationalizations they offered, objectively were subverters of the true faith and the ends for which it stood. They could only be anathematized, cast out, and rigorously separated from the pure and faithful, no matter how few the latter might turn out to be. Such was the mood of the man to whom Lenin came with his fence-straddling draft.

The first few paragraphs of Lenin's own account demonstrate that the hostilities between the two were precipitated by the older man's dissatisfaction with Lenin's draft statement.[13] He angrily denounced it as an "opportunistic" document. Plekhanov had declared war unto the death upon Revisionism. In his view, the breach with Economism was irrevocable. Yet Lenin had the temerity to propose forbearance, the possibility of reconciliation, and even Plekhanov's participation in a publication that offered space to his sworn enemies!* That Lenin could countenance association with opportunists opened him to suspicion of opportunism. At that time, Plekhanov was, indeed, more than a Jacobin: if not quite a Bolshevik, he was more nearly one than the future founder of Bolshevism. At this juncture, he almost broke with Lenin because Lenin did not seem sufficiently "hard" in relation to other groups and factions.

The Spark was not extinguished. At the last moment, it was found possible to devise an arrangement for proceeding with publication plans. The terms make plain that Plekhanov had scored a considerable victory. Once again, as in every previous collaborative effort with younger comrades, the Group managed to salvage a special position for itself. It was agreed that all six—the *troika* and the Emancipation of Labor triumvirate—should jointly constitute the editorial board of *Iskra*, but Plekhanov was conceded two votes. And in case of disagreement between the Group and the other editors, the paper would be bound to publish in full the special opinion of the Group or of each of its dissenting members.[14] The editorship of a second publication, a theoretical and philosophical magazine called *Zaria* (The Dawn), was virtually left to Plekhanov.

Even more important than these organizational arrangements, Plekhanov's views prevailed in the area of policy. The revised version of the editorial statement which was published proved far more uncompromising than the first draft.[15] It contained no words about the virtues of diversity, asserting, on the contrary, that "to establish and consolidate party unity . . . it is necessary first of all to bring about unity of ideas which will

---

* In a brief allusion to the affair years later, Plekhanov indicated that he had forced Lenin and Potresov to "choose between me and Struve." *Sochineniia*, XIX, 93–94.

remove differences of opinion." And lest there be some question as to which ideas were intended, the document named as foes all those upon whom Plekhanov had declared war: the Economists, *Rabochee delo*, the "legal Marxists," and Struve. Apropos of the latter, the statement read: "We utterly reject the half-and-half, vague, and opportunistic emendations which have become so fashionable as a result of the *legerdemain* of Ed. Bernstein, P. Struve, and many others." The new publications, far from functioning as "a storehouse for various views," were to be directed "along the lines of a strictly defined tendency." This meant among other things that material from the pens of "those nonsocialists who are oppressed by the present political system," though admissible, would be put in proper (i.e., Social Democratic) perspective by editorial comment. The orientation of the new publications was summed up in these words: "Before we can unite, and in order that we may unite, we must first of all firmly and definitely draw the lines of demarcation between the various groups."[16]

Although morally degraded by the clash, Lenin carried away a political lesson of inestimable importance. He had been made to grasp the "absurdity" of trying to reconcile the irreconcilable, of attempting to build a broad movement embracing divergent tendencies while holding to a rigorous orthodoxy. Forced to make a choice, he chose orthodoxy, and henceforth the quest for organizational forms which would facilitate its defense figured prominently in his political life. Plekhanov drove Lenin to the left, and after this disturbing encounter no one ever again was able to reproach him for softness. The drawing of "lines of demarcation" became a veritable mania with Lenin. So well did he learn the lessons Plekhanov taught that the pupil soon was to outstrip the master. Only a few years later, the positions the two occupied in their encounter in 1900 were to be reversed.

As a means of minimizing further conflict with Plekhanov, the others contrived to have the *Iskra* editorial center, which Lenin was to direct, situated in Munich rather than Geneva. The tension soon abated, however, and for a time more comradely relations prevailed. No doubt the pressures of Axelrod and Zasulich, who had been dismayed at the discord between their colleagues, helped to bring Plekhanov around. Moreover, having got what he wanted, he could afford to be magnanimous. Perhaps most important of all, Plekhanov's suspicious attitude toward Lenin rapidly yielded to trust and respect as he saw how businesslike, reliable, and efficient his young collaborator was. The first two numbers of *Iskra* came off the press with admirable dispatch, and they successfully passed Plekhanov's critical scrutiny. To Axelrod, Plekhanov wrote early in 1901: "That Petrov [Lenin] is a good fellow I never doubted, and after the journey to Munich [for a conference of editors], even less so. It is only too bad that purely administrative work prevents him from reading and writing much. However, the second number of *Iskra* is nonetheless *very good*. I am reading it with great satisfaction."[17]

Although he wrote of having learned always "to keep a stone in one's sling,"[18] Lenin did not bear a grudge against Plekhanov. Even years later, when their political association had irrevocably ended and they had become avowed enemies, he always took great interest in his former mentor's views on every subject. So reverent was he, and so fertile in providing rationalizations for the "heresies" of the older man, that his comrades laughingly accused him of being in love with Plekhanov.[19] In the year following their clash, Lenin's respect for Plekhanov's acumen was restored and perhaps heightened. Firsthand contacts with the Russian Revisionists and Economists confirmed, in his eyes, the correctness of the position Plekhanov had taken and discredited his own.

More than any other single issue, the relation of the new publications to Struve and his associates had been the bone of contention between Lenin and Plekhanov. The published statement of the *Iskra* editorial policy had the effect of smoking out Struve. Coming abroad toward the end of 1900 for further negotiations, he indicated in no uncertain terms his dissatisfaction with the new turn. Not unnaturally, the editorial statement convinced him that the *Iskra-Zaria* people intended to use him for purposes of their own while denying him any real influence. Balking at this, he made counterproposals designed to enlarge his role and to give him more independence in publishing activities.* Infuriated by Struve's "presumption," Lenin named his redoubtable foe "Judas." The violence of his revulsion stemmed from the discovery that he had been duped. Lenin earlier had been persuaded that the "legal Marxist" Struve, although somehow associated with Revisionism, nevertheless was a genuine socialist, who "was going toward us, and wished to take the first steps." Now Struve "revealed himself in a totally new aspect," with "the coarse huckstering nature of a regular liberal."[20] Lenin was beside himself with rage to learn that two could play the same game. The Social Democrats were not alone in schemes to use others; the liberals, masquerading as socialists, planned to use the Social Democrats. They intended to smuggle their own material into the Marxist organ in an attempt to counter the objectives of its Social Democratic editors. Struve might have had as his slogan this variation on Marx's famous tactic: Alongside the proletariat so long as it is revolutionary in the struggle against absolutism, never ceasing for a moment to blur awareness of the antagonism of the interests of the bourgeoisie and the proletariat.

* For Struve's interpretation of the episode, see his article in *Slavonic and East European Review*, XIII, 77–81. "I resolutely refused," he writes, "to become . . . a mere instrument in the hands of the orthodox Social Democrats."

Plekhanov and Axelrod of course rejected Struve's proposals. They were perfectly ready, as they had been since 1883, to cooperate with the liberals in the struggle against absolutism, provided that the independence of the Social Democrats remained unimpaired. As Plekhanov vehemently put it: "We want to have relations with Judas only as a representative of the democratic opposition. We must refuse to have him work with us as a Social Democrat. . . . His references to 'we Social Democrats' lie like a stone upon my heart."[21] In other words, collaboration was possible only if it did not interfere with the development of proletarian class consciousness; and it would require the firm and definite drawing of "lines of demarcation." In the light of these discussions with Struve, Lenin could now fully appreciate Plekhanov's insistence upon the revision of his draft editorial statement. In his mortification, he was not content with mere demarcation but wished to sever all relations with Struve, and it became Plekhanov and Axelrod's turn to exercise a moderating influence. Over Lenin's opposition, an agreement along the lines they suggested was concluded with Struve. Not long after his return to Russia, however, Struve was arrested while taking part in a demonstration; by the time he was next abroad, a year later, the kind of collaboration earlier envisaged was out of the question.

Lenin's unyielding stand proved to be more than a momentary reaction arising from a fit of pique. This episode brought into the open differences in evaluation and tactical emphasis between him and the Group in regard to the liberals; Lenin was gravitating back to the arch-hostile position he had taken in his meeting with the pioneer Marxists in 1895. The differences were further revealed in mid-1901 by Lenin's proposed rejoinder to the one piece written by Struve that was published under the auspices of *Iskra-Zaria*—a Preface by Struve to a confidential memorandum from Count Witte to the Tsar concerning the relationship of the state and the zemstvos.

Lenin placed his commentary on Struve's remarks[22] against a background discussion of the relations of the liberals to the revolutionists and the government at critical moments since the accession of Alexander II. In his portrayal, the liberals had clearly demonstrated their cowardice and ineffectuality. Lacking the power to exact from the government the liberties they desired, they used the threat posed by the revolutionists as a means of securing satisfaction of their own more moderate demands. They invariably preferred to trust to the good will of the throne rather than throw in unreservedly with the revolutionary forces. The government exploited their simplicity by buying them off with vague promises, and then, after cracking down ruthlessly on the revolutionists, betrayed its pledges. In Lenin's opinion, the earlier generations of liberals stood revealed as "pusillanimous," "senseless," and "treacherous," and the contemporary liberals leaned toward the same discredited tactics. He anticipated little from them but duplicity and treachery.

Plekhanov and Axelrod were taken aback by the malevolence of Lenin's article.[23] They, too, had reservations about the liberals, and preferred, of course, to use them rather than to be used. But they realized, as Lenin did not, that outspoken hostility would make the liberals more rather than less cautious, and might drive them away from the revolutionists and toward the government all the sooner. Not accusations and denunciations were needed but Social Democratic tactics to encourage the liberals to contribute more effectively to the struggle against absolutism. Lenin seemed unable to distinguish between "demarcating" and repelling. So intently did he strive to do the one that, quite without intention, he seemed likely to do the other as well.

At the insistence of Plekhanov and Axelrod, Lenin revised the article considerably, although the published version (which I have cited) still contained remarks highly provocative to the liberal camp. The article bespoke Lenin's sense of outrage at the renewed evidence he found of Struve's hope to use the Social Democrats for the achievement of liberal purposes. The tone sustained throughout the work leaves the reader utterly unprepared for the final paragraphs, which must have been tacked on under pressure from Plekhanov and Axelrod. Only after the liberals have been thoroughly reviled does the article sound the familiar tactical note of the Emancipation of Labor Group:

If the liberals succeed in organizing themselves into an illegal party, so much the better. . . . We shall support their demands, we shall endeavor to work so that the activities of the Social Democrats and the liberals mutually supplement each other. But even if they fail to do so (which is probable [here Lenin's sentiment breaks in again]), we shall not give them up in disgust. . . . An exchange of services between liberals and Social Democrats is going on already; it must be extended and made permanent.[24]

Straining against the tactical injunctions laid down almost two decades before, Lenin in the final analysis yielded only in part to the authority of the pioneer Marxists.* After his break with them a few years later, on other grounds, there no longer existed a restraining force to prevent a virtual declaration of war upon the liberals. That was to be a major feature of the new strategy he advanced in 1905.

In 1901, as *Iskra* became solidly established, the question of its relation to other émigré Marxian groups had to be dealt with. *Iskra* strove to employ the services of Social Democratic groups in various European

---

* Axelrod reproached him for his obstinacy. *Leninskii sbornik*, III, 219.

cities, without at the same time yielding to them a voice in policy. In this, it was more successful than the Emancipation of Labor in earlier years. *Iskra* was obliged, however, to take account of pressures from some émigrés for an agreement among the different Social Democratic groups abroad, and especially between *Iskra-Zaria* itself and the RSDU.

At a meeting in July 1901, attended by representatives of these and some other organizations, an accord was reached. The communiqué issued indicated agreement on condemnation of Bernsteinism and Economism and a rededication to the program of the Emancipation of Labor.[25] The Union appeared to be swinging around in response to a number of developments of the past half-year or so. Not least important had been the decision of the *troika* to join with the pioneer Marxists, and the force subsequently brought to bear upon *Rabochee delo* by the new publications. Not to be overlooked either was evidence that the workers in Russia were moving beyond Economism to political action. In early 1901, with no prompting from Social Democratic agitators, labor forces had joined in student demonstrations against the government. Even the most unrepentant Economist had to admit that the workers were awakening to political consciousness. In March, Krichevsky in *Rabochee delo* hailed this new development and called for a vigorous political campaign. For all that, by the time a congress was convened in October to ratify the July agreement, the Union representatives were hedging, and wanted to introduce "softening" amendments. With that, the orthodox representatives bolted, and the merger scheme collapsed. There followed a lesser amalgamation among the varied groups that sided with *Iskra*: the Russian Revolutionary Organization "Social Democrat" and *Iskra-Zaria*, together with their supporters, formed the Foreign League of Revolutionary Social Democracy.

The process of demarcation was proceeding apace. The new League, in a manifesto written by Lenin, declared it essential for its members to remain "sectists" in order to distinguish themselves from the growing army of revolutionists who were socialists "in name only." The creators of the League, pledging loyalty to the spirit of the party declaration of 1898, affirmed that the problems of the RSDLP remained as they had been formulated almost two decades before by the Emancipation of Labor.[26] Lenin, who but a year before had favored some tolerance of diversity within Social Democracy, now came out as its most extreme antagonist. He was irreconcilable toward those he held responsible for perpetuating division when unity had seemed so close. Having already accomplished the same shift in reference to Struve, he now outdid Plekhanov in intransigence with regard to the RSDU.* The conclusions he had come to after

---

* Plekhanov on this occasion advised against splitting. Martov, *Istoriia rossiskoi sotsial demokratii*, p. 55.

a year of firsthand experience in the emigration with what he took to represent Revisionism (Struve) and Economism (the Union), he set down in the next few months in a famous pamphlet, *What Is to Be Done?*

To the question "What is to be done?" he answered: "Liquidate the Third Period"—the era of "confusion, disintegration, and vacillation" which he associated with the emergence of Revisionism and Economism.[27] Retracing ground that Plekhanov had covered before, his argument echoed his predecessor's much more faithfully than has generally been recognized. Besides, he explicitly and ardently defended Plekhanov and the Emancipation of Labor against all criticism. However, Lenin's evaluation introduced an emphasis not evident in Plekhanov's work, and he went on to draw significant new organizational conclusions. For such reasons, his pamphlet is properly regarded as a milestone not only in his own political development but in the history of Russian Social Democracy as well.

At the very beginning of his Marxian career, Plekhanov had allotted to the intelligentsia a vital role in the socialist movement. The specific character of the task he assigned it suggested a conviction that the proletariat by itself was not likely to attain socialist consciousness. Even though the conditions of labor under capitalism predisposed the workers against that system, the intervention of the intelligentsia was still required to make conscious socialists out of potential socialists. Plekhanov's analysis of the sources of Revisionism and Economism laid major emphasis upon the failure of the intelligentsia, or at least some elements of it, to fulfill its responsibility. Lenin was no less ready to flay the intelligentsia, but he did not stop there. He insisted on placing on public exhibition, and even on holding up to scorn, that which Plekhanov tended to mute or entirely suppress—the responsibility of the workers themselves. Not merely the irresolution and passivity of the intelligentsia, he contended, but also the opportunism of the workers was involved in the rise of Revisionism and Economism.

Lenin spoke with some disdain of the spontaneous, independent activity to be expected of the working class. By itself, the proletariat would never go beyond trade-union consciousness, a level of consciousness entirely compatible with the indefinite tenure of capitalism. A working class with such an orientation, even though it might extend its activity into the political sphere, would still pose no threat to capitalism. Regarding trade-unionist mentality as symptomatic of an accommodation to capitalism, he argued that "working-class, trade-union politics are precisely working-class bourgeois politics."[28] Lenin was saying that the proletariat, on its own, was incapable of anything more than opportunism. Over against the "spontaneity" of the working class, with its unfortunate opportunistic coloration, Lenin set the "consciousness" of the intelligentsia. The intelligentsia must see to it that the movement did not become trapped in the swamp of opportunism. Provided that it was steeped in and loyal to the revolutionary theory of socialism (i.e., provided that it was orthodox), it would chart an unwavering course toward the ultimate goal.

While using somewhat different terminology, and delineating the matter much more sharply, on the whole Lenin's position so far did not appear markedly different from Plekhanov's. Both demanded stronger and more effective Social Democratic leadership and both linked this demand to insistence upon greater attention to theory. Plekhanov thought to achieve these ends through exhortation, greater vigilance, and the rigorous demarcation of the orthodox from every other radical tendency—all measures relative to the intelligentsia alone. Here Lenin broke entirely new ground. To demarcate the orthodox from other tendencies was, in his view, indispensable for the success of the socialist movement. But it had become apparent to Lenin that *the workers themselves,* prone as they were to opportunism, threatened to corrupt the socialist party, and he called for drastic measures against that danger. Drawing the most extreme organizational conclusions, he urged the orthodox socialists to demarcate themselves decisively from the rank and file of the working class. His fear that proletarian opportunism might otherwise inundate it led him to demand the creation of a revolutionary party built on lines alien to the conception of Marx and to the practice of the Marxian parties of Europe.

As a guarantee of the purity of the party and of unswerving pursuit of the chosen ends, the socialists were not to be, as with Marx, "the most advanced and resolute section of the working class [i.e., mass] parties of every country";[29] instead, they were themselves to constitute the party, which would be a small, highly conspiratorial, and strongly disciplined association of professional revolutionists. To be sure, Lenin justified his organizational scheme by reference to the need for a conspiratorial organization if tsarism were to be effectively combated. But it is amply clear that his conception of the party is inseparable from other more general considerations, such as the distinction he drew between "spontaneity" and "consciousness." Into the party he would admit only those possessing a high level of theoretical understanding, and of the most unquestioning, rigorously orthodox kind. Scornfully, he equated freedom of criticism with "freedom for an opportunistic tendency in Social Democracy . . . the freedom to introduce bourgeois ideas and bourgeois elements into socialism."[30] Putting the matter in the most uncompromising terms, he characteristically maintained that in modern society there could be only two ideologies, the bourgeois and the socialist. Hence, *"to deviate from socialist ideology in the slightest degree means strengthening bourgeois ideology."* Since, from his perspective, the workers in the mass were ideologically primitive and therefore susceptible to the influence of bourgeois ideology, they must be excluded from the party.

But that does not mean that Lenin was indifferent to the masses of proletarians. He still considered that for the revolution the masses were indispensable. The task of the party vis-à-vis the masses, in his view, consisted in: (1) raising to its own level and incorporating into the ranks of the professional revolutionists the most capable of the workers; and (2) exercising a guiding influence upon the multitudes who remained outside. While striving to raise workers to their own level, the revolutionists were to guard against being "degraded" to the level of the working masses.[31] Meanwhile, the conscious party must exert itself to the utmost in pushing on the spontaneous labor movement from the outside.

We must have as large a number as possible of trade-union and other mass organizations having the widest possible variety of functions; but it is absurd and dangerous *to confuse* these with organizations of *revolutionists,* to erase the line of demarcation between them . . . to "serve" the mass movement we must have people who will devote themselves exclusively to Social Democratic activities, and . . . such people must *train* themselves patiently and steadfastly to be professional revolutionists.[32]

In what was to become the characteristic operational style of communist parties everywhere, individual members would be deputed to work within mass organizations and seek to secure a dominating party influence over their policies. Here was a scheme by which a carefully selected elite, keeping the controls firmly in its own hands, and organizationally segregating itself from the masses to prevent a dilution of revolutionary militancy, could "utilize" the masses for the achievement of its ends.

Plekhanov made no public outcry against *What Is to Be Done?* until well after the party split at the Second Congress in 1903. It may be seriously doubted that the charges he brought against it then were as clearly conceived in his mind, as he claimed, at the time of the work's publication.[33] He may well have had some early misgivings, but they obviously were more than offset by other considerations. The piece had the merit, in Plekhanov's eyes, of striking hard at the Revisionist and Economist adversaries he himself had been belaboring for years. He could not easily take issue with a work which warmly defended him and the Emancipation of Labor Group and strongly echoed his own sentiments. Lenin had perhaps exaggerated the importance of "consciousness," but the difference between them was only one of degree, not of kind; and the exaggeration was forgivable in the heat of a conflict with a dangerous foe of socialist orthodoxy. In any case, while that conflict continued it would be senseless to point up divisions in one's own ranks. In these years, Plekhanov was hardly sensitive to the dangers of excessive hardness and intransigence. The enemy was on the right, not the left. Under the circumstances, he did not grasp the full implications of Lenin's new organizational ideas; he did not perceive that Lenin and he, as the former observed in distinguishing his views from those of the Economists, were speaking "in different tongues." In addition, differences with Lenin on party organization perhaps seemed academic at the time, inasmuch as the party then existed in name only.

Issues involved in *What Is to Be Done?* were in time to become the subject of a raging public controversy, with Plekhanov and Lenin on opposite sides. In 1902, however, not Lenin's opus but the shaping of the party program was the occasion for the renewal of behind-the-scenes hostilities between the two. Talk of the necessity of drafting a party program commenced in the summer of 1901, as pressures began to develop for the convening of a new party congress. Lenin urged Plekhanov and Axelrod to prepare a draft,[34] but it was Plekhanov's work alone which was submitted half a year later. Far from meeting with general approval, its presentation touched off an internal crisis that for the second time threatened to extinguish *The Spark*.

When in January 1902 Plekhanov unveiled his draft program to a conference of the editors, Lenin and Martov registered strong objections. Never one to take criticism gracefully, Plekhanov was deeply offended by their reaction. To the proposal that each segment of the draft be voted on, he responded by withdrawing it altogether and walking out in a huff. After some attempts at revision, Lenin became convinced that Plekhanov's effort had been wrongly conceived and set to work on a counterdraft. Reactions to his program varied, but from the first Plekhanov took a bitterly negative view. Not one to forgive an "affront" easily, as in his earlier collision with Lenin, he once again created an atmosphere of threats and ultimatums. He advised Axelrod: "If Lenin's version is adopted, I shall be forced to declare that I nevertheless consider it unsatisfactory. There will take place something in the nature of a new schism." He then presented a revised version of his original draft which he pronounced "as different from Lenin's . . . as the heavens from the earth."[35] Lenin evidently found the revision somewhat less than celestial, for he subjected it to a new round of bruising criticism. After further maneuvers and recriminations, Plekhanov at last had his way. To prevent a universally unwanted open split, it was agreed that his reworked draft be taken as the basis for a new editing by a committee which would include neither him nor Lenin. The committee finally drew up a compromise document, which, like most such, satisfied no one completely.

The differences that brought on so grave a crisis ostensibly related both to the form and to the substance of the program. Significantly, those relating to substance emerged only after the program-making process was well advanced; then, owing to the injuries they had already inflicted on each other, the sensitivities of the principals were thoroughly inflamed. Plekhanov had vented his spleen in insisting upon the rejection of Lenin's draft and the adoption of his own. Lenin, as it were, retaliated by taking a hypercritical attitude to the substance of Plekhanov's work. Zasulich, who tried to mediate, was not far off the mark when she accused Lenin of "caviling."[36] As a matter of fact, the substantive "differences" between the two seem to have been more imaginary than real, resulting from personal animosities rather than from fundamental disagreements.

Characteristically, each accused the other of portraying inadequately or incorrectly the peculiarity of Russian capitalism.[37] And both were justified. Each devoted much the greater part of the general section of his respective program to the special features Marx associated with mature, capitalist economies approaching their end.[38] Only then, and with extraordinary brevity, did each turn to the peculiarities of Russian capitalism, before proceeding to the second part of the program—that concerned with specific demands. The latter section of both programs had an unexpectedly different focus, for it turned out that what impended was not the socialist revolution one had been led to anticipate but rather the overthrow of tsarism and the establishment of a democratic republic. Both drafts, in fact, were composed of two disparate parts, connected only by a couple of brief paragraphs on the peculiarities of Russia's socio-economic situation. What these documents revealed above all was the anomalous position of a socialist party, guided by Marxian precepts, in a backward country. Both drafts aimed to instill in the workers socialist consciousness (principled antipathy to capitalism), while projecting a democratic rather than a socialist revolution.

Lenin's other principal substantive criticism of Plekhanov's draft is hardly to be taken more seriously, for it amounted to a lecture to Plekhanov on a point with regard to which he himself had spilled no little ink. The argument here had to do with the political duality of the petty bourgeoisie and the conditions under which alone the Social Democrats could count upon its support in the socialist revolution. At the time of the programmatic dispute under review, no substantial difference between the two existed on this score.

The primary source of the conflict over the program lay in the different styles of the two men, which found expression in the form of their respective programs. Lenin found Plekhanov's draft both excessively verbose and insufficiently precise and concrete in its formulations. This estimate reflected his more general and more important judgment that Plekhanov had produced a document that was too abstract and theoretical. In his most succinct criticism, he charged that it was "not the practical program of a fighting party but a declaration of principles."[39] Believing that the party program should be an agitational document directed to the popular mind, Lenin strove for the utmost in simplicity, directness, and force-fulness of impact. Plekhanov's programmatic description of capitalism cor-responded to the style of a textbook, he objected, whereas his own was calculated to call up in the worker the shock of recognition of his miserable plight, and the passion to fight. Plekhanov indignantly denied the criticism, but a comparison of the efforts of the two tends to bear out Lenin's opinion.

In his Narodnik days, Plekhanov had shown that he could be an energetic and successful practical worker and agitator. His prolonged residence abroad divorced him from activity of that kind and dulled his sensitivity to its requirements. In exile he developed the philosophical interests which increasingly determined the way in which he apprehended the world. So far as the revolutionary movement was concerned, he tended to view it less as an affair of men of flesh and blood than in terms of his-torical process, dialectics, and other such abstract categories. Lenin never so conceived of the movement. He was fond of Goethe's words, "Gray, my friend, is theory, but green is the everlasting tree of life." A keen organizer and agitator, he characteristically took into his hands the lines of communication connecting *Iskra* with Russia; he carried on a voluminous correspondence with *Iskra*'s agents, following with intense interest the shift-ing political orientations of different groups and issuing the most incred-ibly detailed instructions as to ways and means of turning things to *Iskra*'s advantage. Lenin relished practical organizational activity and under-stood how necessary it was to the acquisition of power. In the *Iskra* period, Plekhanov by contrast tended to ignore organizational matters, regarding them as both tedious and inferior in significance to theoretical work. In the years when Lenin was trying to build an organizational base—and in the process creating a considerable personal following—Plekhanov devoted himself to theoretical problems with characteristic intensity. In the con-trast between the organizer-agitator and the scholar-philosopher, though it is by no means an absolute contrast, one obtains some understanding of the later outcome of the rivalry between the two.

Oddly enough, the really important substantive difference between Plekhanov and Lenin arose not in connection with the wording of the draft program but after that matter had already been settled. The new and unexpected controversy centered upon an article of commentary on the agrarian section of the program which Lenin presented for publication.[40] Initially given a generally favorable reception by the editorial board, the piece when revised drew from Plekhanov a severe lashing. The tension engendered was doubly acute, for, apart from the real issues, the new clash represented another bitter skirmish in the continuing personal war between

Plekhanov and Lenin. Still smarting from Lenin's carping criticisms of his draft, Plekhanov now went his adversary one better. His written comments on Lenin's manuscript were patronizing in tone, when not downright scornful. The further he proceeded, the more frequent and barbed his remarks became; and he let scarcely a line pass without introducing changes in style, many of them exceedingly trivial. Adding insult to injury, he asked that various of his proposals for stylistic changes be put to a vote—an unprecedented procedure in the editorial board. Martov hardly exaggerated in protesting that Plekhanov had employed against Lenin phrases and methods ordinarily reserved for enemies.[41]

In mid-May the manuscript reached Lenin once again. At first irritated by the supercilious remarks, he grew incensed at the constant goading, the extraordinary demands, the utter lack of consideration for the author's feelings, and he began peppering the manuscript with tart rejoinders, underlinings, double underlinings, and exclamation points. In one place, where Plekhanov raised a question about the use of quotation marks, Lenin wrote: "Is it so difficult to understand that everyone has his own manner of using quotation marks, or does the author of the comment want to 'put to a vote' quotation marks too? That is like him!"[42] When he had completed his review, Lenin sat down in a white heat and wrote Plekhanov a blistering note:

I have received the article with your remarks. You have a fine idea of tact with regard to your editorial colleagues. You do not hesitate to choose even the most contemptuous expressions, not to mention "voting" on propositions which you did not take the trouble to formulate, and even "voting" on style. I would like to know what you would say if I were to answer your article on the program in the same way. If you have sought to make our work together impossible, then the way you have chosen will very soon attain that end. As for personal as distinct from business relations, you have already completely ruined them, or more exactly: you have achieved their complete cessation.[43]

Whether Lenin actually mailed this letter to Plekhanov is not known. Yet the sentiments it expressed unmistakably signaled still another crisis for *Iskra-Zaria*. Martov shared Lenin's conviction that Plekhanov's behavior was intolerable, and he was alarmed lest it bring a new schism. Accordingly, he sought through Axelrod and Zasulich to impress upon Plekhanov the gravity of the situation and the need to make amends.[44] Potresov urged the most unrelenting pressure, advising Lenin: "Plekhanov will probably not write a *Vademecum*, and if he does, he will destroy himself in the eyes of the public."[45] This time, the *troika* rather than Plekhanov was forcing the issue. In his vindictiveness toward Lenin, he had overplayed his hand. Loyal to him though they were, his old associates could not but agree that he had gone beyond the bounds of decency. They themselves could not countenance a new and infinitely harmful split, could not sacrifice the future of the movement to Plekhanov's pride.

Over a period of two or three weeks, Zasulich and Axelrod used all the powers at their command to bring Plekhanov around. Their unenviable task was to induce the haughty Plekhanov to be contrite—even, if possible, to ask Lenin's pardon. That they ultimately succeeded is attested by the letter that follows. No letter Plekhanov ever wrote cost him so great an effort as his peace offering to Lenin. Beginning with what was for him a quite untypical form of address—Dearest Vladimir Ilyich—he went on:

V. I. [Zasulich] informs me of a remark you made about one place in my programmatic article. . . . If you wish somehow to change it, or better to append a note, then send me a draft annotation, and in the second proofs it will be inserted. . . .

I take this opportunity, dear V. I., to tell you that you have taken offense unjustly, I had no desire to insult you. We both went to extremes somewhat in the argument over program, and that is all. Sometime when we see each other, we will talk of this face to face, "heart to heart" (that is the main thing here), and then—if you wish to be fair—you yourself will see that I, too, had some reason to consider myself offended. But now let us set aside this private matter in the interests of another, a much more important, *common* cause. Believe one thing: I deeply respect you and I think that we are nearer to each other on 75% than to any other members of the "college"; on the remaining 25% there is a difference, but after all, 75 is three times greater than 25, and in the name of harmony it is well to forget about disagreements. . . .

Therefore, once again, do not be angry with me, and if you wish me to give you some sort of satisfaction, write me, and I will do anything that I can in order not to upset a comrade so useful to the cause and whom, believe this, I respect with all my heart."[46]

Lenin responded warmly to what he surely knew was an exceedingly difficult gesture for Plekhanov to make. "A great stone was lifted from my shoulders," he wrote, "when I received your letter, putting an end to ideas of 'civil war.' The more the latter seemed inevitable to us, the more oppressive were such thoughts, since the consequences for the party would have been most unfortunate."[47] To show his reasonableness, Lenin agreed to make such changes as Plekhanov still favored, but Plekhanov for the time being refrained from presenting differing views on the agrarian program. Once again a serious rift within the ranks of the orthodox leaders had been patched up. Nevertheless, personal animosities were accumulating, as were differences on principles and tactics, which could not indefinitely be swept under the rug. The dispute over the agrarian program highlighted one such major disagreement.

That Lenin singled out for elaboration and defense the agrarian section of the party program is a matter of no little significance. His own draft program with its frequent references to the peasants and their plight revealed that he, far more than Plekhanov—and indeed than any of his colleagues—was sensitive to the revolutionary potentialities inherent in the agrarian question. In some of his earlier works, notably *The Development of Capitalism in Russia,* he had emphasized the persistence beyond the Emancipation and into his own time of many aspects of agrarian relationships peculiar to serfdom. It was he who devised for the program a demand especially calculated to galvanize the peasantry—the return of the *otrezki*. These were pieces of land essential to a viable peasant enterprise which some noble landowners had detached and appropriated at the time of the Emancipation, as a means of perpetuating peasant dependence. With the general idea of the return of *otrezki*, Plekhanov and the other editors could have little quarrel. However, disagreement on the terms under which the *otrezki* should be returned was one of the points at issue in the argument about Lenin's article on the agrarian program.

On another matter—Lenin's brief for the nationalization of land—the differences were much more fundamental. It goes without saying that Plekhanov and the others had nothing against such nationalization in its proper time—in the era of the socialist revolution, when the nationalization of *all* the means of production would become imminent. But in his article Lenin unabashedly proposed the nationalization of land as a possible and proper concomitant of the revolution against absolutism.* Such a policy he saw as an essential next step, beyond the return of *otrezki*, for the Social Democratic program in the period of the first revolution. No doubt he expected such a slogan to keep the revolutionary fervor of the peasants alive, thus strengthening the hand of insurgent forces and assisting them in consolidating the democratic revolution. Lenin's scheme envisaged the nationalization not merely of state-, church-, and noble-owned land but of all landed property. However, the level of Russian socio-economic development precluded, he thought, the utilization of this property as the basis for a socialist organization of production. Instead, the land would be leased to individuals, whether peasants or others, under the most favorable terms.

Accustomed to think in terms of distinct historical stages, each with its appropriate forms, Lenin's co-editors could make no sense of his desire to enact the nationalization of land in a revolution destined to be bourgeois in character. That he did not propose a socialist organization of agricultural production hardly mitigated, in their eyes, what was essentially a wrongheaded view. The return of *otrezki* made good sense, for that demand symbolized the need to liquidate the survivals of a feudalistic regime in the countryside. Plekhanov went further, admitting the possi-

---

* *Leninskii sbornik,* III, 352–54. Actually, in some of his earlier writings, Plekhanov, too, had hinted at the possibility of Social Democratic support for nationalization of land in the democratic revolution.

bility that the revolutionary forces might well push for the expropriation of the big landholders and the disposal of their lands at low prices to the rural populace.[48] Social-revolutionary demands such as these were perfectly compatible with a bourgeois-democratic revolution. They would facilitate, as had the great French Revolution, the emergence of a large class of free proprietors. But nationalization of land, which might appropriately be promoted by socialist parties of the more advanced countries of the West, was as irrelevant to Russia's present condition as the demand for an immediate transition to socialism.

To these arguments Lenin remained deaf. Only after Plekhanov had made his apologies did he remove the offending sections, as a token of his desire for harmony. But his stand on the agrarian question in 1905 and after proves conclusively that he had not changed his mind. Here, as in his relation to the liberals, Lenin was improvising tactics significantly different from those advanced earlier by the Emancipation of Labor Group. The others, and Plekhanov at their head, might well find fault with a formula based on the dubious assumption that the demand for the nationalization of land would evoke a positive response among the peasantry. Would not a property-minded peasantry desert a revolution that proclaimed the abolition of private property in land? And what of the urban bourgeoisie? Would it not be apt to draw away from a revolutionary movement that announced the imminent outlawry of certain forms of private property? Was not the nationalization of land a slogan likely to inhibit rather than spur on the bourgeois-democratic revolution that Lenin himself professed a desire to promote? From the point of view of his critics, to introduce demands appropriate to the socialist into the bourgeois-democratic revolution might vitiate the achievement of both.

The whole episode hinted at features of Lenin's outlook that were to become more conspicuous as time went on. His extraordinary militancy sent him upon a restless quest for promising ways and means of releasing revolutionary energy. Plekhanov and other leading Russian Social Democrats were deeply concerned with the same problem, but as a matter of course they took the proletariat as their province. Lenin's single-minded drive to accelerate the revolutionary process brought his attention to focus elsewhere as well. He set himself the task of unleashing the great revolutionary potential he discerned in the peasantry and of harnessing it for the attainment of Social Democratic goals. Lenin's demand for the nationalization of land in conjunction with the first revolution hardly seemed a likely tactic for mobilizing the peasantry. But he would have rejected it—if at all—only for such a pragmatic reason and not on doctrinal grounds. The insistence of his colleagues that nationalization was unalterably associated with the socialist revolution failed to sway him.

Lenin's revolutionary will was pressing against the rigorously deterministic framework within which the pioneers of Russian Marxism had set the revolutionary movement. In Plekhanov's own revolutionary scheme, and more recently in the draft programs of both men, certain fundamental inconsistencies already put a considerable strain on the integrity of the whole. When to that were added elements so at odds with the anticipated character of the first revolution as Lenin's extreme hostility to the liberals and his readiness to call for the nationalization of land, the original revolutionary theory of Russian Marxism could not long be sustained. Having developed the elements of a new revolutionary theory—and it goes without saying that his peculiar organizational ideas represented another major ingredient—Lenin half-consciously was attempting to break out of the restraining confines of Plekhanov's two-stage revolutionary scheme. A time would come when he could no longer be restrained, when he would brush aside theoretical impediments and deliberately set out to harness the whirlwind.

Lenin's special policies concerning the liberals and the peasants were to come into sharp focus in the crucible of revolution itself. His organizational scheme, by contrast, required more or less immediate implementation, for it figured as the means by which the Social Democratic Party would gird itself for the forthcoming battle and ensure its effectiveness when the revolutionary crisis came. Accordingly, the first public clash over what was to become known as Leninism broke out at the 1903 Congress convened to unify and provide the organizational structure of the party. At the center of the tumult that led to the cleaving of the RSDLP into Bolshevik and Menshevik factions were the leading ideas of *What Is to Be Done?*

13

REVOLUTIONARY SCHISM, II

THE SECOND CONGRESS of the RSDLP, convened five years after the first, was in a real sense the culmination of the work of *Iskra*. From its inception that enterprise had been directed to the re-establishment of Marxian orthodoxy as a precondition for the meaningful union of the dispersed elements of the Russian Social Democratic movement into a genuine party. Under Lenin's devoted management, the undertaking functioned effectively from the beginning. In the two and a half years between its inauguration and the convocation of the Second Congress, *Iskra* scored a brilliant success.

The numbers of the paper appeared regularly first at one-month and then at two-week intervals, and, after a mishap involving part of the first issue, safe transport routes were arranged for spiriting the editions into Russia. Nothing like it had been seen since the days of Herzen's *Kolokol*. In fact, copies of *Iskra* reached Russia in much larger quantities than Herzen's paper ever did, and, with its complement of high-powered contributors, it made a stunning impact in the Social Democratic milieu. It was supported by an abundant flow of correspondence from many centers; moreover, it developed a team of agents (there were nine by the end of 1901)[1] who carried the fight for orthodoxy into the local Social Democratic organizations in Russia. Financial difficulties cropped up from time to time, but they were not insuperable. Plekhanov expressed profound satisfaction with the new venture in connection with a query put to him concerning the advisability of an appeal for financial support to English friends of Russian liberty. "*Iskra* must be saved no matter how," he wrote, "so that if it were necessary to appeal to the devil himself for salvation, we would appeal to him."[2]

Under *Iskra*'s persistent pounding the Economist forces were gradually pulverized. The combined operations of relentless published blasts by the heavy artillery from abroad and the aggressive maneuvers of *Iskra*'s agents on the front lines had the effect of bringing one local organization after another into camp. As for the emigration, one sign of the times was the desertion in early 1903 of some of the RSDU leaders, including Ivan'shin;[3] another, the discontinuation of publication of *Rabochee delo*. *Iskra* was making good its bid to become the ideological and organizational center of the party.

Of course, the *Iskra* staff envisaged as a major end a congress that would formally unite the various sections and create the central institutions essential for the coordination of their activities. When as early as mid-1901 pressures for the convocation of such a congress began to increase, however, the editorial board worked feverishly to postpone its calling until their supremacy could no longer be in doubt.[4] On one hand, this entailed redoubled efforts on the part of the agents in Russia to secure a majority of pro-*Iskra* delegates. On the other, the editorial board worked hard and long to prepare the draft party program which it intended should determine the ideological tenor of the congress. *Iskra,* in short, would not participate in a new party congress until the conditions for uniting the party on *its* terms had been made certain. Its active cooperation in preparing the congress that convened in 1903 indicates its satisfaction that the conditions were right, that *Iskra* would prevail.

What was billed as the Second Congress of the RSDLP but was in fact more a founding congress opened in Brussels in July 1903. In mid-stream it shifted to London—a circumstance that calls attention to its extraordinary duration. No other party congress, it may be safely asserted, even began to approach the more than three-week term and the thirty-seven sessions of the 1903 assembly. To find a parallel, one must look to church councils rather than party congresses. And, as with church councils, the long life of this party congress reflected the astounding preoccupation of the Russian Marxists with the niceties of doctrine and organizational principles. In retrospect, is it fanciful to suggest that the 1903 Congress founded a church (or perhaps two churches) rather than a party?

The Congress brought together 43 delegates, representing 26 local organizations. Of the 51 votes they were entitled to cast, 33 were accounted safe for *Iskra*. Economism having collapsed, only two former Economists were at the Congress. It was anticipated that the Jewish Social Democratic organization, the Bund, would be troublesome; but *Iskra* possessed more than enough votes to overrule the Bund's demand for a kind of autonomy for national groups within the party. The power of the orthodox contingent was magnified by the presence in its ranks of the party's major luminaries. The Emancipation of Labor Group, *in toto* (including even Deutsch, who a few years before had escaped from Siberia and rejoined the emigration in Switzerland), was seated at the Congress in recognition of its historic services. On hand was the *troika*, whose members had done so much to establish *Iskra-Zaria* and to make it a potent agency for building the movement. A relative newcomer, who had already demonstrated great literary and oratorical talent—the young Trotsky—also sided with *Iskra*.

Plekhanov opened the Congress with a short address:

Comrades: The Organizational Committee has directed me to open the Second Congress of the RSDLP. I view this great honor to myself only as an endeavor on the part of the Organizational Committee to express its comradely sympathy with that group of veterans of Russian Social Democracy who twenty years ago, in 1883, first began the propaganda of Social Democratic ideas in Russian revolutionary literature. For that comradely sympathy, on behalf of those veterans, I give the Organizational Committee sincere comradely thanks. I wish to believe that at least some of us are fated for a long time yet to fight under the red banner shoulder to shoulder with new, young, and ever more numerous fighters. The state of things now is so favorable for our party that every one of us Russian Social Democrats can exclaim, and perhaps has more than once exclaimed, the words of the humanist knight: *"It is wonderful to be alive at such a time.".* . .

I said that the state of things now is extraordinarily favorable for our party. These words may seem exaggerated in view of the many disruptions, differences, and disagreements which have made themselves felt in the last five years. These disruptions, differences, and disagreements were undoubtedly great and bitter. But they did not prevent our party from becoming—both in the theoretical and practical respects—the strongest of the revolutionary and opposition parties of Russia. In spite of all our differences and disagreements, we have already scored more than one glorious theoretical triumph and have already had many great practical successes. Twenty years ago we were nothing, today we are a great social force—I say this, of course, having in view the Russian scale of things. But strength brings responsibilities. We are strong, but our strength was created by a situation in which we were favored by spontaneous factors. We must give to this *spontaneous* strength a *conscious* expression in our program, in our tactics, in our organization. That is the task of our Congress, which confronts, as you can see, extremely serious and difficult work. But I am sure that this serious and difficult work will be happily carried to its conclusion and that this Congress will constitute an epoch in the history of our party. We have been strong, the Congress will greatly increase our strength. I declare it open and propose that we proceed to the election of the bureau.[5]

Plekhanov's statement was greeted with prolonged applause, and he was immediately chosen by acclamation to be the presiding officer of the meetings.

In predicting that this Congress would mark an epoch in the history of the RSDLP, Plekhanov did not err; but his confidence that the Congress would unify forces and thus greatly enhance the strength of the party could not have been more misplaced. When he delivered his opening remarks,

Plekhanov never dreamed that the 1903 Congress would pass into history as the occasion of the most formidable and irreparable rupture in the whole history of Russian Social Democracy. At the Brussels-London conclave the party was rent in two, bringing into being the Bolshevik and Menshevik factions. What is more, the lines along which the cleavage took place were entirely unforeseeable. The representatives of the Bund and the former Economists bolted the Congress, as might have been expected, when on issue after issue they were defeated. But their departure did not cause the major split at the Congress. Nor did it involve the dissolution of the somewhat unstable alliance between the Emancipation of Labor and the *troika*. Instead, it cut through the one and the other and through the ranks of the less important delegates as well. In a seeming mockery of everything that had gone before, it ranged Plekhanov against the comrades with whose collaboration he had laid the basis of Russian Marxism; it ranged Lenin against his closest associates, the other members of the *troika*; most incredible of all, it aligned *together*, Plekhanov and Lenin, the two whose repeated clashes had made the inner organizational life of *Iskra* so tempestuous.

Unquestionably, Lenin was the guiding genius of the Congress. No one else knew so clearly what he wanted of the Congress and how to get it. So carefully and conscientiously had Lenin made his preparations that the possibility of a slip must have seemed to him more than remote. He had drawn up the agenda, thus determining the questions the Congress would consider. Among them was a proposal for the confirmation of *Iskra* as the official organ of the party. The Congress was to be confronted with a draft program which, in the nature of things, a body of its kind could not drastically alter. He had also prepared for presentation to the Congress a set of party rules, a charter defining the organizational structure and mode of operation of the party. Under his direction, *Iskra*'s agents had secured an *Iskrist* majority, a tightly knit group ready to steamroller any opposition that might arise. Although there was provision for discussion, the composition of the body guaranteed—Lenin thought—that this would be not so much a creative constituent assembly as a rubber stamp for decisions made in advance.

Lenin's main preoccupation was to carry into execution the organizational plan he had outlined in *What Is to Be Done?* The prolonged discussions of the program in 1902 had ended with the smoothing over of differences in the editorial board. But, oddly enough, the organizational question had not been thoroughly debated by the editors in advance of the Congress. That it had not indicates that neither Lenin nor any of his colleagues anticipated serious trouble on this score. Plekhanov's opening speech, with its posing of the task of the Congress in a Leninist fashion, declared his solidarity with his erstwhile rival. In urging the necessity of subordinating spontaneity (the mass movement) to consciousness (the party), he of course echoed the theme of *What Is to Be Done?* At that moment, neither he, nor Martov, nor Axelrod, nor any other of the *Iskra* editors imagined that soon this very matter would become a major source of contention. *Iskra* had staved off the convening of a party congress until the conditions for achieving unity on *its* terms had been achieved. The 1903 Congress revealed that, in spite of their extended collaboration, the editors themselves were not in agreement on the terms.

In the first phase of the Congress, the *Iskra* bloc held firm. In discussions of procedure, preliminary organizational questions, and program, the *Iskra* leaders agreed on every significant point and carried the rank and file with them. The spirited opposition of the Bund and RSDU delegates was unavailing, for in the voting they were regularly overwhelmed. Nevertheless, the confrontation was not without effect upon some of the *Iskra* faction. Whatever their position had been earlier, the stand the Bund and RSDU representatives took at the Congress did not seem so unequivocally reprehensible. The demand of the Bund for autonomy notwithstanding, the dissenters were not utopians of decentralization and democratization. Representatives of both organizations declared themselves centralists;[6] and M. I. Lieber, a principal spokesman of the Bund, replied in the negative to a direct question concerning the feasibility of democracy in local organizations under prevailing conditions.[7] Although the *Iskrists* continued to hold together in their voting, it is apparent from what subsequently happened that, for some, vague clouds of wonder began to break into the blue sky of certainty. Were the adversaries really so unreasonable? Was it proper to put them outside the pale? They did not seem like extremists; perhaps there was some point in their criticism of what they labeled the extremism of the majority.

The central debate on the program could hardly have allayed such doubts. It commenced with a trenchant critique of Lenin's spontaneity-consciousness formula,[8] which A. S. Martynov professed to see mirrored in the program. Forthrightly repudiating the Economism with which he had earlier been associated, he charged Lenin with going to a new extreme in reaction to it. Martynov, who was prepared, as the Economists were not, to recognize the importance of the socialist intelligentsia, reproached Lenin with exaggerating its role and failing to recognize the centrality to the socialist movement of the development of proletarian class consciousness. Pleading for an alteration of the program in this sense, as if to drive a wedge into the massed forces of the majority, he recalled Plekhanov's more positive appraisals of the potential for the development of proletarian class consciousness.

Martynov (seconded by Akimov) had touched on a critical problem in Lenin's theory, one that certainly had troubled his fellow-editors as well. But the demands of factional unity once again took precedence over impulses for an open and impartial effort to grapple with the problem. Unable to deny the force of Martynov's argument, Plekhanov also refused to admit that Lenin had seriously erred—especially since the latter conceded that he had overstated the case for consciousness as a corrective to the deplorable predilection of the Economists for spontaneity. In response to the critics, Plekhanov replied:

Napoleon had a passion for divorcing his marshals from their wives; some marshals yielded to him although they loved their wives. Comrade Akimov is like Napoleon—he wants at all costs to divorce me from Lenin. But I have more character than Napoleon's marshals. I do not intend to divorce myself from Lenin and I hope he does not intend to divorce himself from me.[9]

For the sake of solidarity against an Economist threat that existed no longer, Plekhanov brushed aside a revision of the program that would have brought it more closely into correspondence with the theory he himself had propagated for two decades. The force of Martynov's case, however, was not lost on everyone.

Early exchanges between the Iskrists and the Bund-RSDU representatives hinted that the differences between them could not fairly be reduced to centralism vs. anti-centralism or decentralization. Rather it was a disagreement as to the degree of centralism necessary and desirable for the best interests of the movement. The issue came into sharp focus in a critical session of the Congress concerned with the organization and powers of the party's central institutions. Rejecting pleas for a careful prescription of the powers of the Central Committee, which was to provide practical leadership, Lenin insisted on leaving to the committee itself the definition of its sphere of competence. This was essential, he argued, because the interests of the party might frequently necessitate intervention by the Central Committee in the affairs of local groups.[10] Boggling at this extraordinary demand, representatives of the Bund and the RSDU took the floor to protest against an organizational model which treated the local organizations as mere appendages of the Central Committee. Trotsky, one of the most aggressive agents of the Iskra steamroller, forthrightly asserted that the party statute properly expressed the party's distrust of all its component parts by vesting control of them in the Central Committee.[11] On this issue, the opposition was voted down by a large majority that included not only Plekhanov but Martov as well.

To its opponents, the Iskra bloc's monolithic unity made it invulnerable. They could hardly have imagined that in the second phase of the Congress it would be split down the middle. The first phase had demonstrated how easily the adversaries of *Iskra* could be disposed of. Like many an alliance against a common foe, this one began to disintegrate once the foe had been vanquished. Once his impotence had become apparent, differences the allies had suppressed for the sake of unity began to come into play. Lenin had succeeded too well in the first phase of the Congress. In the second, he could no longer hold his forces together; the polarity Bund-RSDU *vs. Iskra* was superseded by a new alignment.

The battle was joined over the proposed party rules that Lenin presented for the approval of the Congress. Paragraph 1 of these rules, which Lenin himself had drawn up, was destined to be the principal focus of debate. It stipulated: "Anyone is considered a party member who accepts the program and supports the party both materially and by personal participation in one of the party organizations." Prior to the Congress, Lenin had explained his proposal to Martov, who, although finding the definition disquieting, apparently had not regarded the matter as sufficiently weighty to bring up before the editorial board.* Further reflection as to its implications and then the accumulation of disturbing evidence during the Congress, it appears, impelled him to take a stand. At any rate, taking exception to Lenin's formula, Martov presented a counterproposal that substituted for the last requirement individual work under the control and guidance of one of the party organizations. The heat generated in the ensuing debate made it clear that the opposing elements attached great significance to what, on its face, appeared a trivial difference. Not only did the issue create acute discord; it precipitated a schism in the *Iskra* editorial board, and, as it turned out, in the party as well.

Martov, supported by Axelrod, Trotsky, and others, correctly discerned in Lenin's paragraph a device calculated severely to restrict entry into the party. This proposal, an attempt to implement one of the leading ideas of *What Is to Be Done?*, violated their conception of the nature of a socialist party. The Martovists had nothing against a conspiratorial organization of professional revolutionists; indeed, they recognized the need for such an organization *within* the party. But they refused to equate—as they believed Lenin would have them do—the one with the other. Looking ahead to the development of a mass labor party, Martov characteristically asserted: "The more widely dispersed is the name party member, the better. We can only rejoice if every striker, every demonstrator, in answering for his conduct, can declare himself a member of the party."[12] Lenin's rejoinder showed that he was much more concerned with the maintenance of "hardness of line and purity of principles" than with the building of a party of

---

* Haimson, *The Russian Marxists and the Origins of Bolshevism*, pp. 169–70. Martov, many years later, wrote of some dissatisfaction on the part of several of the editors in advance of the Congress. *Istoriia rossiskoi sotsial-demokraticheskoi partii*, p. 68.

large dimensions. In fact, he considered the two incompatible and unhesitatingly rejected Martov's formulation on the ground that it would admit to the party "all elements of dispersion, wavering, and opportunism." In a broad, loose party, it would be impossible to control the members.[13]

Plekhanov had risen to the defense of Lenin's formula before its author.[14] Indeed, in denominating a vote for Lenin's proposal a vote against opportunism, he gave the cue for Lenin's own defense. How could he have done otherwise, when Lenin's stand clearly demonstrated Lenin's assimilation of the lesson Plekhanov himself had striven to impose in the clash between the two which marked the inauguration of *Iskra*? But the solidarity he felt with Lenin on the need for vigilance against opportunism blinded him to implications of Lenin's formula to which he could not easily have reconciled himself. His defense betrayed an interpretation of the disputed paragraph different from that of either its author or his opponents. Whereas the one did not shrink from excluding the mass of workers from the party and the other uncompromisingly opposed such a policy, Plekhanov failed to see that the workers were really involved. He argued that the demands of discipline (associated with work in a party organization) would constitute no bar to the workers, neglecting to observe that the theoretical level Lenin deemed essential for membership would exclude the great majority. For Plekhanov, Lenin's membership rule had merit because it would prevent the entry into the party of those intelligentsia who bridled against discipline because they were infected with "bourgeois individualism." To exclude such persons would mean to bolt the door against opportunism and thus to strengthen the party.

Whatever else may be said of Plekhanov's conduct at the Congress, it was consistent throughout. The same could not be said of Martov and his followers. No one has attempted to solve the riddle that cries out for an answer: How can Martov's support of Lenin on the issue of the powers of the Central Committee be reconciled with his rebellion against the other's formula for party membership? How could Martov and his followers swallow Lenin's patent for archcentralism and a limitless authoritarianism and then strain at a demand for personal participation in a party organization as a requirement for party membership? If, as was certainly the case, pressure to maintain factional unity operated in the first instance, then why did it give way in the second? The impotence of the opposition to *Iskra* already had been made apparent by the time the powers of the Central Committee were up for discussion. By then, too, the Bund-RSDU delegates had already scored a good many points that might have sharpened Martov's dissatisfaction with some of Lenin's formulas. Since he did not break ranks until later, these factors, though undoubtedly real, do not adequately account for Martov's behavior.

The plain truth would seem to be that Martov and his supporters were at the outset relatively insensitive to the dangers implicit in Lenin's arch-centralism. In part, this circumstance is to be traced to the very developments in the socialist movement that strengthened Plekhanov's Jacobin predilections and made Lenin a Bolshevik. Probably more important, their tolerance of an extreme of centralism must be seen against the background of their experience in the *Iskra* enterprise. *Iskra*, as has been stressed, represented an effort on the part of a handful of self-chosen intellectuals to shape the Russian labor movement to a preconceived pattern. Concentrating power in a small clique, it employed fair means and foul to extend its influence, without at the same time admitting into the controlling councils those whom it succeeded in organizing. The activities of *Iskra*'s agents in Russia approximated to the right of intervention in local organizations by the Central Committee that Lenin demanded. Not only Lenin but Martov and the others became accustomed to this style of operation. Inasmuch as it had brought success, there was a natural inclination to carry it over into the formal organization of the party. This Lenin consciously sought to do, and his initiative brought no opposition from his colleagues.

The issue of the narrow party *vs.* the broad was another matter—or so it seemed to the Martovists. They reacted against the aspect of Lenin's organizational scheme that challenged their most deeply held convictions about the proletariat and the party, but they had so far not perceived the inner connection between what they were rebelling against and what they were prepared to go along with. The narrow party conception and Lenin's demand for an all-powerful Central Committee were in reality but two aspects of a single construction. Basic to it was a distrust of the masses, a conviction that socialist consciousness was given to few. And since the ultimate attainment of socialism depended upon those few, its key representatives must be concentrated in the central institutions of the party: the Central Committee must represent socialist consciousness incarnate. In the local organizations, socialist consciousness was apt to be diluted by a greater or lesser degree of opportunism. Therefore, the Central Committee must have control over the local organizations rather than the other way around. To ensure the unwavering pursuit of the ends of the movement, it must have the right to intervene, to counteract and suppress opportunism. The Central Committee must be granted power commensurate with the surpassing importance of its role.

The same premises pointed to the desirability of the narrow party as against the broad. If socialist consciousness were possessed by relatively few—if, therefore, the hardness of the party essential for its victory were constantly threatened from below by opportunism—then it followed that a narrow party would be stronger than a broad. Only in the sequel, however, did Martov and his cohorts grasp the relationship between the narrow party and the all-powerful central institutions, and openly condemn the latter as well as the former. In their minds, the *Iskra* mode of operation had peacefully cohabited with a commitment to a mass party. That the two were incompatible they at last came to recognize in the face of Lenin's drive for the formal sanction of an elitist party. Forced to make a choice, they opted for the broad, proletarian party. By the same token, they tacitly acknowledged that *Iskra's modus operandi* could be justified at most as an improvisation to meet a specific and limited situation. They refused to approve its elevation, as Lenin proposed, to the dignity of a general principle.

In the vote on Paragraph 1 of the party statute, Lenin's proposal was defeated and Martov's adopted by a majority which included, besides a substantial number of Iskrists (including four of the six editors), the Bund representatives and the ex-Economists. Lenin's obsession with opportunism had already led him to the radical conclusion that it was necessary to exclude the mass of the proletarians from the party of the proletariat. The defeat he now suffered moved him to go even further. In *What Is to Be Done?* he had made clear his conviction that the opponents of the exclusivism of the orthodox were bent on taking the party into the "swamp" of opportunism. "You are free," he wrote, "to go . . . into the swamp. . . . And we are prepared to render you every assistance in getting there. . . . But we, too, are 'free' to go where we please, free to fight not only against the swamp but also against those who are turning toward the swamp."[15] Lenin's defeat at the Congress forcefully suggested to him that, all his efforts notwithstanding, the party was blundering into the morass. Even those who had stood closest to him were insufficiently conscious of the pervading danger of opportunism, and to that extent untrustworthy. If they could not be depended upon to take the necessary steps to guarantee the purity of the party, then means would have to be found to keep these "waverers" out of the reach of power. Only the most unquestionably reliable guardians of the purest orthodoxy (that is, those who unerringly followed Lenin's lead) could be depended upon. In short, yet another line of demarcation had to be drawn, one that would cut into the innermost circle of the party.

As it turned out, events conspired to aid Lenin's design. Subsequent to the debate on the party statute, the Bund representatives and the ex-Economists in turn left the Congress.* Their departure transformed

---

* The Bund representatives left after the rejection of their plea for an autonomous status; the ex-Economists, after the vote to recognize the *Iskra* organization as the sole representative abroad of the RSDLP, a move which, they protested, in effect abolished the RSDU.

Lenin's minority into a slim majority—which was the basis for the name Bolsheviks, as against the minority, Mensheviks, by which the factions became known after the Congress. Lenin now maneuvered to secure domination of the party by entrenching himself and his loyal supporters in its central institutions: the Central Committee, the party organ, *Iskra*, and the Party Council (a supreme body to mediate between the other two).

The most emotional scenes of the Congress were played out as Lenin pressed home his advantage. The schism that had rent the editorial board came into sharpest focus in the fight for the future control of *Iskra*. Lenin resorted to a stratagem that evoked an indignant outcry from the minority. Nothing if not audacious, he got one of his followers to move the reduction of the editorial board to three men—Plekhanov, Martov, and Lenin. Lenin's justification of the change—that a smaller editorial staff would get the job done more smoothly and expeditiously—would have been more credible had he not just recently agitated for the addition of a *seventh* person, Trotsky, to the board.[16] Just as the addition of Trotsky was intended to create an anti-Plekhanov majority in *Iskra*, now Lenin sought, by eliminating Martov's adherents—Axelrod, Zasulich, and Potresov—to create an anti-Martov majority. In this manner, the "wavering" elements would be rendered impotent. As Lenin himself declared, by way of retort to Martov's denunciation of his tactics:

I am not a bit frightened by terrible words about "the state of siege within the party" about "exceptional laws against individual persons and groups," etc. In relation to the unstable and wavering elements, we not only can, we are obliged to, create "a state of siege," and our whole party constitution, all our centralism just confirmed by the Congress, is nothing other than a "state of siege" against the numerous sources of political diffuseness.[17]

Since the differences could not be composed (Martov refused to serve), the Congress ended by naming two editors only—Plekhanov and Lenin—and empowering them to add to the board as they saw fit. At the conclusion of the Congress, then, the party was cleft into two; the Bolsheviks were in control of the party's central institutions, and Plekhanov stood in the Bolshevik camp.

Plekhanov's intimate collaboration with Lenin throughout the Congress remains to be elucidated. Beating off efforts to divide him from the author of *What Is to Be Done?*, on every issue without exception he voted with Lenin. He had opened the Congress on a Leninist note, and at the end, with Lenin, he controlled *Iskra*. In the party, which had been given a Leninist complexion, he had been elected president of the Party Council. Not only did he fight staunchly for Lenin's version of Paragraph 1 of the party rules against his fellow editors and old comrades, but he also joined

Lenin in expelling them from the editorial board. Is one justified, then, in concluding that the 1903 Congress witnessed Plekhanov's conversion to Bolshevism?

Even more persuasive than the considerable testimony already supporting this conclusion is the remarkable speech Plekhanov delivered in the heat of the debate on the party program. One of the delegates, Posadovsky, asked the Congress whether the party ought to subordinate its future policy to this or that basic democratic principle, recognizing in it an absolute value; or "must all democratic principles be subordinated exclusively to the interests of the party?" To this question, on which the fate of the Russian revolution would later hinge, Plekhanov answered without hesitation:

Every democratic principle must be considered not by itself, abstractly, but in relation to that which may be called the fundamental principle of democracy, namely, *salus populi suprema lex*. Translated into the language of the revolutionist, this means that the success of the revolution is the highest law. And if the success of the revolution demanded a temporary limitation on the working of this or that democratic principle, then it would be criminal to refrain from such a limitation. As my own personal opinion, I will say that even the principle of universal suffrage must be considered from the point of view of what I have designated the fundamental principle of democracy. It is hypothetically possible that we, the Social Democrats, might speak out against universal suffrage. The bourgeoisie of the Italian republics once deprived persons belonging to the nobility of political rights. The revolutionary proletariat might limit the political rights of the higher classes just as the higher classes once limited their political rights. One can judge of the suitability of such measures only on the basis of the rule: *salus revolutiae suprema lex*.

And we must take the same position on the question of the duration of parliaments. If in a burst of revolutionary enthusiasm the people chose a very fine parliament—a kind of *chambre introuvable*—then we would be bound to try to make of it a *long parliament;* and if the elections turned out unsuccessfully, then we would have to try to disperse it not in two years but if possible in two weeks.[18]

In this speech, which he lived to regret with every sinew of his being, Plekhanov's position was scarcely distinguishable from what came to be the central theme of Leninism. To begin with, he acquiesced in the assumption that democratic rights and the interests of the party might be in conflict, a proposition which seemed preposterous to many of the delegates. How could such a conflict arise, they wondered; for what possible interest could the party stand if not for that embodied in democratic principles? By his remarks, Plekhanov showed that he deemed it possible for the people not to know what were their *true* interests. But on that score, the party, the bearer of socialist consciousness, could not err. It knew that the welfare of the people, secured by the success of the revolution, was the supreme value. Accordingly, the party might legitimately override the will of the people (for example, in bringing about the dispersal of a demo-cratically elected, though "unsatisfactory," parliament) for the people's own good.

From this position it is but a short step, or perhaps no step at all, to the affirmation that every other idea, consideration, group, or institution must give way before the party. The logic is inescapable once the party is com-pletely identified with what is held to be the supreme value. It is the same logic that demanded for the Central Committee, that higher consciousness of the true interests of the proletariat, the power to control local organi-zations of the party. The Plekhanov who spoke these words appeared to have gravitated to the very position against which he had issued a solemn warning in *Our Differences*. If the party were to conceive of itself in the manner he indicated, if it were to strive for the success of the revolution (the winning and retention of power by the party) even though its goals and the goals of the people differed, then would it not—to use his own words of an earlier date—"have to seek salvation in the ideals of 'patri-archal and authoritarian communism,' introducing into those ideals only the change that a socialist caste would manage national production rather than the Peruvian 'Children of the Sun' "?

Admittedly, on the record of the 1903 Congress, the case for Plekhanov as Bolshevik seems very strong. The Congress apparently corroborated his earlier judgment that he stood closer to Lenin than to the other members of the editorial board. Who but he had been responsible for the elitist character of the Emancipation of Labor Group? Was not *Iskra*'s opera-tional style simply an extension of the principles and methods of the Group? And was not Lenin's organizational scheme merely *Iskra*'s opera-tional style writ large? The streak of Jacobinism which distinguished Plekhanov from his other colleagues predisposed him toward Bolshevism. And, as we have observed, his Jacobin tendency was powerfully reinforced in consequence of his struggles against the ideological "heresies" of the turn of the century. Plekhanov's political behavior between 1898 and 1903 was shaped pre-eminently by his violent revulsion against Revisionism. His war against it decidedly strengthened his centralist bent, spurring him to greater emphasis on consciousness and to unrelenting war on oppor-tunism. Not only was the thinking of Plekhanov and Lenin in this period shaped by similar considerations, but without doubt Plekhanov's own writings and conduct contributed heavily to that obsession with oppor-tunism from which issued Lenin's organizational ideas.

At the Congress, as Plekhanov saw it, Lenin was carrying out the tasks that he himself had set before the assembly in his keynote speech. Rather than repugnance at Lenin's activities, he probably experienced puzzlement at the stance of the majority of the *Iskra* board, which appeared to depart from its own tradition. There was point in Lenin's characterization of the Martovists as "waverers," but Plekhanov failed to comprehend why they wavered. He did not see the conflict between Lenin and Martov for what it was—a contest between two fundamentally different conceptions of the party. His Jacobin predilection—and what was another face of the same thing, his extraordinary wariness of a certain kind of ideological deviation —blinded him to that which called forth the stern protests of his colleagues. Whereas they were not insensitive to opportunism, they now detected danger from another quarter, from those who, for fear of opportunism, would radically alter the character of the socialist party. Unable to see how a device to counter opportunism might itself be harmful, Plekhanov was prepared, as were most of the Martovists to begin with, to establish the party permanently along the lines of an authoritarian centralism. Without realizing it, he also gave his blessing to the principle of the narrow party. Thus, in addition to his Jacobin bent, Plekhanov's conduct at the Congress is partly to be explained by his failure to grasp the full implications of Lenin's organizational scheme. Unlike his Jacobinism, this incomprehension implied the potentiality of subsequent conflict with Lenin.

Some further doubt concerning the validity of Plekhanov's identification with Leninism, even if only at the Congress, stems from his attitude toward freedom of criticism. Once the party program had been adopted by the Congress, he drew attention to its binding force on all the members of the party. But, he added: "That does not mean, of course, that a program once adopted cannot be subjected to criticism. We have recognized, do recognize, and will recognize freedom of criticism. But he who wishes to remain a member of the party must, even in his criticism, remain on the ground of the program."[19] Whatever the qualification may mean, the point of view here expressed is well removed from Lenin's equation of freedom of criticism with "freedom for an opportunistic tendency in Social Democracy." Even though at the Congress Plekhanov was not conspicuously tolerant of diversity, he did not condemn criticism on principle as had Lenin. Herein lay another possibility of discord between the two.

Only a short while after the Congress, Plekhanov executed a startling volte-face. Within months, he was reunited with his old comrades and taking up the cudgels against his erstwhile ally. His reversal constitutes decisive evidence that his Bolshevism at the Congress was not nearly so resolute and unequivocal as it appeared to many. Though overshadowed by their evident unity, in retrospect the differences between Lenin and Plekhanov at the Congress are significant. They help to account for what otherwise defies rational explanation.

The Congress over, not a few of the delegates were still at pains to understand the most unexpected turn matters had taken.[20] The bewilderment of many of the principals was emphasized by their profound disagreements as to what had provoked the split. For Lenin, the new division was both perplexing and most regrettable; but he could at any rate take comfort that in the end his views had prevailed. With *Iskra* and the Central Committee in the hands of his supporters, control of the Party Council was also assured, and he could count upon steering the party as he wished. Such a perspective, however, did not reckon with the intentions of Martov and his group to challenge Lenin's supremacy. The Mensheviks would not reconcile themselves to what they viewed as a bid for total control by the other faction on the basis of a slender majority. After the Congress, the Mensheviks not only stood together in a total boycott of *Iskra*, refusing to collaborate in any way, but they also sought to undermine Lenin's position through a campaign in the party organizations. They scored their first success in the Foreign League of Revolutionary Social Democracy, which the Congress had designated the sole officially recognized organization abroad (thus formally ending the organizational life of the Emancipation of Labor Group).

At a congress of the League convened in Geneva six weeks after the conclusion of the party congress in London, the Mensheviks possessed a clear majority. When Lenin, the League's representative at the party congress, reported on the Brussels-London meetings, he was repudiated by the majority. The next day Lenin moved to disband the League congress and to revolutionize the League itself. He set upon it a certain Lengnik, one of his loyal supporters and a member of the Central Committee. Lengnik demanded that the rules of the League be altered, that new members be admitted, and that, pending such changes, the congress be dissolved as incompetent. In this fashion Lenin sought to carry into effect the principle of the right of intervention by the Central Committee into local organizations. The League would have none of it, however, and went forward with its deliberations. The upshot was its conversion into a major instrument for a continuing battle against Lenin.

As the conflict waxed, Plekhanov was caught in an extremely distressing position. To be sure, he had sided with Lenin at the party congress, and he supported him at the League congress; when Lengnik's action against it was appealed, in his capacity as president of the Party Council he ruled against the Menshevik majority in the League. But each step was more difficult for him than the last. After the fracas at the League congress, he could go no further on the same road. Lenin had outstripped his master in intransigence. The positions of the two at the time of their bruising encounter in 1900 were being reversed. The moment was approaching when Plekhanov would break with his disciple because of the latter's excessive hardness. Unable to continue "the state of siege" in the party that Lenin considered indispensable, the old intransigent at last broke down. At a meeting of the Bolshevik caucus, he cried out: "I cannot fire at my own comrades. Better a bullet in the head than a split. There are moments when even the autocracy has to compromise." An ominous voice interjected: "Then it is said to be wavering."[21] The word "opportunism" was about to be flung at Plekhanov. A new line of demarcation was soon to be drawn that would relegate the Father of Russian Marxism to the ranks of the impure.

In Plekhanov's statement just quoted, the middle sentence was decisive. Although no doubt chagrined at having to fire at his long-time associates, Plekhanov rarely allowed sentiment to enter into his political calculations. He certainly had shown little patience with Kautsky's reluctance to fire at *his* old comrade, Bernstein—but then, Plekhanov saw no resemblance between the controversy in the German party and the current Russian one. Having defined the struggle against Revisionism as a matter of life and death for the socialist party, he stridently called for casting out the heretics. A new split in the Russian party, when its future appeared so auspicious, was more than he could bear. That it might split over what he took to be mere organizational differences seemed to him "an inexcusable political mistake, a heinous *political crime*."[22] The specter of a schism led Plekhanov to assume a new and, for him, wholly uncharacteristic role—that of apostle of peace. The reconciliation of the two factions and the restoration of unity now became his preoccupation. In this task he had perforce to urge flexibility and compromise, an attitude hardly compatible with continued solidarity with Lenin.

Plekhanov's shifting position first of all became manifest in regard to *Iskra*, the focal point of his alliance with Lenin. In the interest of party unity he now reversed himself on the question of continuing the old editorial board, and by October was anxiously seeking a way to reinstate the four editors who had been removed by the decision of the party congress. Under the party rules, new editors could be added only by agreement of the elected editors, and Plekhanov was well aware that Lenin would never consent. To exert pressure, he proposed himself to resign. Lenin objected that it would be better for him rather than Plekhanov to resign—otherwise everyone would conclude that he, Lenin, had been in the wrong.[23] With that, Lenin quit the board—surely one of the grossest miscalculations of his entire political career. Plekhanov thereupon quickly recalled the four former editors, and *Iskra* was transformed into a powerful engine for battering down Lenin's remaining strongholds. The change in the composition of the *Iskra* board also automatically introduced two of Lenin's foes, Axelrod and Martov, into the five-man Party Council. In resigning from the board, Lenin may have hoped that Plekhanov could draw the others toward Lenin's side. If that failed, he would still command the party through control of both the Central Committee and the Party Council, for Plekhanov's vote in the latter would ensure Lenin's dominance there. He surely did not expect Plekhanov, instead of winning over the other editors, gradually to fall into line with them. Yet that is precisely what happened.

The shape of things to come was prefigured in the first article Plekhanov contributed to the "new" *Iskra*.[24] Its title, "What Is Not to Be Done," announced that he was putting some distance between Lenin and himself. Yet his criticisms of Lenin were circuitous rather than direct and far milder than those of his co-editors Martov and Axelrod. To this extent, he occupied a middle position appropriate to his self-assumed role of peacemaker. Nevertheless, his critical comments were opposed in spirit to his own position at the Congress and similar in kind to those of the Mensheviks. To Plekhanov's pleas Lenin remained deaf. Recognizing that his plans were going awry, that power was gravitating to his opponents, Lenin desperately but vainly strove to mobilize the Central Committee in order to arrest and reverse the process.[25] Failing in that, he put his case before the party at large in the biting pamphlet *One Step Forward, Two Steps Back*. Plekhanov did not take kindly to Lenin's apparent disregard for his authority, his unwillingness to "listen to reason," his stubborn adherence to conduct seriously damaging to the party. In the course of a year, he assumed an increasingly harsh attitude toward Lenin, moving ever closer to those against whom he had been aligned at the Congress, and he broadened his critique to include not only the organizational but also the tactical and theoretical aspects of Lenin's position.

Initially, Plekhanov singled out as the basis of the party crisis the intransigence of Lenin and his followers. Hardly given to softness and vacillation himself, he thoroughly appreciated the importance of militancy in a revolutionary party. But, from his new perspective, militancy was not always and everywhere a good; its appropriateness depended upon concrete conditions of time and place. Lenin's uncompromising stance, he now thought, militated against party strength and, hence, against the success of the revolutionary cause. It operated as a divisive force which threatened to split the party irrevocably and to exhaust its energies in internecine warfare. Obviously, it was time for a more flexible and conciliatory policy.[26]

Plekhanov understood well the psychological root of Lenin's intransigent attitude. He himself had emphasized repeatedly that the most uncompromising struggle must be waged against every tendency that threatened to corrupt the party, to deflect it from the unwavering pursuit of its goals. But he believed that the defeat of Economism had ended the danger of the corruption of the RSDLP; indeed, the most significant result of the Second Congress had been precisely the attainment of ideological unity. Regrettably, out of the fight against ideological heresies there had grown a morbid sensitivity which was itself dangerous. "Many of us," Plekhanov wrote in a revealing passage, "have become accustomed to thinking that a Social Democrat must be uncompromising if he does not wish to commit the sin of opportunism."[27] The future of the revolutionary movement would be gravely jeopardized if, on such grounds, the party leadership saw fit to impose the discipline of the barracks, to perpetuate a sectarian spirit of exclusivism, to become "utopians of centralism."

In a subsequent article entitled "Centralism or Bonapartism," Plekhanov delineated the sorry fate of the party should it follow Lenin's lead. In so doing, he disassociated himself from the policy of continuous demarcation by which he, and Lenin even more, had thought to ensure the purity of the party. The "hards," he asserted, indiscriminately applying the labels opportunism, Bernsteinism, and Revisionism, "are ready with a light heart to tear away from the party one category of comrades after another as they tear leaf after leaf from an artichoke."[28] Plekhanov now challenged the implied claim of the party center to infallibility and the concomitant right of anathematizing all who differed with it. He aligned himself with the advocates of that freedom of criticism which, in Lenin's eyes, was and could be nothing more than "freedom for an opportunistic tendency in Social Democracy." He considered the Leninist ideal more akin to Bonapartism than to the centralism proper to a proletarian movement; it would succeed in driving from the party all intelligent, self-respecting persons and leave only sycophants.

Months before the appearance of Trotsky's similar critique, which has been much more widely publicized in our time,[29] Plekhanov prophetically sketched the character of future party life should it be grounded on Bolshevik organizational principles:

Imagine that the Central Committee recognized by us all possessed the still-debated right of "liquidation." Then this would happen. Since a congress is in the offing, the C.C. everywhere "liquidates" the elements with which it is dissatisfied, everywhere seats its own creatures, and, filling all the committees with these creatures, without difficulty guarantees itself a fully submissive majority at the congress. The congress constituted of the creatures of the C.C. amiably cries "Hurrah!" approves all its successful and unsuccessful actions, and applauds all its plans and initiatives. Then, in reality, there would be in the party neither a majority nor a minority, because we then would have realized the ideal of the Persian Shah.[30]

Contrasting this monolithic organizational conception with his own model of a party possessing a vigorous inner life, Plekhanov observed that the Bolsheviks "evidently confuse the dictatorship of the proletariat with a dictatorship over the proletariat."[31] It followed that what was needed was not merely a greater flexibility on the part of the leadership, not merely a tolerance of a certain diversity of opinion, but also organizational forms which would limit the authority of the party center. One-sided control from the top down must give way to mutuality of confidence, and, with that, to a continuing interchange of ideas and influence between the party center and the local organizations and rank-and-file members.

Lenin's conduct, and the consequences for the party which Plekhanov thought it entailed, forced the older man into a skeptical attitude to arch-centralism and unlimited intransigence. He was bound now also to re-evaluate his own behavior. His articles of the period are extraordinary for the repeated admissions of error and expressions of regret for actions he had taken in the recent history of Russian Social Democracy.[32] Especially noteworthy is his more charitable treatment of the Economists.[33] They had of course erred, he now argued, but their energetic and successful agitations among the workers constituted an outstanding service. Their outlook had been faulty and one-sided, and it had been necessary to fight and correct it. But they had not, as had those he denominated the theoreticians of Economism, deliberately sought to stifle the development of the political consciousness of the proletariat. Plekhanov now admitted that *he* had overshot the mark in failing to distinguish between loyal if erring comrades and actual foes of the proletariat, in denouncing and, in effect, reading out of the party the former as well as the latter. The fascinating dialectic at work in the party for some years was nearing its climax. Plekhanov, once the comrade-in-arms of Lenin in the war against Economism, now was giving absolution to the latter and joining forces with its former advocates for a struggle against Lenin.

Having initially embarked on a campaign against the consequences of Lenin's outlook (the necessity of shooting at one's comrades, and of refusing to give ground even if that made inevitable the rupture of the party), Plekhanov ultimately was driven to lay bare its roots. Having earlier remained silent about *What Is to Be Done?*, having collaborated intimately in the effort to implement its central ideas at the Congress, in 1904 Plekhanov at last subjected this key work to a searching examination.[34] Now he brought under critical appraisal the theoretical basis of Leninism, its characteristic formulation of the relationship between consciousness and spontaneity.

In *What Is to Be Done?* Lenin conceived of the labor movement and the rise of socialist thought as two distinct, mutually exclusive, entities. The industrial workers at a certain stage organized trade unions for the defense of their interests. But, by themselves, they were incapable of going beyond trade-union consciousness, of transcending the existing order by rising to socialist consciousness. Not only did the workers not create socialist ideology, but it was created "entirely independently" of the spontaneous labor movement. Elements of the bourgeois intelligentsia—a non-proletarian group of high culture—had derived and developed socialism out of current philosophical, historical, and economic theories, and then brought it to the workers from outside. Having conceived the initial relationship between spontaneity (the labor movement) and consciousness (the socialist intelligentsia) in this fashion, Lenin then proceeded—so Plekhanov contended—to take it as a fixed postulate from which he derived his tactical and organizational views: "Excluding socialism from the mass and the mass from socialism, Lenin proclaimed the socialist intelligentsia the demiurge of the socialist revolution."[35] Therefore *it* must constitute the party, while the mass of the workers, essentially opportunistic and alien to socialism, must remain outside. The proletariat, instead of serving as the conscious, historical agent of the socialist revolution, would merely be utilized by the party to achieve *its* ends. Such a scheme required a party in which infinite care was exercised to demarcate the pure from the impure (Plekhanov accused Lenin and his followers of constituting themselves a *super*-intelligentsia which denounced and put outside the pale all those who did not agree with them), and control was exerted from the top down.

In rejecting this narrow construction, Plekhanov attempted first to put the historical record straight. Lenin, he insisted, gave a distorted account of the historical relationship between the labor movement and the emergence of socialist thought. He adduced evidence that Marx and Engels in the West and he himself in Russia arrived at socialism not independently of the rising labor movement but as a response to their awareness of it and of developing class antagonisms. The socialist intelligentsia incontestably did much to impart a socialist orientation to the labor movement, Plekhanov agreed, but not nearly so much as Lenin gave it credit for. It was as incorrect to postulate a working class incapable of rising to socialist consciousness as to divorce the emergence of socialist thought from the struggles of the labor movement. In fact, he argued, experience of the capitalist system not only spurred the workers to self-defense through trade unionism but also aroused in them antagonism to the system itself.* Rather than a passive or opportunistic mass alien to socialism, the "revolutionary bacilli" found a proletariat instinctively socialistic. Their task lay in elevating what was instinctive to the conscious level.

Plekhanov's formulation obviously diminished the role of the socialist intelligentsia. Besides, in what he conceived from the first as a dialectical relationship, the tutelary role of the intelligentsia was gradually reduced as the workers acquired a socialist consciousness, and it would in time be-

---

* A little later, he was to call a "libel" the assertion that the working class, by itself, could never rise above trade-union consciousness. *Sochineniia,* XIII, 184.

come superfluous. This scheme gave scope for vital activity by both the intelligentsia and the mass; it saw consciousness not as the exclusive property of one side and, therefore, implied a broad party; it took as axiomatic the socialist inclinations of the proletariat and its capacity and will to carry out the socialist revolution. Instead of being opposed to each other, consciousness and spontaneity, party and mass, were seen as mutually interpenetrating, ultimately becoming one.

While in the main holding to this scheme in rebutting Lenin's theses, at one point Plekhanov came very close to the Economist position. "If the socialist revolution," he wrote, "is a necessary consequence of the contradictions of capitalism, then it is clear that at a certain stage of social development the workers of capitalist countries would come to *socialism* even if 'left to themselves.' "[36] This affirmation sounds like the ultimate in economic determinism. In reaction to Revisionism, Plekhanov had placed a heavier emphasis than ever on the intelligentsia; in reaction to Leninism, he went to the other extreme, denying completely its indispensability. Even without the intervention of the socialist intelligentsia, he remarked— going further in the heat of the polemic than he had ever gone before, or would ever go again—the socialist revolution was inevitable. His pronouncement in any case had only an academic interest, for he obviously did not propose to have the intelligentsia retire from the scene. Even though it was not indispensable for the socialist revolution, he considered its activity helpful in shortening the time span to the achievement of socialism.

In the end, as might have been expected, Plekhanov denounced Lenin's outlook as a perversion of Marxism. While posing as the incorruptible guardian of orthodoxy, while demanding the most extraordinary organizational arrangements to that end, Lenin himself had deviated hopelessly from "scientific socialism." For Plekhanov, the capitalistic mode of production predisposed the workers toward socialism, and socialist theory itself represented a generalization of the experience of the working class. Although it left room for reciprocal influence of the socialist intelligentsia on the proletariat, his interpretation took the content of the intelligentsia's consciousness to be fundamentally conditioned by the proletariat's situation. To argue otherwise, he contended, was to deny that central truth of Marxian materialism—"being determines consciousness." Lenin's theory bespoke the opposite conviction; it constituted a new embodiment of the idealist doctrine that consciousness determines being. Plekhanov insisted, moreover, that only his own picture of the relationship between the capitalistic mode of production, the proletariat, and the intelligentsia pointed to the immanence of the socialist revolution in the historical process. Those who cast the intelligentsia in the role of "the demiurge of the socialist revolution" by that very act betrayed their disbelief in the inevitability of the proletarian revolution.

Plekhanov's analysis of the revolutionary process squared impeccably with the teachings of Marxism, but the teachings of Marxism did not so easily square with the social reality of the time. Central to all else in his system was his confidence in the inevitability of the socialist revolution. When he wrote "if the socialist revolution is a necessary consequence of the contradictions of capitalism," the "if" figured as a rhetorical flourish rather than as an indication that he viewed the proposition as anything less than a self-evident truth. From this postulate he deduced the development of socialist consciousness among the workers and, at an earlier stage, an instinctive socialism. Doctrines that had to be proved he took as axiomatic, and from them he deduced other principles of major import to his system.

Bernstein, proceeding inductively rather than deductively, had challenged the fundamental Marxian doctrine of the inevitability of socialist revolution. A substantial part of his case rested on the reformist inclinations of the workers, which he regarded positively. Leninism, although it may properly be viewed as a reaction against Revisionism, began with the same premises. What Bernstein regarded positively Lenin castigated as opportunism, but no less than Bernstein he recognized the implications of that phenomenon for the inevitability thesis. From that point on, the two diverged sharply. Bernstein, taking the inclinations of the workers as a guideline, called for transforming the socialist movement into a democratic party of social reform. Lenin, loath to forswear the ultimate socialist goal, was convinced that it could be reached only by revolution. To compensate for the failure of the proletariat to live up to expectations, and the attendant dimming of revolutionary prospects, he proposed transforming the party into a compact, highly disciplined engine of revolutionary consciousness and will. With proper organization and unlimited determination, the party would be capable of surmounting all obstacles, not only the entrenched power of the ruling classes but the slackness and corruptibility of the proletariat as well.

Plekhanov occupied a central position between his opponents to the right and left. In reaction to the challenge of Revisionism, he had moved toward Jacobinism, calling for unrelenting war upon opportunism and for increased stress on consciousness as a guarantee of the ultimate ends of the movement. In this, he set the pattern for Lenin; but Lenin went one step beyond. Unlike Plekhanov, who never squarely faced the issue, Lenin did not ignore the unpleasant implications of worker opportunism. Plekhanov considered that Revisionism meant either the writing off or—what amounted to the same thing—the indefinite postponement of the achievement of socialism. While approving Leninism's dedication to the socialist revolution, Plekhanov feared that its distrust of the mass of the workers and their exclusion from the party would lead the revolutionary movement to a very different destination from the one intended.

In the first case, the ends proper to a Marxian party were sacrificed; in the second, the means. Plekhanov's recognition that in neither instance could the perspectives of Marxian theory be achieved speaks eloquently for his acumen. His own system had the merit of consistency between means and ends, and it kept faith with Marxian teachings. However, his doctrinaire orthodoxy, and his refusal to confront the disturbing facts that conflicted with it, foreshadowed the collapse of his system. The movements launched by Bernstein and Lenin, departing from Marxian orthodoxy, were destined to flourish because each in its way took account of basic political realities. Failing in that, Plekhanov and orthodox Marxism were to go down together.

14

1905: TESTING TIME

PLEKHANOV WAS NEARING his fiftieth year when the Revolution of 1905 broke. Half of those years he had spent in the emigration, his place of residence shifting with the political tides. Expelled first from Switzerland and then from France, he had settled in England—without his family—until, through the intervention of the Swiss socialists, he was permitted in 1895 to return to Geneva. Although he remained under a ban in France and could visit there only by special permission, at any rate he was no longer bothered by the political authorities in Switzerland. Since the mid-nineties, the family had been free from grinding poverty. Rosaliia Markovna, after completing her medical studies, gradually developed a practice that enabled the family to enjoy a modicum of comfort and security.

No one knew better than Plekhanov how much he owed his devoted wife. He had from the first been for her a shining hero, a militant warrior for the good of humanity; and she, a dedicated socialist, gladly devoted her life to his. While raising a family and keeping a home, she continued her early medical studies in order to help him one day be rid of pressing financial worries. She shared in his political struggles, hailing him in victory, consoling him in adversity.* Plekhanov's feeling for Rosaliia is poign-

* Even after his death, her dedication to him did not flag. As once she had taken up medicine to advance his work, she later abandoned it to perpetuate his memory. At the request of the Soviet government, in 1928 she transferred Plekhanov's voluminous papers and library to Leningrad, where, for a decade, she supervised their preservation, classification, and partial publication. During those years, more than once she crossed swords with powerful personages who by the spoken or written word denigrated her departed comrade.

antly conveyed in a letter he wrote from England in 1894, which reveals a tenderness in Plekhanov unsuspected by all but a few intimates:

You already know of course of the death of Alexander III. Russia, it goes without saying, has lost nothing with his death, but . . . I am truly sorry for his wife; it seems she loved him very much and now is living through the greatest distress a person has occasion to experience in life. When you yourself love someone fervently, then you sympathize with the loss of loved persons, no matter who those persons may be.[1]

Since the mid-eighties, Plekhanov had suffered from tuberculosis, and often he was seriously ill. In 1897 such a spell was found to be not just another acute stage in the development of his condition but an independent and serious malady—an angina. Ever alert to her husband's condition, Rosaliia Markovna insisted that Plekhanov take proper care of himself. In 1908 she managed to set up a sanitarium in San Remo, Italy, which made it possible for Plekhanov to escape the cold Geneva winters. Her devoted care undoubtedly much prolonged his life.

Despite his uncertain health, Plekhanov retained his vitality. He continued to adhere to the daily routine he had developed years before with an eye to making the most productive use of the short span allotted to man. Passionately absorbed in the life of the mind, a trait exemplified by the ever greater range of his interests, he managed his own time in accordance with his father's old maxim, "We shall rest when we die."[2] He arose early and was at his desk by eight o'clock. There he would remain until six in the evening, with time out only for dinner, a brief rest, and a vigorous walk. Many days he worked four or more hours at night as well, but ordinarily the end of the day was reserved for interviews with visitors, political conferences, and discussions.

Few things were permitted to interfere with this rigorous schedule. Persons who called during his working hours were sent away. He told the members of his household that if God himself came to the door he should be requested to come back at six. Even in time of illness, he hardly slackened his pace. Instead, he devised a formula, based on thermometer readings, which regulated the type of work he might do. If his temperature was normal, he allowed himself to do anything he liked; when his temperature was above normal but less than 100 degrees, he occupied himself with his studies on art and ethnography or wrote articles not requiring great intensity of concentration; when his temperature was more than 100 degrees, he read contemporary literature or reread Russian and foreign classics. A nature lover and a believer in the wisdom of keeping fit, Plekhanov regularly took long walks. But whether in country or town, he invariably carried with him a book, a notebook, and a pencil. He was a familiar figure in an alley of Geneva's university quarter, pacing back and forth, intent on a book.

Before 1895 it had been impossible for Plekhanov even to think of a private study. After the family fortunes improved, however, he was fitted out with a commodious room in which to house his voluminous library and carry on his work.* There, with his heroes—Engels (Marx, curiously, was absent), Belinsky and Chernyshevsky, Goethe and Voltaire—staring down at him from the walls, he labored in his characteristically meticulous and intensive manner. He never got over the "unfortunate habit" of preparing for every article as though "getting ready to write a dissertation,"[3] so that the preparation generally consumed more time than the writing itself. His insatiable appetite for books is evident from his correspondence, no small part of which consists of requests for materials in one of the five languages he read. If not always, it was surely true much of the time that books and study engaged Plekhanov's interest and energies more than did people and politics. "For a person using it, a book is an inviolable thing,"[4] he once said; and later: "to take a book away from me is equivalent to murder."[5]

His manner of composition was similarly thorough and fastidious. As his wife recalled:

Sometimes, he would dictate the beginning of some article or other. To me this beginning seemed excellent. But he was not satisfied: "No, throw that away, take another sheet." There would follow a new beginning, and then a third and a fourth. I was astonished that with each turn the thought emerged more polished, more beautiful. This exactingness in relation to himself, this care in the working up of his articles, he never forsook to the end of his life.[6]

In spite of his perfectionism, Plekhanov's literary output was enormous. Apart from his abundant commentaries on the eventful times in which he lived, his polemics against rival or deviant political tendencies, and the ever wider range of intellectual disciplines to which he made a contribution, he rarely turned down an invitation from any socialist party or organ to write something. In this he was guided by the rule he had on one occasion suggested to Kautsky: "You are a Marxist, and for a Marxist, as for St. Paul, there is neither Hellas nor Judea. You give all your time to the German workers; give a few hours to the Russian workers, too."[7] As with all workmen in the scholarly guild, however, there were moments when his commitments seemed unbearably tedious. "If you knew how weary I am," he once wrote to Axelrod, "if you knew how fed up I am with this

---

* The room, with all its original furniture, has been restored at the Dom Plekhanova in Leningrad. This institution also contains Plekhanov's papers and his library of 8,000 books and countless periodicals.

eternal, never ending writing. I am definitely condemned by fate to an eternal servitude to literary labor."[8]

His service, for all that, had earned for Plekhanov a great reputation. He counted the leaders of international socialism among his friends, and he himself figured prominently in the affairs of the International. His election to the chairmanship of the Second Congress, and then to the presidency of its supreme body, the Party Council, acknowledged his authority and prestige in the RSDLP. Lenin, even after their break, acknowledged Plekhanov to be a man of "colossal stature." To progressive Russians, Plekhanov had become a living monument. The twenty-fifth anniversary of his participation in the Kazan Square demonstration was commemorated in a number of European cities by resident Russians. As with Herzen and Lavrov before him, many of his compatriots who traveled abroad felt bound to make a pilgrimage to see Plekhanov, to lay eyes on the prophet from whose pen had come the sacred writings of Russian Marxism.

Though surely not indifferent to such homage, Plekhanov had scant time for those who knew little or had nothing interesting to tell him. If a person for whom he had no respect boasted to him that he had been a Marxist at twenty or twenty-two, he was apt to reply, "Well, you've begun to regress at an early age, haven't you?" And to those who dared disagree with his ideas, he might answer tartly, "I was a revolutionary before your father began courting your mother."

Perhaps it was by persons who felt the cutting edge of Plekhanov's tongue that disturbing tales were spread concerning his mode of life. Unaware of his long years of poverty and disregarding the circumstances which explained much of what they saw, some of the young revolutionists were shocked to find Plekhanov living more like a Tambov squire or a bourgeois intellectual than a revolutionary leader. In addition to the comfortable apartment in Geneva, at 6 rue de Candolle, which the Plekhanovs occupied for over twenty years, and where they employed a maid, they possessed winter quarters on the Italian Riviera. Their two daughters, Lydia and Eugenia, were accomplished, well-mannered young ladies, who were educated in European schools and knew nothing of the bohemian life of young Russian radicals. Then there was Plekhanov himself, impeccably groomed and aristocratic-looking. It is impossible to imagine Plekhanov's helping someone—as the story is told of Lenin—to move a great cart of household goods through the streets from one residence to another.[9]

The total lack of bohemianism in Plekhanov and his orderly household led a good many young Russians to suspect that the old Marxist had quite forsaken the revolutionary faith and accommodated himself to the bourgeois world. Though farfetched, this supposition held a grain of truth. Plekhanov, living abroad for long decades, and sensitive to his surroundings, became intimately acquainted with European life and society. He valued its political and cultural attainments, even while exposing its hypocrisies and Philistinism. In spite of its grave faults, he recognized its vast superiority to Russia. He was ambivalent to "bourgeois" life rather than unequivocally opposed to it as were many of the revolutionists; and, indeed, he would have liked nothing better for many years ahead than for his homeland to attain to the levels of the "bourgeois" West.

If some visitors were unfavorably impressed with Plekhanov, others came away quite under the spell of his wide intelligence, his brilliant speech, and his aesthetic sense. The rapt attention with which he was listened to as he spoke in French to audiences of workingmen was often commented on.[10] And Lunacharsky, the future Soviet Commissar of Education, paid a glowing tribute to the life-enhancing effect of Plekhanov's conversation upon those who had the good fortune to know him intimately:

I remember with enthusiasm our long conversations and arguments on philosophical and literary themes, in the course of which I often forgot the problem . . . as, charmed, I listened to this artistic speech, full of quotations, reminiscences, metaphors, in a word, adorned like some many-colored, invaluable incrustation. Georgii Valentinovich's memory was vast, resourceful, amazing, and every conversation with him always enriched you while at the same time giving absorbing pleasure.[11]

Thus, while some found him cold, condescending, and wickedly sarcastic, to others he appeared gracious, erudite, and exhilarating. Each glimpsed a certain aspect of "a man of letters of genius" who was "all too conscious of his genius," "merciless in polemic . . . disdainful, and capricious," because, as one writer has said, "he felt himself intellectually superior to any opposition."[12]

As his twenty-fifth year in the emigration approached, Plekhanov could look back with much satisfaction on what he had achieved. His had been a full measure of suffering and frustration, illness and poverty, but it had not all been in vain. He had laid the foundations of Russian Marxism and in so doing had brought to life a highly dynamic and potentially powerful revolutionary party. At the international level, he had played a leading role in what was then thought to have been the defeat of the Revisionist challenge to Marxian orthodoxy. In the Russian Social Democratic movement, he was in the vanguard of the force that overwhelmed the Economist "heresy." Major problems remained, of course. The newly created Socialist Revolutionary (1901) and Liberal (1903) Parties posed a challenge to the Marxists, and it had to be met; but, of the three, the Social Democrats seemed the strongest, and Plekhanov was confident that it could maintain its lead. To be sure, he was deeply disturbed by the divisions that rent the RSDLP consequent to its Second Congress. Yet, as serious as were his strictures upon Lenin and the Bolsheviks, he discerned a large area of agreement with them and ardently believed in the possibility of reconciliation and reunion. His optimism, rooted in a faith in the inevitability of progress, was not easily shaken. "Come what may," went one of his favorite expressions, "we will surely triumph in the end."

His assurance that all would come out well is not to be dismissed as baseless. Year after year, from the crow's-nest of his Western exile, Plekhanov intently scanned the tide of Russian events, restlessly seeking confirmation of his predictions. By the early years of the twentieth century, it appeared that the "whirring loom of time" had proved important parts of his prognosis. Had not the passing years witnessed the quickening of Russian economic development and the ever deeper penetration of capitalistic organization in industrial life? Had not the "disintegration" of the old-style peasantry continued, as money economy and market relationships expanded into the country? Was it not true that Russia's economic evolution was accompanied by the emergence of bourgeois and proletarian classes? This "Europeanization" of Russian economic and social life, he insisted, made an anachronism of the despotic political system which had been built upon an entirely different socio-economic basis. The relegation of tsarism to the dustbin of history and the Europeanization of Russian political life, he confidently believed, were bound to follow.

In the first years of the century, the crisis of Russian autocracy was apparently maturing. More and more frequently, with greater and greater boldness, and in ever larger numbers, masses of students, workers, and peasants struck, demonstrated, and rioted. The unprecedented dimensions of these disturbances, and the rise of underground political organizations capable of skillfully exploiting them and fomenting new ones, confronted the regime with a threat entirely different in nature from anything known in nineteenth-century Russia. The reforms of Alexander II had been calculated to end unrest and to stabilize the socio-political order. Ironically, a half-century later those very reforms had raised up against the government a host incomparably more dangerous to the regime. Alexander's reforms had, of course, been unavoidable. But neither in the sixties nor after were political changes introduced that might have made possible peaceful development of the national life. By failing to give ground, Russian autocracy unwittingly strengthened the hand of the revolutionists.

In keeping with hallowed tradition, Nicholas II met popular unrest with violence and duplicity. Demonstrators were dispersed by the whips of mounted Cossacks. More insidiously, the regime strove to distract an angry, semiliterate populace by covertly instigating pogroms against the Jews. In yet another gambit, secret government agents endeavored to compete with the revolutionists for the loyalties of the workers. The "police unions" they organized with a view to channeling proletarian discontent into economic moderation and nationalist fervor were to backfire with disastrous consequences. The dissatisfactions of the workers could not be contained within the narrow bounds intended by the managing directors of police unionism. Partly because of genuine sympathy for the workers, partly because of their pressures, Father Gapon, the head of one such organization, led a peaceful procession of petition-bearing proletarians to the Winter Palace on January 9, 1905. On that Bloody Sunday several hundred of the demonstrators were shot down, and the most tumultuous phase of the Revolution of 1905 began. Instead of intimidating the people, the government's fusillade spurred the country—not only workers but peasants and others—into a frenzy of oppositional activities.

From a different direction, another wave, rolling up during 1904, converged with and reinforced the one that broke on Bloody Sunday. For some years, the Tsar had pursued in the Far East a reckless and deceitful policy which at last exhausted the patience of Japan, resurgent since the imperial restoration a few decades before. In February 1904 the Japanese without warning attacked the Russian naval base at Port Arthur, thus opening the Russo-Japanese War. It has been suggested that the Russian government deliberately courted "a nice little war," on the assumption that victory would be easily won, and an accompanying spread of patriotic sentiment would succeed in muffling social protest. If true, the regime blundered inexcusably once again; even if not true, the Tsar's irresponsible conduct of foreign policy in the face of rising internal disorder bespeaks shocking incompetence. In the course of the war, moreover, evidence accumulated that the Alexandrine reforms had failed to achieve not only internal stability but also their other major aim—external strength.

From the first, the war was unpopular with a part of the Russian public. Displeasure was widespread, and it became outspoken protest as Russia suffered one humiliating defeat after another. In a mutually reinforcing cycle, the government lost credit with the politically conscious public, and the latter mounted a vigorous campaign of organized pressure for political reform. The most conspicuous activity came in the last half of 1904 and was initiated by the liberal Union of Liberation and the zemstvo groups and professional organizations from which it drew its strength.[13] Incapable of pursuing a consistent policy (witness the Palace Square massacre a few months later), Nicholas wavered, and appointed as Minister of Interior Prince Sviatopolk-Mirsky,* a man of comparatively liberal persuasion. The Prince's benign attitude gave the forces of discontent further scope for the development of their offensive through congresses and banquets.

---

* In place of the reactionary Plehve, who had been assassinated by a terrorist.

In 1905, then, a wide range of social forces was up in arms against tsarism—not only professional people and students, workers and peasants, but also gentry and businessmen of liberal tendency and elements of the national minorities, who seized the occasion to rebel against oppressive policies of the Russian state.

With all these, and especially the organized political parties, joined in their desire to overthrow or substantially alter the old political order, grounds for cooperation obviously existed. Yet the presence of widely divergent interests and ideologies introduced rivalry as well, and if rivalry took precedence, the chances of overthrowing tsarism would be diminished. With the stakes nothing less than the right to determine Russia's future, a hard-fought competition was waged for influence and power.[14] It was a time when tactics were all-important. Each group had to conduct itself in a way that would ensure both the concentration of ample force for dealing with the Tsar's government and the seizure of the most advantageous possible position for itself in the new order. It was a balance not easy to strike.

For no party more than for the RSDLP was the tactical challenge greater. The Marxists possessed a complete historical prospectus to follow in the master plan of social development worked out by Plekhanov two decades before. Glimpsing some of the complexity of his party's tasks, he had spared no effort to develop suitable tactics, the rational means of reaching the intended ends. The fight against tsarism was to be made a stepping stone to the achievement of a later revolution against the very social order the Social Democrats must first help bring to birth. In regard to this crucial matter, on the eve of the revolution, both factions of the RSDLP ostensibly saw eye to eye. As against this compelling fact, disagreements on organizational questions, and even certain theoretical differences relating to the nature of the party seemed to Plekhanov marginal and inconsequential. Could this fundamental unity survive the jolts and surprises of revolutionary experience itself? Would the course of the revolution conform to his image of it or not? Herein lay the significance for Plekhanov of the Revolution of 1905. It was the most critical event in his career, the testing time for the revolutionary theory on which he staked his political life.

At the outbreak of the Russo-Japanese War Plekhanov was reunited with the majority of the original editors in control of *Iskra*. His increasing hostility to Lenin in the ensuing months was largely the result of Lenin's "divisive" tactics at a time so propitious for the revolutionists. Plekhanov was fully aware of the enlarged possibilities for revolutionary action as Japan inflicted one drubbing after another on Russia. Far from bemoaning the humiliation of Russian arms, the former cadet greeted military defeat as an ally of the revolution. As early as April 1904, he declared: "If the Sevastopol defeat pulled up by the root the system of Nicholas I, then the Port Arthur crash promises to shatter to its foundations the regime of Nicholas II."[15] With victory within reach, the forces of progress must accelerate the gathering of their legions, striking harder and harder, and never resting until the triumphant figure of freedom stood astride the trampled, loathsome corpse of autocracy.

The position Plekhanov took on the war was internationalist, revolutionary, and defeatist. It was dramatized by his conduct at the Amsterdam Congress of the International in August 1904. At the opening session, when the presiding officer called attention to the fraternal solidarity of the proletarians of all countries, symbolized by the presence on the platform of the delegates of the two warring nations, Plekhanov rose and demonstratively shook hands with the Japanese socialist Katayama Sen, to the accompaniment of an enthusiastic ovation. Later, in a speech, he denounced the Russian government for provoking the conflict and hailed its impending doom.[16]

The international socialist movement had a major stake in the developing Russian crisis. The overthrow of tsarist autocracy, generally acknowledged to be a bulwark of European reaction, would facilitate the general advance of socialism. For that reason, more than on any other single issue, the International demonstrated working-class solidarity in the support it rendered (though even that proved ineffectual) to the Russian revolutionists in 1905.[17] Acutely conscious of the awesome responsibility that rested upon the Russian proletariat, Plekhanov did everything in his power to restore unity in the RSDLP. He was conscience-stricken that, because of its internal divisions, his party might be derelict in its obligations to international socialism.

The theoretical basis of Plekhanov's stand on the Russo-Japanese War emerged in an important article he wrote in 1905 entitled "Patriotism and Socialism."[18] The proletarian cannot be patriotic, went the gist of the argument, in a bourgeois fatherland. In modern capitalist society, class struggle creates stronger bonds between the workers of different countries than between workers and their exploiters of like nationality. To work for the genuine welfare of one's country, therefore, did not mean to rush to the colors at the first blast of the trumpets of chauvinism. National ambitions and national honor must give way before higher claims, the claims of humanity as a whole, which were at the heart of the international socialist movement. The sincere socialist must evaluate all international relations according to the principle, *salus revolutiae suprema lex*. He could not dogmatically oppose every war, and once hostilities had broken out, his sympathies must go to the belligerent, whether attacker or defender, whose victory promised in one way or another to enhance the prospects of social-ism. Not blind to the advantages a Japanese victory might bring the Japanese bourgeoisie, Plekhanov nonetheless judged the overthrow of Russian autocracy, which would be facilitated by Japanese victory, of far greater positive significance for the international socialist movement. But Plekhanov immediately qualified his seemingly clear theoretical position, in order to reconcile it with socialist antimilitarism. Inasmuch as wars between civilized peoples in contemporary times seriously damaged work-ing-class interests, the conscious elements of the proletariat were in practice "the most decisive and reliable partisans of peace." Propositions that Ple-khanov took as self-evident in 1904–5 were later to prove clouded with ambiguity and to become the subject of violent controversies in interna-tional socialism in the diplomatic crisis of 1914.

In keeping with his long-held strategy, Plekhanov was most preoccu-pied during the revolutionary crisis of 1904–6 with the question of the relations between the bourgeoisie and the proletariat. In his estimation, the developing upheaval could be only a bourgeois revolution, and, inevitably, the bourgeoisie would have a prominent part in it; but the proletariat was destined to strike the decisive blows. Provided each played its prescribed role, absolutism would be overthrown, the bourgeoisie would become the governing power in a democratic regime, and the proletariat would be in possession of the rights which would enable it to prepare for its economic emancipation later on. As a tactical guide for the attainment of these ends, Plekhanov took Marx's famous slogan: "Alongside the bour-geoisie, to the extent that it is revolutionary in the struggle against absolutism, never ceasing to instill in the proletariat recognition of the antagonism of its interests to those of the bourgeoisie."

In the months of Sviatopolk-Mirsky's so-called "spring," the busy politi-cal activity of the zemstvists and other elements of "society" that he sub-sumed under "the bourgeoisie" gave Plekhanov little cause for complaint. And, after Bloody Sunday, in ringing the tocsin for an armed uprising, he betrayed no doubt that the bourgeoisie would respond favorably to his resounding slogan: "March separately, strike together."[19] This was a capsule statement of his conviction that all opposition groups, while main-taining their principial and organizational independence, must coordinate their activities to maximize the chances of success. Above all, the bour-geoisie and the proletariat must synchronize their blows to shatter the Tsarist edifice.

Soon, however, he began to find fault with his intended ally. By April 1905, Plekhanov, none too gently, was chiding the bourgeoisie and its hangers-on for indulging in a talking spree instead of organizing for action. "If, according to the Bible, the walls of Jericho once fell at the sound of the 'horns of Jubilee,' " he wrote, "in our prosaic time miracles don't happen and the citadel of autocracy will hardly fall at the sound of the innumerable oratorical exercises of our innumerable lovers of freedom."[20] At the same time, he reproved them for failing to neutralize and check the counter-revolutionary tendencies which had cropped up among certain groups of artisans and peasants.

After the October general strike drove the Tsar to promulgate the Manifesto of October 17, with its promise of civil liberties and a representative, legislative Duma, Plekhanov's criticism of the bourgeoisie and its representatives became more pointed. Skeptical, as were many on the left, of the Tsar's promises, he openly warned against antirevolutionary and antiproletarian sentiments current in bourgeois circles, which might ensure the success of Count Witte's efforts to split the revolutionary coalition.[21] In fact, the conservative wing of the liberal movement seceded from the attacking force, formed the Octobrist Party, and thenceforth made common cause with the government. In the course of 1906, Plekhanov came to believe that even the left-liberal Cadet Party, which he took to represent the advanced elements of the bourgeoisie, had almost exhausted its revolutionary fuel. Dominant in the First Duma, which convened in April 1906, the Cadets took a stand sufficiently advanced and intransigent to provoke the Tsar's government to decree its dissolution. In July, in the Vyborg Manifesto, their leaders called for popular support to the Duma, through passive resistance. Plekhanov took issue with the Manifesto on the ground that instead of explaining to the people what it needed to fight for and how, it called for measures which could not possibly be effective against the government.* Presently he criticized the Cadets for abandoning the demand for a constituent assembly and spurning the offer of the Social Democrats to enter into electoral agreements on that platform. Almost more in sorrow than in anger, Plekhanov came to the conclusion that the Cadets feared the sovereignty of the people, and ought properly to be called the Party of People's Semi-Freedom rather than the Party of People's Freedom.[22]

To explain the political behavior of the bourgeoisie, Plekhanov used two different lines of argument. In one, he blamed Lenin's crude tactics for driving the bourgeoisie to the right. He charged that, in choosing only to expose rather than both to support and expose the bourgeoisie, the Bolsheviks had struck a mighty blow against the liberation movement. But he discerned another quite sufficient cause for the equivocal relation of the

---

* Sochineniia, XV, 161–63, 186–87, 194. Plekhanov pointed out that withholding of taxes would have small effect upon the government, since it obtained little revenue from direct taxes. And the abstention of progressively minded youth from service in the army would leave that decisive instrument entirely to the forces of reaction.

bourgeoisie to the revolution. He saw in their unwillingness to fight the Tsarist regime to a finish and their rejection of the demand for a constituent assembly based upon universal suffrage a concern for class interests at the expense of the welfare of the country. For the sake of the landowning elements in its midst, the Cadet Party repudiated the convocation of a constituent assembly, in fear that such an assembly might vote to expropriate the landed estates without compensation.[23] In so arguing, however, Plekhanov was in the peculiar position of scolding the bourgeoisie for conducting itself as he had predicted it would. His earlier judgment that the bourgeoisie would be incapable of sustained revolutionary action was fulfilled better than he had reason to be happy about.

Yet Plekhanov never wrote off the bourgeoisie entirely. Instead, he considered worthy of support any initiative whatever that it might undertake in behalf of political liberalization. For example, while accusing the Cadets of desiring a good deal less than an all-powerful Duma, to the extent that they fought even for a less than fully sovereign institution, he pledged proletarian support.[24] His stand was a logical consequence of an unshakable attachment to Marx's theory of an economically determined sequence of historical stages. In that context, Russia's upheaval could be only a "bourgeois" revolution. His line, he contended, merely implemented Marx's admonition that the proletariat ought to support the bourgeoisie to the extent that it was revolutionary in the struggle against absolutism. So consistently did Plekhanov cleave to the basic premise and the tactic it required that he found himself for the first time in the extreme right wing of the Social Democratic Party. The Bolsheviks described him as an opportunist, pointing derisively to the esteem he enjoyed in the bourgeois press. But even the Mensheviks backed away from a tactic they regarded as self-defeating.[25] They, too, were sensitive to the charge—Plekhanov's repeated denials notwithstanding—that Plekhanov's tactic made the proletariat an instrument of the bourgeoisie. They were highly skeptical of Plekhanov's assurance that the Social Democrats could force the bourgeoisie into a more aggressive stance by helping to intensify what he discerned as a basic opposition between its interests and those of the old order. And, indeed, how could this assurance be squared with his own interpretation of the conservative drift of the bourgeoisie, seen as springing in part at least from its class interests? At one key point—and it was not to be the only one—the revolutionary scheme of the Father of Russian Marxism gave indications of insupportable stress.

After the October Manifesto, the apparent willingness of some of the bourgeoisie to come to terms with the government spurred Plekhanov to designate the peasants "that extraordinarily powerful reserve of the Russian revolution," a potential replacement for the bourgeoisie in the continuing attack.[26] But this idea, which became the core of Lenin's tactics, was for Plekhanov a mere spark that never caught fire. For Lenin's distrust of the bourgeoisie was paralleled, if not equaled, by Plekhanov's distrust of the peasants. If Lenin and the Bolsheviks chose to expose rather than to *support and* expose the bourgeoisie, Plekhanov was certainly more inclined to expose than to support the peasants. To be sure, he welcomed the onset of the *Jacquerie* as evidence that another great stratum of the Tsar's "loyal subjects" was being seduced by "senseless dreams." To be sure, he endorsed the general division of the land, arguing that the success of the peasants' rebellion against the survivals of feudalism would promote the most rapid development of capitalist relationships in the countryside.[27]

But more significant was his monumental neglect of those political groups which sought to express the interests of the peasants. In his writings of the revolutionary years, save for an occasional jab of ridicule, there is scarcely a mention of the Socialist Revolutionary Party. Earlier he had adopted the custom of speaking facetiously of the SR's as "the so-called party of the so-called Socialist Revolutionaries." Probably because of disdain for its theoretical ineptness—Social Revolutionism, according to its historian, was "less an ideology than a state of mind"[28]—Plekhanov seemed unable to take this group seriously. Perhaps the irrationality he discovered in the SR Party appeared to him as an extension of the backwardness and irrationality he professed to see in the peasantry itself. To the Trudoviks, a strong, peasant-based delegation in the First Duma, Plekhanov deigned to devote half an article. But the impression is unavoidable that he was more interested in proving its petty bourgeois character than in finding ways and means of promoting joint action.[29] The enormous earnestness of Plekhanov's discourses on proletarian relations with the bourgeoisie stand in glaring contrast to his quite platonic efforts to build a proletarian-peasant coalition.

In his mind, enthusiasm for the turbulence of the peasantry was tempered by distrust, much as similarly mixed sentiments about the proletariat existed in the minds of many Russian liberals. His distrust was manifested in a number of ways. In opting for support to the insurgent countryside in its drive for land reform, he made it clear there would be no support to the smallholder as against the large, when largeholding represented not a feudal survival but a progressive economic development.[30] This note was a reprise on his oft-repeated belief that the small peasant opposed the "natural" and rational development of large-scale capitalism in an effort to perpetuate his own unstable economy. In a famous speech at the Stockholm Unity Congress of the RSDLP in 1906, Plekhanov attacked publicly, as he had earlier in private, the project for nationalization of land which Lenin now resurrected. But he warned equally against an evident propensity among some peasants to favor the transfer of confiscated land not to private holdings but to the state.[31] This latter tendency he dubbed the *kitaishchina* of the peasantry, an irrational wish to revert to that prior condition of state control of all land, which, in his view, had constituted the economic basis of Russia's oriental despotism.

Finally, and most important, Plekhanov saw the irrationality of the peasantry epitomized in its lack of political consciousness. In certain moving passages of his continuing post-mortem of the revolution he spoke of how the Russian people, through centuries of subjection, had been conditioned for political passiveness.[32] Fervently desiring the land, they had no glimmer of understanding that such an economic reform depended upon the acquisition of adequate political power. They dutifully participated in the Duma elections of 1906, apparently regarding that body as a kind of omnipotent deity which could sweep away all difficulties and fulfill their wants. They failed to understand that the Duma could *become* something significant only if it were strengthened by the resolute support of the people. In a miracle of incomprehension, peasants in the uniforms of the Imperial Army fouled their own nest when they helped bayonet into submission the revolution that would have met their age-old hunger for land. In these grievous failures of the peasantry, Plekhanov saw a fearful drag upon the progress of the country as a whole. The Bolsheviks were sadly wrong, he concluded, in regarding the peasant as "a political adherent and reliable ally of the proletarian."[33] They might seek to manipulate the turbulence of the peasantry for their ends; but turbulence alone was not enough for Plekhanov, who demanded rationality in the historically active masses.

The prophet of the proletariat was left with a terrible dilemma. The bourgeoisie declined to battle militantly for political freedom. And the peasantry, which fought uninhibitedly, was disqualified because of the alleged nonrational character of its struggle. Thus the proletariat was in effect isolated. Perhaps Plekhanov sensed this as early as December 1905, when he privately cautioned against the armed proletarian uprising that shortly broke out under the auspices of the Social Democrats, only to be drowned in blood.[34] More was involved than doubts as to whether the Social Democrats could muster sufficient forces for victory. Plekhanov could not countenance the continuation of the attack by the working class alone, for the alternatives it faced were entirely unacceptable. He rejected any thought that the proletariat alone might destroy absolutism and then hand power to a bourgeoisie which had sat with its hands folded.[35] Even less admissible, in his view, would be the seizure of power by the proletariat, followed by an attempt at the socialist reconstruction of the country. It would be impossible for the proletariat to retain power and to drive on to socialism in the absence of all the economic and social pre-requisites.[36] The dilemma posed by this set of alternatives Plekhanov never squarely faced.

True, the solution to the problem lost some of its urgency, though none of its significance, as the revolutionary tide ebbed and as it became clear that the proletariat did not in any case possess the power to overthrow the old regime. Nevertheless, the failure of the revolution to achieve what he had hoped of it forced Plekhanov to review the tactics of the insurgents. Throughout 1906 and 1907, he publicly pondered the recent events, coming to the sober conclusion that the revolutionary forces had underestimated the enemy and engaged it without sufficient preparation. Forgetting how, after Bloody Sunday, he had waved aside in advance any objection that the era of successful armed uprisings was past, he now emphasized that contemporary governments had far greater powers of resistance than at the time of the French Revolution.[37] That circumstance made mandatory extended and extremely careful preparation before the gauntlet should be thrown down. In particular, it required infinite tact and wisdom, features he found sadly lacking in the tactics of the opposition in 1905.

In laying bare what he identified as its faults of omission and commis-sion, he did not spare those closest to him. The fact that the RSDLP was divided at the outbreak of the revolution had been a crushing disappoint-ment to Plekhanov. In the spring of 1905, the schism gave evidence of deepening. The Bolshevik and Menshevik factions held separate con-gresses, and Plekhanov in mid-1905 responded to such reprehensible con-duct by resigning his posts as editor of *Iskra* and president of the Party Council.* By this dramatic move, he hoped to bring the factions to their senses and to make his plea for unity prevail. For the time being, however, it merely made for a further splintering of the party. About a year later, a Unity Congress of the party was convened in Stockholm, in response to pressures from the rank and file who had flocked into the local organiza-tions of both factions during 1905. But despite Plekhanov's efforts before, during, and after the Congress, the RSDLP was not truly reunited. Ple-khanov's passionate addiction to unity was exceedingly odd in view of his own emphasis on the great differences that had developed between the Bolsheviks and the Mensheviks. They seemed no less substantial than earlier ones between the Revisionists and the orthodox which had prompted him to call for the expulsion of the former from the ranks of the

---

* *Sochineniia*, XIII, 226. Once Plekhanov had severed his relation with *Iskra*, he was free to try an experiment he had talked of earlier, the publication of articles on various themes in a series on the order of Dostoevsky's *Diary of a Writer*. The first of the series, entitled *The Diary of a Social Democrat*, appeared in the spring of 1905. Its continuation throughout the year and its resumption in 1909 advertised Plekhanov's isolation as the revolutionary crisis came to a head and later as well.

Western socialist parties. In 1906, Plekhanov, in Alice-in-Wonderland style, continued to urge unity, at the same time proposing that the names Menshevik and Bolshevik be discarded in favor of Marxist and Blanquist, which would be more indicative of the real and profound differences between the two groups.[38]

The charges that Plekhanov leveled against the Bolsheviks in 1905–6 —and he was to repeat them almost word for word in 1917—are reminiscent of his bill of particulars against the Narodovoltsi two decades before. He accused them of being unable to think dialectically, to understand what goals were historically attainable, to base tactics on real conditions, and to harmonize means and ends. In rejecting objective criteria as the determinants of action and in seeking to achieve unattainable ends by magical means, they deserved to be called "alchemists of revolution."[39] Using intemperate and unseasonable tactics and slogans, they sowed alarm among the bourgeoisie and confusion among the proletariat. He surely had the Bolsheviks in mind—though he may also have been thinking of those Mensheviks who followed Trotsky—when he made the remarkable observation: "The difficulty with us is not in recognizing the antagonism of the interests of the bourgeoisie and the proletariat. In our ranks, the recognition of that antagonism has already attained, one might say, *the firmness of a prejudice.*"[40] He had reason to fear that proletarian class consciousness, to the development of which he had dedicated his life, was overreaching the desired mark, or rather was assuming distorted forms, thus paralyzing the bourgeoisie and creating the frightening possibility that the proletariat might attempt a premature seizure of power.

The Bolsheviks' emphasis upon technical preparation for an armed uprising, coupled with their apparent disregard for the development of the self-activity and consciousness of the workers through trade unions, cooperatives, and electoral activity, seemed to Plekhanov a scandalous betrayal both of the fundamental principles of Marxism and of the only tactic which might result in victory for the revolutionary movement and the proletariat. "If Marx and Engels came incognito to one of those meetings at which our 'Bolsheviks' hold forth with revolutionary eloquence," he wryly observed, "they would be castigated for their 'moderation' and declared to be 'Cadet-like Marxists,' or, in a fit of anger, simply 'Cadets.' "[41] So saying, Plekhanov identified Marx and Engels with himself, for the Bolsheviks had labeled him a "Cadet-like Social Democrat." What appeared to him as the astonishing conduct of the Bolsheviks he explained by the predominance of intelligentsia among them, and indeed in the party generally, leading to a fantastic and one-sided approach which could be corrected only when the workers in great numbers entered into Social Democracy and made of it a mass party.

At the Stockholm Congress, Plekhanov first openly aligned himself with the Mensheviks. The record shows, however, that before and after the Congress he maintained a high degree of independence and not infrequently rebuked the faction to which he nominally belonged. Plekhanov was bound to combat that substantial section of the Menshevik group which, under the influence of revolutionary events and Trotsky's exhortations, appeared ready to break out of the framework of revolutionary strategy elaborated at the commencement of his Marxian career, to which he still held fast. In 1905, for the first time, he directed at the Mensheviks that criticism he would make of the moderate socialist groups collectively in 1917: that they trimmed their tactics in fear of incurring the label of opportunism.[42] In other words, under pressure of the Bolsheviks, they were driven to more radical positions than they deemed right. He also discerned among some of the Mensheviks a fault of which he himself was far from free, an excessive schematism in their projection of the course of the revolution, and in the tactics to be implemented at various points and in various contingencies. In the campaign for the Second Duma, Plekhanov publicly disapproved the party's electoral platform, which he found "infelicitously written" and, more important, "poorly thought out." His maverick behavior evoked not only the censure of the Bolsheviks but chilling silence from the Mensheviks.

Just as in the first instance Plekhanov's hopes for political freedom rested above all on the proletariat, so in his wish to reconstruct the shattered revolutionary legions and to prepare for new offensives he looked again to the proletariat as the keystone. But he was only too aware that if its vanguard had become consciously Social Democratic, a large proportion of the proletariat remained indifferent to the stirring events around them. Even worse, substantial numbers were so poorly oriented that they joined with the extremist, reactionary Black Hundreds, or else came under the influence of the Blanquist *coup de main* advocates. These shocking circumstances would vanish, he felt, under the impact of wise Social Democratic tactics. The Marxian party's overriding task, as always, was to heighten proletarian consciousness,* to facilitate the passage of the proletariat from an algebraic to an arithmetical class, from potentiality to conscious reality. To that end, Plekhanov called first for the promotion of the self-activity of the workers in every possible way. He placed especially great emphasis on trade unions, and, from the first, opposed the boycott of elections for the Duma (favored by the Bolsheviks and many Menshe-

---

* A distinction implicit in Plekhanov's thinking must be borne in mind: that between a "distorted" proletarian consciousness in which antagonism to the bourgeoisie had assumed "the firmness of a prejudice," and that "true" proletarian consciousness which recognized both the antagonism of bourgeois and proletarian interests and the necessity of a capitalist epoch to the ultimate achievement of socialism.

viks). He favored participation in cooperatives, and he argued more than once for the convocation of a worker congress, the pet project of his friend Axelrod. In unions, cooperatives, or electoral campaigns, the people would learn by doing, would probe the social environment and, with the aid of the Social Democrats, become conscious of their interests and how best to promote them. The workers would then take their places in the ranks of Social Democracy and make of it a mass party. They would purge it of the chimerical elements introduced into its ideology by the intelligentsia, and they would refuse to tolerate disunity. As a united mass organization, the RSDLP would be a real threat to autocracy, not only in and of itself, but by stimulating the action of other social groups, first among them the bourgeoisie.

All these recommendations and predictions concerned the fine detail of the revolutionary movement and introduced no change in the fundamental architecture of Plekhanov's projection of Russia's future. That there was wisdom in his suggestions for fuller preparation for new revolutionary offensives may be admitted. But in what must such preparation consist? On the one hand, Plekhanov answered, in Social Democratic tactics calculated to evoke a more robust opposition to the old order from the bourgeoisie. In that event, the proletariat would not be isolated in the attack upon absolutism. "Striking together," the bourgeoisie and the proletariat would carry to its conclusion the work of Russia's first revolution. On the other hand, the Social Democrats must more effectively elevate the class consciousness of the proletariat to ensure that it would "march separately" in the revolutionary conflict. In sum, the tactic for the Social Democrats remained, as before: Alongside the bourgeoisie in the struggle against absolutism, never ceasing to instill in the proletariat recognition of the antagonism of its interests to those of the bourgeoisie. Yet in this very formulation lay the fundamental contradiction in Plekhanov's prognosis, which the events of 1905 had brought into sharp relief.

From the first, Plekhanov had striven to keep the Russian proletariat from serving as a blind instrument of the bourgeoisie in the struggle against absolutism. Instead, it should fight as an independent and class-conscious force, under Social Democratic leadership. He never adequately took into his calculations the possibility that the bourgeoisie might be disinclined to participate in revolutionary action with a group which openly avowed its intention presently to destroy bourgeois society. Again and again, Plekhanov insisted that the socialists must neither hide their ultimate aims nor temporarily abandon their socialist propaganda in order to merge with "society" for the conquest of political liberty.[43]

To do otherwise would be to *dim* the class consciousness of the proletariat, and Plekhanov stoutly maintained that its *increase* was a precondition for the winning of political liberty. Only by socialist propaganda, by arousing hopes for eventual economic emancipation, could masses of workers be moved to take up the cudgels for political freedom. But this argument is less than convincing, for by his own account it had not been socialist propaganda that had drawn the West European workers into the fight against absolutism. That the situation in Russia was potentially similar is evident from Plekhanov's deep concern to deny the liberals leadership of the proletariat. In 1905, as he himself noted, the bourgeoisie was distressed at the influence the Social Democrats enjoyed among the workers, and their own revolutionary ardor was accordingly diminished.

Yet he never clearly recognized that proletarian class consciousness and bourgeois revolutionary militancy were likely to be inversely related. In the West, revolutions had been "bourgeois" just because, and only so long as, the bourgeoisie and its representatives enjoyed uncontested leadership of the opposition movements—the masses, and especially the proletariat, not yet having attained that consciousness which necessarily must precede its constitution as an independent political force. The Revolution of 1905 made clear the impossibility of combining the bourgeoisie with a class-conscious proletariat in a "bourgeois" revolution of the West European kind. It showed that a class-conscious proletariat quickly blighted whatever revolutionary tendencies the bourgeoisie might have. It had brought into bold relief the critical questions: How could a "bourgeois" revolution be carried through without the bourgeoisie? How could a class-conscious proletariat be brought to smash absolutism and then surrender power to a class it had learned to fear and hate?

To these questions Trotsky and Lenin each provided an answer. As Trotsky saw it, the logic of the Russian situation demanded the skipping of an extended interval of bourgeois-democratic rule. The proletariat was not to be deterred either by the passivity or by the counterrevolutionary inclinations of the bourgeoisie from proceeding with the overthrow of absolutism. And once it had disposed of the Tsarist regime, it would turn immediately upon the bourgeoisie in order to inaugurate the socialist phase with all possible speed. Lenin also broke with Plekhanov's scheme, but he did not yet dare to go as far as Trotsky. Still restrained by doctrinal considerations, he could not bring himself to project an immediate transition to socialism. But he decisively rejected a bourgeois regime as the outcome of the first revolution, envisaging instead the establishment of a dictatorship of the proletariat and the peasantry. Precisely what that should entail he never clearly stated; if he had, the basic inconsistency of *his* position would have been revealed.[44]

Plekhanov was unmoved by these attempts to find a way out of the dilemma posed by the events of 1905. He did not even admit the existence of the dilemma, of a new and different situation from the one anticipated in the tactics he had developed decades earlier. Astonishing as it may seem, he who always preached the superiority of the dialectical mode of thought, of the necessity always to take into account the conditions of time and place, failed to detect, let alone resolve, the unique difficulties of the Russian situation.

He persistently failed to recognize the impossibility of finding a tactic that would at once heighten the consciousness of the proletariat and stimulate the bourgeoisie to more aggressive action against the old order. Clinging to his basic premises, he stressed now one, now the other, of this pair of incompatible injunctions. In so far as he reconciled them at all, it was by means of an almost imperceptible shift in emphasis in his interpretation of proletarian class consciousness. If, as he declared, proletarian antagonism to the bourgeoisie had already attained "the firmness of a prejudice," further instruction along that line was obviously unnecessary. But Plekhanov's concept of class consciousness also called for sensitivity to the limits imposed on action by the stage of historical advancement a country had reached. The Social Democrats had the duty of inculcating in the proletariat an awareness that, because of the level of Russian economic development, Russia was ready only for a "bourgeois" revolution. In other words, they were called upon to restrain the revolutionary predilections of the proletariat which they themselves had aroused. That consideration prompted Plekhanov's sharp attacks on the ultrarevolutionary rumblings of both Bolsheviks and Mensheviks, and his eagerness to support any forward initiative by the liberals, no matter how modest. He who had spent his life trying to form the Russian proletariat into an independent political force was now obliged to counsel restraint upon independent proletarian action lest the bourgeoisie be intimidated and the proletariat isolate itself. Yet the timidity of the bourgeoisie, especially after the experience of 1905, ruled out revolutionary initiatives from that sector of society. To accommodate proletarian tactics to those of the bourgeoisie meant to forswear revolution. In effect, Plekhanov said A, while hotly denying that B must inexorably follow. Such was the predicament in which he became entangled as the inner contradictions of his effort to establish an organic link between the bourgeois and socialist revolutions were developed to their limit.

Again and again Plekhanov brought out the stock arguments, indicating wherein and to what extent his rivals had deviated from the canons of Marxism. Yet he realized only too well that support for his own position was declining. In desperation, he endeavored to bring the prestige of the leaders of international socialism into the balance. To a number of them he addressed a series of questions about the character of the Russian revolution and the tactics proper for the Social Democrats. But what was intended to give a fillip to his waning influence turned into one of the most stunning defeats of his career. To his utter consternation, the man he respected above all others in the international socialist movement, Karl Kautsky, replied in a sense absolutely destructive of Plekhanov's position. The dimensions of the disaster may be judged by the fact that Lenin saw fit to translate Kautsky's response into Russian, and to publish it with a Foreword of his own. He hardly exaggerated when he described Kautsky's remarks as "the most brilliant confirmation of the tactics of . . . the Bolsheviks."[45]

The burden of Kautsky's pamphlet was a denial that the French Revolution of 1789 could serve as a model for Russia, that the Russian revolution could possibly be bourgeois in character. The weakness of the Russian bourgeoisie and the emergence of an independent proletarian party spoke for that. Kautsky also stressed the inherent inability of a liberal government to effect a solution of the country's most pressing difficulty, the agrarian problem, in the only way it could be solved—radically. Only confiscation of the landed estates without compensation, and massive state aid to the peasants at the expense of the armed forces and church and state lands, could put Russian agricultural economy on a rational basis. Only by a proletarian-peasant coalition, Kautsky argued, could Russia attain political freedom and at the same time solve the agrarian problem. Like Lenin, Kautsky excluded the possibility of a genuine bourgeois revolution, and yet did not think socialism imminent in Russia:

We shall behave most correctly in relation to the Russian revolution and the tasks it presents us with if we will regard it not as a bourgeois revolution in the usual sense of the word, and also not as a socialist revolution, but as an entirely original process, taking place on the boundary between bourgeois and socialist society, facilitating the liquidation of the first, preparing the conditions for the creation of the second, and in any case giving a powerful impetus to the progressive developments of the countries of capitalist civiliation.[46]

The blow to Plekhanov could hardly have been more devastating. Certain of Kautsky's comments seemed directed specifically at what its author perhaps deemed the obtuseness of his interrogator. "We must recognize," Kautsky said, "that we are confronting entirely new situations and problems, to which not one of the old patterns fits." Moreover, judging it likely that victory would fall to the Social Democratic Party, he warned: "It is impossible to fight while refusing victory in advance." In other words, the proletariat had to fight, and it made no sense whatever to fight unless the leaders were prepared for power. To engage the enemy only if the bourgeoisie did, and unconditionally to forswear power, added up to political bankruptcy.

Though visibly discomfited by Kautsky's analysis of the situation, Plekhanov responded to it no more imaginatively than to the events that had called it forth. By use of tortuous reasoning, he claimed to prove that Kautsky actually agreed with him, and that their differences were only semantic.[47] Similarly he parried the criticisms advanced by Rosa Luxemburg, and they stimulated no change in the direction or content of his thinking. She, not he, was wrong, he urged, in rejecting as outmoded the tactics that Marx and Engels had devised in 1847–48 concerning the relation of the proletariat to the bourgeoisie in the struggle against absolutism.[48]

In 1905, the revolutionary faith to which Plekhanov had devoted his life was put to the test and found wanting. Once before, in the Chernyi Peredel phase of his career, his ideas had seemingly lost their grip on reality and their promise as an instrument for its transformation. To the challenge implicit in the crisis of revolutionary Narodnichestvo, the young Plekhanov had responded creatively. In fathering Russian Marxism, he opened up a new and, as it proved, fruitful avenue of activity for the revolutionary movement. With the Revolution of 1905, Russian orthodox Marxism entered upon a crisis that in the end proved fatal. To this challenge to his second political faith, Plekhanov proved incapable of making a creative response. The fifty-year-old revolutionist no longer had the flexibility of youth. He and his revolutionary system had become inseparable, his commitment to it absolute. It could be shaken neither by events that strikingly refuted basic premises nor by the criticism even of those whose judgment he valued most highly. Plekhanov had become a doctrinaire, a man so blinded by doctrinal allegiances to the true nature of his world that he was incapable of adapting to it.

He could turn nowhere. If the revolution could not be carried out according to his preconceived plan and with the intended results, then why not forswear revolution? But Plekhanov could not renounce a commitment on which he had built his whole life, even when the tactics he commended now seemed incompatible with revolution. His orthodox economic determinism would not permit him to take the path of "revolutionary adventurism" to which Trotsky and Lenin pointed. Still confident that his own calculations were attuned to the historical process, he believed that individuals, groups, or classes daring to violate its iron laws would soon realize their folly. Fixed doctrinal considerations also forbade him from seeking a vital coalition with the peasantry and its spokesmen. How could a more rational society be expected to emerge from an alliance with a numerically superior partner, tradition-bound, sympathetic to irrational and backward forms of social economy, and lacking in political consciousness? Plekhanov could not abandon one of the central elements of his system. Like Luther, there he stood and had to stand, because he could do no other.

It has been argued that Plekhanov's failure to make appropriate adjustments was the result of his long exile and a consequent inability to grasp the situation in Russia.[49] True or not, it must be noted that he did not return to Russia in 1905. Trotsky was the only exiled Russian Social Democrat of any note to return to Russia early in the revolution, and his tireless and brilliant work greatly increased his stature. Every other leader of the party but Plekhanov returned to Russia sooner or later, most of them after the issuance of the October Manifesto, with its promise of civil and political liberty, and before the Tsarist regime succeeded in crushing the revolution.

Plekhanov had anticipated a speedy return to his country in 1905. In December his wife wrote joyously to Axelrod, who had gone on ahead to Finland, of their impending reunion in Russia. "We are overwhelmed with excitement," she exclaimed, "and we cannot wait for the day when at last we shall move from here."[50] Axelrod, meanwhile, was writing that the moment would soon be at hand "when Georgii must come forth in the arena of electoral and parliamentary struggle."[51] Exciting new perspectives were opening up when Plekhanov once again became seriously ill. To comrades in Russia, impatient for his return, he explained that his ailment, chronic inflammation of the pharynx, had become much aggravated that autumn. "Several doctors advise me to have an operation; others would send me to Algeria. All consider a voyage to Russia senseless. I will come, having taken for a short while certain palliatives which will enable me to make the trip."[52] By the time Rosaliia Markovna thought her husband's health sufficiently restored to embark on the journey, word came from Russia advising Plekhanov not to come, lest he be arrested immediately.*

Fortune had decreed for Plekhanov another twelve years of separation from his native land. His illness, as Axelrod said, was "inexcusable mischief." It made Plekhanov miss out on the event he had been awaiting for more than half his life. He told his wife dejectedly, "I feel as though I had deserted the field of battle."[53] His self-flagellation was further provoked by the aspersions cast upon him by other exiles, who could not understand his having let anything prevent his return. In 1917 he would be ready, in full consciousness, to go to his death rather than once again to witness the revolution from afar.

---

* This is according to Plekhanov's daughter, Mme E. Batault-Plekhanova. (Axelrod was still urging Plekhanov to come to Russia, at least for a short visit, in the late months of 1906. *Perepiska Plekhanova i Aksel'roda*, II, 225.)

Inevitably, Plekhanov's doctrinaire stance alienated him from the majority of the Social Democrats, both Bolshevik and Menshevik. His resignation from *Iskra* and from the presidency of the Party Council, though intended as pressure for unification, was more effective in pointing up his apartness. Toward the end of 1905, both factions entreated him to collaborate in the legal newspapers they were setting up in Russia. He did not comply with either request both because of his continuing displeasure with the factionalism in the party and because of basic tactical disagreements (the Menshevik paper *Nachalo* followed Trotsky's line).[54] In 1905–6 most of his political writings were published not in the chief Social Democratic organs but in lesser papers, in his own *Diary of a Social Democrat*, under the auspices of "untitled"—that is, nonfactional—Social Democrats, or in the journal of the Left Democrats, *Tovarishch.*

Both factions were critical of Plekhanov's solicitude for the alliance of the liberals and his early opposition to the boycott of the Duma. His published regrets concerning the decision for the armed uprising that had ended so badly put him further outside the pale. When he violated party discipline by publicly attacking his party's electoral program, the wrath of the Social Democrats was general. After the Bolsheviks assailed him savagely, he was driven to write an article, "It Is the Turn of the Mensheviks to Speak," an anguished protest against their failure to come to his defense.[55] By contrast, Plekhanov received the effusive praises of Miliukov, the leader of the Cadet Party. He publicly welcomed them, but he must have been rather embarrassed by some of the statements, as, for example: "If all the comrades of G. V. Plekhanov understood what the most outstanding of their leaders understands, and if they were as little discomfited as he by the praises of the 'liberal bourgeoisie,' my God, how that would simplify the explanation of our present political problems and how strongly it would advance their solution."[56]

Lauded by friend-enemy and taunted or silently rebuked by those he called comrades, Plekhanov was in an unhappy position. He continued to enjoy esteem for his past contributions, but more and more he was regarded as a kind of historic monument. And he himself was painfully aware of being out of step. Although he stood firm, insisting that he was right and implying that time would vindicate him, in his articles he increasingly acknowledged that most of his readers would not agree with him. It must have been bitter indeed for one who always insisted that only mass movements made history to admit: "The situation of a politically isolated person is oppressive. But it is oppressive only to him for whom it is new. I should not have to accustom myself to it; I have already learned to bear it."[57] His wife was greatly comforted early in 1907 by a letter from

Axelrod, showing that her hero was not "alone," and that Axelrod, too, was "evidently little understood among the younger comrades."[58] Plekhanov himself began to talk feelingly of Ibsen's Dr. Stockmann, a symbol of truth and righteousness, rejected by the people to whose interests he had unselfishly devoted his life. A decade before the tragic denouement, when in his last months he would be harassed by overzealous Red Guards, Plekhanov found it necessary to insist that he was not "an enemy of the people."[59]

FROM POLITICS TO SCHOLARSHIP

Nothing worse can befall a revolutionary leader, Plekhanov once said, than to become captive to doctrinairism. The dictum was never better exemplified than in his own case. His inability to adjust his outlook to Russian realities as manifested in the Revolution of 1905 made the last decade of his life—politically, at any rate—a protracted, painful, and somewhat meaningless epilogue. His performance in the revolutionary years led some radicals to say, with a regretful shake of the head, "Plekhanov is no longer what he once was." His attempts to refute such estimates proved only too well that he had not changed—but the times had. In the area of political affairs Plekhanov had nothing fresh to contribute.

Perhaps in spite of himself, he dimly sensed this and, accordingly, endeavored to direct his energies into more fruitful channels. At any rate, in the years 1908–14, and also after the outbreak of the World War, Plekhanov's attention increasingly was absorbed in artistic and literary, historical and philosophical studies. Admittedly, all these possessed political significance, since they represented efforts to demonstrate the superiority of the Marxian method as a means of comprehending and illuminating human creations and social life and thought. Nonetheless, they indicated a relative de-emphasis of directly political involvements, and entailed as well a decided diminution of his party-political writings. His political tracts of this time, moreover, possess comparatively little intrinsic interest. Correspondingly, in our treatment of this period, we shall deal only cursorily with the vicissitudes of Plekhanov's political life before proceeding to an examination of his varied scholarly endeavors.

The balance of power in Russia, which in 1905 had tipped in favor of the opposition forces, turned sharply to their disadvantage in the succeeding years. The belated rallying to the throne of conservative and reactionary groups, the neutralizing of moderate elements by the extension of limited reforms, and, above all, the return of the armed forces from the Far East, all strengthened the hand of the Tsarist government. In a burst of unusually energetic activity, it ruthlessly stamped out continuing disorders and centers of opposition, and girded itself for the struggle to recover, or at least to restrict as narrowly as possible, the political reforms it had been obliged to grant under duress. With its forces consolidated, and with the aid of a large loan from its ally, France, which allowed it to remain independent of the Duma, the imperial regime once again could ride roughshod over its opposition.

In what amounted to a *coup d'état* before the convocation of the First Duma, Nicholas II unilaterally marked out the constitutional structure of the new political order. He prorogued both the First and Second Dumas when they proved far from compliant to his will. Then, in a flagrant violation of the law of the land, he proclaimed an electoral reform which drastically curtailed the representation of the liberal and radical parties. On the positive side, the Minister of the Interior, Petr Stolypin, prepared an agrarian reform program designed to turn at least a section of the peasantry from a rebellious force into a bulwark of stability. Popularly elected Dumas were dealt with unceremoniously, peasants swung from gallows all over the country, and radical politicians were herded into prisons; but with the revolutionary impulse among the masses nearly exhausted, the opposition was no longer able to rebuff the government. As demoralization set in, there occurred a mass exodus from the ranks of the revolutionary parties, which had grown amazingly when success seemed within reach.

The Social Democratic Party suffered not only a loss of members and the arrest of many leading party workers. The so-called expropriations (bank robberies and the like) perpetrated by Bolshevik agents in order to finance their revolutionary activities besmirched the party in the eyes of many both inside and outside of it. Besides, though the party had been reduced to little more than a paper organization, struggles for control of it went on with unabated intensity. Intrigue was rife and Machiavellianism developed into a fine art, to the shame and dismay of the more idealistic of the Social Democrats. As if that were not enough, various unexpected currents appeared in the RSDLP: a "liquidationist" tendency, calling for the abolition of the underground organization; "God-construction," a philosophical attempt to combine Marxian politics with a more spiritual metaphysical base; and "recallism," a movement to withdraw the small number of Social Democratic representatives from participation in the Imperial Duma. All these provided new occasions for bitter intraparty polemics, new splits, and mutual alienation of men who continued to call each other Comrade while pouring on the invective. But the period also featured repeated efforts to wean the warring Social Democrats from a debilitating sectarianism and to gather up the dispersed forces for new endeavors.

In the early aftermath of the revolution, Plekhanov continued his running battle with the Bolsheviks. If, he insisted, faulty tactics in the camp of the opposition had contributed greatly to the defeat of the revolution, Lenin's faction was the worst offender. Labeling the Bolsheviks by turns Blanquists, Bakuninists, and anarchists, he returned repeatedly to a critical, and often penetrating, analysis of their conduct. The correction of their tactics he took to be an essential condition for the genuine reunification of the party—the objective which above all others consumed his political energy in these years.

For a brief time, Plekhanov's personal position and the prospect of the realization of his major objective were materially improved. His attacks upon the Bolsheviks by implication and sometimes overtly also took in the substantial sector of the Mensheviks—according to Dan, who was one of them, a large majority—which leaned toward Trotsky during the revolutionary years. After the revolution, there occurred a general retreat from the Trotskyist position. The bulk of the Menshevik faction rejoined Plekhanov and Axelrod, thus tacitly admitting the correctness of Plekhanov's much maligned tactics. With Plekhanov, they now eschewed the preparation of a "premature" uprising and turned to more cautious policies, determined, like him, to consolidate what had been won and to exploit the new opportunities for building the organization and developing class consciousness in the proletariat. They willingly collaborated in promoting trade unions and cooperatives and took a keen interest in the work of the Social Democratic faction in the Duma. At the same time, they acknowledged the necessity of supporting and, as occasion required, cooperating with the liberals when the latter pressed for progressive measures.

For a time, then, Plekhanov's isolation was at an end. With the Mensheviks he could continue his campaign to secure the renunciation by the Bolsheviks of their "wrongheaded" tactics, as a prelude to party unification. His satisfaction was but ephemeral, however. Although they had retreated from Trotskyism, such Menshevik leaders as Martynov and Dan, along with many rank-and-file adherents, did not rest long at Plekhanovism. Joining with Axelrod and Potresov, they went on to a new formulation of the organizational question, with which Plekhanov could not agree. From this group stemmed the so-called "liquidationist" tendency, around which revolved much of the intraparty strife of the period.

The opprobrious term liquidationism, originally coined by Lenin, has recently been criticized as a fiction invented for partisan purposes and having no objective foundation.* If liquidationism is taken to mean a desire *completely* to do away with the party in the sense of an illegal, underground organization, that position may perhaps reasonably be argued. It is difficult to see, however, how a denial of the existence of such a *tendency* can be sustained. The pre-1905 inclinations of the Mensheviks, disillusionment with the tactics many had supported during the revolution, and revulsion at the "expropriations" and the sordid intraparty squabbles and grabs for power all contributed to such a tendency.

At the Second Congress and after, Menshevik antipathy to a conspiratorial party of professional revolutionists had become apparent. Axelrod and others never stopped appealing for the promotion of the "self-activity" of the working class, the end of which they envisaged as the emergence of a truly proletarian party. The retreat of many of the Mensheviks from their 1905 policy reinforced this attitude, signaling as it did an abandonment of any hope of a resumption of revolution in the near future. A conspiratorial organization, if appropriate for the preparation of armed uprisings, seemed little adapted to the tactics the Mensheviks now favored. The exploitation of opportunities already won for developing a strong working-class organization was for the most part a legal activity. Such activity would lay the basis for a genuinely Marxian, because proletarian, party—a party infinitely preferable to the discredited organization of radical intelligentsia which passed for the party of the proletariat. Instead of rebuilding what had become an object of contempt, why not start fresh and gradually construct something worthy of the proletariat and better designed for the achievement of its purposes? Out of such materials and reflections was the liquidationist tendency concocted. Not to be overlooked, besides, is the fact that the Bolsheviks in these years usually controlled the Central Committee of the party and, more often than not, the underground apparatus. In that context, "liquidationism" figured as an attempt of the Mensheviks to sever organizational ties that had become intolerable fetters; if they remained in the party and subject to its discipline, they would be forced to act in ways opposed to their fundamental inclinations.

Among the elements that went into the liquidationist tendency were several also included in Plekhanov's baggage.† Nevertheless, Plekhanov's forcefully negative attitude toward the tendency does not constitute an

---

* Schapiro, *The Communist Party of the Soviet Union*, Chapter 6. Much of the material Schapiro presents in the chapter serves as a refutation of this position.

† In a letter to Axelrod in early 1907, Plekhanov spoke of the "inevitability" of a (final) split with the Bolsheviks. A year later, he canvassed the possibility that the Mensheviks might bolt the "so-called party." *Perepiska Plekhanova i Aksel'roda*, II, 229, 250.

enigma.* Liquidationism simply could not be squared with his total out-look at a number of critical points. First of all, the new "deviation" ap-peared to abandon the idea of revolution. In this it may be viewed as a logical inference from Plekhanov's tactical calculations, which he himself refused to draw. If a *proletarian* revolution were to be shunned for the near future, and if the Social Democrats were to give tactical support to a bourgeoisie to which revolution was anathema, then a revolution of any kind was impossible. Accordingly, an underground organization was un-necessary, and the Social Democrats could devote all their efforts to legal activity. Plekhanov pointedly noted, however, that the events of 1905-7 had not in fact made it possible for the RSDLP to emerge openly as a political party because of continuing Tsarist harassment. Therefore it had no alternative—unless it were prepared for suicide—but to continue its underground existence.[1] On the larger issue, Plekhanov had drawn the wine, but he refused to drink it. No matter how strongly the logic of his premises might impel him, he was too deeply committed to revolution to renounce it. Thus, one of his slogans during this period was, "Long live Menshevism without liquidationism—that is, revolutionary Menshevism."[2]

The liquidationist tendency, besides, smacked too much of Economism for Plekhanov's comfort.[3] If, after his break with Lenin, he assumed a more charitable view of the Economists, he had by no means changed his atti-tude to their "errors." The promotion of the self-activity of the workers was highly desirable, but without strong Social Democratic leadership might it not take the line of least resistance and restrict itself to economic struggles alone? Liquidationism, as Plekhanov saw it, bore within itself the seeds of Revisionist opportunism.† Here, it would appear, the experi-ence of 1905 had once again reduced his confidence in the working class. At the least, he evidently did not think it had yet attained sufficient ma-turity to guarantee a consistently "sound" policy without outside guidance. His opponents, he felt, were not sufficiently sensitive to this circumstance. In addition, he associated with the liquidators a regression to the uncoordi-

---

* It is so described in Schapiro, p. 115. Although the doctrinal grounds for Plekha-nov's opposition to liquidationism were more than ample, a personal factor also played a part. As a member of the editorial board of a Menshevik group engaged in preparing a large work on social movements in recent Russian history, he came into a sharp col-lision with Potresov. Potresov, charged with treating the rise of Marxism, allotted to Plekhanov much less space and attention than Plekhanov thought proper. Besides, in emphasizing the role of Struve and legal Marxism, Potresov—so Plekhanov claimed—displayed an intolerable "retrospective liquidationism." In the dispute, Plekhanov dis-played that combination of egotism, irascibility, and intolerance that had shocked some of the Russian Social Democrats in earlier intraparty conflicts. See the article "O moem sekrete," *Sochineniia*, XIX. Other materials on this struggle are included in the same volume and in *Perepiska Plekhanova i Aksel'roda*, II, 267–83.

† Indeed, Plekhanov spoke of liquidationism as "a variety of Revisionism." *Sochi-neniia*, XIX, 83.

nated and primitive methods of work characteristic of the Economist period. Where individuals and groups set to work without prior laying of plans, designation of objectives, and provision for a central organization to coordinate activities, chaos was bound to follow. Could that mode of operation conceivably advance the movement toward its goals?

At best, Plekhanov judged, liquidationism must prove seriously disruptive. Experience might readily demonstrate the indispensability of an underground organization to those who attempted to follow the admonitions of the liquidators. Realization of the need for central planning and coordination would be borne in on the practical workers in the localities; and they could not but be aware of the absence of the conditions necessary for the legal existence of the party. Knowing all that, if they persisted in ignoring the already existing underground party, then they were bound to establish a second. Hence, if liquidationism managed to avoid the dangers of opportunism and chaos, it would succeed in making the party schism definitive, at an incalculable cost to the proletariat. The new deviation inevitably drew Plekhanov's hostility, inasmuch as he considered the preservation and unification of the party a *sine qua non*. Sincere and intelligent Social Democrats, he understood, desired the reconstruction of the party along lines that would facilitate the implementation of correct (that is, Menshevik) tactics. But they erred grievously when, in disgust with the antics of the Bolsheviks, they were goaded into leaving the party. Reconstruction was to be achieved not by forsaking the party but by winning control of it.*

Plekhanov professed to have been conscious of a liquidationist tendency among the Mensheviks as early as the London Congress of the party in mid-1907.† He had rebuffed its spokesmen in the Menshevik caucus, with the apparent approval of the great majority. Only two years later, when, as he said, its advocates had become so numerous as to jeopardize the very existence of the party, did he see fit to attack it openly. It was by concentrating on his tactical agreement with the Mensheviks that he managed to postpone as long as he did an action that must have been exceedingly difficult to take. For, in letting his shafts fly against liquidationism, he cut himself off once again from the main body of the Menshevik faction,

---

* Most of these ideas were already present in his first essay against the liquidators. See *Sochineniia*, XIX, 5–20.

† As a matter of fact, he had drawn attention to something approaching it as early as 1905. At that time, he criticized the Mensheviks for permitting an unreasonable degree of decentralization in their organization. They reminded him of the king in the fairy tale who, at night, would throw out of the window a piece of cloth torn into innumerable fragments, to find on the following morning a completely sewn garment. The Mensheviks, he protested, were ready to tear their organization to pieces, but they would not have it whole on the morrow. *Ibid.*, XIII, 317–18.

thereby condemning himself to renewed isolation. He could hardly have taken such a step unless he thought the danger very grave. Thereafter, in answer to the refrain Plekhanov sang in season and out, his opponents nicknamed him "the bard of the underground."

Plekhanov's war against the liquidators brought him into a partial community of interest with the Bolsheviks. If no less hostile to their tactics than before, in these years of reaction he deemed tactical questions secondary to the organizational question, in which the very existence of the party appeared to be at stake. The possibility of collaboration with the Bolsheviks increased after Lenin in 1909 purged his faction of the "recallists," a group which, in Plekhanov's opinion, deviated as unforgivably to the left as the liquidators did to the right. If the liquidators seemed prepared to become completely legal, the "recallists," in effect, denounced every form of legal activity as opportunism and demanded its complete cessation. Plekhanov contributed to various Bolshevik publications, but the collaboration could not last. His polemics against the liquidators might be convenient for the Bolsheviks, but he had no intention of embracing Lenin's tactical line, and it was galling to the Bolsheviks to have their publications used by an eminent personality as a vehicle for criticizing their tactics. Besides, Plekhanov never stopped working for a reunification of the party that would include elements which, in Lenin's estimation, were irrevocably outside the pale.

On the whole, then, in these years, Plekhanov was politically alone. Repelled alike by Menshevik organizational views and Bolshevik tactics, he defended a suprafactional middle ground, justifying his conduct in these words:

My tactical views were completely worked out when neither the Bolsheviks nor the Mensheviks had yet seen the light, that is, in the period of the rise of the Emancipation of Labor Group. Since that time, no essential change has taken place in them. If I have sometimes supported the Bolsheviks and sometimes the Mensheviks, that occurred for the simple reason that sometimes the one and sometimes the other were right *from my point of view*.[4]

In truth, the Bolsheviks and Mensheviks had deviated from his position. Lenin had broken with Plekhanov's two-stage revolutionary scheme. As for the Menshevik majority, although he qualified his differences with it as organizational, he definitely discerned in its organizational position a harbinger of Revisionism. Although they professed continued allegiance to his original revolutionary prospectus, their actual tactics (which represented an attempt to come to terms with Russian realities as they had been made apparent in 1905–6) were in his view out of harmony with it. While both the Bolsheviks and the Mensheviks sought in their own ways to meet the times, Plekhanov stubbornly clung to his old ideas, castigating all deviators as if to say, "Le marxisme, c'est moi."[5] His predicament was the predicament of orthodox Marxism in the early twentieth century: caught between Revisionism and Bolshevism, it was losing the ground out from under it.

With the exception of a small group of "nonfactional" Mensheviks, the Russian Social Democrats declined Plekhanov's repeated invitations to be reconciled on his terms. Finally, in 1912, the split in the RSDLP became definitive. Thereafter, two distinct organizations, each claiming to be the legitimate party, vied for the loyalty of the proletariat. For all that, two years later Plekhanov was still pressing for party unity. Largely at his urging, the Bureau of the Socialist International had been persuaded to negotiate—without success, as it happened—a closing of the breach in the ranks of the Russian Social Democrats. As the holocaust of 1914 began, Plekhanov and a little band of loyal supporters had just recently inaugurated yet another forlorn little splinter of a newspaper. On its masthead was inscribed the proud device: *Edinstvo* (Unity).

PHILOSOPHY

Probably no other follower of Marx and Engels took philosophy as seriously as did Plekhanov. Kautsky might admit the possibility of reconciling Neo-Kantianism with Marxism.[6] Lenin might tolerate the God-constructionism of Bogdanov because he considered such matters "completely irrelevant to the social revolution."[7] But, to Plekhanov's way of thinking, such casualness betrayed an inadequate comprehension of Marxism. As he wrote:

Marxism represents a complete and rigorously materialistic world-view, and he who loses sight of this completeness . . . risks a very poor understanding even of those particular aspects of this teaching which for one reason or another attract his attention. . . . A *complete* world-view differs from an *eclectic* one in that *each* of its aspects is connected in the closest way *with all the others,* and therefore one cannot with impunity eliminate one of them and replace it by something arbitrarily drawn from a *different* world-view.[8]

No aspect of Marxism could afford to be neglected, then, and least of all its philosophical basis—for Plekhanov paid philosophy the tribute of being the "science of the sciences."[9] It was not merely an academic matter but a subject that should be studied closely by the socialists if they wished to acquire a solid foundation for their socio-political views. If they were derelict in that, he feared that their movement would be penetrated by ideas seriously damaging to its integrity and success. Nothing less than constant vigilance and a militant defense of materialism would insulate it against subversion.

Defend it Plekhanov did, but a certain ambivalence pervades the corpus of his philosophical writings. His polemics against the Narodniks, the Neo-Kantians, Bogdanov, and others who dared to contradict or propose alterations in Marxian materialism have about them a quasi-religious air. In his relation to such critics, Plekhanov followed the example of St. Bernard, to whom he once likened himself. " 'I have an evangel,' said the saint, 'and if an angel came down from heaven and began to contradict it—anathema to that angel!' "[10] However, Plekhanov did not rest his case for dialectical materialism* on denunciation alone. The expository essays in which he set forth the various aspects and applications of Marxian thought breathe a spirit more akin to science than to religion.† They reflect a mind committed to a particular method, to be sure, but genuinely devoted to the search for truth. Dedicated as Plekhanov was to the scientific ideal, it was impossible for him to interlard his works with deliberate distortions in the manner of many later "Marxist" writers. His keen sensitivity and lively imagination enabled him to employ the method—even though he admitted it was still far from perfect—often with striking results. No doubt this was due in part also to the liberal interpretation he made of the method as a tool of investigation. "Marx," he wrote, "although he explains all social movements as the outcome of the economic development of society, very often explains them thus only *in the last analysis*, implying that a considerable number of intermediate 'factors' are operative."[11] Such an approach did comparatively little to hobble the investigator, since it permitted wide scope for research and interpretation. Perhaps this feature explains why, in spite of his commitment, Plekhanov appeared to remain "inwardly free."[12] Sometimes his studies led him to conclusions more or less at odds with one or another Marxian precept,‡ and on a few occasions he did not flinch from pointing out the contradiction.

In the last analysis, Plekhanov wished the worth of Marxism to be judged according to the maxim, "The proof of the pudding is in the eating." Upon Marxian scholarship he laid the task of proving that the pudding had no peer. But that would never be accomplished, he warned, merely

---

* According to R. N. Carew-Hunt, Plekhanov evidently was the first person to use the expression "dialectical materialism" (*Marxism Past and Present* [New York, 1955], p. 5). The Russian Marxist seems to have used the expression for the first time in 1891 in an essay on Hegel. See *Sochineniia*, VII, 52.

† This is particularly true in such works as his *Essays on the History of Materialism, The Role of the Individual in History,* and *Fundamental Problems of Marxism.* All three are available in English translations.

‡ See the trenchant critique of his *Role of the Individual in History* in Sidney Hook, *The Hero in History,* pp. 82–101. Hook credits Plekhanov with "independence of thought" and with "a refreshing willingness to follow the lead of evidence." But in the end he takes him to task for claiming to have proved what the evidence he adduces in fact refutes.

by endless reiteration of general principles, such as that the anatomy of a society is rooted in its economy. Instead:

It is necessary to know how to make scientific use of scientific ideas; one must render a satisfactory account of all the living functions of the organism, the anatomical structure of which is determined by the economy; it is necessary to understand how it moves, how it is nourished, how emotions and concepts that arise in correspondence with its anatomical structure become such as they are, how they change together with changes occurring in its structure, etc.[13]

In a word, "it must know how to give a materialist explanation to all sides of human life."[14] No one applied himself more assiduously to the task than Plekhanov himself, his inquiries ranging into fields as varied as history and aesthetics, anthropology and literature, epistemology and art.

Recognizing that the work was only beginning, he expected it to advance with great rapidity, for the avowedly Marxist scholars were not alone. In his view, a great many scientific investigators, whatever their attitude to philosophical materialism, were furnishing abundant support for it in their various researches. That he had read remarkably widely and had striven to assimilate to his system the findings of many leading students was evident in such stimulating essays as his "Letters Without Address" and "Fundamental Problems of Marxism." Among other places, he had discovered supporting evidence in the work on biological evolution of Darwin, Haeckel, Huxley, and De Vries, in the anthropological studies of Tylor, Ratzel, and Frazer, and in the psychological inquiries of Forel.*

Apart from such "proving" investigations by Marxist and non-Marxist scholars alike, Plekhanov saw great value for his cause in studies of the history of philosophy, and it was to this aspect that the greater part of his own philosophical works was devoted. He commenced a series of such works in 1891 with an essay commemorating the sixtieth anniversary of the death of Hegel.† This piece, which evoked high praise from Engels and Kautsky, contained the germ of his subsequent book-length studies on the history of philosophy. Hegel held an eminent place in Plekhanov's pantheon, and from him Plekhanov acquired many of the basic patterns of his way of thinking, including his manner of studying the history of philosophy itself. Individual philosophies were to be seen not as acciden-

---

* All these, and a good many more, are pressed into the service of Marxism in his "Fundamental Problems of Marxism" (in *Sochineniia*, Vol. XVIII). A present-day anthropologist, Morris Opler, recently called attention to Plekhanov's surprisingly comprehensive grasp of the anthropological materials of his time. See his article in *American Anthropologist*, LXIV (1962), 533.

† *Sochineniia*, VII, 29–55. My brief treatment of Plekhanov's philosophical views, or rather certain aspects of them, is based on the whole body of his philosophical works, not simply on those written in the period 1907–14. The same will hold true for the sections of this chapter dealing with his historical and literary views.

tal constructions but as necessary products of their times. To fight against the systems of one's predecessors was senseless, for each of them must be understood as a different stage in the development of a single philosophy.* "Every particular philosophy is the daughter of its own time, and 'the latest philosophy is the result of all the preceding and must contain the legitimate principles of all within itself.'"[15] Viewing the history of philosophy from that perspective, Plekhanov saw in dialectical materialism the culmination of all previous philosophical thought; it was "the most developed, the richest, and the most concrete" of all systems.[16]

His summation of the proof of that proposition was embodied in his celebrated book, *On the Development of the Monistic Conception of History*, in which Hegel figured as a bridge between the materialist thinkers of the eighteenth century and "modern materialism." On these, Plekhanov had already written one of his most original scholarly works, *Essays on the History of Materialism*.† There his attention focused first of all upon Holbach and Helvétius, whom he selected as the leading thinkers of their time. In his view, they warranted that distinction both because their outlook was consistent with the most advanced science of their age and because they stood on the political left. However, if Plekhanov valued their defense of philosophical materialism, he perceived in their outlook certain serious defects which made them powerless either to solve basic historical problems or to give an accurate representation of social reality.

As sensationalists, they took man to be a product of his natural and social environment. But when they endeavored to explain the development of social institutions, like the men of the Enlightenment generally, they identified opinion as the causal factor.[17] Besides being contradictory on their face (environment determines man, man determines environment), the two propositions were inconsistent in that they comprised a materialistic interpretation of man and an idealistic formula for history. Alternatively, eighteenth-century thinkers explained the history of humanity by reference to the peculiarities of human nature; but such references only created new difficulties. How could human nature, conceived as a constant, serve to explain something that was characterized by change?[18] Basically, Plekhanov found the position of the eighteenth-century materialists inadequate because it was metaphysical, in the Hegelian sense of the word. It fell far short of being a satisfactory tool of analysis, for it lacked a conception of development, tending instead to see his-

* Plekhanov lived up to this preachment better in relation to those whose ideas had in some degree entered into dialectical materialism than to others. To a friend he wrote: "That it is necessary to insult Kant I have always thought and have never ceased thinking. Dangerous old man!" *Literaturnoe nasledie Plekhanova*, I, 354.

† Although this work was not published until 1896, Plekhanov had completed it before his study of "the monistic conception of history."

tory as the result of the disorderly play of chance.* It was excessively abstract, making little use of the principles it espoused to illuminate the rich tapestry of real life. And it viewed phenomena as discrete, disconnected, separated from one another by an impassable gap. Accordingly, men like Holbach and Helvétius were unable to render an adequate account of the development of social institutions and social thought and their mutual interrelations.

In Plekhanov's reading of the history of philosophy, it was Hegel who deserved the credit for overcoming the deficiencies of these predecessors. Hegel could not be content with the resolution of apparent contradictions by offhand references to interaction that explained nothing. Instead, he attempted to find the sources of the interacting elements (social institutions and ideas) in something more profound.[19] He decisively departed from the dualisms and eclecticism of antecedent and contemporary philosophies, with all their contradictions and inconsistencies. Proclaiming the Absolute or the progressive fulfillment of Reason the demiurge of the historical process, he took his stand foursquare on the ground of monism. But, in Plekhanov's estimation, that breakthrough to "consistency" by no means exhausted Hegel's services. As against his predecessors, Hegel recognized the interrelatedness of all the varied manifestations of social life in a given epoch. And in his insistence upon the empirical study of history, he expressed his rejection of sterile formulae that unlocked none of the secrets of the human past.

In sum, Hegel had cast metaphysical thinking down from its throne and supplanted it with dialectics, a method of studying phenomena not only in their mutual connection but in their development. When applied to society, that method, according to Plekhanov, "brought about a complete revolution." Out of it came the wonderfully stimulating conception of "the history of humanity as a process regulated by law."[20] It followed that men could discover those laws and penetrate to the essential structure of what had appeared to be merely the disorderly play of chance. Moreover, they might even predict the future. With Hegel's "revelation," the grand perspective opened out that man might break through the bonds of blind necessity and enter into the realm of reason and freedom.

Plekhanov envisaged the history of philosophy itself as a kind of dialectical process that corresponded to the evolution of society. As Holbach and Helvétius once were in the vanguard of philosophical thought, so Hegel occupied that position later by virtue of having negated their "errors," transcended their systems, and moved onto a higher plane with

---

* Characteristically, they expected the righting of the wrongs in their society to be carried out by a "sage on the throne," whose timely appearance was at the mercy of chance. *Sochineniia*, VIII, 63.

his dialectical and monistic philosophy. But although it enormously advanced philosophical thought, the Hegelian system itself was not free of inadequacies. Hegel merited eternal glory for having first mooted the existence of laws of history, but his idealistic approach played him false when he undertook to discover them. It had required the reintroduction of materialism in a modernized form to set right side up the relationship between being and thought which Hegel—according to the Marxists—conceived in an inverted fashion. The Left Hegelian, Feuerbach, had refurbished materialism so that it could take its rightful place,* and to Marx and Engels belonged the mighty achievement of having synthesized that materialism with Hegel's dialectical method.

Marx and Engels "correctly" proclaimed the primacy of the material factor, the prevailing mode of production, as the determinant of the character of society. The varied spiritual phenomena, including the ideas generated in a given epoch, constituted a superstructure reared on the socio-economic base. In standing Hegel "right side up," Marx and Engels also eliminated the inconsistencies of the eighteenth-century materialists. They "demonstrated" that both man's social environment and his ideas are derived from something more basic than either: the productive system of society. As for human nature, it could not be construed as a constant. "Acting by means of his labor upon the nature that exists outside of him, man [unconsciously] brings about changes in his own nature."[21] As with Hegel, the authors of dialectical materialism found the mainspring of historical development outside of man. But, in their system, it was not Reason or the Absolute but changes in the mode of production that provided the impetus to historical development.

As well as in the history of philosophy, Plekhanov obviously took a deep interest in philosophy of history. He thought of the historical process as a movement conforming to law and independent of human will. Yet he rejected the inference that men's opinions and actions had no bearing on the process: there could be no history without men. If one's actions ran counter to the course of historical movement, one would be placed in the ludicrous position of a Don Quixote.[22] But the fulfillment of the historical process Plekhanov envisaged presupposed certain definite kinds of human action. If the process were truly to qualify as objective and in accordance with law, these human actions, we would suppose, must be automatically forthcoming. Plekhanov did so construe the matter, at least in his general

---

* Plekhanov considered modern materialism to be closely affiliated to the outlook of Spinoza, agreeing with Feuerbach as to the nonessentiality of its theological component. "This Spinozism," he wrote, "freed from its theological lumber by Feuerbach, was the philosophy which Marx and Engels adopted when they broke away from idealism. . . . The Spinozism of Marx and Engels was materialism in its most modern form." See *Sochineniia*, XVIII, 189.

theoretical pronouncements; yet on the crucial question of the development of proletarian consciousness he vacillated no little throughout his Marxian career. To keep faith with his cherished dictum "being determines consciousness," he was obliged to argue that the growth of proletarian consciousness depended upon the development of capitalism alone. But only once, in the heat of a polemic, did he intimate that the activity of the socialist intelligentsia could be dispensed with. For the rest, he took its activity to be essential. If the latter proposition could not be reconciled with what he took to be the central principle of Marxian materialism, he did manage to close the circle of historical inevitability with a deterministic explanation of the initiatives of the socialist intelligentsia: "If I am inclined to take part in a movement whose triumph seems to me a historical necessity, this only means that I consider my activity likewise to be an indispensable link in the chain of conditions whose aggregate will necessarily ensure the triumph of the movement which is dear to me."*

It might be concluded from this that Plekhanov considered all human conduct determined, his outlook thus constituting a closed system. Further examination reveals certain fundamental inconsistencies. In the passage just quoted, Plekhanov refers to his own activity as an indispensable link in the chain of conditions, and he also tacitly admits that he participates in the movement because he is so inclined. This formulation would seem to admit of the possibility that he and many others could refrain from participation, thus preventing the triumph of the movement. In other words, the door seems to be left open for free will to affect the course of history. Lest this example seem somewhat tenuous, it may be pointed out that Plekhanov allotted to passion an extraordinarily important role in the historical process. As he wrote: "Not one great step in history was ever made without the assistance of passion, which, multiplying tenfold the moral forces and exercising the intellectual capacities of the historical actors, itself constitutes a great progressive force."[23]

If challenged to reconcile this statement with his historical scheme, Plekhanov no doubt would have treated passion, too, as determined by objective factors. Still, even if he did not consciously recognize it, his political conduct implicitly acknowledged an area of genuine freedom. There was, for example, his letter to Axelrod at the time of the Revisionist controversy, conceding that Bernstein was partly right but denouncing him for employing his data in a sense damaging to revolutionary socialism. It

---

* *Sochineniia*, XVIII, 245. Immediately following this statement, Plekhanov points to the similar position of American Protestantism, in which no contradiction is seen between belief in determinism and being "a man of action." The same parallel is drawn in an interesting article by R. V. Daniels, "Fate and Will in the Marxian Philosophy of History," *Journal of the History of Ideas*, Vol. XXI (1960).

would hardly have made sense to denounce Bernstein except on the assumption that he could have behaved otherwise. Plekhanov considered it the duty of a socialist leader to combat any and all constructions that threatened to impair the achievement of his ultimate goal. But Bernstein, another socialist leader, saw fit to behave differently. Significantly, in his lexicon of invective, Plekhanov reserved the epithet "passionless" for those he despised most, including Bernstein.* His savage attack upon Bernstein surely bespoke a fear that Revisionist thinking might deflect the historical process in unforeseen and undesirable ways. It might operate against the attainment of a level of proletarian *élan* sufficient for carrying through the socialist revolution. Revisionism threatened to deprive the socialists of that belief in their ultimate triumph which was itself a major source of their strength. Plekhanov would hardly have been so disturbed about Bernstein if, as he professed to believe, the passion requisite for the fulfillment of his historical scheme must be automatically forthcoming.

His failure to resolve successfully the problem of free will and determinism had its parallel in his thinking about evolution and revolution, to which it was related. In common with many nineteenth-century thinkers, Plekhanov recognized the idea of evolution as a key principle of social analysis. But he took issue with those who sought to make of it a sovereign principle. Rejecting the inference that "history makes no jumps,"[24] he insisted on the organic relationship between evolution and revolution. After all, he observed, quite a few revolutions had occurred in history. And they had occurred not in spite of evolution but because evolution had prepared the way for them. In his words:

There can be no sudden change without a sufficient cause, and this cause is to be found in the previous march of social evolution. But, inasmuch as this evolution never ceases in societies that are in the course of development, we may say that history is continually preparing for such sudden changes and revolutions. It goes on doing this assiduously and imperturbably . . . hence these political catastrophes are absolutely inevitable.[25]

We must grant that evolution may prepare, and not infrequently has prepared, the way for revolution. Where dominant social forces refused to give place to other elements thrown up in the course of social evolution, the new groups sometimes embarked upon a struggle that culminated in successful revolution. But Plekhanov was guilty of an unforgivable flaw in logic in the passage just cited. Although the revolutions that occurred were surely prepared by the previous march of evolution, it by no means follows that evolution inevitably brings revolution in its wake. The quality

---

* For example, in 1898, he wrote to Axelrod: "I loved Hegel because . . . he was full of theoretical passion. In Bernstein, this passion is absent and in its stead there is a mass of self-satisfied vulgarity." *Perepiska Plekhanova i Aksel'roda*, I, 201.

of social evolution might vary considerably in dependence upon the predilections of men. In the nineteenth century, some ruling groups had considered it the better part of wisdom to throw in with social reform rather than to defend to the last every jot and tittle of their prerogatives. In behaving flexibly, they inhibited the development of revolutionary passion in the proletariat, or at least made for its early subsidence. By their conscious action, in exercise of their free will, some men had altered the course of the historical process envisaged by the Marxists. The dialectics of an ever sharpening opposition, inevitably bringing on a catastrophic upheaval, were simply not at work in England and elsewhere. Plekhanov's conduct in the face of Revisionism suggests a man frantically endeavoring to compensate by his passionate efforts for the failure of the historical process to follow the path he alleged to be objective and independent of human will. His philosophical premises made it impossible for him to grasp the meaning of Revisionism and its powerful appeal to the workers of such countries as England and Germany.

The same deficiencies of Plekhanov's system were operative in regard to the Bolsheviks, but in the opposite direction. Here, too, men's deliberate actions served to vitiate the materialization of the "objective" historical process. In Russia, where the ruling groups were indeed inflexible, social evolution did appear to be preparing the way for revolution. Plekhanov's detestation of Russia's socio-political order kindled in him a passion to overthrow it. He had turned to the emerging proletariat as the only force capable of achieving that objective. His own revolutionary passion was generally kept in check by his awe of "the laws of history," his conviction that they could not be violated with impunity. In Lenin, revolutionary passion burned so hot that everything else had to give way before it. He was prepared to inflame or to exploit already inflamed passions of the people, proletarian or peasant alike, to the point where they would strike down state, aristocracy, and bourgeoisie and make it possible to skip a whole historical stage. In singing his paean to passion as a factor in history, Plekhanov did not reckon with passion of this order. Both in 1905 and in 1917, he was placed in the awkward position of striving to cool passions which were "unlawful," which threatened to upset the "inevitable" working out of the "objective" historical process. As with freedom and determinism, Plekhanov never succeeded in bringing evolution and revolution into a workable balance. To be more exact, his orthodox Marxism which purportedly did just that was repudiated by the actual course of historical development. In Western Europe the balance was upset in favor of evolution, in Russia in favor of revolution; revolution failed to materialize in the first case, and evolution was radically abridged in the second.

Apparently dialectical materialism, like other philosophies before, was not without its deficiencies and contradictions. Discerning though it might be, even in the hands of so talented a practitioner as Plekhanov Marxism fell far short of being the last word in social science.

Plekhanov's strong historical bent, evident early in his career, became if anything more pronounced as he grew older. A substantial portion of his writing was historical in nature, whether it dealt with the evolution of philosophical thought, with Western or Russian historiography (Guizot, Thierry, Pogodin, and others), or with such figures of the Russian intelligentsia as Chadaev, Belinsky, Herzen, and Chernyshevsky (on whom he wrote an entire book). He began work in 1909 on what was to be his historical magnum opus, *The History of Russian Social Thought*. The initial contract with the publisher, Mir, called for a study, apparently in one volume, extending from the beginnings through the Revolution of 1905. As Plekhanov proceeded, however, the prospectus became ever longer, Mir announcing in 1917 that the completed work would come to no less than seven volumes.[26] When Plekhanov died the following year, he had succeeded in completing only the first three. His chapter on Radishchev, which would have brought him up to the end of the eighteenth century, was unfinished.

Plekhanov set out in the opening words of his Preface the principles according to which he had constructed his work:

In the researches here presented on the history of Russian social thought, I took off from that basic proposition of historical materialism that consciousness does not determine being but being consciousness. For that reason, I first of all turned to a review of the objective conditions of time and place which have determined the course of development of Russian social life. . . . Conditions of place, I call *geographical*, and conditions of time—the *historical* setting of the given process.[27]

Elsewhere, he further clarified his method, asserting that the task of the investigator of social thought was by no means fulfilled when he had presented the ideas and ideals of various figures. The more fundamental obligation was to determine the "sociological equivalent" of the different outlooks, "where they got them, why they arose at a given stage of social development."[28] Plekhanov's explicit formulation of his premises was an admirable practice. However, the obtrusive and didactic manner in which he continually reiterated it throughout was an offensive feature of a work that has a great many merits.

In the long Introduction of some 120 pages, which is perhaps the most stimulating portion of the entire work, Plekhanov critically examines the researches of a number of leading Russian historians. As in his studies of the history of philosophy, he scrutinizes the works of his predecessors from the perspective of historical materialism, with a view to separating sound perceptions from unsound. The former then could be incorporated into an account that was fresh, "true," and consistent because rendered throughout from the Marxian historical standpoint. That he should have proceeded in this manner is not surprising. But the results are remarkable in several respects. Many of the leading ideas in his conception of Russian history were taken over almost bodily from the work of "bourgeois" students. Clearly recognizable in Plekhanov's history are the ideas of Solov'ev on colonization, of Kliuchevsky on the rise of the imperial state, of Brückner on the influence of the Mongols, of Chicherin on the peasant commune. On the other hand, he tears to shreds the thesis of Pokrovsky, a Marxist investigator and, later, the dean of Soviet historians, about the "commercial capitalist" nature of Muscovite society.

Plekhanov, of course, also criticizes certain features of the historical approaches of men like Kliuchevsky and Solov'ev. But, on certain decisive points, his own historical construction exemplifies the very thing he criticizes in others. For example, in his view Kliuchevsky misrepresented the truth when he explained certain differences between the West and Russia by the precedence of "the political 'moment' over the economic in the West," whereas the two were mixed in the Russian historical process. "In actuality," Plekhanov objected, "the political 'moment' never and nowhere precedes the economic; it is always conditioned by the latter, which, however, in no way prevents it from exerting upon the economic a reverse influence."[29] Yet, in his refutation of Pokrovsky, Plekhanov unwittingly appears to give precedence precisely to the political over the economic "moment." That the Tsar in Muscovite times was deeply involved in commercial activities, was indeed the "first merchant," proved not that Russia then was a land of commercial capitalism, he argued, but the reverse. The monopolization of trade advantages by the crown was a feature of civilizations with relatively little commerce. In Russia, it sprang from the expanding fiscal needs of the state, which, in turn, grew out of military exigency.[30] In Plekhanov's history as in Kliuchevsky's, the security problem, therefore, figured as a major determinant of the character of the Russian state. Did not such interpretations, in effect, suggest the primacy of the political "moment"—of state requirements—over the economic?

Plekhanov would probably have replied that he had never denied the reciprocal action of elements of the superstructure on economic life, and also that, "in the final analysis," it was the economic backwardness of the country which forced the state to become so concerned with economic life. But where reciprocal action is admitted, it could be asked, how is it possible to know what is determining "in the final analysis"? In this case, why stop arbitrarily with Russia's economic backwardness? What caused it?

Elsewhere, Plekhanov himself pointed to the constant spoliations of the steppe nomads—another political factor—as a major hindrance to the economic development of the country.[31] More than likely, Plekhanov would have sought to undercut this argument with the discovery of yet another economic factor. His plea for reciprocal action and his insistence upon the determining role of the economic "in the final analysis" is tantamount to a declaration that his system of historical interpretation does not admit of the possibility of disproof.

Though apt to be dogmatic and unyielding where philosophical principles were concerned, in empirical research Plekhanov dutifully followed the lead of evidence. That characteristic lends distinction and value to his work, even though the results may not always have served very well as a proof of the validity of his principles. Notable instances may be cited of his independence of thought and freedom from dogmatism. Beginning with a conception of the origins of the Russian peasant commune that took as gospel the pronouncements of Marx and Engels on the subject, Plekhanov came around later to a diametrically opposite view.[32] Initially he envisaged the peasant communes of Moscow-Petersburg times as the foundation upon which Russian despotism had been erected; subsequently—influenced by the studies of the non-Marxists Chicherin and Efimenko—he regarded them as an improvisation of the Russian state to serve its fiscal needs.

In another striking case, he argued from evidence for a principle that could doubtfully be reconciled with Marxism, at least as it has been represented by contemporary exponents:

The movement of humanity on the path of culture is not at all a straight-line movement. With the transition to a higher stage of economic development, a given tribe (or state), of course, makes a more or less significant step forward. But not in all respects. Certain aspects of its life may regress thanks just to the fact that it has made—generally speaking—a progressive step.[33]

As an example, he pointed out that hunting peoples show incomparably greater skill in the plastic arts than do herdsmen and primitive agriculturalists. Similarly, though modern civilization was much more highly developed economically than ancient Greece, the latter far outstripped the former in aesthetic sensitivity.*

Remarkable though these points are, the most startling statement to be found in the *History of Russian Social Thought* is Plekhanov's characterization, in the Introduction, of class relationships: "The course of development of any given society divided into classes is determined by the

---

* The principle he espoused here notwithstanding, it never occurred to him that political democratization need not inevitably follow the penetration of the capitalist mode of production.

course of development of these classes and their mutual relations—that is, in the first place, their *mutual struggle* where the internal social structure is concerned; and, secondly, their more or less friendly *cooperation* in the case of the defense of the country against external attacks."[34] Although to a non-Marxist this statement might seem to overstate the case for class struggle, coming from a Marxist it represented a large concession. Contradicting the famous opening line of the *Communist Manifesto,* it admitted that there was something more to history than class struggles. Other than its dissent from a fundamental proposition of "scientific socialism," Plekhanov's formulation comes as a shock because nothing in his earlier writings seems to anticipate it. Certainly, it runs counter to the thoughts expressed in his important article "Patriotism and Socialism" (1905); and in this shift we may perhaps discern part of the basis of his different attitudes to the Russo-Japanese War and the World War. It is difficult to imagine how any experience in his political life after 1905 could have caused this change in point of view. Rather, it must have resulted from his historical researches, which brought him to an appreciation of the national interest as a potent factor in the international dimension of a people's history.* That dimension could not be neglected, he thought; yet it could not be comprehended adequately by the investigator who everywhere and always took class struggle as the organizing principle of his history.

Plekhanov's organization of the main body of his opus also comes as something of a surprise. His various concessions notwithstanding, one still anticipates an exposition of the interplay of social ideas, deriving from the conflict of interest between the exploited and the exploiters. Instead, successive chapters take up "the movement of social thought under the influence of the struggle between the spiritual and temporal power," "between the boyars and the service nobility," "between the boyars and the clergy," "between the Tsars and the boyars." That these subjects may be comprised under class struggle in the Marxian sense is more than doubtful.† Obviously, such social conflicts constitute exceedingly important elements in history, and Plekhanov very properly chose to treat them. In so doing, however, he in effect admitted that class struggle in the generally understood sense far from encompassed the whole even of the internal side of a people's history. Subsequent sections of his work deal mainly with conventional themes—such as the Time of Troubles, the schism in the church, and the reforms of Peter the Great—but often in an unconventional manner.

* In the body of his work, Plekhanov adduced the principle with reference to the Time of Troubles. *Sochineniia,* XX, 251.

† Each of the four elements mentioned did not bear a distinct relationship to the means of production, the criterion according to which a class is defined in Marxian thought. Nor can these struggles be subsumed under the rubric oppressed *vs.* oppressors.

Although it is not without some arid stretches, as a whole Plekhanov's history presents many arresting insights that deserve to be better known.

Seen in the context of Russian historiography, Plekhanov's *History of Russian Social Thought* represents a fresh and illuminating attempt to answer a question with which Russian thinkers had wrestled for decades. Yet he may have been the first investigator to attempt a more or less systematic reply to the question, Is Russia Western or Eastern? His response was bound to be complex, for, as he acknowledged, the countries of the West, like those of the East, varied a good deal in their social development. Complexity was compounded by unintended equivocation. On the one hand, Plekhanov set up West and East as two more or less polar models of development; on the other hand, his eagerness to subsume all forms of historical development under a comprehensive scheme pressed him toward the dissolution of the polarity East-West. Taking the West, and particularly France, as the primary model, he argued that the developmental patterns of the Eastern despotisms, though different, were not entirely so. For example, they too, had passed through something like a feudal phase.[35]

Plekhanov's estimate of Russia's changing cultural situation—the basic theme of his survey of Russian history—is summarized in this interesting passage, which follows the comparison of France and the Eastern despotisms:

The same must be said in comparing the historical development of France with the historical development of Russia; there can be no talk of the *complete* uniqueness of the Russian historical process; such uniqueness generally is unknown to sociology; but if not *completely* unique, the Russian historical process nevertheless is distinguished from the French by certain extremely important features. And not only from the French. In it there are peculiarities very noticeably distinguishing it from the historical process of all the countries of the European West and reminiscent of the process of development of the great Oriental despotisms. Further—and significantly complicating the question—these same peculiarities pass through a sufficiently original process of development. They now increase and now diminish, as a consequence of which Russia seems to waver between the West and the East. In the course of the Moscow period of its history, they attain much greater dimensions than in the Kiev period. And after the reforms of Peter I, they again decline—at first slowly, then more and more rapidly. This new phase of Russian social development—a phase at first of slow and superficial and then ever accelerating and deepening Europeanization of Russia—is far from being complete in our time.[36]

Paradoxically, the features that Russia shared with the West Plekhanov took to be fundamental; those it had in common with the East, thus distinguishing it from the West, he called secondary. Nonetheless, in the main he assimilated Russian historical development to the Eastern rather than the Western pattern. Indeed, for two decades prior to the beginning of his major historical opus, he had been working out a conception of

Russia as an "Oriental (sometimes semi-Oriental) despotism."* By that term he designated a distinct institutional complex which, so far as he knew, had grown up only in a number of great Oriental civilizations such as Ancient Egypt, China, and India. Its most conspicuous feature was an omnipotent state authority (the despot and his governing apparatus), which, through its control of the means of production, reduced all classes of the population to utter dependence and impotence. Unlike other writers before and since, Plekhanov did not associate this development with the long period of Mongol rule over Russia,† but with the rise of the principality of Moscow to supremacy in Russia. During that period and after, the peculiarity of the Russian order was noted by numerous Western visitors. In the sixteenth century, for example, Herberstein commented that the Tsar "has power over both secular and spiritual individuals and, free in his arbitrary will, disposes of the lives and property of all."[37]

With Kliuchevsky, Plekhanov saw the emergence of Russian autocracy (a more familiar term, but too often confused with absolutism) as a consequence of financial stress. Moscow's aggrandizement and the development under its aegis of a centralized state apparatus required large expenditures. Apart from the need to support an expanding administrative machinery and the pomp of an imperial court, external pressures demanded the maintenance of a large military establishment.‡ Since the need was great and available resources small, draconic measures were required and they were instituted without apologies and without regrets. In what was an overwhelmingly agricultural country, the state arrogated the right to virtually all landed property. The peasant was deprived first of his property in land and then of his property in himself, that is, of his freedom.[38] The nobility as well, whether the newly created elements or the old boyar aristocracy, were converted into slaves of the state. The right to hold peopled lands—that is, to secure the wherewithal to live—was made dependent upon service to the state.§

---

* See my article in the *Journal of the History of Ideas*, Vol. XIX, 1958. There I incorrectly stated that Plekhanov never set forth a systematic account of Russian history from that perspective. His *History of Russian Social Thought* is such an account. My article, based on gleanings from a quarter of a century of Plekhanov's writings prior to his magnum opus, demonstrates that its main outlines were perceptible in his thinking before he began writing his *History*. In no important respect does the *History* depart from the sketch of Plekhanov's historical views presented in the article.

† At most, he conceded to the impact of the Mongols an indirect influence (see *Sochineniia*, XX, 247–48). For a comprehensive study of Oriental despotism which, in its treatment of Russia, puts the chief emphasis on Mongol domination, see Karl A. Wittfogel, *Oriental Despotism, a Comparative Study of Total Power*, pp. 219–25 and *passim*.

‡ *Sochineniia*, XX, 87 and *passim*. Plekhanov saw similar pressures pushing Russia in the same direction in the Kievan period as well. *Ibid.*, p. 57.

§ *Ibid.*, p. 66. The same sort of pattern of imposed dependence, according to Plekhanov, was also applied to the urban dwellers. *Ibid.*, p. 90.

Into this familiar pattern, Plekhanov introduced a characteristic note. Throughout, he emphasized the backwardness of Russia's economy as compared with that of the West, explaining much of the difference between the two on that basis. Specifically, through the greater part of its history (and particularly in the Moscow period), Russian society was sustained by natural economy.* This was an agricultural economy of small, self-sufficient units of production, employing primitive techniques and achieving only low levels of productivity. In the final analysis, the emergence of Oriental despotism in Russia was the result of this economic factor. Primitive though peasant agriculture was, it constituted the only productive activity of any consequence. The erection of a Leviathan state on such a basis could be accomplished only if the state-builders were able to squeeze from the tillers of the soil an extraordinary share of their meager output. In turn, this was attainable only if the state assumed control of landed property and, with that, of the power of life and death over its subjects.

Another cardinal feature of Russian Oriental despotism to which Plekhanov called attention was its stability. He had in mind not merely the relative absence of social ferment and upheaval but, more generally, a pace of social development so slow as to be almost imperceptible. The two features were intimately related, and both stemmed from the character of the economic system. Natural economy involves traditionalism in techniques of production, endless repetition of inherited methods, the absence of all dynamism. Where the motive force of historical development has lapsed into stagnation, social relationships and the political, intellectual, and moral life of the people are also unchanging. The patterns of social life become set into such a fixed mold that no other socio-political order is conceivable to those who live within its framework. That was why popular rebellions in Russia were generally directed not against the system as such but against extraordinary abuses emanating from some "Antichrist" or "false Tsar," who had somehow gained control of the throne.[39] In spite of all evidence to the contrary, the peasants persisted in looking upon the "legitimate" Tsar as a paternalistic protector. This irrationality was but one facet of the brutalized, dehumanized condition to which the masses fell under Oriental despotism. A stagnant agricultural economy; a populace dispersed among a multitude of communal organizations without organic ties to one another; an overwhelmingly peasant people, traditionally oriented and intellectually and morally degraded by the conditions under which they lived—such, in Plekhanov's estimation, was the socio-

---

* Taking over Solov'ev's idea of the importance of colonization as a factor in Russian history, Plekhanov modified it to read colonization "under the conditions of natural economy." (Sochineniia, XX, 87). He argued that in Kievan times, as well as later, natural economy prevailed. Ibid., pp. 57–62.

economic basis of Russia's Oriental despotism. So long as it endured, despotism was secure.[40]

As for the other elements of Russian society, each was brought into subservience to the state. The church progressively lost its independence, as did the boyars, the *dvoriane* (newer nobility), and the urban dwellers. Moreover, each group became psychologically adjusted to the system. The dvoriane might inveigh against boyars, and boyars against clergy, but all three in the main submissively acknowledged the omnipotence of the ruler. With almost no exceptions, dissidents from other classes followed the pattern of the peasants. Boyars might bridle against extraordinary cruelty and arbitrariness of a Tsar; Cossacks beyond the frontier might lash out at a system that threatened their freedom; the dvoriane might play at "palace revolutions." But none of them could replace the socio-political order with a different and workable one.* That system, Plekhanov contended, was not to be understood as the product of the will of this or that individual—although he identified Ivan the Terrible as the formulator, and a principal implementer, of Russian Oriental despotism. It represented a natural and inevitable consequence of basic economic fact.[41]

Plekhanov perceived a curious dialectic at work in the long sweep of Russian history. In the context of Russian economic backwardness, the need for external security had led to the creation of an Oriental despotism. Once in being, this system served as a further impediment to economic development. Meanwhile, countries to the west of Russia, favored by a more lively economic growth, increased their power and thus posed new threats to Russian security.[42] The stimulus eventually given to a more rapid development of Russian society came not from within but from contact with her more virile neighbors. For self-preservation, if for no other reason, she had been forced to borrow techniques and ideas from the West. These borrowings, intended to bolster Russia's traditional order, instead proved to be its undoing. Having imparted to the West its dynamic character, they became agencies for Russia's transformation from an Oriental-barbaric into an Occidental-civilized society.

This historical construction necessarily assigned a momentous role to Peter the Great. Plekhanov's conception of the import of Peter's work, together with his own views of Russian development from the great Tsar's time to his own, he summarized as follows:

Old Muscovite Russia was distinguished by its completely Asiatic character. Its social life, its administration, the psychology of its inhabitants—everything in it

---

* *Sochineniia*, XX, 236–37. In the eighteenth century, the dvoriane managed to secure a special position for themselves. But, owing to fear of a boyar oligarchy on one side and peasant rebellion on the other, they continued to support the autocratic principle. *Ibid.*, XXI, 185.

was alien to Europe and very closely related to China, Persia, and Ancient Egypt. . . . Peter only added European extremities to a body which nevertheless remained Asiatic. However, the new extremities exercised an enormous influence on the nature of the old body. For the support of the post-reform order, money was needed. The Petrine reform gave impetus to the development of commodity production in Russia. Moreover, for the support of the post-reform order at least some factory industry was needed. Peter laid the basis for that industry in our country and by the same token threw onto Russian soil the seed of entirely new economic relations. For a long time, the industry established by Peter had a rather sorry existence. . . . Nevertheless, it accomplished its work of regenerating the Russian social *corpus,* which was strongly facilitated by those international relations without which the work of the brilliant Peter would have been unthinkable. The success of Russian economic development is evident from the fact that while the Petrine reform demanded the stabilization of serfdom, the reforms of Alexander II presupposed its abolition. The beginning of the new . . . economic order is usually dated from February 19, 1861. We see that it was inaugurated as early as Peter the Great. But of course the 19th of February gave a most powerful stimulus to the development of this order. Now we are irrevocably drawn into the economic movement of civilized humanity and there shall be no dawn for old Muscovite Oblomovism.[43]

In this construction, the key point has to do with the planting of the seeds of a new economic order by Peter the Great, the creation of especially favorable conditions for growth under Alexander II, and the luxuriant blooming of that order in the last half of the nineteenth century. The new economic system, of course, was capitalism. In Plekhanov's view, Russia had passed successively from primitive natural economy in Muscovite Russia to a system modified by the introduction of elements of money economy and commodity production in the first century and a half of the Petersburg period, to the triumph of this economy and mode of production over the primitive Muscovite economic system during the last half of the nineteenth century—that first period of Russia's age of capitalism.* The "Europeanization" of Russia's economic system inescapably altered its social structure as well, fostering the growth of industrial towns peopled with bourgeois and proletarian classes. In these new forces, whose Western counterparts had struggled for political and civil liberty, Plekhanov discerned the promise of the overthrow of Russia's Oriental despotism and the "Europeanization" of its political life.

In the realm of ideas, the Westernization of Russia had for a long time affected only the upper classes. Even prior to the time of Peter the Great,

---

* Plekhanov maintained that even such economic advances as the Russian state was impelled to sponsor were brought into the pattern of Oriental despotism so far as possible. When Peter the Great introduced industry, instead of bringing in free labor with it, he endeavored to adjust it to serfdom. When the peasants were finally emancipated, they were delivered from noble control but remained "fully dependent" upon the state. *Sochineniia,* XX, 122, 124–25.

a few scattered individuals who came to know something of the West experienced disharmony with their native social milieu and fled.* They were the forerunners of the nineteenth-century intelligentsia whose values, shaped by Western practices and theories, brought them into conflict with Russian reality. Instead of fleeing, however, they strove to bring about the reconstruction of Russian life along lines "closer to their heart's desire." One of the great indirect results of the opening of "the window on the West" was the stimulation of Russian social thought. In the nineteenth century, in contrast to earlier eras, there were ample alternative models upon which Russia could pattern a new national life; but what the would-be architects lacked was the social support needed in order to carry through the work of "negation" that must precede construction.† In this was the pathos of the intelligentsia: their abhorrence of Russian reality was equaled only by their inability to alter it.

The great mass of the Russian people, the peasants, long remained unaffected by the Westernization process. Steeped in "Asiatic barbarism," they were utterly alien to the ideals of the Westernized intelligentsia. Cultural contact had brought advanced social and political thought to Russia before the materialization there of the socio-economic developments that had first given rise to it in the West. If the need was to "Europeanize the barbarians,"[44] it could not be done at the behest of the intelligentsia. Advanced ideas could be made flesh only when economic development had changed the character of social life; when it had brought into being social forces which, by their nature and interests, would strive for their realization. That, indeed, was the historic significance of capitalism in Russia.

Although not neglecting the bourgeoisie, Plekhanov qualified the proletariat as the Europeanized mass force that would at last fulfill the passionate wish of the intelligentsia to negate the old order. But the peasants, even in the early twentieth century, still remained comparatively un-

---

* *Sochineniia*, XX, 268, 278–79. Elsewhere, Plekhanov wrote of Ordyn-Nashchokin, one such individual: "He was one of the first victims of Moscow's turn from the East to the West" (*ibid.*, X, 146). Other advanced men of the eighteenth and early nineteenth centuries, Plekhanov contended, experienced a kind of nausea with respect to their social environment. *Ibid.*, X, 147; XXII, 52–53.

† This was a key concept in Plekhanov's interpretation of the intellectual odyssey of Belinsky, and it figured in his analysis of the plight of Herzen, Chernyshevsky, and others. These men are not covered in the *History* proper. References to them and works on them may be found in various volumes of the *Sochineniia*. A concentration of historical articles on social thought in nineteenth-century Russia appears in Vol. XXIII. Since these materials would very likely have found their way into later sections of the *History* had it been completed, they are considered a part of it here. For the point on negation, see X, 349; XIV, 286ff.; XXIII, 139–41, 424–25.

affected. In an aside, Plekhanov succinctly summed up the recent revolution in these terms: "The explosion of 1905–6 was a consequence of the Europeanization of Russia. Its 'failure' was a consequence of the fact that the process of Europeanization had as yet worked out far from all over Russia."[45] The revolution that began so auspiciously foundered on the irrationality of the peasants. Still manifesting the psychology of the enslaved masses under Oriental despotism, even when they acted with extreme violence, they were objectively conservatives. They did not yet understand the necessary conditions of their liberation, and, still worse, could be utilized by their own enemies to hamstring the efforts of those who did. In these latter views, one readily observes how Plekhanov's historical outlook converges with his thinking on contemporary Russian society and its problems.

Parenthetically, Plekhanov's position on the agrarian question becomes clearer against this background. In the course of drafting the party program, as well as in 1905–6, Plekhanov had adamantly opposed Lenin's proposal for the nationalization of land in the first revolution. Yet, both in *Socialism and Political Struggle* and during the famine of 1891–92, he had argued *for* nationalization.[46] In the decade between the famine and the *Iskra* attempt to compose a party program, Plekhanov's conception of Russia as an Oriental despotism had matured. At its base was state control of landed property, an arrangement which forced the entire population into dependence upon the state. Even after the Emancipation, Plekhanov thought, peasant dependence continued, if in a somewhat mitigated form. The penetration of capitalism into the countryside eroded it further. In his estimation, the progressive forces in Russia must adopt an agrarian program that would destroy once and for all the economic basis of despotism. A summary statement of his position appeared in an article of 1906:

A division of the land among the peasants unquestionably would have many inconveniences from our point of view. But as compared with nationalization it would have the enormous superiority of striking the definitive blow at the old order under which both the land and the tiller of the land were the property of the state, and which was nothing else but a Muscovite edition of the economic order lying at the base of all the great Oriental despotisms. But nationalization of land would be an attempt to restore in our country that order which first received some serious blows in the eighteenth century and has been quite powerfully shaken by the course of economic development in the second half of the nineteenth century.[47]

In his *History*, the individual thinkers or works Plekhanov selected as characteristic of their times and of a given class outlook seem occasionally to have been arbitrary, and his treatment of them not infrequently leaves the reader somewhat dissatisfied. Often the ideas of a given writer are analyzed without due attention to the social milieu, to preceding Russian thought, and to foreign currents, their treatment instead approximating to a philosophical criticism.* In his studies of leaders of the nineteenth-century intelligentsia, Plekhanov had interesting observations to impart. Unfortunately, as the critic Ivanov-Razumnik noted, he developed the habit of treating them all *"sub-specie Marxism."* According to Plekhanov, this writer commented,

all the tragedy of Herzen consisted . . . in that he did not attain to the understanding of the dogmas of the Marxian teaching of truth. . . . And that is characteristic, for it is not to Herzen alone that M. Plekhanov applies his universal diagnosis; no, all the errors of all the thinkers, publicists, artists, consist in their not knowing or in misunderstanding Marxian truth, which alone saves.†

In spite of its faults, Plekhanov's work stands as one of the outstanding syntheses of Russian history. His employment of the comparative method yielded many insights not readily available to other investigators. It furnished a perspective from which the peculiarities of Russian historical development stood out in bold relief. Certainly, his emphasis upon its affinities with Oriental societies carries conviction. It makes intelligible much that is otherwise perplexing in Russian history. Not to be underestimated either are his contributions to our understanding of how economic factors helped to shape the course of development of Russian civilization. Among other things, his derivations of psychological and institutional complexes from basic socio-economic circumstances are especially valuable. These features convey more of a sense of the wholeness of Russian civilization than is found in almost any other account. In these respects, Plekhanov demonstrated striking intuition, frequent flashes of bril-

---

* In other cases, excessively long forays into tangential areas impair the proportion and unity of the work. A case in point is his treatment of Rosicrucianism in the third volume.

† *Literatura i obshchestvennost'*, pp. 127–28. A bitter polemic was carried on between Plekhanov and Ivanov-Razumnik, who had himself written a *History of Russian Social Thought*. In Plekhanov's judgment, Ivanov-Razumnik's work possessed little value because the author did not understand that social thought in a society divided into classes necessarily reflected the viewpoint of one class or another. Ivanov-Razumnik charged Plekhanov with failure to fulfill the most important function of the historian of social thought. The historian, he said, could not be content with finding the "sociological equivalent" of this or that ideology; he must go on to determine the "ethical or philosophical equivalent" of various sociological manifestations. In other words, for him ethics represented an independent realm and in no case could be treated as merely a part of the superstructure of a particular mode of production. For Plekhanov's side of the polemic, see the article, "Ideologiia meshchanina nashego vremeni," *Sochineniia*, Vol. XIV.

liance, and no little originality. His *History of Russian Social Thought* can still be read with great profit today.

ART

Although Plekhanov is widely known as the Father of Russian Marxism, he is less well recognized as the parent of Marxian literary criticism. Marx and Engels defined the relation of art to the total complex of human life only in the most general terms. They also threw off a few obiter dicta in regard to criticism.[48] But no one before Plekhanov seriously applied himself to the construction of a systematic theory of art and art criticism consistent with the point of view of historical materialism. Plekhanov made his first excursion into literary criticism in 1888 with a study of Gleb Uspensky. It was the first of a series on the "belletrist Narodniks," a group of writers who had expressed a warmly sympathetic attitude to the peasants in their tales of popular life. Apropos of the piece on Uspensky, Axelrod exclaimed excitedly to a visitor that it was "a brilliant adaptation of the Marxian method to literary criticism. We've had nothing like it."[49] In this, and in subsequent works on Karonin (1890) and Naumov (1897), there began to emerge the principles that Plekhanov presently elaborated into an explicit theory.

His views on the nature of art and the duty of the critic were in several respects identical to his corresponding views on philosophy, political theory, and other branches of thought. In each instance, the observer had before him a social phenomenon, a product reflecting the strivings and moods—in a word, the consciousness—of a particular society or, in a class-divided society, a particular class. Consciousness, of course, was determined by being, by the conditions of social life, and, ultimately, by the prevailing mode of production. Accordingly, for the art historian or critic to denounce this or that artistic expression of the consciousness of a given society or class made as little sense as for the historian of philosophy to fight against the systems of his predecessors. He must approach his subject with scientific detachment, his duty neither to condemn nor to absolve but to explain.* Above all, he must be able to discover the social roots of a given work. In Plekhanov's words: "As an advocate of the materialist outlook, I submit that the first task of the critic is to translate the idea of a given work from the language of art to the language of sociology, in order to find what might be called the sociological equivalent of a given literary phenomenon."[50]

The passage calls to mind his similar definition of the task of the historian of social thought. But it also suggests a major difference Plekhanov

---

* *Sochineniia*, XXIII, 177. Of course, he quoted here the famous critical principle of Taine. Plekhanov carried the same idea over into his historical work. *Ibid.*, XX, 5.

made out between art and the various branches of social thought. Each possessed a distinctive language, the latter communicating by means of logical argument ("syllogisms"), the former by images. Since both were derived from the same milieu and were but different forms of expression of a single social reality, the one could be translated into the other. In a number of aspects, however, Plekhanov took art to be a more complex and elusive subject than the social disciplines. Unlike the latter, the production and appreciation of art were characteristics of man as a biological species. The creation of art stemmed from the play instinct that man shared with other, more primitive, animals. Besides, man possessed a native faculty for responding with pleasure to beautiful objects. These faculties, plastic in nature, were molded by differing social environments to give different results. The forms and content of art varied widely, as did taste, according to the differing conditions of time and place from which they sprang.*

The difficulty of determining the sociological equivalent of different forms of art also varied greatly. Where primitive art was concerned, the problem was relatively simple. Anthropologists had reported numerous cases among primitive peoples of dances imitating the motions of hunting and cultivating activities. Similarly, ornaments and pictures were fashioned in imitation of animal prey, flocks, and the like. The evidence pointed to the priority of labor to play and to the determining role of the productive activity of society upon the character of its art.[51] In more advanced societies, Plekhanov recognized, the problem was infinitely more complex. A knowledge of the economic life of France in the eighteenth century would hardly explain the origin of the minuet. That dance could not be related directly to the productive activity of society, because it was a dance expressive of the psychology of a nonproductive class. Plekhanov was willing to concede the primacy of the psychological factor over the economic in such a case, but he insisted on the ultimate determinacy of the latter. The appearance of nonproductive classes, he observed, was itself a result of the economic development of French society.[52] The reasoning might be lame, but the formulation had the advantage of not restricting the critic too narrowly. He was given ample scope for the interpretation of specific forms or works of art in terms of causes more proximate than the economic.

Once the critic had determined the sociological equivalent of a piece of art, he still had before him the second and scarcely less important part

* These ideas are developed particularly in "Letters Without Address," *Sochineniia*, Vol. XIV; see pp. 5–7 and *passim*. This piece appears in English translation, along with the essay on French literature and art to be discussed below, and the title essay, in *Art and Social Life* (London, 1953). Plekhanov's conception of the aesthetic faculty as more or less autonomous enabled him to approve Kant's aesthetic views. *Sochineniia*, XIV, 118–19.

of his job. The materialist critic, as Plekhanov urged, "must not bolt the door against aesthetics"; on the contrary, he was bound to go on to the "evaluation of the aesthetic virtues of the particular work."[53] In so doing, he assimilated into his method what was valuable in the work of his "idealist" predecessors, while transcending them by adding another dimension to criticism that gave it wholeness. But what were the criteria by which the critic determined the artistic worth of a given work? Plekhanov was wary of a priori, abstract definitions of the ideal in art. After all, art had existed before criticism. Hence, criticism must determine not what art should be but what it is.* Proper criteria were to be derived not from abstract speculation but from the study of art.

His first principle stemmed from his definition of art. Since it involved the immediate perception of truth through images, a work qualified as art only if it did in fact communicate thoughts and feelings in that manner rather than by proof through syllogisms. According to his second principle, also implicit in his definition of art, an artistic work must be truthful, must correspond to reality. For Plekhanov, truthfulness was indispensable, because where truth was absent so was beauty. Beauty consisted in truth and simplicity. "A false idea," he wrote, "spoils a work of art, since it brings a lie into the psychology of its characters."[54] The third principle was that the idea embodied in a work of art should be concrete rather than abstract and should embrace the whole of a subject rather than just one or another of its sides. Finally, the work must possess unity: unity of form, unity of content, and a harmonious integration of form and content.[55] A great work of art, then, faithfully reflects reality through images which successfully realize the idea embodied in it. As further qualifications, Plekhanov added that the value of a work is determined also by the loftiness of the mood it expresses; and only ideas promoting communion between men are capable of inspiring the artist.[56]

Although the total approach to art outlined here represented something new, Plekhanov was indebted for many of its elements to a number of distinguished predecessors. The most important of them were: Hegel, in whose aesthetics "there were many germs of the materialist view of art"; Belinsky, to whom he was indebted for his aesthetic criteria, and whom he once called "the most brilliant of all the Russian writers";[57] and Hippolyte Taine, the French historian and critic, whose work he profoundly admired. All three, in one way or another, had recognized the interdependence of art and the whole complex of human life and thought. All three perceived

* *Sochineniia*, XXIII, 157. Taking this stand, Plekhanov nevertheless came around to acceptance of the aesthetic code of Belinsky, which, he contended, the famous critic arrived at partly a priori. Perhaps Plekhanov could not avoid so doing, for, as Herbert Bowman has observed: "Every systematic statement of what art is offers the materials for a systematic statement of what art should be." See *Vissarion Belinski, 1811–1848: A Study in the Origins of Social Criticism in Russia*, p. 3.

the necessity of viewing art historically, with Belinsky and Taine approaching to a materialist interpretation. The critic's need of scientific detachment Plekhanov of course borrowed from Taine. In the works of Taine he also noted many brilliant examples of the reflection of society in art which no doubt had prompted him to formulate the first task of the critic as he did. Yet, in his estimation, the French writer still fell short of a proper conception of the relation between art and society. When Taine spoke of the environment as the determinant of the form and content of art, he meant the psychological environment. Plekhanov himself, as we have seen, recognized the force of that factor. But Taine went no further, failing to connect psychology with the social structure, and the social structure with its economic base. Perceptive though he was, Taine became entangled in inextricable contradictions because "having said A, he was unable to go on and say B."[58] Plekhanov's brand of literary criticism may be defined as a synthesis of the critical conceptions of Belinsky and Taine with the sociological ideas of Marx.

A few examples will serve to illustrate Plekhanov's method. In a study of French dramatic literature and painting in the eighteenth century,[59] he threw a good deal of light on the succession of schools by relating them to the movement of society in the period, by determining their sociological equivalents. Classicism in literature and painting had triumphed during the reign of Louis XIV, a period in which the consolidation of absolute monarchy brought with it the creation of an elegant court life. New canons of taste emerged as the court aristocracy rose to particular prominence and self-consciousness. Looking askance at the buffoonery and naïveté of the popular medieval theater, they favored an art concerned with elevated personages, in a sublime and dignified style. In the drama, Corneille achieved eminence with tragedies depicting the great ones of ancient times in postures which gave edification to those of his own. In painting, the arbiter of taste, Le Brun, celebrated the greatest hero of his time in a series of resplendent tableaus. The Sun King, looking out from them, was attired in classical costume.

Winning ascendancy in the seventeenth century, classicism remained in vogue up into the French revolution. But—and this was the principal question Plekhanov undertook to answer—how was one to account for the persistence of conservative style and taste in a revolutionary milieu? His answer was both penetrating and subtle. In the reign of Louis XV, classicism lost its vitality and became decadent even as did the governing forces. The earlier refinement gave way to affectation, respect for martial virtues to softness and voluptuousness. The transition was most strikingly reflected in art in the succession from Le Brun to Boucher. Boucher, no less lionized than his predecessor, glorified feminine beauty rather than masculine prowess. Indeed, the male sex was represented in his paintings mainly by cupids. The decadence of the ruling elements, evident first of all in the area of politics, called forth irate opposition from the spokesmen of the rising bourgeoisie, in the arts as well as in the writings of various publicists. A new school protested against the "corruptness" and "depravity" of the noble idlers by celebrating the moral virtues. Dramatists like Nivelle de La Chaussée and Beaumarchais and painters like Greuze shifted attention from ancient to contemporary times and from the seats of the mighty to the hearth of the middle-class family. No longer an object of derision, as in Molière, the bourgeois was held up in the new genres of drama ("sentimental comedy") and painting as a man worthy of respect and admiration —hard-working, upright, and the epitome of the domestic virtues.

Representing as it did a flattering portrait of a rising class soon to gain power, the new tendency might have been expected to triumph over the classical forms and taste of the adversary. Yet, after a tentative advance, the exponents of morality on the stage and on canvas were driven from the field. In the several decades prior to 1789, the bourgeoisie embraced classicism wholeheartedly. Far from symbolizing reconciliation with the aristocracy, however, this phenomenon expressed a movement from a merely oppositional to a revolutionary mood. The increased dissatisfaction and growing aggressiveness of the Third Estate demanded another model than the honest bourgeois of the sentimental comedy, admirable though he might be in his way. He would no longer do because he was utterly divorced from politics. Besides, it was difficult to imagine him engaged in heroic action. To find appropriate models, artists in sympathy with the insurrection in the making reverted to ancient times; but the new school infused the classical forms with a different content. In the resurrected classicism, interest centered upon republican heroes rather than reigning figures—men who loved liberty and were prepared for any sacrifice for the good of the country. Such were the new models placed before the bourgeoisie in Saurin's tragedy *Spartacus* and in David's remarkable portrait of Brutus. Classicism had been taken over by the protagonists of the bourgeoisie and made to serve its purposes. After the revolution, when the social situation had drastically altered, classicism lost its interest for the new ruling class, and soon it was eclipsed.

Although in this essay Plekhanov considered French literature and painting chiefly from the sociological angle, his writings as a whole offer abundant examples of his aesthetic criticism. His analysis of the work of the "belletrist Narodnik" Naumov[60] is particularly instructive. For one thing, it brings to the fore Plekhanov's attitude toward the expression of ideas in literature or other forms of art. The Marxist critic, of course, had nothing against that practice; on the contrary, a work without ideas could not be dignified as art. However, the idea expressed must not "carry the impress of vulgarity"; it must be rendered artistically.[61] In a generally severe judgment on Naumov, Plekhanov's chief point concerned the author's sacrifice of artistic presentation to propagandistic aims. It was a sin that Plekhanov imputed to many another writer as well, and it is particularly noteworthy that he never allowed himself to be swayed by the specific ideological content of a work. He could laud Tolstoy's novels and puncture such a work as Gorky's *Mother* while recognizing the first author as the spokesman of the noble class and the second as a would-be poet of the revolutionary proletariat. [*]

He sympathized with Naumov's purpose—the unmasking of the exploitation of the peasantry—but he criticized the execution as being unrealistic. Naumov's characters were not living people but "anthropomorphic abstractions" whom the author endowed with speech. They revealed themselves to the reader not through their responses to situations in which they were placed but through dialogues of a painfully unreal kind. In these, one character puts extremely naïve questions to another so that the latter can expound his ideas at length. One witnesses an incredible scene in which a kulak candidly explains to his victim why he exploits him. Instead of having a character use words conveying irony, Naumov tells the reader repeatedly that he spoke "with irony." Obviously, Naumov failed to measure up to Plekhanov's standard of truthfulness. Even more fundamentally, however, his work in the main did not conform to the most basic requirement of art. Plekhanov might have said of Naumov what he later wrote apropos of Gorky as the author of *Mother*: Gorky had to understand "how poorly the role of propagandist, that is, a person speaking chiefly in the language of logic, suits an artist, that is, a person speaking chiefly in the language of images."[†]

Plekhanov's criticism implicitly took Naumov to task on the form-content relationship as well, a matter to which he addressed himself explicitly elsewhere. Contradicting a widely held view, Plekhanov argued that Russian literature of the eighteenth century was far from devoid of content. But, as in newly developing literatures generally, mastery of form lagged behind content. The satire of Kantemir, for example, possessed no few ideas, but the form in which they were presented made Kantemir's work practically unreadable for the modern man.[62] On the other hand, the Marxist critic found the art of his own time "impoverished" precisely

---

[*] *Sochineniia*, XXIV, 224; XIV, 192. Similarly, he found the work of the Russian poet Nekrasov wanting in artistic execution, although he admired its sentiment, as he had in student days; see *ibid.*, X, 377–95.

[†] *Ibid.*, XIV, 192. Plekhanov later evaluated subsequent works of Gorky more favorably; see the article in *ibid.*, XXIV, 257–76.

because of its paucity of content. The avoidance of ideas and concentration on form, on "effects," was a characteristic feature of an art in decline. These qualities of contemporary art—and he included not only Cubism and Futurism but also Impressionism in his negative evaluation—were associated in his mind with the decadence of the bourgeoisie.* The flight to "art for art's sake" expressed the inclination of a class that had once welcomed ideas to escape from unpleasant reality now that class struggle threatened it with extinction.[63] As for Impressionism, Plekhanov acknowledged that it had produced many outstanding landscapes, but he added, somewhat irrelevantly, that landscapes did not comprise the whole of painting. The text for his sermon against Impressionism was the statement of one of its practitioners: "Light is the principal personage in a picture." A painter conceiving his art in that fashion was bound to strive for effects, Plekhanov protested, to communicate sensation but not yet emotion or thought. Consequently, his work was necessarily superficial, never breaking through the outer crust of phenomena to reveal man and the great variety of his experience.[64] Such was the fate of the great majority of artists who took refuge in the fashionable *fin-de-siècle* cult of archsubjectivism.

Possibly the most ambitious of Plekhanov's sorties into the field of criticism is his interesting study of Ibsen.[65] In all his critical writings, no better exemplar of his method will be found. In Plekhanov's estimation, the Norwegian dramatist had "no peer among his contemporaries," and yet his plays had about them a certain artificial and inartistic quality. This inadequacy might seem perplexing, for certainly Ibsen was a man of ideas and a playwright of great talent. Plekhanov undertook to solve the enigma by translating the images of the plays into the ideas for which they stood and then disclosing their shortcomings. Characters such as Brand, he recognized, bespoke the dramatist's ardent identification with the "revolt of the modern spirit." On close examination, however, the ends of the revolt were proved to be so nebulous as to justify calling it a revolt without a cause. To be sure, Ibsen made amply clear his contempt for stifling irrational conventions, for triviality and opportunism, for cant and hypocrisy. But, in Plekhanov's view, his positive aims, couched as they were in such vague generalities as "the free mind" and "being true to oneself," were almost meaningless. He deemed Ibsen's works less than completely artistic because the idea so many of them embodied was abstract rather than concrete; they made the moral law an end in itself and gave man nothing more to strive for. Ibsen's unsatisfactory conception of ends was reflected in vague artistic images.

* Cubism he defined as "nonsense cubed"—that is, raised to the third power. *Sochineniia*, XIV, 171.

In the second part of the study, Plekhanov endeavored to determine the social roots of Ibsen's peculiar predicament. Turning to an examination of the milieu in which Ibsen grew up, he discovered there the basis of his revolt. Reared in provincial Norway, the lively and imaginative youth felt hemmed in and stifled by the banality and boredom of a Philistine society that instinctively mistrusted originality. He came to detest the society from which he had sprung, yet he was never able to free himself of it. Indeed, it determined the character of his revolt. According to Plekhanov, the distinguishing social feature of Ibsen's Norway was its essentially petty bourgeois character. Against the tyranny of a hidebound public opinion, Ibsen staked out for the unusual individual not merely the right to existence but a decided superiority over the unthinking herd. But this was to pose the question much too narrowly, to respond only to one limited aspect of social reality. Such an approach took no cognizance whatever of the economic basis of society and its social structure, which happened to be the fundamental data.

In the end, Plekhanov discovered in Ibsen's social environment extenuating circumstances which largely exonerated him. The somnolent, self-satisfied mediocrity of his milieu had understandably aroused his disgust. But this society, owing to the stage of development at which it stood, offered no hope of correction through basic and general reconstruction. As a petty-bourgeois country in an early stage of capitalist development, Norway possessed practically no working class in Ibsen's formative period. With no progressive social force on the scene, Ibsen could find no way out for his country through politics. Accordingly, he turned to ethics and became a moralist. His Dr. Stockmann thundered not against the people indiscriminately—much less against a proletariat that did not yet exist—but against the Philistine petty bourgeoisie who dominated the life of society. Yet that same petty bourgeois environment precluded Ibsen's advance beyond negation to a positive, concrete, social ideal. He could go no further than the consecration of the free mind and purity of will. Having interpreted Ibsen's moral-intellectual orientation "dialectically," Plekhanov could not refrain from adding an unhistorical though characteristic *non sequitur*. The free mind and purity of will of which Ibsen sang, he agreed, were highly desirable. "But there is here not the slightest trace of politics. *And without politics there can be no socialism.*"[66]

In practically all Plekhanov's writings on art, there are to be found acute observations. But, as one proceeds through the body of his work in this field, one is apt to gain diminishing satisfaction. This paradoxical situation mirrors the ambiguity of Plekhanov's approach to artistic phenomena. Analysis of art from the sociological angle yielded many arresting and valuable insights. However, the framework of his sociological approach was too confining. After explicitly rejecting the "Procrustean bed" of idealist aesthetics, Plekhanov chose to press all art into the Procrustean bed of the Marxian historical process and the class struggles appropriate to its successive phases of development. Even in the hands of such a talented student as Plekhanov, this feature of the method in the long run could not but produce tedious results. Besides, this reductionism made it impossible to do justice to the full gamut of artistic expression, as is evident in Plekhanov's dubious strictures on Impressionism. On the other hand, his method provided for virtual autonomy of the aesthetic judgment, a circumstance which more or less liberated the critic in at least one dimension of his work. He exploited this freedom to good advantage, the value of his criticism undoubtedly owing a great deal to his personal aesthetic sensitivity. On principle, he never consented to subordinate aesthetics to utility. Where artistic realization was concerned, his criticism dealt out even-handed judgment alike to political friend or foe.

This "objectivism" of Plekhanov's method, his refusal *deliberately* to subordinate aesthetics to utility, determined its ultimate fate in the U.S.S.R. With the onset of totalitarian integration in the late 1920's, his critical method, which until then had predominated, was brought under severe attack and "corrected."[67] The intent was to remove a serious impediment to the dignifying as artist of the pamphleteer, he whose real nature could not be concealed by the fact that he drove home his logical arguments "not in treatises and articles but in novels, short stories, and plays."[68] Besides, Plekhanov had declared in no uncertain terms against the conversion of the muse of the artist into a "state muse." When that happened, he maintained, art displays the most obvious signs of decline and loses much of its truth, strength, and appeal.[69] For all that, the denunciation of his aesthetic approach speaks less for the complete objectivity of Plekhanov's method than for the unconditional character of the Soviet demand for the surrender of art to politics.

In point of fact, Plekhanov deceived himself no little in imagining his aesthetic judgment to be detached and scientific. Plenty of instances could be cited wherein, all his admonitions to the contrary notwithstanding, his estimate of specific works verged on condemnation rather than explanation. Much more important, it was impossible for him to keep his sociological and aesthetic evaluations in water-tight compartments. They constantly flowed together, with one unvarying result—the subordination of aesthetic judgment to political preference. Art must be truthful in its representation of reality—so read one of the principal points of his aesthetic code. But Plekhanov's criticism breathed the conviction that the Marxian point of view alone was capable of penetrating and grasping social truth in all its many-sidedness. Consequently, no matter how talented an artist might be, his work could never completely measure up to Plekhanov's standards unless he looked at the world through Marxian spectacles. A large part of his criticism—as the analysis of Ibsen illustrates —is devoted to showing how the artist fell short of a fully adequate realization because he did not apprehend the great "truth" of his time.

These observations are particularly true for his judgment of contemporary art, his work on earlier periods approximating much more closely to the detachment of which he was an exponent. To be sure, he rejected the imputation that he believed artists "ought" to be inspired by the emancipation movement of the working class.[70] Yet, in effect, he admitted the charge when he wrote: "One can confidently state that the powers of any true artist today are enhanced if he is imbued with the great emancipatory ideas of our time."[71] He could not conceal his disappointment at the failure of the overwhelming majority of artists so to identify themselves. It is clear that his sociological conceptions decidedly did influence his aesthetic judgment. But if in some respects Plekhanov's critical essays fell short of what he claimed for them, they nonetheless have much to offer to both Marxian and non-Marxian students of criticism.

16

FROM INTERNATIONALISM TO NATIONALISM

IN THE EARLY YEARS OF the twentieth century, inter-
national tension became a feature of modern life that has persisted almost
without interruption to our time. As one crisis followed another in rapid
succession, national passions became inflamed, the arms race gained in
intensity, and possibilities for diplomatic maneuver narrowed. If war
came, there was reason to fear that the ramifications of the alliance system
and of far-ranging imperial rivalries would make it world-wide in scope.
No less alarming, recent advances in technology promised to wreak
destruction of life and property on an unheard-of scale. With a view to
averting the catastrophe, the Socialist International from the turn of the
century onward devoted ever more attention at its congresses to antiwar
policies and plans. Against the nationalist folly that threatened to plunge
the world into the abyss, the socialist organization proposed to pit the
international solidarity of the working class.

As early as 1900, the Paris Congress of the International called for
the mobilization of a common struggle against militarism and colonialism.
Seven years later, when the international situation appeared to have
deteriorated further, the Stuttgart Congress moved the question of war
and peace to the very center of its deliberations. The 1907 congress
pieced together a resolution on the prevention of war that remained
the basic guide down to 1914. Congresses subsequent to the one at
Stuttgart endeavored without success to secure general agreement on
such specific measures as an international general strike, to be taken in
the event of a war crisis. This lapse notwithstanding, the members of the
International believed that by their labors, and especially with the 1907
resolution, they had concocted an effective antidote to war.[1] With a
certain lack of realism, they were inclined after 1907 to view the preven-

tion or the localization of hostilities as a consequence of their own efforts.[2] This illusion was cruelly destroyed in 1914, when the International proved powerless to halt the slide of Europe down the incline to war. In the crisis precipitated by the Sarajevo incident, the working classes rallied to the colors of their respective "bourgeois" states and prepared to fight their proletarian brothers of different nationality. The outbreak of the World War was the death knell of the International and its noble dream.

No leader of the International was more fervently dedicated than Plekhanov to the ideal of international proletarian solidarity. During the Russo-Japanese War, by word and deed, he demonstrated where his allegiance lay. His defeatist attitude to Russia's war effort and his famous gesture to Katayama at the Amsterdam Congress in 1904 exemplified the principles of socialist internationalism the successive congresses espoused. That his views had not changed by the eve of the World War is evident from an open letter he wrote in 1912 to a French socialist newspaper:

For us the interests of the proletariat are the highest law, and war is entirely contrary to that interest. . . . Yes, we are for peace. . . . We know that there exists in the world but one force capable of maintaining peace—the power of the organized international proletariat. Let them cry if they will about the paradox; it is nonetheless incontestable that only the *war of classes* can be opposed with success to *war between peoples*.[3]

Less than two years later, the writer of these lines delivered a rousing war speech to a group of Russian volunteers about to take up arms for France against Germany.[4] To an astonished visitor, he announced that, were it not for his advanced age, he himself would go to the Front in defense of Russia.[5]

In a certain sense, Plekhanov had dimly foreseen and warned against the disaster that overwhelmed the International in 1914, although he could never have dreamed that he would come to the defense of Tsarist Russia. Along with some others, he had repeatedly urged the expulsion of the Revisionists from the international organization, on the ground that they did not share the Marxian outlook upon which it purportedly was based. His pleas went unheeded by an organization that preferred unity to orthodoxy, numbers to rigorous discipline. In this, the International mirrored the behavior of most of its constituent parties. Like the German Social Democratic Party, its strongest section, the International condemned Revisionism, refused to oust its advocates, and in the end succumbed to it.

Although its partisans may have argued to the contrary, the general tendency of Revisionism undeniably ran counter to internationalism. In the view of the Revisionists, the bourgeois state, by a process of evolutionary development, was gradually transformed into a socialist state. The state, accordingly, could hardly be condemned out of hand as a mere instrument of the ruling class for the preservation of its dominance. Partly a workers' state already, owing to the reforms it had enacted in their behalf, it was destined in due course to belong entirely to the people. The working class could not be indifferent to the destruction by foreign conquest of an institution to which their hopes for complete emancipation were pinned. In other words, Revisionism tended to foster nationalism, in spite of the internationalist pledges of its exponents.[6] For all that, had Plekhanov's admonitions been heeded, had the International moved to expel the Revisionists, it might well have wrecked itself in the effort before 1914. Social reform, Revisionism, and nationalism were all facets of a single social process. The Revisionists could not have been excluded without at the same time excluding a substantial portion of the working class, the group for which the organization claimed to speak.

On the other hand, there was the remarkably militant resolution of the Stuttgart Congress on ways and means of avoiding war, which was passed by a unanimous vote of the Congress. The aggressive tone of the resolution (based on a draft by Bebel) emerged particularly in the last paragraphs, which represented an amendment offered by Rosa Luxemburg, Lenin, and Martov:

> If a war threatens to break out, it is the duty of the working class and of its parliamentary representatives in the countries involved, supported by the consolidating activity of the International Bureau, to exert every effort to prevent the outbreak of war by means they consider most effective, which naturally vary according to the accentuation of the class struggle and of the general political situation.
>
> Should war break out none the less, it is their duty to intervene in favor of its speedy termination and to do all in their power to utilize the economic and political crisis caused by the war to rouse the peoples and thereby to hasten the abolition of capitalist class rule.[7]

That these guidelines, devised by representatives of its left wing, should have carried unanimously seems to speak for the efficacy of the International as an antiwar agency. Plekhanov was one of those who expressed keen satisfaction with a formula which, as he said, appeared to cover all contingencies.[8]

The resolution won unanimous support, however, largely because it was a catchall. The delegates took great satisfaction in what they had concocted; but time would disclose that, in seeking to satisfy all factions, they had brewed a self-contradictory and ineffectual nostrum. To begin with, Bebel's resolution identified rivalries among the capitalist states as the cause of war. This proposition clearly pointed to the necessity of a categorical condemnation of all armed conflicts. The resolution fell short of that in deference to those important elements who were convinced of the need to distinguish between aggressive and defensive wars.[9] At the Copenhagen Congress in 1910, these forces secured official recognition of the right of national defense against attack.[10] How an aggressor might be identified unmistakably and how national defense could be reconciled with proletarian internationalism were questions that went unanswered. This important qualification of the general line constituted a Pandora's box, out of which incalculable mischief would spring in 1914.

Moreover, the militant and straightforward policy line of the last paragraphs of the resolution was deprived of a good deal of its force by the preceding assertion that action to be taken would necessarily vary with the occasion and with the background of the different parties.[11] The amendment of the Russian Social Democrats might readily be understood to include the possibility of recourse to insurrection, and Plekhanov was one of those who endorsed it on that score.[12] But it was not so taken by the German Social Democrats, who flinched even from much less aggressive initiatives. At the 1910 congress they turned aside a proposal in support of an international general strike as a means of preventing or stopping war.[13] Pleading that the passage of such a resolution might result in the persecution of their party by the German state, they betrayed a defensive psychology hardly compatible with the bold words of the resolution. It was not clear at the time, but the Germans would appear to have been flatly opposed to the general strike on principle, and not merely for the reasons they gave. Plekhanov defended the German position, however, while sniping at the British and French, parties which had advanced the general strike scheme. Considering the Germans more reliable than the others, he saw no need to describe in detail what actions should be taken in the event of war. "One may affirm without fear of error," he wrote, "that it would be precisely the class-conscious German proletariat that would know how best to use on behalf of the revolution the situation that would be created in Europe by a war, let us say, between Germany and England."[14] His implicit confidence in the German Social Democratic leadership made him oddly insensitive to the great need for agreement on common action if it were to be effective, and he blithely disregarded the deterrent value of a specific threat on governments apt to pursue reckless foreign policies.

With no accord reached either on insurrection or on the general strike, the International was left with comparatively ineffectual means of implementing its antiwar policy. It could count only on mass demonstrations of workers, votes by their parliamentary representatives against war credits, and coordination of the activities of the various parties through its Bureau. If these devices were not entirely inconsequential, they still fell far short of a panoply of weapons capable of rendering international proletarian solidarity an effective barrier to war. Even the limited means provided for might not be fully utilized, owing to the character of the International's constitution. Since it was a loose association of autonomous national parties, its decisions could not be made binding on its constituent elements. Perhaps the moral bonds among the leaders of the national sections, based upon common allegiances and friendly personal relations, seemed the surest guarantee against internecine warfare. But, in the acute crisis of mid-1914, the pressures of nationalism snapped whatever bonds united the socialist parties. Their carefully erected antiwar positions collapsed almost at once, and they marched willingly down the road to Armageddon.

In the spring of 1914, Plekhanov's wife was considering the enlargement of the sanitarium she had established earlier at San Remo. Plekhanov, though deep in the preparation of his historical magnum opus, was still sensitive to the political weather; he advised Rosaliia to postpone her plans, for he had a premonition that war was coming.[15] The assassination of Archduke Francis Ferdinand confirmed his fears. A month later, after the Austrian declaration of war, he sped from Paris, where he had been gathering material, to Brussels to attend a special meeting called by the Bureau of the International. He must have been indignant and heartened by turns, as various leaders reported on the position their respective parties would take. Viktor Adler must particularly have excited his scorn by capitulating, apparently without a struggle, to the nationalist fever that had swept Austria into war. A war against Serbia was popular in Austria, Adler observed, and it would be difficult for the socialists there to take any action against it.[16] So far as the Austrians were concerned, all past pledges in favor of international proletarian solidarity seemed to count for nothing.

Other leaders, particularly Hugo Haase, the chairman of the German party, made statements of a more encouraging kind. To a mass meeting in Brussels sponsored by the Belgian organization, Haase gave a speech in keeping with the most aggressive part of the Stuttgart resolution. "Austria alone is responsible for the war," he said. "Evidently Austria is counting on Germany, but the German socialists declare that secret treaties do not bind the German proletariat. The German proletariat declares that Germany must not intervene even if Russia intervenes." Affirming that the French proletariat was of a similar mind, he continued: "Let our foes destroy one another. Perhaps the poor classes, suffering need and exploitation, will at last awake and establish a socialist society."[17] Plekhanov's confidence in the Germans had not, it appeared, been misplaced.

Jean Jaurès followed with a speech hardly less satisfying than Haase's from the internationalist point of view. Two weeks before, at a special congress of the French Socialist Party, he had called for an international general strike to prevent the outbreak of war. At Brussels, he responded warmly to Haase's declaration, and gave an equivalent pledge on behalf of the French workers. The German Socialist commitment, it was assumed, would have the effect of forcing the German government to exercise a moderating influence on Austrian policy. Jaurès promised pressure on the French government to compel a similar restraint on Russia's part. But, he announced, "if Russia should not take notice, our duty is to say: 'We know but one treaty—the treaty that binds us to the human race.'"[18] These declarations gave real encouragement to those, like Plekhanov, who hoped much from the action of the international socialist movement. If, through German and French action, Austrian and Russian policy could be moderated, then the war might be localized and perhaps even brought to a speedy termination.

On the day after the Bureau concluded its meeting, Jaurès was assassinated in Paris. It was a severe blow to the International and the peace effort. Plekhanov learned of the tragedy in London, where he had gone with his wife after the Brussels meeting. Rosaliia later reported that when Plekhanov read the news he "turned deathly pale." "It seemed to me," she wrote, "that he would lose consciousness. 'What is the matter with you?' I asked him. 'Why has this news upset you so?' 'You cannot imagine what kind of war this will be,' he replied. 'It will be a slaughter of peoples and its cruelty will surpass all that mankind has experienced until now.'"[19] Dejectedly, the pair left immediately for Paris, the City of Light, which now seemed dark and gloomy. Yet the cause of peace still did not seem lost. The words spoken at Jaurès's funeral by Hermann Müller, the representative of the German Social Democratic Party, reaffirmed the internationalist stand of Haase at Brussels. And, with the death of Jaurès, leadership of the French party passed to Edouard Vaillant and to Jules Guesde, who was an orthodox Marxist and an old friend whom Plekhanov actually regarded more highly than Jaurès.

Few today would agree with Plekhanov's estimate of the two men, but it hardly mattered by then who was at the helm of French socialism. Jaurès could no more have stopped the headlong flight to war than Guesde did, for the course of events was being determined not in Paris but in St. Petersburg and Berlin. When Russia ordered mobilization as a warning to Austria that she would not tolerate the crushing of Serbia, Germany countered by declaring war on Russia, and soon after on France. Jaurès had considered it mandatory for his party to collaborate in national defense against aggression. Abandoning internationalism, Guesde now adopted the same line and announced the readiness of the French socialists to vote for war credits. Germany's ultimatum to Belgium, demanding unimpeded passage for its troops, dispelled any remaining doubts of the French socialists. Meanwhile, the resistance of the German Social Democrats was crumbling. They dutifully complied with the order of the Imperial Government to refrain from further demonstrations, and on the day of the ultimatum to Belgium the party cast its votes in the Reichstag in favor of war credits.

Unexpected though the conduct of the German party was, it had its equal in Plekhanov's behavior at the outbreak of the war and after. His position may have been partly determined by the circumstances in which he found himself when war came. The crisis caught him in the capital of the country whose revolution he revered and whose culture he loved. Perhaps he was affected by the panic that gripped Paris with the German declaration of war, and readily fell in with the spirit of patriotism that infected not only the populace in general but Guesde and his circle as well.[20] The latter—and Plekhanov was close to them—were convinced of the need to defend France not just because it was their homeland but because its fate was bound up with the cause of human progress. The land of the Great Revolution, the land that stood closest to socialism, must be guarded at all costs against the onslaught of German imperialism.

Plekhanov became an ardent proponent of the Allied fight against the Central Powers. He approved the vote of the French socialists in favor of war credits. And he who had a decade before denounced one of their leaders, Auguste Millerand, for accepting a portfolio in a bourgeois cabinet now gave his blessing to Guesde for doing the same thing. He who for almost forty years had been calling upon the Russian people to overthrow the Tsarist government now besought them to defend it. His efforts to rally Russian volunteers for service with the French army seemed to symbolize a complete break with his principles. It is hardly surprising that his conduct caused first disbelief and then dismay among his followers and former followers, the majority of whom had taken an antiwar stand.

Returning to Switzerland soon after France entered the war, Plekhanov was confronted with what were to be the two major socialist positions on the conflict other than his own "defensism." He summoned to Geneva Angelica Balabanoff, one of his devoted disciples, who now held a prominent position in the Italian Socialist Party, and to her astonishment—for she assumed the answer to be implicit in the premises of Marxism—asked her what her attitude and that of her party would be to the war. She replied: "We shall do our utmost to prevent Italy from entering the war and to end the war as soon as possible. So far as I am concerned, I shall of course do all in my power to assist the party." Plekhanov's eyes flashed angrily as he rebuked her: "So you would prevent Italy from entering the war! How about Belgium? Where is your love for Russia?" To this unexpected outburst, she replied:

What do you mean—my love for Russia? Must my attitude toward war change because Russia is involved? Would other imperialist governments not act as Germany has done in Belgium if it were necessary to gain their ends? Wasn't it you who taught me the real causes of war? Didn't you warn us that this slaughter was being prepared and that we must oppose it?[21]

"So far as I am concerned," Plekhanov said, "if I were not old and sick I would join the army. To bayonet your German comrades would give me great pleasure."

In this exchange, Balabanoff upheld the internationalist position characteristic of the centrists among the European socialists. They condemned the war, strove for neutrality, and sought to bring the hostilities to an end. Plekhanov had little more patience with this position than with that of the extreme Left, which he encountered soon after.

In October, Plekhanov went to Lausanne to address a gathering of Russian Social Democrats that included Lenin. The Bolshevik chief had already heard something of his former mentor's attitude but had refused to credit the story. It was "simply impossible" for him to believe that Plekhanov, the intransigent Marxist, had become a defensist.[*] As Lenin listened to Plekhanov's speech, however, he recognized that the impossible had come to pass. He had no intention of permitting Plekhanov's case to go unchallenged. Approaching the speakers' table, he began by commending Plekhanov's analysis and condemnation of the behavior of the German Social Democratic Party. But, echoing the words of Müller's funeral oration, and of Angelica Balabanoff's declaration, he insisted that none of the belligerent states was innocent. The congresses of the International had correctly identified capitalism as the source of international conflict, and they had laid down the proper course for the socialists to take. The socialist parties—French, British, and Belgian as well as German—had abdicated their responsibilities, succumbing to chauvinist intoxication. So far, his position did not differ substantially from that of the centrists. Then, advancing what was to be the theme of the left wing, he declared it essential to convert the international war that had just begun into a struggle of the proletariat for the overthrow of the ruling class.[22]

As against these positions, Plekhanov developed his own fully in a long pamphlet called *O voine* (On the War). Not for a moment did he concede

---

[*] Lenin at times thought that Plekhanov's military education accounted for his war position. Krupskaia, *Memories of Lenin*, II, 144.

that his stand involved any significant departure from internationalism and Marxian orthodoxy. Changes that others might call important reversals of his established position, he considered mere tactical changes demanded by drastically altered conditions. Were not the exponents of the dialectical method bound to adjust their tactics to changing circumstances if they hoped to achieve their goals—which remained unaltered?

He admitted, though less vehemently than before, that war in contemporary times stemmed from capitalism, and that all the states had pursued imperialistic policies.[23] Yet, in his view, this admission by no means settled the question of war guilt, which he took to be of great moment. Those socialists who held all the powers responsible for the war simply disregarded the facts. Was not the German government to blame for the deterioration of the international situation in the years prior to the outbreak of the war? Had not Germany stood behind the ultimatum Austria served upon Serbia? And which of the Allied powers had committed so reprehensible an act as the rape of neutral Belgium?[24] Plekhanov had no doubts whatever as to the responsibility of the Central Powers, and especially Germany, for the war. Germany, in proving most willing to use force, had branded itself the aggressor. For the socialists to make no distinction as between the attacker and the defender, he contended, was to betray a lamentable failure of moral sense.

Of course, neither Plekhanov nor anyone else in the international socialist movement had all the facts on which to base a judgment. Yet it is apparent that Plekhanov's assessment of responsibility discriminated against the Central Powers, while turning a blind eye to the complicity of the Allied states. He justified the intrigues of the Serbian nationalists in Bosnia on the ground of the right of union of people of common nationality; as for Austria, it had seized upon the assassination of the Archduke as a pretext for carrying out its desire to crush Serbia.[25] That, of course, was true, but Plekhanov overlooked the connection between the Serbian intrigues and the determination of the Hapsburg regime to destroy its neighbor. Having condemned Austria and its ally Germany for supporting the ultimatum to Serbia, he went on, incredibly, to rationalize Russia's conduct. Arguing more like a Russian statesman than a revolutionary socialist, he maintained that Russia had no alternative but to come to Serbia's assistance if it "did not wish to lose all influence in the Balkans."[26] With that he implicitly vindicated Russian mobilization, and yet denounced Germany's declaration of war—the response thereto.

In Plekhanov's account, the German Social Democratic Party shared with the German government the role of villain. Plekhanov's intense disillusionment with the party he had honored above all others is apparent in everything he wrote during the war. He could not find words sufficiently abusive to communicate the full measure of his contempt. The Germans had betrayed his trust that they could be counted on to do the right thing in a crisis. Their failure to resist the policy of "blood and iron" proved the counterfeit nature of their earlier protestations against public commitment to the general strike tactic. They had betrayed their pledges to the International and the solemn promises of Haase and Müller made only days before the German declaration of war. "Strikebreakers on a grand scale," they had destroyed international proletarian solidarity, the best hope of staving off a general conflict. Plekhanov confessed that he had at first been unable to believe reports in the "bourgeois" press of Social Democratic support of war credits in the Reichstag.[27]

He labeled their justification—the right of German self-defense—spurious, seeing no resemblance between the German position toward Russia and the French position toward Germany. Together with the French socialists, he had credited the French government with good faith, accepted official news reports uncritically, and been caught in the patriotic impulse to national self-defense. He made no allowances for the German socialists, who were subject to much the same circumstances. Of course, he acknowledged, a great wave of chauvinism had passed over the country; but the duty of genuine socialists consisted in providing leadership for resistance to it rather than capitulation. Instead of fulfilling their responsibilities, the German Social Democrats had made an unholy alliance with rapacious German imperialism. Opportunism triumphed, as the party pursued a monstrous policy of seeking advantages for the German working class at the expense of peoples to be brought under German domination.* Entering upon class collaboration, and supporting national aggrandizement, the German socialists had disgracefully abandoned their principles for the sake of material gains. This aggression by the Central Powers, Plekhanov maintained, dictated the necessity of national defense for their victims. Clearly, he considered the rupture of the proletarian united front, and the collaboration of the German party with imperialistic militarism, to have rendered inapplicable the internationalist final paragraphs of the Stuttgart resolution. He invoked instead the International's legitimization of socialist support to a war of national defense.† On that basis, he endorsed

---

* O voine, p. 73. Plekhanov's hostility to the German party owed something to an exasperating interview he had shortly after the outbreak of the war with Max Quarck, a Social Democratic deputy to the Reichstag. Quarck identified German victory with the progress of socialism, and complained of the poor reception the Belgians were giving the German troops (Louis Dumur, "Socialistes Allemands," La Guerre mondiale, Geneva, December 12, 1914). According to Plekhanov's daughter, her father's retort was, "Did you expect to be greeted with beer and pretzels?"

† One is reminded here of his dictum in The History of Russian Social Thought that antagonistic classes may engage in "more or less friendly cooperation in the case of the defense of the country against external attack."

socialist approval of war credits in the parliaments of the Allied states, and even the entry of socialists into governments of national unity.

He would not have been in character, however, had he rested his case simply on the right of national defense; as might have been expected, he linked the defense efforts to the values and ends of socialism. Military victory for Germany, he argued, would be disastrous for socialism in both the triumphant and the defeated countries. In the first case, it would strengthen the right wing of the Social Democratic Party, which had forfeited its claim to a place in the comity of truly socialist organizations. Countries that might be subjugated to German imperialism would, at the least, be retarded in their economic development, if not deprived of their national independence. In either case, the prospects of socialism would be greatly diminished. A decisive defeat for German imperialism, on the other hand, would shift control of the German party to the more trustworthy and militant left wing. As for the other countries, obviously their march toward socialism would be far easier if they could be spared the burden of onerous exactions, or, worse yet, foreign domination.

Plekhanov's analysis of Russia's position in the war is, of course, of special interest. According to Vaganian, Plekhanov at the outset approved of the Social Democratic vote in the Duma against war credits.[28] The commitments of his whole adult life evidently made him unable at first to invoke his defensist stand with reference to Russia. But it was not long before he rectified the inconsistency. His reasoning may well have been that if France was fighting a just war, then Tsarist Russia, its ally, must also be on the side of the angels. It was a syllogism that he never propounded openly, however. Instead, he took the line that Russia, too, was fighting a defensive war. A German victory, he asserted, would constitute a stunning setback to the progressive movement of Russia. German imperialism intended to exploit the nations it conquered, and their economic development would surely be brought to a standstill, with the inevitable halt of social and political progress as well.[29]

Those who held that a Russian defeat would bring disaster only to its ruling classes, he remarked, were sadly mistaken. The working people, in fighting against Germany, really defended their own interests. For, he said, "Russia belongs to its working people. He to whom the interests of this population are dear cannot remain indifferent to the fate of Russia."[30] He conceded the possibility that a Russian victory might strengthen the hand of Russian reaction, but he was confident that it would do so only temporarily; in any case, the loss to the progressive forces would be far less than in the event of a German victory. For the Russian workers to deny their support to the war effort would be tantamount to aiding the ruling classes of the invading power—which would have far worse consequences.

Plekhanov rejected the plea of those who saw in a Russian defeat the opportunity to advance the revolutionary cause. Curiously, he suggested that a German defeat would shift the political balance in Germany to the left, whereas a Russian defeat would have the opposite effect in Russia. Perhaps he viewed the matter in this light because, while well-informed on the annexationist schemes of the German military, he evidently took at face value the purely defensive professions of the Allied powers. On that basis, he might assume for a defeated Germany results different from those in store for Russia if it fell before the Kaiser's forces. He saw no likelihood of a revolution for Russia because, as he concluded somewhat prematurely, the Russian people were at one with the government in their determination to repel the invader.[31] Even as the war progressed and popular opposition to it in Russia increased, Plekhanov did not shift to a revolutionary policy. Instead, he sought to stem the revolutionary tide and to rekindle the will to an effective national defense.

The veteran revolutionist feared the outbreak of a revolution which might disrupt the life of the country and impair its war effort.* It is probable that he opposed a revolutionary policy also because he had little reason to anticipate a revolution cut to his specifications. The bourgeois parties, the most ardent proponents of the war, had lost whatever revolutionary sympathies they might once have had. Yet he could not conceive of a revolution that did not involve both the bourgeoisie and the proletariat. On the other hand, it was the Bolsheviks who hailed defeatism, and Lenin might be able to exploit popular discontents to his reprehensible ends. Once again, as in 1905, the specter of a premature seizure of power rose to haunt Plekhanov. Such an attempt, he repeated endlessly, would be the very worst thing for the interests of the working class.

He envisaged three possible alternatives: German victory with attendant economic enslavement of Russia; Russian victory with a possible concomitant strengthening of the reactionary party; and Russian defeat followed by a Bolshevik seizure of power. In *O voine* he did not actually sum up the results of his reflections, but they came to this: win or lose, Russian progress was likely to suffer a setback. A defensist with regard to the war, Plekhanov had become a defeatist with regard to the revolution. As between the second and third possibilities, he considered the second preferable, for a government victory would at any rate allow for the evolutionary development of the Russian economy which was essential to the fulfillment of his revolutionary scheme.

In time, Plekhanov sensed the unacceptability from the political point of view of a set of such unpromising alternatives as he had sketched. In

---

* This is admitted even by Kamenskaia, whose sketch of Plekhanov's career was written under the guidance of Plekhanov's wife. *Anarchisme et socialisme,* p. xxxiii.

September 1915 he attempted to establish a more heartening connection between the national defense and the political progress of Russia. Aware of the growing impotence of the government, he nevertheless urged continuing popular support of the war effort, foreseeing the transfer of power in some unspecified manner from tsarism to the people. As he wrote: "The liberation of Russia from the internal foe (the old regime and its defenders), attained in the process of self-defense against foreign invasion—such is the great goal to which all particular and secondary considerations must be subordinated."[32] Although perhaps somewhat more encouraging, this recommendation suffered from a certain incongruity. The Russian people, whose interests were bound up with progress, were invited to advance those interests by striving for the military victory of a reactionary state.

In all this, one is hard put to recognize Plekhanov, the militant soldier of revolutionary Social Democracy. His objections to the contrary notwithstanding, the tactics he promoted during the war years could not be reconciled with the precepts and aims he had upheld for the preceding three decades. The shock of the war had jolted him into taking positions far removed from those he had long defended. The Plekhanov of the war period supported class collaboration instead of class struggle; a war among nations instead of international proletarian solidarity. He counseled the necessity of defending the existing state, instead of preparing for its overthrow, since that would bring unintended and undesirable results. His position, although he steadfastly refused to recognize it, was the mirror image of the Revisionism against which he inveighed so feelingly. As if to prove the case, in *O voine* he quoted with approval Kant, the thinker whom he had seen fit to castigate so roundly during his bout with Revisionism.[33]

His astounding reversal began with his revulsion at the "betrayal" of the German Social Democrats, which impelled him to switch from internationalism to justification of national defense. The legitimacy of national defense became the fixed point of his policy. And, once having deceived himself that national defense was a means to the socialist ends he cherished, his penchant for consistency drove him to draw the logical implications and to follow them without wavering.* In truth, national defense became the end to which he subordinated socialism. If, as he said, Marx and Engels justified the right of self-defense, they contradicted themselves in doing so. The *Communist Manifesto* proclaims without qualification: "The working-

---

* What was implied in *O voine* he stated explicitly some time later: "Once the revolutionist has been placed by historical circumstances in a situation which requires him, for the good of his cause, to support war against German imperialism, I will go all the way, untroubled by any tactical 'loyalties'." *Prizyv*, No. 17 (January 22, 1916), p. 8.

men have no fatherland!" Indeed, Plekhanov himself affirmed at the time of the Russo-Japanese War that in a capitalist society the state belonged to the bourgeoisie. To concede that it was the duty of the worker to support national defense was to assert that the worker did possess a stake in the nation. In making this concession, Plekhanov backed into the Revisionist position and was obliged to accept all the implications that went with it. His invariable criterion until then for judging the aptness of any given tactic from the socialist point of view was whether or not it assisted in the development of proletarian class consciousness. He continued to use the same phrases, but it was clear that the wartime tactics he commended militated against that development, and, hence, against the prospects of socialist revolution. Yet he still considered himself a revolutionary socialist, never grasping the incompatibility of the defensist position with revolutionary Social Democracy. The supreme irony was that he failed to recognize where his premises had taken him. While advancing an essentially Revisionist line, and approving the same in the French party and elsewhere, he never ceased to denounce the German party for abandoning orthodoxy.

The extent of Plekhanov's break with Marxian orthodoxy is especially apparent in the new attitude he adopted toward Kant. Ever the stout defender of the philosophical foundations of Marxism, his changed orientation to Kant signaled a fundamental shift in his outlook. Whereas he had once seen in Kantianism a philosophy inimical to the interests of the proletariat, he now envisaged a kind of synthesis between it and Marxism. It was Kantian ethics in particular that now exercised a strong attraction on him. He found noble and appealing Kant's dictum that every person must be treated as an end in himself and never as a means. But he saw no inconsistency between this principle and a movement which sought to do away with an economic system that treated man as a mere means. In international politics, the bourgeoisie were impelled to expansionist policies that violated the right of self-determination of peoples. As Plekhanov saw it, Kant's dictum when applied to international politics demanded the defense of national independence. No less than an individual, a people must be treated as an end rather than a means. Correct proletarian policy, therefore, required support of the right of self-determination. "The economy of the new societies recommended by Marx," he said, "has united the 'external policy of the proletariat' with *the moral law* of Kant."[34]

In embracing the ethics which he had once condemned, Plekhanov no doubt believed he was merely adding moral cement to a Marxian edifice which remained essentially unaltered. In fact, he was displacing fundamental elements of his system with principles drawn from another. Kantian ethics, as Plekhanov once remarked, had about them an absolute quality. They represented a philosophical idealism that could not be reconciled with Marxism because they did not depend on conditions of time and place. Marxian socialism based itself not on ethical grounds but on historical necessity. It was an end to which all other ends were allegedly subordinate in the historical process. How could ethics, a freely chosen guide to conduct, be squared with a system that viewed man's behavior as determined by conditions external to him? He who upheld the inviolability of the individual and of the nation and yet claimed to be a Marxist could do so only at the cost of consistency.* The right of national defense, which on the political level brought Plekhanov to a Revisionist stance, had its philosophical counterpart in Kantian ethics.† One who endorsed the latter could not at the same time be a Marxist, but he could still favor socialism. For him, it could be a rationally chosen ethical ideal. Socialism figured in just that way for Eduard Bernstein.

Bernstein, it is well worth noting, early in the war arrived at a position similar in certain respects to that of Plekhanov. In the crisis of August 1914 he voted "with a heavy heart" for war credits, on the supposition that Germany must defend itself against a Russian attack. He differed from others in his party, and particularly those in the Revisionist right wing, in not being carried away by exaggerated patriotism. Bernstein, unlike the multitude who had rallied to his banner chiefly for pragmatic reasons, was a man of deep ethical sensibility. Before the end of 1914, he had learned of the universal revulsion abroad against the German Social Democrats and of the truth about Germany's rape of neutral Belgium. His consternation was intensified by the amazing growth of chauvinism among his colleagues, extending as it did even to the justification of territorial aggrandizement. His moral revolt led him in late 1914 to denounce German chauvinism and annexationist schemes. In March 1915 he voted against war credits for the first time, and thereafter he was a leader of the German socialist group that fought for an early end to the war and a just peace.[35]

Aside from the pamphlet *O voine*, Plekhanov's political writings of the war years appeared mainly in the weekly newspaper *Prizyv* (The Call), which was founded in the autumn of 1915. Published in Paris, it brought him into collaboration with a mixed bag of right-wing Social Democrats and, ironically, right-wing Socialist Revolutionaries. Among them were the SR's N. D. Avksent'ev, I. Bunakov, and A. A. Argunov, and the former

---

* Plekhanov himself had once written: "With the aid of eclectic thinking, one can unite Marx not only with Kant but also with the medieval 'realists.' For consistent thinkers, the illegal cohabitation of Marx with the philosophy of Kant appears as a sort of monstrosity in the full sense of the word." *Sochineniia*, VIII, 393.

† Probably he found his way to Kant in the search for a philosophical justification of the right of national defense. In *O voine*, the philosophical argument depends more on Kant than on Marx.

Social Democratic members of the Second Duma, G. A. Alexinsky and Belousov. The author of the announcement of publication of the new organ was anonymous, but the work bears Plekhanov's unmistakable stamp. Characteristically, and significantly, the first of a series of twelve propositions it affirmed was the right of self-defense against attack. The keystone of *Prizyv's* outlook was an unqualified belief in the guilt of the Central Powers. The importance to Plekhanov, before all else, of the defeat of the reactionary and imperialistic coalition led him to take the most unlikely positions in the pages of *Prizyv*. His attitudes, if consistent with the task he gave highest priority, conflicted jarringly with the principles with which he had been identified throughout his adult life.

His colleague Avksent'ev argued for abstention of the Left party representatives in the Duma vote on war credits, on the ground that to do otherwise should suggest to the masses confidence in the government. Plekhanov, though acknowledging the desirability of democratizing the war effort, advised a vote in favor of war credits. Evincing either a surprising naïveté or a lack of candor, he argued that to vote in the contrary sense might, for lack of funds, hamper the Russian war effort.[36] When the Minister of the Interior dealt with the workers in a most provocative way, Plekhanov urged forbearance. The workers must not permit themselves to be provoked into refusing to collaborate in the war effort, for such action would foul their own nest: "Everything that weakens the power of resistance of our country now works to the advantage of political reaction. Everything that increases this power works to the advantage of political progress."[37] In the matter of bringing about the desired democratization of the regime, his line was reminiscent of his tactics in 1905, though even more moderate. The forces of the Left, for their own best interests, must support the "responsible opposition" rather than launch revolutionary initiatives that must inevitably meet with failure. In a highly schematic representation based on French revolutionary experience, he saw the Left triumphing ultimately if it now supported the moderate opposition; whereas if it attempted to take control at once, it would soon be compelled to give way to the more powerful forces of the Right.[38] Ostensibly a strategy designed for achieving radical ends, Plekhanov's line in practice required extremely moderate conduct on the part of the revolutionists. It placed him at the extreme right of the RSDLP, alienated from virtually all his former associates in the party.

There was, however, by no means general agreement among Social Democrats with the war views of Lenin. Almost no one was prepared to give himself wholeheartedly to the Allied cause,[39] but most of the Social Democrats occupied the ground between Lenin and Plekhanov, where stood also the other centrist elements of the International. In the centrist view, since none of the powers could be absolved from guilt, there was no justification for support of one coalition against the other. What was needed was a strategy consistent with proletarian internationalism. In the first place, it required the reweaving of the severed ties between the socialists of the warring blocs. Then, together, the various parties could mobilize the proletariats within their own countries for pressure upon the belligerent governments. The aim of such actions should be the speediest possible termination of the war, upon the "just" basis of no annexations and no indemnities.

Socialists of this persuasion were prominent in the Zimmerwald and Kienthal congresses of 1915 and 1916 in Switzerland.[40] The successive congresses reflected the growth of antiwar feeling, with increasing numbers splitting themselves off from the defensist right wings of their parties. The centrist faction dominated the two congresses, although the Kienthal resolutions gave evidence of the rising influence of the Leninist Left. Plekhanov turned his back on all such assemblages. For example, in July 1916 he vehemently opposed the convening of a congress, arguing that it would never do for the socialists of the Allied powers to meet with the socialists of the "imperialist" powers.* For decades, he had ruled out collaboration between the proletariat and its "bourgeois exploiters." Now, in order not to impede such collaboration in the Entente countries, he adamantly rejected discussions among the socialists of the belligerent states. His former stand had been based on a conviction that nothing should be allowed to confuse the workers and retard the growth of their *class* consciousness. His wartime stand was designed to prevent a confusion that might reduce their *national* consciousness and the unity of the nation. Yet he dubbed the Zimmerwald-Kienthal elements "pseudo-internationalists," while reserving to himself and those who shared his views the badge of internationalism. In a scheme in which black was made to appear white, and vice versa, he declared that resistance to German imperialism was the only form of action that corresponded to internationalism and the class interests of the proletariat.

Plekhanov's specific indictments of the Zimmerwald-Kienthal resolutions were twofold. First, declarations in favor of a speedy peace on the basis of no annexations and no indemnities were less than worthless; action, not words, was needed. Totally oblivious of hints abroad of the annexationist aims of the Entente, he saw no need for guarantees of the benign motives of the Allied powers. If the socialists of the "victimized" countries wanted a just peace, they should lend all their energies to the expulsion

---

* *Prizyv*, No. 43 (July 22, 1916), p. 7. Earlier he had argued against the convening of the International Socialist Bureau for similar reasons. Plekhanov to Liubimov, February 19, 1916 (unpublished letter in the possession of Mme E. Batault-Plekhanova).

of the invader. As for the socialists of the Central Powers, they should contribute not pledges but action against their imperialistic masters. Second, he could see no sense in efforts to develop concerted pressure on the belligerent governments.* On the contrary, he feared that the Zimmerwald-Kienthal resolutions, if implemented, would have effects opposite to those intended. After their unspeakable "perfidy," could anyone seriously trust the German Social Democrats to carry out their part of a bargain? And in the Allied countries, Zimmerwald-Kienthal propaganda might very likely weaken the resolve of the workers, and hence the national defense efforts of their countries. Not only was little to be expected in the way of revolutionary action from the German working class, but the German militarists would be encouraged by wavering in the Allied forces to press their advantage. Accordingly, well-meaning declarations could easily have the effect of abetting the imperialistic ambitions of Germany instead of promoting a just peace. Plekhanov's recommendations to the socialists of the Allied countries might be succinctly summarized as follows: Vis-à-vis your own ruling class, words but no action; vis-à-vis the foreign foe, action but no words. From the socialists of the Central Powers he demanded action against their ruling classes, an atonement for which no words could possibly be an adequate substitute.

The events of 1914 and the succeeding war years made upon Plekhanov an indescribably destructive impact. Coming on top of the defeat of his expectations in the Revolution of 1905, the outbreak of the war and the collapse of the International were almost more than he could bear. In the first case, his revolutionary scheme for Russia had suffered a stunning blow; in the second, his implicit faith and confidence in the International —and especially its strongest and seemingly most orthodox section—had proved unjustified. He who thought of himself as the most militant of revolutionists found himself in the extreme right wing of Russian Social Democracy in 1905–6, and, in the war years, in the extreme right of the International as well.

Although Plekhanov's war stand alienated him not only from Lenin and the Bolsheviks but also from Martov, Axelrod, and even Zasulich, it endeared him to many West European socialist leaders whose orthodoxy and reliability he had formerly questioned. If he still felt uneasy in their company, he could console himself that he remained at one with his old

---

* *Prizyv*, No. 43 (July 22, 1916), and No. 56 (December 16, 1916) contain Plekhanov's arguments against Zimmerwald-Kienthal. He was no more favorable to peace overtures from any source. He wrote to his daughters on December 31, 1916: "As for the German proposals, as well as those of Wilson and the Swiss Federal Council, we cannot at all enter into negotiations with an enemy who treads our soil" (unpublished letter in the possession of Mme E. Batault-Plekhanova).

comrade Guesde. But was that enough? Did it begin to offset the pain and bewilderment he felt at the vast gulf that had opened between him and Kautsky, the two leading theoreticians—as he thought—of the Second International? So deeply wounded was he by the action of the German party and the incomprehensible behavior of its theoretical head, that he could scarcely bring himself to mention Kautsky's name in his wartime writings.

For a man who prided himself on the possession of a special insight into the nature of reality, these unforeseen and unimaginable developments were profoundly upsetting. No less disturbing was his realization that his position enjoyed little support in Russia. By his stand on the war, Plekhanov increased his political isolation and reduced to the vanishing point his chances of exerting influence on the course of events in Russia. He endeavored in his writings to convey the impression that his confidence was unruffled, that his outlook needed no revision, that all would yet go his way; but he could not conceal his growing uncertainty. It appears in his admission that socialism, although it would surely come, was further off than he and others had anticipated.[41] It appears as well in his more favorable appraisal of Kant, which implied a shift away from socialism represented as an historically inevitable and scientifically validated society. The march of events perhaps had suggested to Plekhanov a wider range of possibilities for the development of human society than was admitted by Marxian determinism. And yet, while he seemed to allow for greater freedom of action for men, it was too late for him to effect an adjustment in his outlook that would deprive determinism of its central place.

That he was failing, that events were passing him by, Plekhanov surely knew at one level of his consciousness. His divorce from the comrades to whom he had been closest added immeasurably to his grief. A description of Plekhanov in the summer of 1916, written by Aptekman, an old comrade of Narodnik days, shows a broken man. Aptekman had become a Marxist under Plekhanov's immediate tutelage and was devoted to his master. He was surprised by an unexpected visit from Plekhanov, whom he had not seen for almost two years. The defensist had come to talk about the politics of the war with his disciple, who, using the method of thought learned from Plekhanov, had long since arrived at internationalist conclusions. Even before the strained conversation began, Aptekman was overwhelmed with sorrow by the appearance of his old and well-loved comrade.

Lord, such a face! Tormented, suffering. . . . A dark face. . . . His deep-set eyes dimmed. A martyr, plagued by doubt, by inner division, having lost his way, having lost his very self . . . having betrayed his very self . . . I had never seen him thus. This was not physical suffering, not ordinary spiritual

distress, but something profound, tragic, weighing upon his strong, ardent soul.
. . . "What torments him so? What is it that so tears him apart?" . . . glimmered through my mind while glancing at him. "He is wounded, unquestionably wounded, this indefatigable warrior."[42]

He who had worked with Plekhanov in the vibrant, full-souled days of agitations among the workers of St. Petersburg saw before him in 1916 "an eagle with broken wings."[43]

17

1917: THE PROPHET REJECTED

THE WORLD WAR PLACED an intolerable strain on Russia's political and social order. Had Russia remained at peace for several decades after 1905, reforms instituted in the wake of the revolution might conceivably have had their intended effect. But time to test this hypothesis was denied the country. Pursuing an adventurous foreign policy which ignored the requirements of internal development, the Tsarist regime stumbled into a catastrophic conflict in which it perished.

The ineptitude it displayed in its foreign policy was equaled only by its failure to cope with the problems the war created.[1] At the outbreak of hostilities, much of the opposition rallied to the government, and the peasants at least passively accepted the necessity of sacrifices. But thanks to the government's military and administrative incompetence, the honeymoon was short. In 1915, various segments of the populace once again went into opposition; their numbers grew and they became increasingly difficult to hold in line. By early 1917, large areas of Russian territory had been overrun, and the morale of the soldiers had been shattered. The situation at the rear was hardly better. The peasants bitterly resented the government's insatiable demands for army recruits. No less bitterly did they resent the imposition of fixed prices on agricultural but not manufactured products, and they countered by withholding grain from the market. When the government seized the grain, the peasants were outraged. Meanwhile, the urban masses were plagued by food shortages and sharply rising prices. Driven to desperation, Russia's people at last rebelled. In February 1917 war-hating soldiers refused to put down antigovernmental demonstrations of hungry workers. With that, the discredited regime fell.[2]

In some ways, the overthrow of the old regime made Russia's outstanding problems more acute than ever. The revolution was followed by the virtual dissolution of the old governing apparatus and the complete break-down of discipline in the armed forces. With the time-honored restraints gone, a people upon whom order had been imposed from above got out of control. There was no way for the new Provisional Government to restore order by force, and, in any case, such a policy was out of the question. As never before in Russian history, no group could long hold the reins of power unless it was prepared to meet the importunate demands of the people.

At the same time, these demands were becoming more radical. With the disappearance of the repressive machinery of the old order, Russia's masses turned increasingly to the left, seeking not only the redress of grievances that grew out of the war but the fulfillment of aspirations of longer standing. The first and most insistent demand was for the termina-tion of the war, but the land-hungry peasants could not long be kept from seizing the holdings of the nobility, nor the urban workers from exacting substantial concessions from their employers. With the overthrow of the Tsarist regime, not only the political system but class relationships and property rights became subject to drastic change.

Hard on the heels of the February Revolution, two rival political au-thorities were formed: a Provisional Government, established by moder-ately liberal elements of the landholding, industrial, and professional classes; and a series of people's councils, or soviets, set up by radical poli-ticians and parties in Petrograd and throughout the country. These coun-cils, elected by workers and soldiers and, in the rural areas, by peasants, were the focal point of interaction between the masses and the radical parties. Based as they were upon numbers, and enjoying the confidence of the troops, the soviets disposed of enormous power in comparison with the Provisional Government. But at first the soviet leaders declined to use it, or rather used it with great restraint. The Mensheviks and the Socialist Revolutionaries, who at first dominated the soviets, distrusted the Provisional Government but did not wish to displace it and make the soviets the exclusive center of political authority. Instead, they envisaged the soviets as organs of pressure, thinking to impose upon the Provisional Government a program of democratic political and social reform.

The soviets and the policies they advanced were the peculiar outcome of the juxtaposition of relatively backward Russia to the West, and the consequent rise of socialist parties in a country still under a virtually auto-cratic rule. The fall of the old political order was sure to be followed by the emergence of independent organizations of the popular masses. Yet, from the point of view of the revolutionists, the country's retarded socio-economic development ruled out an immediate transition to socialism. Hence, the soviets were obliged to operate in an area somewhere between a bourgeois-liberal and a socialist order; to push for the satisfaction of popular demands compatible with bourgeois society while refusing to take the power that lay within reach as a prelude to the proclamation of the socialist order.

The moderate socialist leaders of the soviets accordingly found themselves in a dilemma. As spokesmen for the masses, they were bound to be responsive to the demands of the masses. But they also recognized the existence of limits beyond which the liberal Provisional Government could not be pushed without upsetting the precarious balance between the two political authorities. If the masses were given their way, they would drive out the liberal and conservative elements and force their own leaders to take power "prematurely." On the other hand, if the moderates urged restraint, they ran the risk of losing their following to the Bolsheviks, who, after Lenin's return, had no qualms about displacing the Provisional Government. In fact, the moderate socialists in the course of 1917 were obliged by popular pressure to participate in the Provisional Government—to accept ministerial posts as well as to support increasingly radical government policies. As a result, numerous conservative and liberal elements withdrew their support of the Provisional Government and some backed an attempted military coup by General Lavr Kornilov. But while they alienated these forces, the moderate socialists, who gained a majority of places in the government after popular upheavals in April and July, 1917, succeeded no better than the original government coalition in satisfying the masses. With the exception of an interlude after the so-called July Days, the people fell increasingly under the spell of the Bolsheviks. The climax came in October with the transference of power to Lenin's party.

Although the Bolsheviks thought of themselves as a proletarian party, working-class support did not clinch their victory in 1917. To be sure, the workers were anxious to improve their conditions. But they had won substantial gains—for instance, the eight-hour day—well before the Bolsheviks gained control. After Lenin's return to Russia in April 1917, the Bolsheviks encouraged the proletarians to press for an immediate transition to socialism, and some factory seizures occurred. But it was the war and the agrarian question that proved decisive. Had the post-July Provisional Government with its moderate socialist majority dealt with these problems to the satisfaction of the soldiers and peasants—that is, had it withdrawn from the war and announced a satisfactory program of land reform—it is difficult to see how the Bolsheviks could have taken power. The Bolshevik slogan "Peace, Land, and Bread," which found wide sympathy, has no evident connection with socialism. The Bolshevik victory is to be attributed more to skillful exploitation of general popular dissatisfaction than to their championing of proletarian socialism. The Bolsheviks' success was facilitated by the character of their organization, which had been designed from the first for the manipulation of mass forces by a tightly knit elite; and by the political insight of their leader, a man not to be deterred by doctrinal considerations from seizing power when the opportunity presented itself. No less an authority than Trotsky affirms that the Bolsheviks would not have won without Lenin.[3]

In 1917, three main views emerged. The original governing coalition, representing conservative and liberal opinion, anticipated the establishment by a popularly elected constituent assembly of a liberal democratic political system. It recognized the inevitability of socio-economic reform as well, but, consisting as it did of representatives of the landowning and business classes, it was opposed to such radical measures as the transfer of land to the peasants without compensation* and the satisfaction of worker demands that threatened to reduce profits markedly or simply make private business enterprise unprofitable. The foreign policy of the Provisional Government was directed by a succession of foreign ministers drawn from the conservative-liberal camp, who kept faith with the war aims and commitments of the Tsarist regime.[4]

On the constitutional issue there was little difference between the moderate socialists and the conservative-liberals, but the two parted company on the land and war questions. The socialists, echoing peasant sentiment, opposed compensation to the big landlords, although they were willing to let the matter await final settlement by the constituent assembly.[5] They favored larger concessions to the industrial workers than the entrepreneurs were disposed to grant, but sought to curb extreme demands and disorders of the working class. As for the war, the moderate socialists straddled the centrist and defensist positions. A declaration of the Petrograd Soviet soon after the fall of the old regime called for a speedy peace with no annexations and no indemnities.[6] However, the moderate socialists saw no alternative but to maintain the Front until such a peace could be concluded. They hoped the war might be terminated by bringing the united pressure of the peoples of the belligerent countries to bear upon their governments, and to that end they became prime movers in the effort to re-establish ties by convening an international socialist congress at Stockholm. This effort was foiled by the Allied governments and the Russian foreign minister.[7]

Upon his return to Russia in April 1917, Lenin charted for the Bolsheviks a policy sharply opposed to those of both the conservative-liberals and the moderate socialists. In essence, he now embraced Trotsky's scheme

---

* Even the Cadet Party, the most advanced section, stood for compensation. Its agrarian program appears in Browder and Kerensky, *The Russian Provisional Government,* II, 605–8.

for telescoping the bourgeois and socialist revolutions, ruling out not only an extended interval of bourgeois-democratic rule but also the "dictatorship of the proletariat and peasantry" which he had designated in 1905–6 as the political regime transitional to socialism. In his April Theses,[8] he demanded the immediate termination of the war and the immediate satisfaction of the socio-economic wants of the peasants and workers. The goals which the Russian people so greatly desired could be achieved, he contended, only by the transfer of all power to the soviets. The soviets were to displace the Provisional Government, thus becoming the sole source of political authority. They were in no case to be superseded by a parliamentary regime, for that would be a step backward. Apart from the obvious appeal of such a program, it had the further advantage of offering simple and direct solutions, ignoring whatever difficulties might lie in the way of their implementation and whatever unpleasant consequences might follow.

On the very eve of the February revolution, Plekhanov had written in an American newspaper that strikes and other forms of working-class struggle in Russia would under existing conditions be criminal.[9] At the same time, he protested against the blindness of official policy as evidenced in the arrest of the labor members of the War Industries Committee, men who had loyally promoted the collaboration of the industrial workers in the war effort. To Guesde, he communicated his fear that this move might lead to serious trouble, and he urged that the French government make representations against the folly of its Russian ally.[10] As it happened, the arrest of the labor members of the War Industries Committee provoked a call for a protest strike on February 14, which was answered a day later by 100,000 workers in Petrograd.[11] Without a doubt, this event figured as an important prelude to the series of strikes and demonstrations which a few days later brought down the Imperial Government.

Word of the overthrow of the Tsarist regime reached Plekhanov at his winter residence in San Remo. Incredulous at the news, which was brought to him by a neighboring pharmacist, he immediately went out to seek confirmation in the press. Yes, it was true, the event he had long predicted and to which his life was dedicated had taken place. Yet the prophet of the revolution could not exult in the fulfillment of his prophecy. He must surely have felt a surge of excitement, enthusiasm, and pride, but his views on the war had led him to call for something like a moratorium on political and class struggle. He had insisted that the left wing should support the "responsible opposition," which pressed for change by legal and peaceful procedures. Yet the inflexibility of the Tsarist government and the disinclination of the moderates to use force made almost inevitable a resort to the more radical measures that Plekhanov had declared criminal. When the upheaval came, he initially found it inconvenient, untimely, fraught with danger.

So detached did he feel at first from the eruption in Petrograd that he saw no reason not to stay in San Remo, continuing work on his *History of Russian Social Thought*.[12] Within days, however, he had changed his mind. It was impossible to concentrate on his writing, especially when telegrams began arriving from Russia, urging him to come home and take the place of leadership he so richly deserved in the new order. Perhaps, after all, he was not so out of touch with the main currents of Russian life as he had been led to believe. Besides, he evidently reasoned, the revolution might after all not militate against a Russian victory in the war. After the revolution of 1789, the French soldiers had performed miracles. The new Russian government, based on popular forces as the old was not, might mount a far more energetic and effective war effort than its predecessor.

Moreover, Plekhanov soon gained the impression that the revolution was achieving what he had designated the highest goal in September 1915: "The liberation of Russia from the internal foe (the old regime and its defenders), attained in the process of self-defense against foreign invasion." True, the internal foe had been driven out by violence rather than by peaceful pressure, but this was a quibble. What mattered was that the state was in the hands of the "responsible opposition" which Plekhanov had urged the Left parties to support. There was evidence, too, that the revolution had neatly resolved the seemingly insurmountable problems placed before Plekhanov's revolutionary system by the events of 1905. The earlier revolution had cast grave doubts on the workability of his tactics, on the possibility of combining the bourgeoisie with a class-conscious proletariat in a revolution against absolutism. Though he would have none of them, the more realistic courses after 1905 involved the forswearing of revolutionary methods, since they could not attain the desired results, or the promoting of a revolution aimed at establishing a proletarian (or possibly a proletarian-peasant) regime. In 1917, almost miraculously, something rather like what he anticipated had come to pass: the working class had played a decisive role in the overthrow of absolutism, and yet power had ostensibly passed to the bourgeoisie. In short, Plekhanov regarded the February Revolution as Russia's long-awaited first revolution, its bourgeois revolution. Following a brief interval of hesitation, he bestowed his blessings upon it.

Plausible as this judgment must have seemed, it was, of course, fundamentally wrong. The overthrow of the Tsar had been accomplished by the proletariat with the help of the soldiers. True, the moderate elements of the State Duma were responsible for establishing and staffing the Provisional Government. But it made little sense to describe as a "bourgeois" revolution an upheaval in which the bourgeoisie, neither during the revolutionary days nor after, had behind it a mass force. Indeed, the "bourgeois" Provisional Government had no real power save what was accorded it on sufferance by the socialist leaders of the soviets.

Eight days after the overthrow of the Tsar, Plekhanov and his wife left San Remo on the first leg of the journey home. Plekhanov's illness had become worse over the years, and to go north in winter was risky. In England, whence he was to travel east on a French transport, he caught a severe cold, and his friend Deutsch urged him to wait until his health improved. Plekhanov refused. "I must go. An old soldier of the revolution must be at his post when he is called."[13] Undoubtedly, he was thinking of his failure to return in 1905, a decision for which he had never forgiven himself. His wife was aware of the danger but could not oppose him. In London, she bought an oxygen tank thinking they might later need one and be unable to obtain it.[14] Both recognized that he might be going to his death, but they also knew that his destiny lay in Russia.

The Allied governments facilitated his return home in the hope that he would help to invigorate the failing Russian war effort.* Indeed, Plekhanov returned to Russia in the company of a delegation of Western socialist leaders charged with the same mission. Men like Marcel Cachin of France and Will O'Grady of England were to greet the Russian revolution and welcome Russia into the family of nations fighting "for justice and democracy against imperialism and reaction."[15]

Plekhanov arrived in Petrograd on March 31, 1917. Hours before his train pulled into the Finland Station, a great crowd began collecting. Factories, regiments, and various social organizations had sent their delegations. There were units of the workers' militia, a brass band, and countless miscellaneous citizens. A part of the station had been reserved for representatives of the political parties, the soviets, and the Allied embassies. When Plekhanov stepped from the train, a sea of red banners greeted his eyes and a cry of welcome broke from the crowd. To the accompaniment of the Marseillaise and the continuing shouts of the throng, he was escorted by a delegation of his followers, the Edinstvo (Unity) group, to the waiting room. There, he was greeted on behalf of the soviets by N. S. Chkeidze, a member of their Executive Committee, with the words: "We hope you will take among us the pre-eminent place that belongs to you by right, and will for a long time continue to work for the realization of the ideals of socialism." At the People's House, to which he then proceeded, he was showered with further warm salutations. After

* The defeatists, who were denied transit by the Allies, received a more sympathetic hearing from the Germans. Thus Lenin and others returned to Russia via Germany in the famed sealed railroad cars. Warth, *The Allies and the Russian Revolution*, pp. 37–43.

his brief remarks, he was hoisted onto the shoulders of admirers who conveyed him to the automobile assigned to take him to his quarters. The vehicle could scarcely make its way through the mass of people who had turned out to see him.[16]

Stirring and poignant thoughts passed through Plekhanov's mind. Here was Petersburg, the scene of his first action in the revolutionary movement. There, the Kazan Square, where forty years before he had hurled his defiance at the autocratic regime that now lay in ruins. The workers who had done so much to tear it down were the blood and bone of those among whom long ago he had carried on his first successful agitations. Those heartening experiences among the Petersburg proletariat had predisposed him toward Marxism. And now his prophecy that political liberty in Russia should be won by the working class or not at all had been vindicated. The great city he had fled in 1880 to escape arrest now gave him a hero's welcome; and Tsar Nicholas, the scourge of the revolutionists, was under arrest.

Plekhanov was profoundly moved by the reception he was given. After thirty-seven years of bitter exile, it was comforting to be acclaimed by the people to whose welfare he had dedicated his life. After decades of political isolation, it was balm to receive the sympathy and reverence that flowed to him from all sides. Plekhanov was so overwhelmed that he may have failed for a time to grasp the meaning of what was going on around him. Petrograd paid its homage to the Father of Russian Marxism, to the man who had given his life to the struggle against despotism and exploitation. But the masses of Petrograd—and of Russia generally—still knew little of the country's political groupings, of the position of the parties and of leading individuals on the key issues of the day. Indeed, those issues were as yet not very clearly defined. Those who understood Plekhanov's position on the war and sympathized with it were few in number. Would he be able to translate the great personal prestige he enjoyed into support for his political program? Could he close the gap between the "undiscriminating" masses and his "conscious" followers, symbolized at the Finland Station by the contrast between the huge turnout and the tiny size of the Edinstvo group?

For a brief moment, it appeared that he might. At least he seemed to have sufficient common ground with the soviets to join with them and, from an inside position, to work for bringing the leaders and the masses to see things as he did. The two central premises of his politics in 1917 were the unequivocally bourgeois character of the historical phase Russia was just entering, and the necessity of pursuing the war to a victorious end as a precondition for Russian progress. On the first score, the moderate socialist leaders of the soviets concurred with him. The restraint they exercised in relation to the "bourgeois" Provisional Government was a tribute to the powerful impress Plekhanov's two-stage revolutionary scheme had made upon the thinking of the revolutionary intelligentsia. On this vital issue, the pioneer Marxist could hardly find fault with the initial stand of the soviet leadership.

Policy on the war was another matter. The overthrow of tsarism made Plekhanov a more ardent and outspoken defensist than ever. In the hope of acquiring influence in the soviets, however, Plekhanov trimmed his sails on the war issue just after his arrival in Russia. In an address to the Petrograd Soviet,[17] he warmly endorsed the appeal this organization had issued a few days before to "the peoples of all the world." The appeal echoed his sentiments when it declared: "We will firmly defend our liberty against all reactionary assaults both from within and without." But the Soviet manifesto also summoned all peoples "to take into their own hands the decision of the question of war and peace." Calling for "a decisive struggle against the acquisitive ambitions of all countries," the Soviet proclaimed the determination of the "Russian democracy" to "oppose the policy of its own ruling classes by every means." Clearly, this declaration resembled the Zimmerwald position much more than it did Plekhanov's own, and he was mistaken if he thought it mere rhetoric. In laying the blame for the war upon "the acquisitive ambitions of all countries," the manifesto in effect denied the contentions of those, like Plekhanov, who portrayed Russia as an injured party fighting a legitimate war. It soon became clear that Plekhanov and the soviet leaders were in basic disagreement.

The soviets, holding the ruling classes of all countries responsible for the war, proposed to mobilize the forces of international socialism on behalf of a just peace. In Plekhanov's eyes, German imperialism was to blame, and he saw no other way of attaining an acceptable peace than by forcibly overcoming the enemy. But he feared that soviet denunciations of the war and the war policy of Russia's "ruling classes" might well destroy what remained of the morale and fighting capacity of the troops. After rebellious soldiers persuaded the Petrograd Soviet to publish Order No. 1, a decree which accelerated the breakdown of army discipline by denying the authority of the officers, Plekhanov objected strenuously and called again and again for its repeal.* The revolution itself, he warned, was

---

* He early warned of the disasters that would befall Russia if "the army fell into disarray in consequence of the breakdown of discipline." When word of the July offensive reached the capital, he spoke glowingly of this "day of resurrection." He regarded the dismissal from his post of Minister of War Savinkov, the forceful SR who aimed to restore discipline in the armed forces, as a step that would transform "the Government of National Salvation" into "the Government of National Doom." *God na rodine,* I, 32, 219; II, 93.

being placed in jeopardy by soviet policies with regard to the armed forces and the war.

Plekhanov's pleas were totally ineffective, for he asked of the soviet leadership what was politically impossible. They could not give unqualified support to the war when the soldiers, who comprised one of the principal forces in the soviets, were clamoring for its end. If the centrist policy could not command popular support, his defensist position, with its faulty premises, had absolutely no chance of success. He was guided by the example of the French Revolution, but he overlooked what a modern scholar has cogently noted, that "in 1792 war broke out in the third year of the revolution, while in 1917 revolution broke out in the third year of the war."[18] The Russian soldiers were sick of fighting, and so far, they had gained no tangible advantages from the revolution. Peace and a share of the land meant more to them than the defense of an abstraction called "the revolution."

In internal affairs also, Plekhanov opposed the main body of popular revolutionary forces. In May 1917 he advised the All-Russian Peasant Congress to put an end to the widespread disorders in the countryside and to leave the settlement of the agrarian question to the discretion of the forthcoming constituent assembly. True to his earlier pronouncement, Plekhanov himself recommended that private landholding be retained, and he deplored the resolution passed by the Congress in support of nationalization of land. He even urged that some compensation, however modest, be given the expropriated large landholders as a magnanimous gesture to save them from utter impoverishment.[19] His unprecedented solicitude for the landed aristocracy may again have reflected the Kantian ethical influence. It surely was related to his concern for the preservation of national unity; he favored the curbing of class hostilities in the face of what he regarded as a mortal threat to the revolution.

In industrial relations, Plekhanov took much the same line. He cautioned the workers—for their own sake—against making excessive demands upon the entrepreneurs:

Of course, the workers must energetically defend their interests. . . . But here, too, it is essential to remain on realistic ground, carefully avoiding dangerous utopias. If our proletariat presented to the capitalists demands whose fulfillment would render the further operation of the enterprises unprofitable, then the enterprises would be closed, the workers would be deprived of wages, and there would be famine in the country. And this at a time when it is waging war against a powerful, rapacious, and merciless opponent.[20]

At first his admonitions were addressed almost exclusively to the workers. Later in 1917, he frequently advised the entrepreneurs—for *their* sake—to make reasonable concessions to the workers. For example, in August, he asserted: "The best means of struggle against the spread of utopian [i.e., Bolshevik] slogans among the Russian proletariat appears to be a system of wide social reforms, worked out through an all-round, well-thought-out agreement between the revolutionary democracy and the commercial-industrial bourgeoisie."[21] The peasants and workers heeded Plekhanov no more than the soldiers did. In the course of 1917, they moved ever leftward while his position remained fixed.

In 1917, Plekhanov did everything he could to stem the class struggle that he had devoted his life to promoting. This seemingly odd conduct followed inevitably from his attitude to the war. The defense of the homeland was indispensable to the salvation of Russia and the Russian revolution, and the threat posed by Germany could be repelled only by a rapprochement of all social forces except those sympathetic to the old order. From the moment of his return to Russia he had favored a coalition government, a kind of *union sacrée,* as the political expression of such a rapprochement. He greeted its establishment in May,* he spoke in its behalf until July, and after the July Days he publicly wrung his hands at the temporary refusal of "the representatives of commerce and industry" to participate further in the coalition.[22] From then on until the Bolsheviks seized power, he pleaded day in and day out for moderate policies which would allow for a stable coalition.

Of course, Plekhanov's revolutionary scheme itself dictated the same tactics to which his war outlook drove him. His revolutionary prospectus called for an extended interval of bourgeois democracy and capitalistic economic development. But, as he advised the Russian workers, there could be no capitalism without capitalists. The proletariat must not drive the entrepreneurs too hard, he insisted, lest it be obliged to take power prematurely; and Engels had declared that no worse fate could befall the working class. The conclusion seemed inescapable. Plekhanov, a lifelong champion of the proletariat, was compelled to urge that its class enemy, the bourgeoisie, be spared—for the proletariat's own sake! How painfully applicable to him were the words he once wrote of Ibsen: "The greatest tragedy of his fate was that he, a man who valued consistency above all else, was destined to become entangled in unending contradictions."[23]

Plekhanov in 1917 favored order, class conciliation, and unrelenting pursuit of the war. Understandably, he regarded Lenin and the Bolsheviks, who espoused diametrically opposed policies, as depraved. He called the April Theses "ravings" which showed a senseless determination to push on immediately to the socialist revolution.[24] After all, Plekhanov

---

* *God na rodine,* I, 90. Circumstances made it mandatory, he considered, that the working class "advance to the fore not that which divides it from other classes and strata but that which unites it with them." *Ibid.,* p. 34.

protested, since the capitalistic phase of Russia's development had only just begun, such a program was irreconcilable with Marx's famous dictum: "Not a single social order disappears before all the productive forces for which it provides ample scope are developed; and new, higher productive relations never take the place of the former before the material conditions for their existence are worked out in the womb of the old society."

In 1917 as in 1905, but even more vehemently, Plekhanov posed as the upholder of Marxian orthodoxy while branding Lenin an anarchist, a Bakuninist, an "alchemist of revolution." What remained of scientific socialism, he asked, if one disregarded the historical process that established the limits of social action? How could the Bolshevik leader be considered a Marxist when he left entirely out of his political calculations Russia's level of economic development?[25] Lenin's program seemed to Plekhanov the negation of Marx and a return to the utopian socialism of an earlier day. Like the Narodovoltsi, Lenin proposed to substitute the will of the revolutionists for the objective laws that determined the course of history. Again and again, Plekhanov recalled Engels's warning of the misfortunes the working class should draw upon itself if it were to attempt a premature seizure of power.

He never hoped to dissuade the Bolsheviks in 1917; he hoped only to prevent the spread of their influence among the masses. He spared no effort to discredit them in his writings and speeches, even giving currency to the dubious rumor, spread through Petrograd during the July Days, that Lenin was a German agent. Subsequently, Plekhanov damned his former disciple as "a demagogue to the tip of his toenails";[26] but he was not content with mere verbal assaults, particularly in the face of Bolshevik connivance in armed demonstrations against the government. He applauded Kerensky's measures against the Bolsheviks after the July Days, and later berated the Provisional Government for insufficient determination and vigor in suppressing "anarchy." A forceful policy was mandatory, he declared, "where the weapons of criticism give way to criticism by means of weapons."[27]

Plekhanov reserved some of his most bitter polemics for the centrist political leaders and groups which from February on occupied the dominant place in the soviets and thus exercised the widest influence over the masses. In his judgment, their policies, though ostensibly anti-Leninist, actually played into Lenin's hands. He called Mensheviks like Chkeidze and Tseretelli and Socialist Revolutionaries like Chernov "semi-Leninists."* He might have granted that they were also semi-Plekhanovists, but that was just the trouble: if they really opposed Lenin and his policies, as they professed to do, they ought to have been consistent Plekhanovists

* He first used the term in May. *God na rodine*, I, 111.

and not sought to construct a program out of mutually contradictory materials. Their effort to find a middle course did much to destroy the Plekhanovist position politically, and at the same time it helped to undermine their own authority and opened the way for Lenin's sweep to power.

In the breasts of the "semi-Leninists," Plekhanov descried a persistent struggle between two conflicting spirits, which he personified as Ivan and Peter:

Ivan thinks our Social Democracy is obliged to defend Russia, which has been attacked by Germany. On that account, Peter brands him a social patriot and, pronouncing himself an internationalist, declares national self-defense the cause of the bourgeoisie. Ivan is convinced that in the interest of the speedy conclusion of peace, the army must go over to the offensive. Peter propagandizes fraternization of the Russian armies with the Germans. Ivan stands for a coalition ministry. Peter repeats that entry into such a ministry is a betrayal of the cause of the proletariat. Ivan considers that the famous call "Workers of all countries, unite!" tacitly includes the invitation: "Workers of all countries, quickly turn your back on those who stand under the banner of capitalist imperialism!" Peter is profoundly disturbed by those who, following this invitation, turn their backs on Scheidemann and Company [the German Majority Social Democrats who supported the war]: he sees in this a violation of international socialist solidarity.[28]

The two points of view were clearly incompatible, Plekhanov argued, and any attempt to combine them could only bring disastrous results.

Although the centrists had committed themselves at least conditionally to the cause of national defense, they undermined it with their Zimmerwaldist propaganda, laying war guilt indifferently on the bourgeoisie of all the belligerent countries. Most of them supported the coalition government, but they immediately endangered it by representing their entry into the cabinet as a way of carrying on the class struggle. Though they freely admitted Russia's unreadiness for socialism, their conduct and words made the continued existence of capitalism precarious in the extreme. Constantly casting aspersions on the "exploiting classes," they spurred on the "anarchistic" and "nonconscious" elements of the population which ultimately provided the basis of Lenin's victory.[29]

Irreconcilably opposed as Plekhanov was to the Bolsheviks, and alienated as he was from the moderate socialists, he quickly lost his prestige and influence in the revolutionary camp. He did not take an active part in the work of the soviets, and it was not simply because of ill health. Apparently he was offered a seat in the Soviet Executive Committee but declined it when the soviet leaders refused his request that a second place be allotted to one of his Edinstvo followers.[30] As his views became known, Plekhanov was regarded by most moderate socialists as an object of distrust. The divide between them was emphasized during the political maneuvering that accompanied the May crisis. At that point, a cabinet shake-up brought into the Provisional Government a group of moderate socialists of the Zimmerwald persuasion. Plekhanov was apparently considered for the post of Minister of Labor, only to have his name vetoed by the Soviet Executive Committee.[31] Much the same procedure was repeated at the time of the July crisis.[32] He held no post in the soviets throughout 1917, and in the government he had only the chairmanship of a commission for the improvement of the conditions of the railroad workers.[33] What a calamity was this for a man who was used to dealing with grand political strategy and universal historical laws! With good reason, he lamented: "I am on the margin of life here."[34]

Plekhanov would have accepted a ministerial post only on condition of labor support, and this was denied him. The soviet leaders opposed him for fear his authority would be employed against them by the more conservative elements of the Provisional Government, that he would be used as "a living shield against attacks from the left."[35] Their concern was no doubt justified. As a minister, they had reason to believe, he would use his long association with the revolutionary movement to legitimize tactics which were inadmissible from the soviet point of view. In 1905, the Bolsheviks had labeled Plekhanov a Cadet-like Marxist; in 1917 many Mensheviks followed suit, calling him simply a Cadet.[36] In truth, the policies he advanced in 1917 were almost indistinguishable from those of the Cadets.

Nevertheless, his conduct does not prove that he had abandoned socialism for bourgeois liberalism. His decades in the West had awakened in him an appreciation of liberal political values, but they had not reconciled him to bourgeois society. That his immediate program in 1917 coincided with that of the Cadets followed from the character of his two-stage revolutionary scheme. The Cadets lauded him because he appeared to fall in with their plans for the consolidation of the democratic revolution on a nonsocialistic basis. His long-range goals still conflicted with theirs, though not so sharply as had been the case earlier. His attitude toward the war, the dilution of his Marxism with Kantianism, and the moderateness of his policies both before and after the February Revolution suggest a mellowing that he himself refused to acknowledge. If the Provisional Government had resisted the Bolsheviks and succeeded in establishing a stable democratic order, Plekhanov would more than likely have become a Revisionist.

In 1917, his newspaper, *Edinstvo*, did not, he candidly admitted, find favor among those to whom it was directed.[37] He deliberately avoided his former comrades, whose views in most cases were now sharply at odds with his own,[38] and the leading soviet personages stayed away from him so as not to compromise themselves with the masses.[39] By contrast, he was praised by the liberal and conservative forces, against which he had long contended, for the nationalistic and moderate program he advocated in 1917, for urging the restoration of authority in the army, and for favoring strong measures against the Bolsheviks. General Kornilov expressed a wish to have Plekhanov enter the cabinet of the regime with which he proposed to replace the Kerensky government.[40] For a man who had devoted his life to the revolutionary movement, this was perhaps the ultimate reproach. He was barred by the organs of the revolution from entering the government. Only the forces against whom he had inveighed all his life—he also denounced Kornilov for his attempt at a coup—were ready to advance him to a position of power.

In August, not long before the Kornilov affair, Plekhanov went to Moscow to address the State Conference called by Kerensky. The contrast between his reception then and the rousing welcome he had received in Petrograd five months earlier emphasized the swift decline of his popularity. At Moscow, his arrival went unnoticed. No quarters had been reserved for him, and he and his wife tried one hotel after another without finding a room. At last, they were reduced to accepting the hospitality of N. Vol'sky, a radical with whom Plekhanov had crossed swords years before.[41] Plekhanov already had a sense of impending disaster. Deeply disturbed, he sought to bring the events going on around him into a meaningful relation to the history of the revolutionary movement and to his own life. While at Vol'sky's he asked to see a copy of Herzen's *Past and Thoughts*, and looked up the place in which Herzen described a youthful vow taken by him and his friend Ogarev to avenge the deaths of Russia's first revolutionists, the martyred Decembrists. He read the moving passage aloud and afterwards proposed an expedition to the near-by Sparrow Hills, that "sacred place in the history of Russian social thought," where the oath had been spoken.[42]

With Vera Zasulich, one of the few comrades with whom he was reunited in 1917, and a few others, Plekhanov went up to the Sparrow Hills. He did not succeed in finding the precise location, but he was enchanted by the panoramic view of the city and deeply moved by the associations of the place. Growing very pale, he suddenly seized Zasulich by the hand and exclaimed:

Vera Ivanovna, ninety years ago, approximately on this spot, Herzen and Ogarev took their vow. About forty years ago, in another place—do you remember?— I and you together also vowed that for us the good of the people would be the highest law all our lives. Our road now is obviously headed for grief. The moment is rapidly approaching when we—rather, about us—will be said: "That is all." That will come probably sooner than we expect. While we still breathe, let us ask ourselves, let us look one another directly in the eye: did we fulfill our vow? I think we fulfilled it honestly. Isn't that true, Vera Ivanovna, honestly?[43]

Undeniably, Plekhanov had fulfilled his vow. His anguish was caused rather by his recognition that he had not fulfilled himself. He whose career was marked by sublime confidence that his ideas and actions were attuned to the historical process stood by, an impotent observer, while events moved on to ends very different from those he had worked for all his life. He was assailed by the harrowing thought that his lifelong optimism had been misplaced, that the outlook upon which he had built his life had somehow played him false.

Ten weeks later the Bolsheviks seized power. Plekhanov's response came in the form of an open letter to the Petrograd workers published in *Edinstvo*,[44] a poignant and penetrating commentary on the October *coup*. He was opposed to the transfer of power to the soviets, not because he opposed the working class but because of his devotion to its interests. Who but Plekhanov, he reminded them, had made the prophecy: "The revolutionary movement will triumph in Russia as a movement of the working class or it will not triumph at all"? Could anyone truly believe that he, Plekhanov, who had struggled for decades against overwhelming odds for the creation of that proletarian movement, had gone over to the bourgeoisie when the workers had become strong?

In a trenchant analysis, the old warrior proved that, though vanquished politically, he still possessed a keen understanding of social dynamics. A dictatorship of the proletariat, he urged, could succeed only if the working class comprised a majority of the population. The support of the peasantry would not compensate for the weakness of Russia's working class, for the peasants wanted land, not the overthrow of capitalism. Since their own economic activity had a capitalistic character, they would oppose the building of socialism, leaving the proletariat isolated and powerless to achieve its objectives. Nor could the numerical inferiority of the Russian working class be compensated for by a socialist revolution in Germany; no such revolution would be forthcoming. A premature seizure of power, then, must have disastrous consequences: not a socialist revolution but a civil war which would result in the loss of the precious positions conquered in the February Revolution. Russia's continued engagement in war with Germany, while divided against itself, further heightened the likelihood of a devastating defeat for the proletariat and the greatest misfortunes for the country. Russia's plight forbade the seizure of power by one class, let alone one party; it demanded instead the coalition of all forces opposed to the restoration of the old regime.

A few days after the open letter appeared, the further publication of *Edinstvo* was banned. Two or three more numbers were issued under another masthead before the revolutionary authorities finally silenced the Father of Russian Marxism. The apprehension that Plekhanov had expressed to Zasulich about the end coming sooner than they supposed grew after October. One day while walking on the banks of the Neva with the Belgian socialist Brouckère, Plekhanov pointed out the fortress of Peter and Paul, in which many a revolutionist had been imprisoned during the now fallen Tsarist regime. "In three months it will be my turn," he said.[45]

That fate he escaped, but he suffered lesser indignities. Not long after the Bolsheviks took power, a detail of soldiers and sailors from the soviet of Tsarkoe Selo, the Petrograd suburb in which Plekhanov lived, burst into his apartment without knocking.[46] They announced that they were looking for arms and demanded to see the head of the household. Ignoring Rosaliia Markovna's reply that her husband was ill in bed, they pushed on to his room, where they ordered Rosaliia to open trunks and drawers for them to search. Finding nothing, they were about to leave when one sailor returned to the charge. Waving his revolver in Plekhanov's face, he cried: "Surrender your arms, or if we ourselves find them, I will kill you on the spot." The sick man replied: "It is not difficult to kill a person, but you'll find no weapons all the same." After further threats and rude remarks, the detail left.

They had not recognized Plekhanov. And though, as he later confided to his wife, he had expected to breathe his last (he asked for a cup of black coffee during the visit so that he might be firm on his feet when led out to be shot), neither he nor his wife revealed his identity, lest that should make matters worse. For months, demagogues had depicted him as a traitor and a counterrevolutionary. Plekhanov was not molested again, for when word of his ordeal got out, the Soviet government issued a decree for "the protection of the person and property of Citizen Plekhanov."

Before the decree appeared, Rosaliia Markovna moved her husband, for safety's sake, to the French Red Cross Hospital in Petrograd. She feared for his life even there, when shortly afterwards a band of soldiers and sailors entered the hospital and slew two former ministers of the Provisional Government. In January 1918, she moved her husband once again, this time to a sanitarium in Terioki, Finland, and there he spent the last months of his life. Though his health was shattered, he maintained his alertness and lucidity of thought almost to the end. And, though bitterly disappointed at the turn affairs had taken, he still showed spirit and courage. Six days before he died, he suddenly awakened from a deep sleep. With an energetic motion of the hand, and his eyes burning with fever, he said in a loud whisper, "So they won't acknowledge my services. I'll show them!"[47] Three days later, his face was so contorted with suffering that Rosaliia Markovna could not look at him without weeping. When he noticed her tears, he scolded her, saying: "What is the matter with you, Rosa? Aren't you ashamed! You and I are old revolutionists and we must be firm." "That is how," he said, raising his arm and clenching his fist. Unafraid to die, he comforted his wife with these words: "And, then, what is death? A transformation of matter." And turning his glance toward the window, "Do you see that birch which leans tenderly against the pine? I, too, perhaps will one day be transformed into a similar birch. What is so bad about that?"[48]

Plekhanov died on May 30, 1918. His body was taken from Finland to Petrograd, where it lay in state for several days at the building of the Free Economic Society. Throngs of people, few of whom had been willing to follow his political lead in 1917, came to pay him homage in death. Many workers, disregarding the advice of the Bolshevik Party that they stay away from Plekhanov's funeral, swelled the crowd that accompanied his bier on the seven-kilometer procession to its final resting place. He was buried in the Volkhov cemetery, next to his beloved relative, Belinsky. On his gravestone, at his own request, appeared the words from Shelley's *Adonais*: "He is made one with nature." Even his gravestone bore witness to his materialist outlook.

The Bolshevik Revolution was the final crushing blow to Plekhanov and his revolutionary theory, a theory based on his conviction that Russia and the West were fundamentally similar. Conceding the peculiarities of his country's earlier institutional development, Plekhanov saw in capitalism the agency that must transform its economic life and social structure, bringing them into correspondence with modern Western forms. The Europeanization of Russia's social life, he confidently believed, would lead to the Europeanization of Russia's political system. This conception bears witness to the rationalistic cast of Plekhanov's thought, to the predilection, anchored in his Marxian creed, for finding universal patterns in the history of human societies. In his quest for unity, simplicity, and certainty, he tended to lose sight of the substantial differences in the modern history of the various countries comprised in the "West." France, for example, had been the scene of the classic "bourgeois" revolution, whereas Germany's attempt at such a revolution ended in failure. Blurring this all-important distinction, Plekhanov arbitrarily took the French model to represent the Western pattern of historical development. Then, elevating the French experience into a universal, he projected for Russia a revolution of the same kind and a similar outcome. In reality, Russia in 1900 was more like Germany before 1848 than France before 1789. Coming much later than the comparable campaign in Germany, the movement for the overthrow of Russian absolutism was even less likely than its predecessor to follow the French pattern.

In laying down the foundations of Russian Marxism, Plekhanov charged the Narodniks with a failure to apprehend rightly Russian socio-economic reality and the tendency of its development. Unquestionably his indictment hit the mark on a number of key matters, above all on the score of the appearance in Russia of an expanding capitalistic productive system and its concomitant, an industrial working class. Yet he went too far in dismissing the Narodniks' insistence on the peculiarities of Russia, too far in imagining that Russia would be transformed by capitalism into a replica of "Western" society. His adversaries may not have identified them accurately, but genuine and substantial differences in Russia's traditions and social structure set it apart from the countries of the West, and not least from France before 1789.

Having missed out on a long-range development of commercial enterprise and urban life, Russia did not possess, as France did, a numerous and affluent bourgeoisie, an independent social force sensible of its own importance and confident in its strength and its ability to govern. Besides being weak, Russia's middle class was inhibited from pressing resolutely for political power, as its French counterpart was not, by its awareness of the existence of an aggressive and demanding working class whose challenge it might immediately have to confront. In France, the bourgeoisie enjoyed practically uncontested leadership in the Revolution; a genuine proletariat had hardly appeared as yet, much less constituted itself an independent political force. Finally, Russia in the early twentieth century, as distinct from France in the late eighteenth, combined within its borders both the agrarian order of a backward country and a modern industrial economy in the early, most exploitative phase of its development. It possessed a potential for releasing at one and the same time the revolutionary energy of a highly discontented peasantry and a militant industrial proletariat. Plekhanov never gave adequate weight to these differences.

Moreover, even if these differences had not existed, the probability of the Russian revolution's following the French pattern would have been remote. As E. H. Carr has pointed out: "In history the drama cannot repeat itself because the *dramatis personae* at the second performance are already conscious of the prospective *dénouement*."[49] It seems likely that the Russian bourgeoisie declined to play its assigned role at least in part because of fears inspired by the turbulent activities of the proletariats of Western countries in the nineteenth century. Plekhanov thought the bourgeoisie to be incapable of sustained revolutionary activity, but his own initiatives made matters worse, for by working to heighten the class consciousness of the proletariat, he decreased the readiness of the bourgeoisie to fight for the overthrow of absolutism.

Since Russia's unreadiness for socialism constituted one of the major points in Plekhanov's critique of the Narodniks, he was faced with the paradoxical task of devising a program for a socialist movement in an economically retarded country which had not yet settled scores with absolutism. He sought to solve this problem by converting what initially seemed an insurmountable hurdle into a distinct advantage, by establishing an organic connection between the socialist revolution and the "bourgeois" revolution which must precede it. He proposed to make the first revolution instrumental to the second, the connecting link being proletarian class consciousness. This should be awakened at the earliest possible moment—specifically, in conjunction with the campaign for the destruction of absolutism—and continuously increased in breadth and depth up to the achievement of socialism. In this manner the socialists, while working for the "bourgeois" revolution, would at the same time be pressing toward their ultimate goal.

Hence Plekhanov's preoccupation with the relations between the proletariat and the bourgeoisie in the struggle against absolutism. In the West, "the people" had struck the decisive blow against absolutism only to have the bourgeoisie pre-empt the spoils of victory. In Russia, to avoid that result, Plekhanov proposed a critical modification: the socialists rather than the bourgeois liberals should summon the workers to the assault on absolutism, thus guaranteeing their participation not as "blind tools" but as an independent, class-conscious force. Under socialist leadership, the workers would fight alongside the bourgeoisie against absolutism and yet harbor no illusions about the relation of their long-run interests to those of their comrades in arms. They would view the revolution against absolutism not as an end in itself, but as a means of acquiring both economic advantages and the political rights wherewith to pursue more effectively their ultimate goal of socialism.

Plekhanov never saw that his modification threatened to disrupt the orderly Marxian sequence of economically determined historical stages. An unresolvable contradiction lay embedded in that all-important element of his system, his concept of class consciousness. Plekhanov's class-conscious proletariat was to understand (1) the role of the class in society; (2) its real interests and the tactics proper to their fulfillment, and (3) the limits imposed upon action by the stage of historical, and especially economic, development the society had reached. To expect any mass group to assimilate and to be guided by such a set of principles, to be capable of such a comprehensive sociological and historical sensitivity, required the kind of confidence that only a faith in historical inevitability could give.

The achievement of proletarian class consiousness, in so far as it involved a grasp of the antagonism of proletarian and bourgeois interests, lay well within the realm of the possible. But the events of 1905 demonstrated the impossibility of combining a class-conscious proletariat with the bourgeoisie in a revolution on the earlier Western model. The bourgeoisie fulfilled all too well Plekhanov's prediction that it would prove incapable of sustained revolutionary action. On the other hand, he was moved to fear that working-class opposition to the bourgeoisie had already attained the "firmness of a prejudice." Here was a premonition of 1917, when few workers saw any compelling reason for conceding power to those they had been taught to regard as their class enemies. Plekhanov's insistence on the coincidence of bourgeois and proletarian interests in 1917 was heard incredulously by those who "knew" from his teaching, directly or through his disciples, that such a coincidence could not exist.

In laying down Social Democratic strategy, Plekhanov did not realize that his proposed "improvement" on Western historical experience could not be made without causing a series of compensatory adjustments. Anticipating Trotsky's "law of uneven development,"* he thought to capitalize on Russia's backwardness to the benefit of the socialist cause, although in a definite and limited way. He failed to deduce the corollary "law of combined development," which projected as the consequence of unevenness a different historical destiny for backward countries, including even the skipping of whole historical stages. Plekhanov's own political activity in reality contributed to the deflection of the historical process he envisaged. He criticized Lenin countless times for disregarding the "objective conditions" of Russian society,† yet his own voluntarism in regard to the Russian historical process differed from Lenin's only in degree. Nor did he point the way for the Bolshevik chief in this sense alone. His response to Revisionism figured heavily in impressing upon Lenin the surpassing importance to the movement of the socialist intelligentsia. The irrepressible will to socialism in a sector of the intelligentsia, a class-conscious proletariat, and an unanticipated and extraordinarily revolutionary upsurge of peasants and soldiers, which was exploited by the Bolsheviks

---

* In a generally stimulating treatment, Meyer (*Leninism*, Chapter 12) mistakenly portrays the Mensheviks—Plekhanov is included by implication—as believing that Russia must recapitulate the *entire* course of the development of Western Europe. This view leaves out of account Plekhanov's linkage of the two revolutions and his intention of shortening the time span between them.

† It is interesting to note that in the early history of the Communist International, Lenin advanced with reference to such colonial countries as India and China tactics recalling Plekhanov's two-stage revolutionary scheme, which he had decisively broken with in 1917. Ranged against Lenin's tactic of supporting bourgeois-led national liberation movements, and calling instead for Communist leadership, were such Asian figures as the Indian M. N. Roy; Xenia J. Eudin and Robert C. North, *Soviet Russia and the East, 1920–1927* (Stanford, Calif., 1957), pp. 36–42, 63–67. A similar controversy arose in the 1920's with respect to the Chinese Communist movement, with Stalin favoring Communist support for the Kuomintang and Trotsky emphasizing the need for independent, aggressive Communist initiative.

with consummate skill—this combination shattered Plekhanov's famous two-stage revolutionary scheme.

After October, to those who spoke of a filial connection between Plekhanov and Lenin, Plekhanov replied that the Bolshevik leader was at best an illegitimate son. At the very last, however, he seems to have grasped the inner connection between his own revolutionary system and the Bolshevik Revolution. According to Deutsch, who spent many hours with his dying comrade, Plekhanov repeatedly put to him the question that "deeply tormented him": "Did we not begin the propaganda of Marxism too early in backward, semi-Asiatic Russia?"[50] In the end he appears to have understood his own complicity in what had happened, recognizing its relation to his insistence upon the vital link between the Russian bourgeois and socialist revolutions. He was tortured by the thought that, after all, it had been a mistake to launch a Marxian movement in a backward country; a wedding of that kind could not but produce results other than he had anticipated.

In the light of the events of 1917, he felt he had seriously overestimated the extent of the Europeanization of Russia. This is evident in his question to Deutsch. And even before the Bolshevik seizure of power, he told Vol'sky that what was European in Russia corresponded only to "the spots on an elephant."[51] The success of Lenin's "demagoguery" he attributed to an insufficient level of proletarian consciousness, another way of saying insufficient Europeanization. A summary judgment on the Bolshevik Revolution affords a glimpse of his last thoughts on this point:

The revolution through which we are living is not a revolution in the European sense of the word, but a bloody epilogue to the reforms of 1861. The soldier is a peasant who has joined the revolution only in order to get the land of the landlords, and he has no interest in the remaining [i.e., the political] conquests of the revolution. He goes against and annihilates the bourgeoisie as if, to his mind, they are the same as the landlords. Lenin, Trotsky, and others, who for twenty years went with the Marxists, essentially became Narodniks after the February Revolution. They are acting according to the program of L. Tikhomirov and are following the advice of Bakunin, who found that the revolution must rely not on the organized workers, who are infected with statism, but on the nonconscious masses, the criminal element, etc.*

---

* Zaria, No. 5-6 (1924), p. 144. How Plekhanov continued to the end to think in terms of the French Revolution may be seen from a letter written by his wife, under his inspiration, on November 24, 1917: "We are suffering not from the terror of the Montagnards, no! It is those against whom Robespierre stormed who have seized power. It is the Hébertists, the Bakuninists, the anarchists. The Convention wanted a France united, strong, and indivisible, while our present regime allows great Russia to be torn to pieces. The Convention would not treat with an enemy that tramped the French soil. Our regime allows Germany to place a yoke on the neck of the Russian people and is ready to abandon to Germany whatever it wishes, while assuring the poor Russian people that this is internationalism."

Plekhanov, bitterly disappointed, believed that the workers were sadly mistaken in imagining they were breaking through to a golden age. But when, shortly after the Bolsheviks took over, he was invited to occupy a ministerial post in a counterrevolutionary coalition, he flatly replied: "I have given forty years to the proletariat, and I will not shoot it down when it is going along the wrong road; and I advise you not to either."[52]

Plekhanov's judgment was vindicated to no small extent by postrevolutionary developments. Despite his many errors, he knew what conditions were essential for the erection of that stable, humane, and democratic socialist order to which he dedicated his life. That those conditions were wanting in Russia, the aftermath of the Bolshevik Revolution showed only too well. The warnings of his open letter to the Petrograd workers and the few articles he wrote thereafter pointed the course Soviet Russia was to take.

As he had predicted, the German revolution did not materialize, and Russia was left to its own resources. Had the Allies not won the war, the terms inflicted upon Russia by Germany in the Treaty of Brest-Litovsk would have had calamitous consequences. That treaty had hardly been signed when a civil war broke out that racked the land for three years, reducing it to a condition not far from barbarism. When the war ended, the country was ruled by the dictatorship of a small minority, as Plekhanov had predicted it would be if the Bolsheviks prevailed. As he had also foretold, the proletarians—or rather those who claimed to speak for them—were incapable of overcoming the prevailing social and economic patterns of Russian life, and in 1921 the New Economic Policy reintroduced free enterprise for peasants and small businessmen. As for Lenin and Trotsky, they all but admitted to error in having forced the pace of history. In effect acknowledging the validity of Plekhanov's warnings, on countless occasions they inveighed against Russia's "peasant barbarism" which at every turn hindered the advance toward that socialist society which was to have been the most rational, the freest, and the most abundant in human history.

When, toward the end of the twenties, the first Five Year Plan was launched, the resistance of the peasantry battered down, and the integration of Soviet society on a totalitarian basis begun, the shape of things once again proved Plekhanov's prescience. Was not this a case of a successful revolutionary clique holding power tenaciously, even though recognizing the divergence between the people's aims and its own socialist objectives? Where that occurred, he had written in 1885, the revolutionary group might attempt to organize national production along socialist lines, in the absence of both objective conditions for and popular approval of socialization. In that case, "it would have to seek salvation in the ideals of 'patriarchal and authoritarian communism,' introducing into those ideals only the change that a socialist caste would manage the national production instead of the Peruvian 'Children of the Sun' and their officials." Was not the Stalin regime an "authoritarian communism"? Did it not aspire to make the populace utterly dependent, through state control of the means of production?

As for the character of party life as it developed under the aegis of Stalin, what could be a better description than Plekhanov's critique of the implications of Lenin's organizational plans, written in 1904?

Imagine that the Central Committee recognized by all of us possessed the still-debated right of "liquidation." Then this would happen. Since a congress is in the offing, the C.C. everywhere "liquidates" the elements with which it is dissatisfied, everywhere seats its own creatures, and, filling all the committees with these creatures, without difficulty guarantees itself a fully submissive majority at the congress. The congress constituted of the creatures of the C.C. amiably cries "Hurrah!" approves all its successful and unsuccessful actions, and applauds all its plans and initiatives. Then, in reality, there would be in the party neither a majority nor a minority, because we would then have realized the ideal of the Persian Shah.

Desiring the attainment among the masses of the highest possible degree of political awareness and sensitivity, Plekhanov had in 1885 written lines that might be read as an indictment of contemporary Soviet society: "And even if there came into being a state which—without giving you political rights—wanted to and could guarantee your material welfare, in that case you would be nothing more than 'satiated slaves, well-fed working cattle.'"[53]

Plekhanov's defeat symbolized the defeat as well of the orthodox Marxian outlook which he upheld throughout his life. The failure of his spirited campaigns against the two major deviations, Revisionism and Bolshevism, are to be attributed not just to his own inadequacy but to the inadequacy of Marxian doctrine when applied to the changing societies of Europe in the early twentieth century. Reformism destroyed the chances of socialist revolution in the West. Plekhanov's own political career demonstrated better than anything else the inappropriateness of the formulas of orthodox Marxism to backward countries such as Russia. His attempt to steer between the Charybdis of reformism and the Scylla of Bolshevism ended in disaster.

Though Plekhanov was the foe of utopianism in the socialist movement, his own aspirations turned out to be utopian. Having once denominated philosophy "the science of the sciences," he became wedded to philosophical positions that played him false. It proved impossible to maintain the balance, essential for the fulfillment of his vision, between determinism and will, evolution and revolution. Both in the West and in Russia, the march of events made a mockery of Plekhanov's abiding belief in history as an objective process conforming to knowable laws, and independent of human will. Yet with the ambiguity so characteristic of human history, Plekhanov has proved right in a way. In the West, reformism modified capitalism but failed to achieve the socialist transformation its proponents anticipated. And in Russia Plekhanov's warnings against a premature seizure of power subsequently came back to mock the "outlaws" who had triumphed over him in 1917.

NOTES

(Full titles and publication information will be found in the Bibliography.)

CHAPTER 1

1. An enormous literature has been produced on the intelligentsia. A good brief account appears in Seton-Watson, pp. 18–24.

2. Two new universities and five institutions for advanced professional training were founded between 1862 and 1870. See W. H. E. Johnson, *Russia's Educational Heritage* (Pittsburgh, 1950), pp. 145–46.

3. The sources for this account of Plekhanov's early life are: Arzaev, Preface to Plekhanov, *God na rodine*; Frencher, "Na rodine G. V. Plekhanova"; Kamenskaia, Preface to Plekhanoff, *Anarchisme et socialisme*; R. M. Plekhanova, "Kak organizoval svoi umstvennyi trud G. V. Plekhanov" and "Plekhanov i rabochie"; Deutsch, "Molodost' G. V. Plekhanova"; V. V. Pozdniakova-Plekhanova, "Detstvo i otrochestvo G. V. Plekhanova," in Deutsch, *Gruppa "Osvobozhdenie Truda,"* Vol. I; M. C. Aleksandrov, "Odin iz pervykh uchitelei Plekhanova," in *ibid.,* Vol. V; Semashko, "O detskikh godakh G. V. Plekhanova" and "Zamechaniia po povodu biografii G. V. Plekhanova sostavlennoi Iu. Arzaevym"; Smirnov, "G. V. Plekhanov v Voronezhskoi Voennoi Gymnazii"; Aptekman, "Pometki O. V. Aptekmana na stat'e o G. V. Plekhanove." I am also indebted for information on a number of points to Mmes Eugenia Batault-Plekhanova and Lydia Savoureux-Plekhanova and to the staff of the Dom Plekhanova in Leningrad.

4. Semashko, *Proletarskaia revoliutsiia,* 1922, No. 5, p. 303.

5. Frencher, p. 45.

6. Cited by Aleksandrov, *Gruppa,* V, 37.

7. *Sochineniia,* X, 389.

8. *Poems of Nicholas Nekrassov,* trans. Juliet Soskice (London, 1929), p. 190.

9. Arzaev, p. xi.

10. Notes of interview with Plekhanov's daughters, Paris, Summer 1959.

11. Haimson, pp. 31–32. Haimson's interpretation is borrowed from Deutsch, "Molodost' G. V. Plekhanova," p. 127.

12. Deutsch, "Molodost' G. V. Plekhanova," p. 129.

13. Frencher, p. 37.

14. Kropotkin, p. 240.

CHAPTER 2

1. The best general work available on populism is Venturi's *Roots of Revolution*. An earlier work on the same subject is Footman's *Red Prelude*.

2. For an excellent recent study of Bakunin's anarchist views, see Pyziur, *The Doctrine of Anarchism of Michael A. Bakunin*.

3. A detailed study of the Zurich community of Russian students and their part in the revolutionary movement is Meijer's *Knowledge and Revolution*.

4. "Plekhanov v Gornom Institute," in Deutsch, *Gruppa*, IV, 408.

5. Akselrod, "Sergei Kravchinskii," in *Rabochii klass i revoliutsionnoe dvizhenie v Rossii*, p. 98.

6. Material on Axelrod is drawn from his autobiography, *Perezhitoe i peredumannoe*. On his first meeting with Plekhanov, see pp. 156–57; also Aptekman, "Pometki O. V. Aptekmana na stat'e o G. V. Plekhanove."

7. *Sochineniia*, III, 128.

8. Deutsch, "Molodost' G. V. Plekhanova," p. 125.

9. Letter to the author from Dom Plekhanova, Leningrad, October 30, 1958.

10. Notes of interview with Plekhanov's daughters, Paris, Summer 1959.

11. Cherniavskii, pp. 7–8.

12. In his long autobiographical piece, "Russkii rabochii v revoliutsionnom dvizhenii," *Sochineniia*, III, 148-54.

13. The description of the Kazan demonstration given here is based upon the accounts of Cherniavskii and Plekhanov. The rendition of the speech is from Cherniavskii, p. 14. The government reconstruction of the demonstration, based upon an extensive inquest, substantially agrees with the accounts of the revolutionists. See Basilevskii, ed., *Gosudarstvennye prestuplenie v Rossii v XIX veke*, II, 1–146, but especially 4–7.

14. Deutsch, "Kak G. V. Plekhanov stal marksistom," p. 97. Plekhanov testified directly as to his antipathy to German Social Democracy at the time in "O bylom i nebylitsakh," the transcript of an interview he gave to Deutsch in 1907, published for the first time in *Proletarskaia revoliutsiia*, 1923, No. 15, and subsequently reprinted in *Sochineniia*, XXIV, 300.

15. Aptekman, *Iz istorii narodnichestva 70-kh godov: "Zemlia i Volia,"* pp. 94–99 (hereafter cited as *Zemlia i Volia*).

16. *Ibid.*, p. 99.

17. R. M. Plekhanova, "Pereferiinyi kruzhok 'Zemli i voli,'" in Deutsch, *Gruppa*, IV, 106, 112.

18. Aptekman, *Zemlia i Volia*, pp. 111–12. Plekhanov touches on his Saratov experience in *Sochineniia*, XXIV, 94–95, 300–302.

19. Aptekman, *G. V. Plekhanov*, p. 20; also *Zemlia i Volia*, p. 119.

20. This characterization of the period was made by Plekhanov retrospectively in *Sochineniia*, I, 161.

21. See N. Rusanov, *Iz moikh vospominaniakh* (Berlin, 1923), pp. 180-86.

22. Plekhanov, *God na rodine*, II, 253–55.

23. See *Sochineniia*, III, 155–58.

24. It is reprinted in *Literaturnoe nasledie G. V. Plekhanova*, I, 380–81.

25. All these manifestoes are found in *ibid.*

26. The relationship between the programmatic efforts of 1877 and 1878 is discussed by S. Valk in the introductory essay in *Arkhiv "Zemli i Voli" i "Narodnoi Voli,"* pp. 6–10. The relevant documents are reprinted in this work.

27. Plekhanov discusses his role in this incident in *Sochineniia,* III, 159–71.

28. Aptekman, *G. V. Plekhanov,* p. 22; *Sochineniia,* III, 162.

29. *Sochineniia,* III, 166.

30. *Ibid.,* XXIV, 97–98, 303.

31. *Ibid.,* III, 171–81.

32. *Ibid.,* X, 399–407.

CHAPTER 3

1. See, for example, Popov, "Zemlia i Volia nakanune voronezhskogo s'ezda," pp. 23–27.

2. Aptekman, *Zemlia i Volia,* pp. 125–26, 136; *Sochineniia,* XII, 352–53.

3. *Sochineniia,* XXIV, 98–99.

4. *Ibid.,* I, 69.

5. My analysis of the development of terrorism and of the conflict between the terrorists and the Derevenshchiki is based upon Aptekman's *Zemlia i Volia;* the articles by Popov, Morozov, and Frolenko in *Byloe,* 1906, Nos. 8 and 12, and 1907, No. 1; Tikhomirov's *Vospominaniia;* Plekhanov's "O bylom i nebylitsakh," in *Sochineniia,* Vol. XXIV; and Figner.

6. Tikhomirov, *Vospominaniia,* p. 133.

7. *Ibid.,* pp. 127–28; R. M. Plekhanova, "Pereferiinyi kruzhok," in Deutsch, *Gruppa,* IV, 107.

8. *Sochineniia,* XXIV, 307.

9. Cited in Venturi, pp. 639–40.

10. *Sochineniia,* XXIV, 305.

11. Aptekman, *Zemlia i Volia,* p. 136.

12. Cited by Aptekman, *ibid.,* p. 165.

13. Cited by Aptekman, *ibid.,* p. 182.

14. *Ibid.,* p. 175.

15. Morozov, pp. 8–9.

16. Accounts of the meeting are given in *Sochineniia,* XXIV, 304–6; Morozov, p. 6; Popov, "Zemlia i Volia," pp. 21–22; Aptekman, *Zemlia i Volia,* pp. 183–84.

17. *Sochineniia,* XXIV, 306.

18. The account of the Lipetsk meeting is based mainly upon Morozov, pp. 10–15.

19. *Ibid.,* p. 11. Morozov takes credit for the formulation of the Lipetsk program, but Frolenko, who also attended, considers it a product of several men's efforts (see "Kommentarii," p. 27).

20. The facts in the account of the Voronezh congress are drawn principally from Aptekman, *Zemlia i Volia,* pp. 189–94; the interpretation is largely my own.

21. The letter is reproduced in *ibid.,* pp. 189–90.

22. *Sochineniia,* XXIV, 105, 137; Deutsch, "Kak G. V. Plekhanov stal marksistom," pp. 111, 113.

23. *Sochineniia,* XXIV, 105-6, 137.

24. The remainder of this paragraph is based upon Morozov's greatly fore-

shortened description of the Voronezh meeting, pp. 16–19. What he says here is confirmed by Figner, p. 132.

25. *Sochineniia*, XXIV, 307–10.

26. Popov, "Zemlia i Volia," p. 33; Aptekman, *Zemlia i Volia*, p. 194.

27. Popov suggests most of these considerations.

28. R. M. Plekhanova, "Nasha zhizn do emigratsii," in Deutsch, *Gruppa*, VI, 65–69, 71–73; also *ibid.*, IV, 115.

29. Plekhanova, "Nasha zhizn," pp. 72–73.

30. Deutsch, "Kak G. V. Plekhanov stal marksistom," p. 113.

31. Aptekman, *Zemlia i Volia*, p. 201. The following treatment of the fate of Chernyi Peredel is based mainly upon Aptekman's account, pp. 201–21.

32. Axelrod's notes on his association with Chernyi Peredel appear in his *Perezhitoe i peredumannoe*, pp. 333–69, 381–89, and *passim*.

33. *Sochineniia*, I, 108.

34. Aptekman, *Zemlia i Volia*, pp. 206–8.

35. *Sochineniia*, III, 184–86; 201–2.

36. R. M. Plekhanova, "Nasha zhizn," *Gruppa*, VI, 96–97. Her characterization of Khalturin reflects Plekhanov's sentiments.

37. *Ibid.*, pp. 88–92.

CHAPTER 4

1. Cited in Nevskii, *Ocherki po istorii rossiskoi kommunisticheskoi partii*, I, 177.

2. Chagin, p. 10. The material presented on the penetration of Marxism into Russia is largely drawn from Chagin's work. See also *Perepiska K. Marksa i F. Engel'sa s russkimi politicheskimi deiateliami* (hereafter cited as *Perepiska Marksa i Engel'sa*).

3. Karl Marx, *Capital* (New York, Modern Library), p. 20.

4. On this point, see Shul'gin, pp. 171–73.

5. *Perepiska Marksa i Engel'sa*, p. 206.

6. Deutsch, "Molodost' G. V. Plekhanova," p. 139.

7. Plekhanov refers to this in *Sochineniia*, III, 140–41.

8. Deutsch, "Kak G. V. Plekhanov stal marksistom," p. 102.

9. Bakunin, pp. 223–24.

10. *Sochineniia*, I, 19.

11. *Ibid.*, p. 57.

12. *Ibid.*, p. 12. Riazanov was the editor of Plekhanov's collected works (*Sochineniia*). By contrast, Vaganian places greater emphasis upon Bakunin's influence at this time. See his *G. V. Plekhanov*, p. 36.

13. *Sochineniia*, I, 56–57.

14. *Ibid.*, p. 59.

15. *Ibid.*, p. 62.

16. *Ibid.*, pp. 67–70.

17. *Ibid.*, pp. 59–60.

18. *Ibid.*, p. 61.

19. *Ibid.*, p. 29.

20. *Ibid.*, p. 57.

21. Pyziur, pp. 98–99.

22. *Sochineniia*, X, 399.

23. *Ibid.*, I, 76–77.

24. R. M. Plekhanova, "Nasha zhizn," *Gruppa*, VI, 94.

25. *Sochineniia*, I, 103.

26. *Ibid.*, pp. 102–3.

27. *Ibid.*, p. 103.

28. *Ibid.*, p. 106.
29. *Ibid.*, p. 117.
30. *Ibid.*, III, 197.
31. R. M. Plekhanova, "Nasha zhizn," *Gruppa*, VI, 102–3, 110–11.
32. *Perezhitoe i peredumannoe*, p. 347.
33. *Sochineniia*, I, 138.
34. Deutsch, "Kak G. V. Plekhanov stal marksistom," pp. 122–23.
35. *Sochineniia*, XIII, 26.

CHAPTER 5

1. Concerning Axelrod's experiences with Chernyi Peredel in Russia and his negotiations on program with the Geneva comrades, see his *Perezhitoe i peredumannoe*, pp. 347–57, 368–69.
2. *Sochineniia*, I, 137–39.
3. Deutsch, "Kak G. V. Plekhanov stal marksistom," pp. 121–24.
4. R. M. Plekhanova, "Nasha zhizn," *Gruppa*, VI, 107–9.
5. *Dela i dni*, No. 2 (1921), pp. 84, 88, 89.
6. *Ibid.*, p. 86.
7. Deutsch, "Kak G. V. Plekhanov stal marksistom," p. 133.
8. Plekhanov's association with Guesde is touched on in R. M. Plekhanova, "Nasha pervaia vstrecha s Zhiulem Gedom," in Deutsch, *Gruppa*, I, 95–100.
9. *Ibid.*, pp. 96–98.
10. *Literaturnoe nasledie G. V. Plekhanova*, I, 202–20.
11. Deutsch, "Kak G. V. Plekhanov stal marksistom," p. 120.
12. *Ibid.*
13. *Ibid.*, pp. 120, 127–28.
14. It may be read in translation in *The Russian Menace to Europe*, ed. Blackstock and Hoselitz, pp. 203–15.
15. *Sochineniia*, I, 124–25.
16. Bernstein, "Karl Marks i russkie revoliutsionnery," pp. 9–10, 16–17; Potash, pp. 50–51.
17. Shtein, pp. 236–38.
18. Cited in Iakovlev, *Iz istorii politicheskoi bor'by v 70-kh i 80-kh gg.* (Moscow, 1912), p. 470.
19. Marx and Engels, *Correspondence, 1846–1895* (New York, 1934), pp. 390–91.
20. Marks i Engels, "Predislovie k russkomu izdaniiu 'Manifesta Kommunisticheskoi Partii," *Sochineniia*, Vol. XV.
21. See Engels to Zasulich, April 1885, in Deutsch, *Gruppa*, III, 24–27.
22. *Sochineniia*, XXIV, 178–79.
23. *Chernyi Peredel, organ sotsialistov-federalistov* (Moscow, 1923), p. 199.
24. This circumstance he recognized in a brief remark in his notebook (*Literaturnoe nasledie G. V. Plekhanova*, I, 203).
25. Akselrod, *Perezhitoe i peredumannoe*, p. 369.
26. *Sochineniia*, I, 124–25.
27. *Ibid.*, pp. 125–27.
28. *Ibid.*, pp. 125–26.
29. *Ibid.*, pp. 128–30.
30. *Ibid.*, p. 131.

31. *Ibid.*, p. 135.
32. *Ibid.*, p. 133.
33. *Perepiska Marksa i Engel'sa*, pp. 240–41.
34. *Literaturnoe nasledie G. V. Plekhanova*, I, 206–7.
35. *Ibid.*, p. 207.
36. *Ibid.*
37. *Ibid.*, VIII, 210.
38. *Sochineniia*, XXIV, 178.
39. *Ibid.*, I, 150–51.
40. *Literaturnoe nasledie G. V. Plekhanova*, VIII, 211.
41. *Dela i dni*, No. 2 (1921), p. 91.

CHAPTER 6

1. *Sochineniia*, II, 22.
2. Cited by Axelrod in *Rabochii klass i revoliutsionnoe dvizhenie v Rossii*, p. 60.
3. Deutsch, "Kak G. V. Plekhanov stal marksistom," p. 129.
4. See Axelrod's speech in Nevskii, ed., *Gruppa "Osvobozhdenie Truda" v period 1883–1894 gg.: Istoriko-revoliutsionnyi sbornik*, II, 67 (hereafter cited as *Istoriko-revoliutsionnyi sbornik*, II).
5. *Sochineniia*, I, 136.
6. *Istoriko-revoliutsionnyi sbornik*, II, 67.
7. The letter appears in *Byloe*, 1906, No. 3, pp. 33–37.
8. *Gruppa*, II, 219.
9. Deutsch, "Kak G. V. Plekhanov stal marksistom," pp. 138–39.
10. *Ibid.*, p. 138; *Gruppa*, IV, 134.
11. Akselrod, *Perezhitoe i peredumannoe*, pp. 393–99.
12. *Dela i dni*, No. 2 (1921), p. 86.
13. Akselrod, *Perezhitoe i peredumannoe*, pp. 387–88; Deutsch, "K voznikoveniiu Gruppy 'Osvobozhdenie Truda,' " pp. 198–200.
14. Deutsch, "O sblizhenii i razryve s narodovol'tsami," pp. 6–7.
15. Akselrod, *Perezhitoe i peredumannoe*, Chapter 16. For an indication of his swing toward Social Democratic ideas, see his article of 1881 reprinted in *Istoriko-revoliutsionnyi sbornik*, II, 73–85.
16. Deutsch, *Gruppa*, III, 143–51.
17. *Ibid.*, p. 145.
18. Deutsch, "O sblizhenii i razryve s narodovol'tsami," p. 17.
19. *Gruppa*, III, 144, 148.
20. Deutsch, "O sblizhenii i razryve s narodovol'tsami," pp. 15–20.
21. *Dela i dni*, No. 2 (1921), pp. 90–91.
22. "O sblizhenii i razryve s narodovol'tsami," p. 35.
23. *Perezhitoe i peredumannoe*, p. 425.
24. *Sochineniia*, XIII, 29–30.
25. *Ibid.*, p. 31.
26. *Ibid.*, p. 30.
27. *Ibid.*, p. 32.
28. *Dela i dni*, No. 2 (1921), p. 93.
29. *Ibid.*, pp. 93–95.
30. *Ibid.*, p. 96.

31. Deutsch, "O sblizhenii i razryve s narodovol'tsami," pp. 37–39.
32. *Gruppa*, I, 175.
33. *Ibid.*, p. 178.
34. *Ibid.*, p. 179.
35. *Ibid.*, p. 180.
36. *Ibid.*, pp. 245–46, 253.
37. *Istoriko-revoliutsionnyi sbornik*, II, 402–3. Tikhomirov later argued in the same vein, when trying to persuade Lavrov that the loss of Plekhanov and his group would not be so important. *Gruppa*, I, 250.
38. Tikhomirov, *Vospominaniia L'va Tikhomirova*, pp. 156–57; Deutsch, "O sblizhenii i razryve s narodovol'tsami," pp. 48–51.
39. *Dela i dni*, No. 2 (1921), p. 98.

CHAPTER 7

1. *Brief History of Russia* (New York, 1933), I, 230.
2. *Sochineniia*, II, 28, 39.
3. *Ibid.*, p. 86.
4. *Ibid.*, p. 41.
5. Lavrov, "Sotsializm i politicheskaia bor'ba," p. 65.
6. Tikhomirov, "Chego nam zhdat' ot revoliutsii," pp. 227–62.
7. *Sochineniia*, II, 102.
8. *Ibid.*
9. *Ibid.*, p. 71.
10. *Ibid.*, p. 158.
11. *Ibid.*, pp. 173–74, 133–34.
12. *Ibid.*, p. 103.
13. *Ibid.*, pp. 148–52, 236.
14. *Ibid.*, p. 34.
15. *Ibid.*, pp. 235, 290.
16. *Ibid.*, p. 268.
17. *Ibid.*, p. 103.
18. *Ibid.*, p. 27.
19. *Ibid.*, p. 231.
20. *Ibid.*, pp. 236, 239.
21. *Ibid.*, p. 130.
22. *Ibid.*, p. 238.
23. *Ibid.*, p. 230.
24. *Ibid.*, pp. 189–94.
25. *Ibid.*, p. 271.
26. *Ibid.*, pp. 205–14.
27. *Ibid.*, pp. 217, 226–27.
28. *Ibid.*, p. 225.
29. *Ibid.*, p. 263.
30. *Ibid.*, pp. 34, 270.
31. *Ibid.*, p. 238.

32. For a more detailed discussion of this matter and that treated in the following paragraph, see my article, "Plekhanov on Russian Capitalism and the Peasant Commune," *American Slavic and East European Review*, XII (1953), 468–71.
33. *Sochineniia*, II, 244–45, 258.
34. *Ibid.*, p. 264.
35. For further discussion of this point, see "Plekhanov on Russian Capitalism," pp. 472–73.
36. *Sochineniia*, II, 130.
37. *Ibid.*, p. 260.
38. *Ibid.*, pp. 79, 290, 303.
39. *Ibid.*, p. 287.
40. *Ibid.*, pp. 66, 79, 296.
41. *Ibid.*, p. 84.
42. *Ibid.*, p. 303.
43. *Ibid.*, p. 335.
44. *Ibid.*, pp. 78–79.
45. *Ibid.*, pp. 330, 290–92, 308–9.
46. *Ibid.*, p. 357; italics mine.
47. *Ibid.*, p. 79.
48. *Ibid.*, pp. 81, 294.
49. *Ibid.*, pp. 62, 313.
50. *Ibid.*, pp. 78, 79, 239, 402.

51. *Ibid.*, p. 370.   52. *Ibid.*, p. 203.
53. *Ibid.*, pp. 200, 370.   54. *Ibid.*, III, 378–79.
55. *Ibid.*, II, 359. The remark concerning sustained action by the bourgeoisie was made in 1890, but the idea was implicit in his earlier writings.
56. *Ibid.*, pp. 343–44, 347. Although this idea was stated in just these words for the first time in 1889, Plekhanov had held it in 1883.
57. *Ibid.*, pp. 157–58.   58. *Ibid.*, pp. 346, 84.
59. *Ibid.*, pp. 365–66.   60. *Ibid.*, p. 346.
61. *Ibid.*, pp. 87–88, 404.   62. *Ibid.*, pp. 337–38.

CHAPTER 8

1. This paragraph is based largely on Ivanov-Razumnik's brilliant account of the mood of society in the eighties in *Istoriia russkoi obshchestvennoi mysli*, II, 291–333.
2. V. B., "Vospominaniia Peterburzhtsa o vtoroi polovine 80x godakh," *Minuvshie gody*, 1908, No. 10, p. 169.
3. *Istoriko-revoliutsionnyi sbornik*, II, 185.
4. Deutsch, *Gruppa*, I, 11.
5. Cited in "Bibliografiia," *Katorga i ssylka*, 1933, No. 10, pp. 134, 136–37.
6. Cited by Plekhanov in *Sochineniia*, IV, 277.
7. Akselrod, "Gruppa 'Osvobozhdenie Truda,' " p. 97.
8. Marx and Engels, *Correspondence, 1846–1895*, pp. 390–91.
9. *Perepiska Marksa i Engel'sa*, pp. 249–52.
10. The details of Deutsch's arrest, extradition, and exile are given in his memoir *Sixteen Years in Siberia*.
11. Akselrod, "Gruppa 'Osvobozhdenie Truda,' " p. 97.
12. Deutsch, *Gruppa*, II, 88–102. Another similar letter by Deutsch appears in *Literaturnoe nasledie Plekhanova*, I, 225–29.
13. *Gruppa*, I, pp. 20–21, 41–44; "Iz perepiski Gruppy 'Osvobozhdenie Truda,' " pp. 194–97.
14. For material on the Blagoev circle and its relation to the Emancipation of Labor Group, see Sergievskii, *Partiia russkikh sotsial-demokratov. Gruppa Blagoeva*, and "Gruppa 'Osvobozhdenie Truda,' i marksistkie kruzhki." These works should be used with caution. See also Blagoev, "Kratkie vospominaniia iz moei zhizni"; Sergievskii, "Kogda i po kakomu povodu byl napisan Plekhanovym 'Proekt Programmy Russkikh Sotsial-Demokratov' "; N-skii, "K istorii 'Partiia russkikh sotsial-demokratov' v 1884–1886 gg."; "Programma pervogo v Rossii S.D. Kruzhka," *Byloe*, 1918, No. 13.
15. *Byloe*, 1918, No. 13, pp. 49–52.
16. *Perepiska Plekhanova i Aksel'roda*, I, 21.
17. *Gruppa*, VI, 131–32.
18. A good deal of material on this group appears in *Ot Gruppa Blagoeva k soiuzu bor'by*, ed. Ol'minskii. See also Brusnev's account, "Voznikovenie pervykh sotsial-demokraticheskikh organizatsii," pp. 16–32.
19. *Perepiska Plekhanova i Aksel'roda*, I, 71–73.
20. *Gruppa*, I, 27–32. *Perepiska Plekhanova i Aksel'roda*, Vol. I, provides much information on the relations between the Group and the younger Marxists in Switzerland.
21. *Perepiska Plekhanova i Aksel'roda*, I, 44.

22. *Sochineniia*, II, 358, 361.
23. *Gruppa*, II, 163.
24. Material on this theme may be found in *Perepiska Plekhanova i Aksel'roda*; Akselrod, "Gruppa 'Osvobozhdenie Truda' "; and Deutsch, *Gruppa, passim.*
25. *Perepiska Plekhanova i Aksel'roda*, I, 43.
26. G. Bakalov, p. 45.
27. "Pis'ma k Libknekhtu," pp. 211–12.
28. *Literaturnoe nasledie Plekhanova*, IV, 269.
29. *Perepiska Plekhanova i Aksel'roda*, I, 94.
30. For this paragraph, see *Gruppa*, IV, 241–43; E. Kuskova, p. 144; *Perepiska Marksa i Engel'sa*, pp. 277ff.
31. *Perepiska Plekhanova i Aksel'roda*, I, 80–81.
32. Sergievskii, *Partiia russkikh sotsial-demokratov. Gruppa Blagoeva,* and "Gruppa 'Osvobozhdenie Truda.' " Sergievskii's position does not enjoy official support in the U.S.S.R. A recent Soviet study finds that there can be "no doubt of the intellectual influence of the first Russian Marxian organization on the rise and formation of the ideology of all the Social Democratic organizations in the years from the eighties to the early nineties." Polevoi, p. 516.
33. *Istoriia russkoi obshchestvennoi mysli*, II, 335.
34. *Istoriko-revoliutsionnyi sbornik*, II, 116–17 and *passim.*
35. *Ibid.*, p. 185.
36. L. Akselrod-Ortodoks, "Iz moikh vospominanii," pp. 30–32.
37. For an account of this group, see Aleksandrov, " 'Gruppa Narodovol'tsev.' "
38. *Istoriko-revoliutsionnyi sbornik*, II, 189–90.
39. *Ibid.*, p. 189.
40. *Ibid.*, p. 186; Lavrov, "Vospominaniia o S. M. Ginsburg," pp. 230–31.
41. Excerpts from its program appear in Poliakov, pp. 246–49.
42. *Perepiska Plekhanova i Aksel'roda*, I, 27, 44.
43. *Ibid.*, p. 59.
44. L. Fedorchenko, "Pervye shagi sotsial-demokratii v Kieve," p. 25.
45. *Sochineniia*, IX, 24.
46. L. Akselrod-Ortodoks, *Etiudy i vospominaniia*, p. 9.
47. See Thun, p. 256, and Nevskii, *Ocherki po istorii rossiskoi kommunisticheskoi partii.*
48. *Perepiska Plekhanova i Aksel'roda*, I, 243; Ol'minskii, pp. 74–75.

CHAPTER 9

1. This summary comes from Ivanov-Razumnik, *Istoriia russkoi obshchestvennoi mysli*, II, 335.
2. For an incisive study of Russian liberalism and its relation to these and other events, see George Fischer, *Russian Liberalism.*
3. Plekhanov developed this approach in a long pamphlet called *On the Problems of the Socialists in the Struggle with Famine in Russia.* It is reproduced in *Sochineniia*, Vol. III. Lavrov sketched a somewhat similar position in his postscript to I. Sergeevskii's *Golod v Rossii* (Geneva, 1892).
4. For certain sections of this chapter, I have found useful Iu. Martov's *Zapiski sotsial-demokrata* and *Istoriia rossiskoi sotsial-demokratii.*

5. Struve, p. 579.

6. Martov, *Zapiski*, pp. 141–43.

7. V. I. Lenin, *What the "Friends of the People" Are and How They Fight the Social-Democrats* (Moscow, 1946), pp. 80–82.

8. Cited by Andrew Rothstein in his Preface to the English edition of Plekhanov's *In Defense of Materialism* (London, 1947), p. 10.

9. *Istoriko-revoliutsionnyi sbornik*, II, 186–87.

10. Cited by Liadov, I, 105.

11. *Perepiska Marksa i Engel'sa*, p. 272.

12. The story of Potresov's visit to Plekhanov on this occasion is told in Riazanov's Preface to *Sochineniia*, VII, 7.

13. *Proiskhozhdenie bol'shevizma*, p. 194.

14. Cited in *History of the Communist Party of the Soviet Union (Bolsheviks)* (Leningrad, 1938), p. 12.

15. Martov, *Zapiski*, p. 245.

16. *My Life as a Rebel*, p. 18.

17. *The Origins of Russian Communism* (London, 1937), Chapter 1 and *passim*.

18. It fills most of *Sochineniia*, Vol. VII. An English edition, under the title *In Defense of Materialism*, trans. A. Rothstein, was published in London in 1947.

19. "Obosnovanie narodnichestva v trudakh g-na Vorontsova," *Sochineniia*, Vol. IX.

20. Martov, *Zapiski*, pp. 186–88, 225–38, 264–71.

21. *Sochineniia*, IX, 316.

22. Cited in *Perepiska Plekhanova i Aksel'roda*, I, 29.

23. *Sochieneniia*, III, 395–97, also, 414–16. For similar statements of his Narodnik days, see *ibid.*, I, 126, 128–29.

24. "Russkii rabochii v revoliutsionnom dvizhenii," *ibid.*, III, 127–205.

25. Martov, *Zapiski*, p. 150.

26. *Ibid.*, pp. 254–55.

27. *Perepiska Plekhanova i Aksel'roda*, I, 113.

28. *Ibid.*, pp. 265–75.

29. *Ibid.*, p. 274.

30. Martov, *Zapiski*, pp. 266–67.

31. *Ibid.*, pp. 272ff.

32. *Ibid.*, pp. 290ff.

33. This account is based for the most part on the report submitted by the Russian delegation to the London Congress of the International in 1896. See *Sochineniia*, IX, 352–67.

34. Martov, *Istoriia*, p. 28.

35. *Gruppa*, V, 219–20.

36. Struve (July 1934), p. 72.

37. Many of them are included in *Perepiska Marksa i Engel'sa*.

38. *Friedrich Engels' Briefwechsel mit Karl Kautsky*, ed. Benedikt Kautsky (Vienna, 1955), p. 98.

39. *Voinstvuiushchii materialist*, No. 4, 1925, pp. 219–21.

40. *Sochineniia*, IX, 343.

41. Axelrod MS, Chapter 17, p. 22; see also *Perepiska Plekhanova i Aksel'roda*, I, 149.

42. *Engels' Briefwechsel*, pp. 318, 320.

43. *Literaturnoe nasledie Plekhanova*, I, 279.
44. *Gruppa*, V, 163–64, 168–70.
45. *Perepiska Plekhanova i Aksel'roda*, I, 150.
46. *Sochineniia*, XXIV, 320.
47. *Perepiska Plekhanova i Aksel'roda*, I, 160.

CHAPTER 10

1. *Sochineniia*, IX, 367.
2. *Perepiska Plekhanova i Aksel'roda*, I, 156.
3. *Ibid.*, pp. 172–73.
4. See, for example, the program of the Emancipation of Labor Group in *Sochineniia*, II, 359–60.
5. *Ibid.*, IV, 115.
6. *Gruppa*, IV, 251.
7. *Ibid.*, pp. 283, 286–87.
8. *Ibid.*, p. 297.
9. *Ibid.*, V, 158.
10. *Ibid.*, p. 216.
11. This account of Bernstein's ideas is based upon the English edition of his book, *Evolutionary Socialism* (London, 1909).
12. *Perepiska Plekhanova i Aksel'roda*, I, 189.
13. *Ibid.*, pp. 192–95.
14. *Gruppa*, VI, 196.
15. *Ibid.*, V, 224–25.
16. *Sochineniia*, XI, 35.
17. *Perepiska Plekhanova i Aksel'roda*, II, 60–62; *Gruppa*, III, 256.
18. *Ibid.*, VI, 258.
19. Bernstein's claim was made in his famous book. The "substantiation" was not made publicly but came to Plekhanov's attention by way of Kautsky. See *Perepiska Plekhanova i Aksel'roda*, II, 64–65.
20. *Sochineniia*, XII, 455.
21. *Perepiska Plekhanova i Aksel'roda*, II, 74.
22. *Gruppa*, VI, 257.
23. *Sochineniia*, XI, 132.
24. *Ibid.*, pp. 129–30.
25. *Perepiska Plekhanova i Aksel'roda*, I, 195.
26. *Sochineniia*, XI, 89.
27. *Ibid.*, VIII, 397–402, and elsewhere in the same article.
28. *Ibid.*, XI, 317–18.
29. *Ibid.*, pp. 113, 130–31.
30. *Ibid.*, pp. 58–59, 219, and *passim*.
31. This was particularly true of his polemic against Struve, in *ibid.*, pp. 182–240.
32. *Ibid.*, p. 220.
33. *Ibid.*, p. 119.
34. *Sochineniia*, XVI, 236.
35. *Literaturnoe nasledie Plekhanova*, I, 297.
36. A stimulating discussion of "the decay of German Marxism" is presented in Plamenatz, *German Marxism and Russian Communism*, Chapter 8.

CHAPTER 11

1. Much of it is spread across the pages of *Perepiska Plekhanova i Aksel'roda*, I, 122ff., and II, *passim*.
2. *Ibid.*, I, 134.
3. *Ibid.*, pp. 122–35.
4. *Gruppa*, VI, 204–5.
5. *Ibid.*, pp. 207–8
6. *Perepiska Plekhanova i Aksel'roda*, I, 174–75; Kuskova, pp. 136, 143.
7. A similar period of great internal stress had taken place about a year earlier. *Perepiska Plekhanova i Aksel'roda*, II, 28–35; *Gruppa*, VI, 207–12.
8. *Perepiska Plekhanova i Aksel'roda*, I, 152–53, 200, and *passim*.
9. *Ibid.*, II, 25.
10. *Ibid.*, pp. 78–79.
11. *Ibid.*, pp. 80–81.
12. *Ibid.*, p. 82.
13. *Ibid.*, p. 39.
14. *Gruppa*, V, 149–51.
15. *Ibid.*, VI, 226.
16. *Perepiska Plekhanova i Aksel'roda*, II, 72.
17. *Ibid.*, p. 86.
18. *Leninskii sbornik*, IV, 8–9, 22, 23; *Letters of Lenin*, pp. 86–87.
19. *Gruppa*, II, 318.
20. *Perepiska Plekhanova i Aksel'roda*, II, 99.
21. *Ibid.*, p. 98.
22. *Gruppa*, VI, 140–41. This interesting letter provides good evidence of the strength of Economism in the labor movement.
23. *Sochineniia*, XII, 42.
24. *Ibid.*, pp. 41–42.
25. *Ibid.*, pp. 33, 29.
26. It appears in *Sochineniia*, Vol. XII.
27. *Ibid.*, p. 473.
28. *Ibid.*, p. 33.
29. *Ibid.*, p. 519.
30. *Ibid.*, p. 520.

CHAPTER 12

1. Iu. Martov, *Zapiski*, p. 411.
2. The article, written for *Rabochaia gazeta*, was published for the first time in *Leninskii sbornik*, III, 19–24.
3. *Leninskii sbornik*, I, 33–47.
4. For this and the following paragraph, see Martov's memoir in *ibid.*, IV, 49–61, and the same author's *Istoriia rossiskoi sotsial-demokratii*, pp. 48–52.
5. *Perepiska Plekhanova i Aksel'roda*, II, 104–5.
6. For Struve's account of these negotiations, see his article, "My Contacts and Conflicts with Lenin."
7. *Leninskii sbornik*, IV, 62–75.
8. *Ibid.*, p. 73.
9. *Ibid.*, I, 66–69; this also appears in *Letters of Lenin*, pp. 112–15.

10. Interview with Plekhanov's daughter, Mme E. Batault-Plekhanova, Paris, Summer 1959.

11. *Gruppa*, VI, 296–301, 158; *Perepiska Plekhanova i Aksel'roda*, II, 133.

12. *Ibid.*, p. 118.

13. *Leninskii sbornik*, I, pp. 33–35.

14. *Ibid.*, p. 71.

15. *Ibid.*, IV, 62–75.

16. *Ibid.*, p. 68. Haimson, pp. 118–19, does not distinguish between the two drafts, intimates that the clash between Plekhanov and Lenin had no substantive grounds, and gives the impression that Lenin called for a rigorous demarcation from the very first.

17. *Perepiska Plekhanova i Aksel'roda*, II, 146.

18. *Leninskii sbornik*, I, 41.

19. Cited by Kamenev in *ibid.*, pp. 27–28.

20. For Lenin's view of the matter, see his *Sochineniia*, IV, 67–68.

21. *Leninskii sbornik*, III, 126. Axelrod conveyed to Struve the only admissible terms for collaboration. *Perepiska Plekhanova i Aksel'roda*, II, 141–42.

22. Lenin, *Sochineniia*, IV, 123–57.

23. *Perepiska Plekhanova i Aksel'roda*, II, 154, 157–58.

24. Lenin, *Sochineniia*, IV, 156–57.   25. *Ibid.*, p. 537.

26. *Ibid.*, p. 538.   27. *Ibid.*, pp. 499–501.

28. *Ibid.*, p. 434.   29. *Communist Manifesto*, p. 22.

30. Lenin, *Sochineniia*, IV, 368.   31. *Ibid.*, p. 461.

32. *Ibid.*, p. 458.

33. Plekhanov, *Sochineniia*, XIII, 135. That he and Axelrod both had reservations about *What Is to Be Done?* is evident in *Perepiska Plekhanova i Aksel'-roda*, II, 165.

34. *Leninskii sbornik*, III, 192–93; *Perepiska Plekhanova i Aksel'roda*, II, 155.

35. *Ibid.*, 166–67; see also *Leninskii sbornik*, III, 285.

36. *Ibid.*, II, 74.

37. *Ibid.*, p. 86; *Literaturnoe nasledie Plekhanova*, I, 357.

38. The two programs may be compared in *Leninskii sbornik*, Vol. II.

39. *Ibid.*, p. 65.

40. The article and materials relating to the controversy are to be found in *Leninskii sbornik*, Vol. III.

41. For his fascinating letter, see *ibid.*, pp. 423–27.

42. *Ibid.*, p. 381.

43. *Ibid.*, p. 422.

44. *Ibid.*, pp. 423–27.

45. *Ibid.*, IV, 118, 128.

46. *Ibid.*, III, 429–30.

47. *Ibid.*, p. 433.

48. Plekhanov, *Sochineniia*, XII, 237.

CHAPTER 13

1. *Pis'ma P. B. Aksel'roda i Iu. O. Martova*, I, 46.

2. *Leninskii sbornik*, III, 156.

3. *Pis'ma Aksel'roda i Martova*, I, 79.

4. See, for example, the letter in *Leninskii sbornik*, IV, 172.

5. *Vtoroi s'ezd R.S.D.R.P., protokoly*, pp. 5–6.

6. *Ibid.*, pp. 118, 171.   7. *Ibid.*, p. 160.

8. *Ibid.*, pp. 108–19.   9. *Ibid.*, pp. 136–37.

10. *Ibid.*, pp. 163–64.   11. *Ibid.*, p. 169.

12. *Ibid.*, p. 263.   13. *Ibid.*, pp. 276–77.

14. *Ibid.*, pp. 271–72.   15. Lenin, *Sochineniia*, IV, 369.

16. *Pis'ma Aksel'roda i Martova*, p. 79.

17. *Vtoroi s'ezd R.S.D.R.P.*, p. 374.

18. *Ibid.*, pp. 181–82.

19. *Ibid.*, p. 426.

20. See, for example, the Martov and Axelrod articles in *Iskra*, Nos. 53, 55, and 57 (1903); Martov, *Bor'ba s "osadnym polozheniem,"* which includes a number of important documents; various of Lenin's writings such as "Rasskaz o II s'ezde R.S.D.R.P.," *Leninskii sbornik*, VI, 220–34, and "Shag vpered dva shaga nazad," *Sochineniia*, Vol. VII; Plekhanov, "Nasha programma," *Gruppa*, VI, 44–49.

21. Wolfe, pp. 254–55.

22. *Gruppa*, IV, 48–49.

23. Plekhanov, *Sochineniia*, XIII, 43.

24. *Ibid.*, pp. 3–10.

25. *Letters of Lenin*, pp. 186–91, 194–99, and, especially, 201–4.

26. This was the gist of his argument in the article "What Is Not to Be Done," *Sochineniia*, XIII.

27. *Ibid.*, p. 7.

28. *Ibid.*, p. 88.

29. Most notably by Wolfe, pp. 253, 293–94, and Deutscher, pp. 88–97.

30. Plekhanov, *Sochineniia*, XIII, 90.

31. *Ibid.*, p. 91.

32. See, for examples, *ibid.*, pp. 54, 92, and 135–40.

33. Expressed most fully in his article "Something on Economism," *ibid.*, pp. 14–22.

34. In his long article, "The Working Class and the Social Democratic Intelligentsia," *ibid.*, pp. 116–40.

35. *Ibid.*, p. 134.

36. *Ibid.*, p. 121.

CHAPTER 14

1. Unpublished letter dated October 1894 in the possession of Mme E. Batault-Plekhanova.

2. A good deal of the biographical material in this section is based upon interviews with Mme Batault-Plekhanova, Summer 1959, and an unpublished article by R. M. Plekhanova, "Kak organizoval svoi umstvennyi trud G. V. Plekhanov."

3. *Dela i dni*, No. 2 (1921), p. 84.

4. *Literaturnoe nasledie Plekhanova*, VIII, 209.

5. *Perepiska Plekhanova i Aksel'roda*, II, 68.

6. *Gruppa*, VI, 100–101.

7. *Ibid.*, V, 218.

8. *Perepiska Plekhanova i Aksel'roda,* I, 113.

9. Valentinov, *Vstrechi s Leninym,* pp. 137–40.

10. Balabanoff, p. 19; A. Lunacharskii, "Pamiati G. V. Plekhanova," p. 2.

11. Lunacharskii, "Pamiati G. V. Plekhanova," p. 3.

12. Ralph Fox, *Lenin* (New York, 1934), p. 86.

13. See Chapter 5 of Fischer, *Russian Liberalism.*

14. See Treadgold for an extended account of the rival parties and their struggle.

15. *Sochineniia,* XIII, 96.

16. *Ibid.,* pp. 372–74.

17. David Thomson, *Europe Since Napoleon* (New York, 1957), p. 388.

18. *Sochineniia,* XIII, 263–72.

19. See the article of the same name in *ibid.*

20. *Ibid.,* p. 215.

21. *Ibid.,* pp. 333–34, 345.

22. *Ibid.,* XV, 162, 195–97, 338.

23. *Ibid.,* pp. 162, 286.

24. *Ibid.,* p. 338–39.

25. *Ibid.,* pp. 140, 58.

26. *Ibid.,* XIII, 350.

27. *Ibid.,* pp. 241, 246–48; XV, 30.

28. Radkey, p. 3 and *passim.*

29. *Sochineniia,* XV, 202–16.

30. *Ibid.,* p. 40.

31. *Ibid.,* pp. 67–76.

32. Plekhanov developed this theme most fully in "Zametki publitsista," *ibid.,* XV, 415–27.

33. *Ibid.,* p. 439.

34. *Gruppa,* V, 232–34.

35. *Sochineniia,* XIII, 183.

36. *Ibid.,* XV, 268.

37. *Ibid.,* XIII, 191; XV, 306. Engels had made this point and several others germane to the Russian situation in his 1895 Preface to *The Class Struggles in France.*

38. *Sochineniia,* XII, 452–55; XV, 154.

39. *Ibid.,* XIII, 174; XV, 108, 220–21.

40. *Ibid.,* XV, 95.

41. *Ibid.,* p. 251.

42. *Ibid.,* p. 58.

43. *Ibid.,* XIII, 192–93, 341.

44. Dan, pp. 366–68.

45. Kautsky, p. 4.

46. *Ibid.,* p. 32.

47. *Sochineniia,* XV, 295–97.

48. *Ibid.,* pp. 392–94.

49. This is the theme of the early study by the Soviet writer V. Vaganian, *G. V. Plekhanov.*

50. *Perepiska Plekhanova i Aksel'roda,* II, 211.

51. *Ibid.,* p. 209.

52. *Gruppa,* V, 231–32.

53. Cited by Kamenskaia in the Preface to Plekhanoff, *Anarchisme et Socialisme,* p. xxxiv.

54. *Gruppa,* V, 231–34; IV, 346–49.

55. *Sochineniia,* XV, 359–62.

56. Miliukov, p. 222.

57. *Sochineniia,* XV, 360.

58. The letter, dated February 20, 1907, is now in the International Institute of Social History in Amsterdam.

59. *Sochineniia,* XV, 15.

CHAPTER 15

1. *Sochineniia,* XIX, 280–81.
2. *Ibid.,* p. 20.
3. *Ibid.,* pp. 36, 281.
4. *Ibid.,* XIX, 283.
5. This characterization was made by Ivanov-Razumnik, *Literatura i obshchestvennost',* p. 176.
6. *Gruppa,* V, 227.
7. Schapiro, p. 109.
8. Plekhanov, *Sochineniia,* XVI, 294.
9. *Gruppa,* VI, 257. A comprehensive study of Plekhanov's philosophical views—which, unfortunately, I have been unable to read—is G. Petrovic, *Filozofski pogledi G. V. Plehanova* (Zagreb, 1957).
10. *Sochineniia,* XIX, 89.
11. *Ibid.,* XVIII, 225.
12. The phrase is borrowed from Zenkovsky, II, 740.
13. *Sochineniia,* VIII, 185.
14. *Ibid.,* p. 169.
15. *Ibid.,* VII, 34–35; VIII, 132.
16. *Ibid.,* VIII, 146.
17. *Ibid.,* pp. 68–73.
18. *Ibid.,* pp. 73, 146–47.
19. *Ibid.,* VII, 35.
20. *Ibid.,* VIII, 129.
21. *Ibid.,* p. 147.
22. *Ibid.,* p. 398.
23. *Ibid.,* VII, 289.
24. *Ibid.,* VIII, 128.
25. *Ibid.,* III, 51.
26. Information on successive changes in the conception of the work appears in Riazanov's Preface to *ibid.,* Vol. XX.
27. *Ibid.,* p. 3.
28. *Ibid.,* XIV, 272.
29. *Ibid.,* XX, 26.
30. *Ibid.,* pp. 259–60.
31. *Ibid.,* pp. 37–38.
32. See my article "Plekhanov's Russia: The Impact of the West upon an 'Oriental' Society," in which this point is developed.
33. *Sochineniia,* XX, 44.
34. *Ibid.,* p. 13.
35. *Ibid.,* p. 11. For a statement unequivocally expressing the qualitative difference between the Western and Eastern models, see *ibid.,* XVIII, 216–17.
36. *Ibid.,* XX, 12.
37. Cited in *ibid.,* p. 79.
38. *Ibid.,* pp. 68–69, 75.
39. *Ibid.,* XXI, 175.
40. *Ibid.,* XX, 76–77.
41. *Ibid.,* pp. 184–85, 201.
42. *Ibid.,* pp. 252–54.
43. This passage, quoted for the succinctness with which it covers a complex process, comes not from the *History* but from an earlier writing (*ibid.,* X, 154–55). It is, however, a central theme of the *History.*
44. *Ibid.,* XX, 120.
45. *Ibid.,* p. 114.
46. *Ibid.,* II, 87; III, 411.

47. *Ibid.*, XV, 31ff. See also Plekhanov's speech on the agrarian question at the Stockholm Unity Congress in 1906, in *ibid.*, pp. 67–76.

48. For a brief discussion of their views, see Rufus Mathewson, *The Positive Hero in Russian Literature* (New York, 1958), Chapter 8. Isaiah Berlin comments briefly on Marx's literary tastes in *Karl Marx, His Life and Environment,* pp. 262–63.

49. Aptekman, *G. V. Plekhanov,* pp. 45–46.

50. *Sochineniia,* XIV, 183–84.

51. See the third of the "Letters Without Address," in *ibid.*

52. *Ibid.*, XVIII, 223.

53. *Ibid.*, XIV, 189.

54. *Ibid.*, p. 159.

55. The principles are set out in *ibid.*, XXIII, 156–57.

56. *Ibid.*, XIV, 138, 149.

57. *Ibid.*, XXIII, 207; VIII, 361.

58. *Ibid.*, XIV, 34–36; XVIII, 234–35.

59. *Ibid.*, XIV, 95–119.

60. *Ibid.*, X, 110–32. Plekhanov's essays on other "belletrist Narodniks" occur in the same volume.

61. *Ibid.*, XIV, 85.

62. *Ibid.*, XXI, 208–9.

63. This is the burden of the last part of "Art and Social Life."

64. *Sochineniia,* XIV, 168–70.

65. *Ibid.*, pp. 193–237.

66. *Ibid.*, p. 233.

67. For a brief account of the "correction" see Rubin, "Plekhanov and Soviet Literary Criticism."

68. *Sochineniia,* XIV, 137.

69. *Ibid.*, p. 136.

70. *Ibid.*, p. 178.

71. *Ibid.*, p. 179.

CHAPTER 16

1. Cole, III, 69. I have found the first one hundred pages of this volume very helpful in composing this section.

2. Fainsod, p. 19.

3. *Le Socialisme,* No. 2, 1912.

4. Vaganian, *Plekhanov,* p. 664.

5. Balabanoff, p. 120.

6. The manner in which French socialism was influenced along these lines is well shown in Weinstein, *Jean Jaurès: A Study of Patriotism in the French Socialist Movement.*

7. The full text of the resolution may be found in Gankin and Fisher, pp. 57–59.

8. *Sochineniia,* XVI, 363–64.

9. Cole, pp. 65, 66.

10. Gankin and Fisher, p. 73.

11. *Ibid.*, p. 58.

12. *Sochineniia,* XVI, 363–64.

13. Cole, pp. 83–84.

14. *Sochineniia*, XVI, 363.

15. Kamenskaia Preface to Plekhanoff, *Anarchisme et socialisme*, p. xxxi. Also R. M. Plekhanova, "Italiia i Gorky."

16. Cole, p. 92.

17. Vaganian, *Plekhanov*, pp. 658–59.

18. Fainsod, p. 23.

19. R. M. Plekhanova, "Italiia i Gorky," p. 16.

20. Vaganian emphasizes this factor in his interpretation of Plekhanov's war position; *Plekhanov*, p. 664.

21. Balabanoff, p. 120.

22. *Ibid.*, pp. 144–46. A somewhat different version of this meeting is given in Aptekman, *G. V. Plekhanov*, pp. 89–90.

23. Plekhanov, *O voine*, p. 66.

24. *Ibid.*, pp. 8, 10.

25. *Ibid.*, p. 62.

26. *Ibid.*, p. 8.

27. *Ibid.*, pp. 9–10.

28. Vaganian, *Plekhanov*, p. 669.

29. *O voine*, pp. 29–31.

30. *Ibid.*, p. 71.

31. *Ibid.*, pp. 71–72.

32. *Izveshchenie*, September 1915. This was a leaflet announcing the publication of the newspaper *Prizyv*.

33. *O voine*, pp. 49–51.

34. *Ibid.*, p. 51.

35. Gay, pp. 268–87.

36. *Prizyv*, No. 17 (January 22, 1916), pp. 2–8.

37. *Ibid.*, No. 19 (February 5, 1916), pp. 1–2.

38. *Ibid.*, No. 3 (October 17, 1915), pp. 2–4.

39. Schapiro, pp. 141–47.

40. These are treated at length in Fainsod, *International Socialism and the War*. Many of the relevant documents appear in Gankin and Fisher, *The Bolsheviks and the World War*.

41. *O voine*, p. 85.

42. Aptekman, *G. V. Plekhanov*, p. 52.

43. *Ibid.*, p. 95.

CHAPTER 17

1. A good account of the impact of the war upon Russia is Florinsky, *The End of the Russian Empire*.

2. For the events of 1917, the following works are extremely helpful: Chamberlin, *The Russian Revolution*; Trotsky, *History of the Russian Revolution*; Sukhanov, *The Russian Revolution, 1917*; Browder and Kerensky, *The Russian Provisional Government, 1917*.

3. Trotsky, *History of the Russian Revolution*, I, 329–31.

4. Warth, p. 89.

5. The soviet policy is given in Browder and Kerensky, II, 604–5.

6. *Ibid.*, pp. 1077–78.

7. Warth, p. 88.

8. Browder and Kerensky, III, 1205–7.

9. Trotsky, *History of the Russian Revolution*, I, 227. I have been unable to

find the article to which Trotsky refers, but Plekhanov's position at the time as well as his letter to Guesde cited hereafter makes Trotsky's assertion entirely credible.

10. Plekhanov to Guesde, February 16, 1917 (unpublished letter in the possession of Mme E. Batault-Plekhanova).

11. Schapiro, pp. 153–54.

12. Interview with Plekhanov's daughters, Paris, Summer 1959.

13. Shub, p. 4.

14. R. M. Plekhanova, "Poslednie dni G. V. Plekhanova," p. 135.

15. Sukhanov, pp. 260–63. Actually, the foreign socialists were themselves affected by the fervent internationalism of the Russian revolution, and some returned to their countries to preach an international socialist congress for peace; see Fainsod, pp. 125, 128–32.

16. This paragraph is based on the account given in *Plekhanov v svobodnoi Rossii* (Petrograd, 1917), pp. 4–6.

17. Plekhanov, *God na rodine*, I, 10–11.

18. Lewis B. Namier, "History and Political Culture," in *The Varieties of History*, ed. F. Stern (New York, 1956), p. 377.

19. *God na rodine*, I, 149–51.

20. *Ibid.*, pp. 129–30.

21. *Ibid.*, II, 85.

22. *Ibid.*, pp. 130, 132.

23. *Sochineniia*, XIV, 222.

24. *God na rodine*, I, 27.

25. *Ibid.*, pp. 27–28.

26. *Ibid.*, II, 33–34.

27. *Ibid.*, p. 28.

28. *Ibid.*, p. 108.

29. *Ibid.*, I, 108–11, 232–33; II, 94–95, 176–78.

30. Letter from Alexander Kerensky to the author, February 4, 1962.

31. R. M. Plekhanova to her daughters, May 20, 1917, (unpublished letter in the possession of Mme E. Batault-Plekhanova).

32. Letter of R. M. Plekhanova to her daughters, July 31, 1917. A suggestion of negotiations between Kerensky and Plekhanov appears in Browder and Kerensky, III, 1428.

33. *Ibid.*, II, 756.

34. Interview with Plekhanov's daughters, Paris, Summer 1959.

35. Victor Chernov. *The Great Russian Revolution* (New Haven, Conn., 1936), p. 206.

36. *God na rodine*, II, 149.

37. *Ibid.*, p. 38. Sukhanov (p. 260) speaks of *Edinstvo* as a "tiny, little-read, and completely uninfluential paper."

38. Aptekman, *G. V. Plekhanov*, p. 96; Balabanoff, p. 290.

39. Sukhanov, p. 260.

40. Browder and Kerensky, III, 1557.

41. Interview with N. Vol'sky, Paris, Summer 1959.

42. Valentinov, p. 288.

43. Ibid., pp. 288–89.

44. *God na rodine*, II, 244–48.

45. De Brouckère, "Le Mort de Plekhanoff," *Les Droits des peuples*, July 21, 1918.

46. The fullest account of this episode, based on information provided by Plekhanov's wife, is given in the Arzaev Preface to *God na rodine*, I, xlii–xliv.

47. R. M. Plekhanova, "Posledie dni G. V. Plekhanova," p. 137.

48. *Ibid.*, pp. 138–39; letter from R. M. Plekhanova to her daughters, June 1918; Kamenskaia Preface to Plekhanoff, *Anarchisme et socialisme*, p. xxxvi.

49. E. H. Carr, *The New Society* (London, 1951), pp. 5–6.

50. Quoted by Kuskova, p. 139.

51. Vol'skii, "Besedy s Plekhanovym v avguste 1917."

52. R. M. Plekhanova, "Plekhanov i interventsiia." According to this account, General Krasnov, through his agent Savinkov, asked Plekhanov to become Premier.

53. *Sochineniia*, II, 365–66.

BIBLIOGRAPHY

MANUSCRIPTS

Axelrod MS at the International Institute of Social History, Amsterdam.
R. M. Plekhanova MSS in the possession of Mme Eugenia Batault-Plekhanova in Paris:
"Italiia i Gorky."
"Kak organizoval svoi umstvennyi trud G. V. Plekhanov."
"Plekhanov i interventsiia."
"Plekhanov i rabochie."
Unpublished correspondence in the possession of Mme E. Batault-Plekhanova in Paris.
N. Vol'skii, "Besedy s Plekhanovym v avguste 1917." An unpublished MS in the possession of its author, Paris.

PERIODICALS

Prizyv. Paris, 1915–17.
Sotsial-Demokrat. Literaturnoe-politicheskoe obozrenie. Geneva, 1888. Vol. I.
Sotsial-Demokrat. Trekhmesiachnoe literaturnoe-politicheskoe obozrenie. Geneva, 1890–92. Nos. 1–4.

BOOKS, PAMPHLETS, AND ARTICLES

Akimov-Makhnovets, V. P. "Pervyi s'ezd R.S.D.R. Partii," *Minuvshie gody*, 1908, No. 2.
Akselrod, P. B. "Gruppa 'Osvobozhdenie Truda,'" *Letopisi marksizma*, 1928, No. 6.
———. Istoricheskoe polozhenie i vzaimnoe otnoshenie liberal'noi i sotsialisticheskoi demokratii v Rossii. Geneva, 1898.
———. Iz arkhiva P. B. Aksel'roda. Materialy po istorii russkogo revoliutsionnogo dvizheniia. Vol. II. Edited by Voitinskii, Nikolaevskii, and Tsederbaum-Dan. Berlin, 1924.

——. Perezhitoe i peredumannoe. Berlin, 1923.

——. Rabochii klass i revoliutsionnoe dvizhenie v Rossii. St. Petersburg, 1907.

Akselrod, P. B., and Plekhanov, G. V. Perepiska G. V. Plekhanova i P. B. Aksel'-roda. Edited by Berlin, Nikolaevskii, and Voitinskii. 2 vols. Moscow, 1925.

Akselrod-Ortodoks, L. Etiudy i vospominaniia. Leningrad, 1925.

——. "Iz moikh vospominanii," Katorga i ssylka, 1930, No. 2.

Aleksandrov [Ol'minskii], M. C. " 'Gruppa Narodovol'tsev', 1891–1894," Byloe, 1906, No. 11.

Aptekman, O. V. Chernyi Peredel. Moscow, 1923.

——. G. V. Plekhanov. Leningrad, 1925.

——. Iz istorii narodnichestva 70-kh godov: "Zemlia i Volia." Rostov-on-Don, 1907.

——. "Pometki O. V. Aptekmana na stat'e o G. V. Plekhanove," Katorga i ssylka, 1928, No. 5.

Arkhiv "Zemli i Voli" i "Narodnoi Voli." Moscow, 1932.

Arzaev, Iu. Preface to G. V. Plekhanov, God na rodine. Paris, 1921.

B——, V. "Vospominaniia peterburzhtsa o vtoroi polovine 80-kh godov," Minuvshie gody, 1908, No. 10–11.

Bakalov, G. "G. V. Plekhanov v Bol'garii," Letopisi marksizma, 1928, No. 5.

Bakunin, M. Gosudarstvo i anarkhiia. 1873.

Balabanoff, Angelica. My Life as a Rebel. New York, 1938.

Baron, Samuel H. "Plekhanov's Russia: The Impact of the West upon an 'Oriental' Society," Journal of the History of Ideas, Vol. XIX (1958).

Basilevskii, B., ed. Gosudarstvennye prestuplenia v Rossii v XIX veke. Stuttgart, 1903.

——. ed. Literatura partii Narodnoi Voli. Paris, 1905.

Baturin, N. Ocherki istorii sotsial-demokratii v Rossii. 2d ed. Moscow, 1922.

Berdyaev, Nicolas. The Russian Idea. New York, 1948.

Berlin, Isaiah. Karl Marx, His Life and Environment. 2d ed. New York, 1959.

——. Review of Plekhanov's In Defense of Materialism in Slavonic and East European Review, Vol. XXVIII (1949).

Bernstein, Eduard. Evolutionary Socialism. Translated by Edith Harvey. London, 1909.

——. "Karl Marks i russkie revoliutsionnery," Minuvshie gody, 1908, No. 10–11.

"Bibliografiia," Katorga i ssylka, 1933, No. 10.

Blagoev, D. "Kratkie vospominaniia iz moei zhizni," Proletarskaia revoliutsiia, 1927, No. 1.

Blagoevtsy–Redaktsiia "Vestnika Narodnoi Voli," Byloe, 1918, No. 13.

Bogucharskii, V. Iz istorii politicheskoi bor'by v 70-kh i 80-kh gg. XIX veka. Moscow, 1912.

Bowman, Herbert E. Vissarion Belinski, 1811–1848: A Study in the Origins of Social Criticism in Russia. Cambridge, Mass., 1954.

Browder, Robert P., and Kerensky, Alexander F., eds. The Russian Provisional Government, 1917. 3 vols. Stanford, Calif., 1961.

Brusnev, M. "Voznikovenie pervykh russkikh sotsial-demokraticheskikh organizatsii," Proletarskaia revoliutsiia, 1923, No. 2.

Bunyan, James, and Fisher, H. H. The Bolshevik Revolution, 1917–1918. Stanford, Calif., 1934.

Carr, E. H. A History of Soviet Russia. London, 1950. Vol. I.

Chagin, B. A. Proniknovenie idei marksizma v Rossiiu. Leningrad, 1948.
Chamberlin, William H. The Russian Revolution. 2 vols. New York, 1935.
Cherniavskii, M. M. "K 50-letiiu kazanskoi demonstratsii 1876 goda," *Katorga i ssylka*, 1926, No. 7–8.
Chernomordik, S. "K 50-letiiu Gruppy 'Osvobozhdenie Truda,' " *Katorga i ssylka*, 1933, Nos. 10 and 12.
Cole, G. D. H. The Second International, 1889–1914. Vol. III, Part I of A History of Socialist Thought. London, 1956.
Dan, F. I. Proiskhozhdenie bol'shevizma. New York, 1946.
Daniels, R. V. "Fate and Will in the Marxian Philosophy of History," *Journal of the History of Ideas*, Vol. XXI (1960).
Deutsch, Lev, ed. Gruppa "Osvobozhdenie Truda." 6 vols. Moscow, 1924–28.
———. "Iz otnoshenii G. V. Plekhanova k narodovol'tsam," *Katorga i ssylka*, 1923, No. 7.
———. "K voznikoveniiu Gruppy 'Osvobozhdenie Truda,' " *Proletarskaia revoliutsiia*, 1923, No. 4.
———. "Kak G. V. Plekhanov stal marksistom," *Proletarskaia revoliutsiia*, 1922, No. 7.
———. "Molodost' G. V. Plekhanova," *Byloe*, 1918, No. 13.
———. "O sblizhenii i razryve s narodovol'tsami," *Proletarskaia revoliutsiia*, 1923, No. 8.
———. "Pis'ma G. V. Plekhanova k P. L. Lavrovu," *Dela i dni*, No. 2 (1921).
———. Sixteen Years in Siberia. Translated by Helen Chisholm. London, 1903.
———. "V. I. Ignatov," *Proletarskaia revoliutsiia*, 1923, No. 9.
Deutscher, Isaac. The Prophet Armed. New York, 1954.
Dumur, L. "Socialistes allemands," *La Guerre mondiale* (Geneva), Dec. 12, 1914.
Engels, Friedrich. Fridrikh Engel's o Rossii. Geneva, 1894.
Ermanskii, O. A. Iz perezhitogo. Moscow, 1927.
Fainsod, Merle. International Socialism and the World War. Cambridge, Mass., 1935.
Fedorchenko, L. "G. V. Plekhanov," *Katorga i ssylka*, 1923, No. 7.
———. "Pervye shagi sotsial-demokratii v Kieve," *Katorga i ssylka*, 1926, No. 6.
Figner, Vera. Zapechatlennyi trud. Moscow, 1932. Vol. I.
Fischer, George. Russian Liberalism: From Gentry to Intelligentsia. Cambridge, Mass., 1958.
Florinsky, Michael T. The End of the Russian Empire. New Haven, Conn., 1931.
Footman, David. Red Prelude. New Haven, Conn., 1954.
Frencher, A. A. "Na rodine G. V. Plekhanova," *Proletarskaia revoliutsiia*, 1922, No. 8.
Frolenko, M. F. "Kommentarii k stat'e N. A. Morozova 'Voznikovenie Narodnoi Voli,' " *Byloe*, 1906, No. 12.
———. "Lipetskii i Voronezhskii s'ezdy," *Byloe*, 1907, No. 1.
Gankin, Olga H., and Fisher, H. H. The Bolsheviks and the World War. Stanford, Calif., 1940.
Gay, Peter. The Dilemma of Democratic Socialism. New York, 1952.
Gerasimov, V. Zhizn russkogo rabochego polveka tomu nazad. Petrograd, n.d.
Gorki, Maxim. Days with Lenin. New York, 1932.
Haimson, Leopold. The Russian Marxists and the Origins of Bolshevism. Cambridge, Mass., 1955.

Hook, Sidney. The Hero in History. Boston, 1955.

"Ispol'nitel'nyi komitet—Aleksander III," in Byloe, 1906, No. 3.

Ivanov-Razumnik, V. Istoriia russkoi obshchestvennoi mysli. 2 vols. 2d ed. St. Petersburg, 1908.

———. Literatura i obshchestvennost'. 2d ed. 1911.

"Iz perepiski Gruppy 'Ozvobozhdenie Truda,' " Krasnaia letopis', 1924, No. 2.

Kamenev, Iu., ed. Sotsial-demokraticheskie izdaniia. Ukazatel' sotsial-demokraticheskoi literatury na russkom iazyke: 1883–1895. Paris, 1913. Vol. I.

Kamenskaia, M. Preface to Plekhanoff, Anarchisme et socialisme. Paris, 1924.

Kareev, N. I. "Novaia popytka ekonomicheskogo obosnovaniia istorii," Russkoe bogatstvo, 1894, No. 1.

Kautsky, Karl. Dvizhushchie sily i perspektivy russkoi revoliutsii. Moscow, 1907.

Keep, J. L. H. The Development of Social Democracy in Russia, 1898–1907. Unpublished thesis, University of London, 1953. Microfilm copy at the University of California, Berkeley.

Kizevetter, A. "Novyi trud G. V. Plekhanova po russkoi istorii," Golos minuvshego, 1916, No. 1.

Knizhnaia letopis', 1934———.

Kol'tsov, D. "Konets 'Narodnoi Voli' i nachalo sotsial-demokratii," in A. Thun, Istoriia revoliutsionnykh dvizhenii v Rossii. 2d ed. Petrograd, 1920.

Koz'min, B. N. "Neizdannye pis'ma G. V. Plekhanova k P. L. Lavrovu," Literaturnoe nasledstvo, Nos. 19–21 (1935).

———. "Odin iz pervykh literaturnykh opytov G. V. Plekhanova," Katorga i ssylka, 1923, No. 7.

Kremer, A. Ob agitatsii. Geneva, 1896.

Kropotkin, P. Memoirs of a Revolutionist. Boston, 1899.

Krupskaya, N. K. Memories of Lenin. Translated by E. Verney. 2 vols. New York, n.d.

Kuskova, E. "Davno minuvshee," Novyi zhurnal, Vol. LIV (1958).

Lavrov, P. L. Review of Sotsializm i politicheskaia bor'ba in Vestnik Narodnoi Voli, No. 2 (1884).

———. "Vospominaniia o S. M. Ginsburg," Golos minuvshego, 1917, Nos. 7–8.

"Lavrov-Ginsburg perepiska," Katorga i ssylka, 1928, No. 2.

Lenin, V. I. Sochineniia. 3d ed. Moscow, 1935. Vols. I–VI.

———. Letters of Lenin. Translated and edited by Elizabeth Hill and Doris Mudie. New York, 1937.

Leninskii sbornik. Edited by L. Kamenev. Moscow, 1924–38. Vols. I–IV, VI, XI.

Liadov, M. Istoriia rossiskoi sotsial-demokraticheskoi partii. St. Petersburg, 1906. Vol. I.

Lunacharskii, A. "Neskol'ko vstrech s G. V. Plekhanovym," Pod znamenem marksizma, 1922, No. 5–6.

———. "Pamiati G. V. Plekhanova," Plamia, 1918, No. 7.

Malakhovskii, V. "Plekhanov o sushchnosti narodnichestva," Proletarskaia revoliutsiia, 1928, No. 1.

Martov, Iu. Bor'ba s "osadnym polozheniem." Geneva, 1904.

———. Istoriia rossiskoi sotsial-demokratii. 3d ed. Moscow, 1923.

———. "Voina i G. V. Plekhanov," in Protiv voiny. Moscow, 1917.

———. Zapiski sotsial-demokrata. Moscow, 1924.

Martov, L. "Obshchestvennye dvizheniia i umstvennye techeniia v period 1884–1905 gg.," in Vol. V of *Istoriia literatury XIX veka*, edited by Ovsianiko-Kulikovskii. Moscow, 1911.

Marx, Karl, and Engels, Friedrich. The Communist Manifesto. New York, 1932.

———. The Russian Menace to Europe. Edited by Paul Blackstock and Bert F. Hoselitz. Glencoe, Ill., 1952.

Masaryk, Thomas G. The Spirit of Russia. 2 vols. 2d ed. London, 1955.

Meijer, J. M. Knowledge and Revolution. Assen, Holland, 1955.

Meyer, Alfred. Leninism. New York, 1962.

Mikhailovskii, N. K. "Literatura i zhizn," *Russkaia mysl'*, 1892, No. 6.

———. "Literatura i zhizn," *Russkoe bogatstvo*, 1894, No. 2.

Miliukov, P. God bor'by. St. Petersburg, 1907.

Mindlin, I. B. "Perekhod G. V. Plekhanova ot narodnichestva k marksizmu," *Voprosy istorii*, 1956, No. 12.

Moiseenko, P. A. "Vospominaniia o Morozovskoi stachki," *Proletarskaia revoliutsiia*, 1924, No. 1.

Morozov, N. "Voznikovenie 'Narodnoi Voli,' " *Byloe*, 1906, No. 12.

N——skii, B. "K istorii 'Partii russkikh sotsial-demokratov' v 1884–1886 gg.," *Katorga i ssylka*, 1929, No. 5.

Nevskii, V. I. "Gruppa 'Osvobozhdenie Truda,' " in Ot "Zemli i Voli" k Gruppe "Osvobozhdenie Truda." Moscow, 1930.

———, ed. Gruppa "Osvobozhdenie Truda." Bibliografiia za 50 let. Moscow, 1934.

———, ed. Gruppa "Osvobozhdenie Truda" v period 1883–1894 gg. Istoriko-revoliutsionnyi sbornik. Leningrad, 1924. Vol. II.

———. Ocherki po istorii rossiskoi kommunisticheskoi partii. Petrograd, 1923. Vol. I.

Nikolaevskii, B. "Programma pervogo v Rossii sotsial-demokraticheskogo kruzhka," *Byloe*, 1918, No. 13.

Ol'minskii, M. C., ed. Ot Gruppa Blagoeva k soiuzu bor'by. 1921.

Otvet redaktsii "Rabochego dela" na "Pis'mo" P. Aksel'roda i "Vademecum" G. Plekhanova. Geneva, 1900.

Pamiati G. V. Plekhanova. Petrograd, 1918.

"Perepiska G. V. Plekhanova, P. B. Aksel'roda i V. I. Zasulich s L. Iogichesom (Grozovskim, Tyshko) 1891–92," *Proletarskaia revoliutsiia*, 1928, Nos. 11–12.

Perepiska K. Marksa i F. Engel'sa s russkimi politicheskimi deiateliami. 1947.

"Pis'ma G. V. Plekhanova k Engel'su," *Pod znamenem marksizma*, 1923, No. 11–12.

"Pis'ma marksistov k N. K. Mikhailovskomu," *Byloe*, 1918, No. 13.

Pis'ma P. B. Aksel'roda i Iu. O. Martova. Materialy po istorii russkogo revoliutsionnogo dvizheniia. Berlin, 1924.

"Pis'mo G. A. Lopatina o besede s F. Engel'som o Rossii," *Golos minuvshego*, 1923, No. 2.

Plamenatz, John. German Marxism and Russian Communism. London, 1954.

Plekhanov, G. V. God na rodine. 2 vols. Paris, 1924.

———. "Kongressu germanskikh sotsialistov," *Voinstvuiuschii materialist*, No. III (1925).

———. Literaturnoe nasledie G. V. Plekhanova. 8 vols. Moscow, 1934–40.

———. O voine. 2d ed. Petrograd, n.d.

———. "Pis'ma," *Voinstvuiushchii materialist,* No. I (1924).

———. "Pis'ma k Libknekhtu," *Voinstvuiushchii materialist,* No. IV (1925).

———. Sochineniia. 2d ed. Edited by D. Riazanov. 24 vols. Moscow, 1923–27.

"G. V. Plekhanov i shpionskie zabavy," *Krasnyi arkhiv,* No. V.

G. V. Plekhanov v svobodnoi Rossii. Petrograd, 1917.

Plekhanova, R. M. "Poslednie dni G. V. Plekhanova," *Zaria,* 1924, Nos. 4–5.

Pod znamenem marksizma, 1923, Nos. 6–7. [Almost all the articles in these issues are devoted to Plekhanov.]

Polevoi, Iu. Zarozhdenie marksizma v Rossii. Moscow, 1959.

Poliakov, A. S. "Vtoroe 1 marta," *Golos minuvshego,* 1918, Nos. 10–12.

Popov, M. R. "K istorii rabochego dvizheniia v kontse semidesiatykh godov," *Golos minuvshego,* 1920–21.

———. "Zemlia i Volia nakanune voronezhskogo s'ezda," *Byloe,* 1906, No. 8.

Potash, M. "Marks i Engel's o narodnicheskom sotsializme v Rossii," *Proletarskaia revoliutsiia,* 1929, No. 12.

Potresov, A. "G. V. Plekhanov," *Byloe,* 1918, No. 12.

Pyziur, Eugene. The Doctrine of Anarchism of Michael A. Bakunin. Milwaukee, Wis., 1955.

Radkey, O. H. The Agrarian Foes of Bolshevism. New York, 1958.

Rakhmetov, V. "K voprosu o menshevistkikh tendentsiakh v Gruppe 'Osvobozhdenie Truda,'" *Proletarskaia revoliutsiia,* 1928, No. 9.

Riazanov, D. Plekhanov i Gruppa "Osvobozhdenie Truda." 3d ed. Petrograd, 1918.

Robinson, G. T. Rural Russia Under the Old Regime. 2d ed. New York, 1949.

Rubin, Burton. "Plekhanov and Soviet Literary Criticism," *American Slavic and East European Review,* Vol. XV (1956).

Schapiro, Leonard. The Communist Party of the Soviet Union. New York, 1960.

Semashko, N. "O detskikh godakh G. V. Plekhanova," *Katorga i ssylka,* 1923, No. 7.

———. "Zamechaniia po povodu biografii G. V. Plekhanova sostavlennoi Iu. Arzaevym," *Proletarskaia revoliutsiia,* 1922, No. 5.

Sergievskii, N. L. "Gruppa 'Osvobozhdenie Truda,' i marksistkie kruzhki," in *Istoriko-revoliutsionnyi sbornik,* Vol. II. Leningrad, 1924.

———. "Kogda i po kakomu povodu byl napisan Plekhanovym 'Proekt Programmy Russkikh Sotsial-Demokratov,'" *Proletarskaia revoliutsiia,* 1928, No. 1.

———. Partiia russkikh sotsial-demokratov. Gruppa Blagoeva. Moscow, 1929.

———. "Pervyi transport literatury Gruppy 'Osvobozhdenie Truda,'" *Krasnyi arkhiv,* No. XVIII.

———. "Plekhanov i Gruppa Blagoeva," *Proletarskaia revoliutsiia,* 1928, No. 8.

Seton-Watson, Hugh. The Decline of Imperial Russia. London, 1952.

Shtein, V. M. Ocherki razvitiia russkoi obshchestvenno-ekonomicheskoi mysli XIX–XX veka. Leningrad, 1948.

Shub, D. "G. V. Plekhanov v 1917 godu," *Russkaia mysl',* No. 3 (June 5, 1958).

Shul'gin, V. "K voprosu o proniknovenii marksizma v Rossiiu v 40–60 godakh XIX veka," *Istorik-marksist,* 1939, Nos. 5–6.

Smirnov, I. "G. V. Plekhanov v Voronezhskoi Voennoi Gimnasii," *Katorga i ssylka,* 1929, No. 12.

Smirnova, V. "G. V. Plekhanov v mezhdunarodnom sotsialisticheskom dvizhenii (1883–1900)," *Voprosy istorii,* 1956, No. 12.

Struve, Petr B. "My Contacts and Conflicts with Lenin," *Slavonic and East European Review*, Vols. XII and XIII.

Sukhanov, N. N. The Russian Revolution, 1917. Translated and edited by J. Carmichael. New York, 1955.

Tikhomirov, L. "Chego nam zhdat' ot revoliutsii," *Vestnik Narodnoi Voli*, No. II (1884).

———. Plekhanov i ego druz'ia. Leningrad, 1925.

———. Vospominaniia L'va Tikhomirova. Moscow, 1927.

Thun, A. Istoriia revoliutsionnykh dvizhenii v Rossii. 2d ed. Petrograd, 1920.

Treadgold, D. W. Lenin and His Rivals; The Struggle for Russia's Future, 1898–1906. New York, 1955.

Trotsky, L. The History of the Russian Revolution. 3 vols. New York, 1932.

———. Our Revolution. Translated by M. Ol'gin. New York, 1918.

———. Vtoroi s'ezd rossiskoi sotsial-demokraticheskoi partii. Geneva, 1903.

Vaganian, V. G. V. Plekhanov. Moscow, 1924.

———. Opyt bibliografii G. V. Plekhanova. 1923.

Valentinov, N. "Tragediia G. V. Plekhanova," *Novyi zhurnal*, Vol. XX (1948).

———. Vstrechi s Leninym. New York, 1953.

Venturi, Franco. Roots of Revolution. London, 1960.

Vol'fson, S. Plekhanov. Minsk, 1924.

Vtoroi s'ezd R.S.D.R.P., protokoly. Moscow, 1959.

Warth, Robert D. The Allies and the Russian Revolution. Durham, N.C., 1954.

Weinstein, Harold. Jean Jaurès: A Study in Patriotism in the French Socialist Movement. New York, 1936.

Wetter, Gustav A. Dialectical Materialism. New York, 1958.

Wittfogel, Karl A. Oriental Despotism. A Comparative Study of Total Power. New Haven, Conn., 1957.

Wolfe, Bertram. Three Who Made a Revolution. New York, 1948.

Zenkovsky, V. V. A History of Russian Philosophy. Translated by G. L. Kline. 2 vols. New York, 1953.

Zinov'ev, G. G. V. Plekhanov. Petrograd, 1918.

INDEX

INDEX

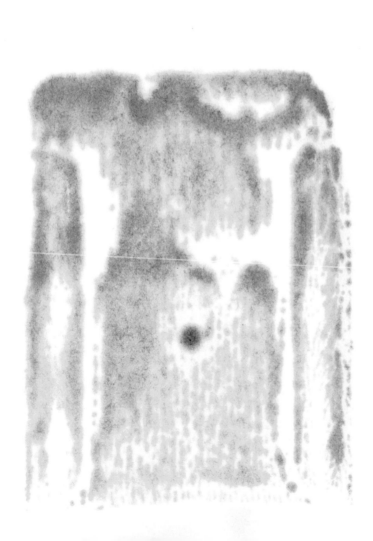

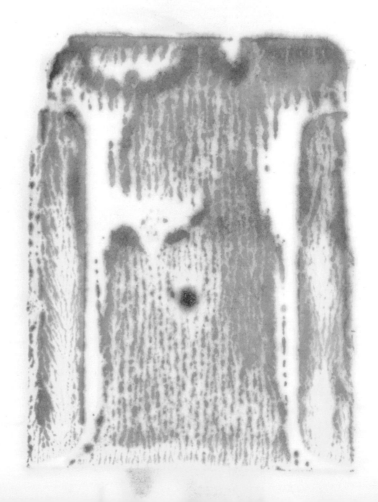